COMMAND CULTURE

COMMAND CULTURE

Officer Education in the U.S. Army
and the German Armed Forces, 1901–1940,
and the Consequences for World War II

JÖRG MUTH

University of North Texas Press
Denton, Texas

10 9 8 7 6 5 4 3 2 1

Permissions:
University of North Texas Press
1155 Union Circle #311336
Denton, TX 76203-5017

The paper used in this book meets the minimum requirements of the American
National Standard for Permanence of Paper for Printed Library Materials,
z39.48.1984. Binding materials have been chosen for durability.

Library of Congress Cataloging-in-Publication Data

Muth, Jörg, 1967-
    Command culture : officer education in the U.S. Army and the German Armed
Forces, 1901/1940, and the consequences for World War II / Jörg Muth. -- 1st ed.
    p. cm.
    Includes bibliographical references and index.
    ISBN 978-1-57441-303-8 (cloth : alk. paper)
    1. United States. Army--Officers--Training of--History--20th century. 2.
Germany--Armed Forces--Officers--Training of--History--20th century. 3.
Military education--United States--History--20th century. 4. Military
education--Germany--History--20th century. 5. United States.
Army--Recruiting, enlistment, etc.--History--20th century. 6.
Germany--Armed Forces--Recruiting, enlistment, etc.--History--20th century.
I. Title.
    U408.M87 2011
    355.5'5097309041--dc22

                                                    2011011192

Contents

Acknowledgments

Even after finishing my master's with an outstanding grade and publishing a successful book, support or advancement was denied me in Germany. All kinds of specious reasons were given to me at that time. The real reason for the rejections was most likely that the academic system in Germany, just like in the U.S. Army, as will be pointed out in this study, has a hard time dealing with mavericks and rejects them rather than making good use of them.

I owe a debt of gratitude to Ronald Smelser who invited me to finish my doctoral dissertation—on which this book is based—in the United States. The present work was made possible only through his invitation. He is therefore ultimately responsible for providing me with the means of gaining the Ph.D. for which I have worked so long and so hard.

Edward Davies gave me the welcome that I generally expected but that I got only from him. He had an open ear for all my problems and even ended other phone calls immediately so he could talk to me. Thanks also to Ben Cohen for helping me along the last few yards and John Reed for the military history talk and bull sessions.

In my "early years," the steep hierarchies at a German civilian university would have been unbearable to me without the nearly daily visits at my ersatz university, the Military History Research Center (*Militärgeschichtliches Forschungsamt*, MGFA) in Potsdam. Here, I was always welcome and the academic civilian, but especially the academic military, personnel, in rank from lieutenant up to the commander of the facility, discussed all aspects of military history with me, treating me as an equal and with great respect, even when I was still an undergraduate. My *Ersatzdoktorvater*, Arnim Lang, editor-in-chief of the MGFA, helped to publish my first book just the way I wanted it to be and never doubted that I would finally finish my dissertation. His encouragement over the long years was invaluable.

I am indebted to Beatrice Heuser for writing the mother-of-all-letters-of-recommendation that finally got the ball rolling.

Thanks to Roger Cirillo for getting me started when I arrived in the United States for my first research trip. The advice, literature, and contacts he gave me were priceless and long lasting.

Gerhard Weinberg and Edward Coffman have never hesitated to give me most valuable professional counsel when I asked for it and relentlessly wrote letters of recommendation for me. The latter are one of the banes of the academic system and utterly useless unless the writer is personally known to the addressee, which is rarely the case. Both men, however, were always gracious to me and never made me feel any dependency.

It is a sad fact that whenever I finish a book one of those individuals who lent me major support did not live to see the finished product because he died. Before the publication of my first book, my good friend Rolf Wiemer died and this time it was Charles Kirkpatrick, an expert on the U.S. Army and its officer corps, with whom I had a lively email exchange until his untimely death. Charles gave me priceless advice, answered all my questions with great patience, and his eagerness to read my finished study was an honor to me. It is my great wish and hope that I will finally reach a position where I can concentrate on writing a book in a timeframe where every contributor will still be able to read it.

A great thanks to Walter Hudson for vouching for me and getting me established at Fort Leavenworth.

Thank you to Robert Black, Darla Thompson, Elizabeth Merrifield, Paul Barron, Peggy Stelpflug, Alan Aimone, Iris Thompson, Oliver Sander, Wilson Heefner, Casey Madrick, Tino Tolonen, Lewis Sorley, Alicia Mauldin, and Lynn Beahm for helping me with the photos for the book.

I am very grateful to past and present friends and colleagues of the advisory board of H-War and the editors. They have always treated me with the greatest professionalism, courtesy, and kindness. Their regard was especially precious because these things were in short supply elsewhere.

I am indebted to Craig Baker, my boss at Blue Coat Systems. He always had an understanding of my insane work schedule and he let me do my job at Blue Coat with the greatest latitude and flexibility. His support was so important to me and the completion of this book that he should be named the honorary sixth member of my Ph.D. committee.

Many thanks to my good friend Janet Valentine for the opportunities and for always showing true multicultural understanding for her odd German colleague.

Keith Pinney, Julie Scott, and the staff of the Cross Culture Club are an invaluable asset to the international students at the University of Utah and make life in Utah bearable for them. I am very grateful for the good times in the house of the CCC.

Thanks to my best friend, Michael "Bakerman" Sanetra, for unwavering phone calls and making me laugh in the darkest times.

The book is dedicated to my parents, Annemarie and Ernst Muth, whom I have not seen in four-and-a-half years.

The German Historical Institute made it possible for me to conduct research at the National Archives II, College Park, Maryland; the Dwight D. Eisenhower Presidential Library, Abilene, Kansas; the Harry S. Truman Library, Independence, Missouri; and the Combined Arms Research Library, Fort Leavenworth, Kansas.

At the National Archives II, I was rendered great support and assistance by Timothy Nenninger, Robin Cookson, Larry MacDonald, and Les Waffen.

At the Eisenhower Library, David Haight acted as my "personal" archivist with great knowledge and dedication. His help and determination beyond the call of duty even opened the gates to another library whose leadership had stubbornly refused me access to its special archives collection with the ridiculous excuse that I was a "civilian."

The United States Military Academy's History Department honored me by selecting me as a fellow for its annual military history summer seminar. The ample and gracious stipend I received enabled me to conduct research at the Special Archives Collection of the West Point Library with the knowledgeable assistance of Alan Aimone.

I am grateful to the Department of History of the University of Utah for awarding me the Burton Fellowship and getting me a teaching assistantship for the last year of my dissertation. The anonymous donor of the fellowship provided me with an additional travel and research grant, which came at a time when it was badly needed. I am much obliged to him or her.

I am indebted to the United States Army Military History Institute for awarding me the Matthew B. Ridgway Research Grant that enabled me to conduct research at its facility in Carlisle, Pennsylvania. Rich Baker was instrumental in making my research productive. It was not intentional, but is only fitting, that Matthew Ridgway is now on the cover of this book.

The most amazing financial support came from the George C. Marshall Foundation when it awarded me the prestigious George C. Marshall/Baruch Fellowship. It allowed me to dig up incredible material, for once without suffering financial hardships for the trip. I am grateful to Paul Barron for all his support during my stay and Wesley Taylor, former president of the George C. Marshall Foundation, for saying the right words at the right time.

As I have diligently researched, I have tried to diligently name everybody who helped me. Because of the long years over which this project stretched and the many moves from location to location, it is possible that I have lost notes. Those who would like to appear here or in the footnotes when a new edition is printed may send me an email to jmuth@ gmx.net.

Introduction

"He who has not fought the Germans does not know war."
—British military aphorism[1]

During the course of World War II, the supreme commander of the Allied forces, General Dwight David Eisenhower, USMA 1915, had already resolved that he would not write his account of the events but leave that to historians and those who were compelled to justify themselves. Directly after the war's conclusion, however, various Allied commanders stepped into the limelight and criticized in interviews and publications the American war effort and the leadership of the U.S. officer corps, which irked the Americans greatly. Walter Bedell Smith, Eisenhower's close friend and former chief of staff, tried to persuade him to write his account and published some articles in newspapers explaining and justifying some of Ike's decisions during the war.[2] Much later they were bundled together into a book.[3]

Another book, although written by an officer who barely had commanded anything, heavily criticized several American officers for their conduct and lack of leadership during the war, especially General Mark Wayne Clark, USMA 1917, Ike's friend and the commander of the Fifth Army in Italy.[4] The author, Captain Harry C. Butcher, was designated

1

as the Supreme Commander's "naval aide" by General George Catlett Marshall, VMI 1901, then chief of staff of the army, who sensed correctly that, because of the heavy burden of responsibility Eisenhower carried, he might occasionally need a friend to talk to who had no real place in the chain of command. In the theaters of war, Butcher was often seen by field commanders as a nuisance because he roamed around and assumed authority he did not really possess, but it was well known that he had the ear of Eisenhower. Though on the "suggestion" of Ike, Butcher erased some sharp criticism from his book, the final product was still somewhat harsh on a number of commanders.[5]

Adding to the finger pointing about conduct and leadership was the publication of George Smith Patton's, USMA 1909, manuscript of his wartime thoughts. It was never intended for publication in this form but could not be revised or edited because Patton died in a car accident in 1945.[6] His widow deemed the thoughts of her late husband nevertheless so important that the manuscript was made public. Patton's critique of and sometimes ranting about allied commanders and his fellow officers proved just as harsh as Butcher's, but Patton's success as a combat commander and his personal ties with many U.S. and Allied commanders greatly enhanced his critical evaluations. The bickering among the former commanders persuaded Eisenhower to publish his own account, which remains one of the most balanced views of World War II from the American side at the operational and strategic level.[7]

The argument moved briefly to a new stage when in 1946 congressmen from Texas forced Mark W. Clark to testify in front of a committee regarding his orders to the 36th Infantry Division—a former Texas National Guard outfit—to cross the Rapido River. This operation, conducted January 20 to 22, 1944, attempted to relieve pressure on the troubled Anzio beachhead in Italy yet resulted only in very heavy casualties and no gain. Still, few doubted that Eisenhower's close friend and now victorious army commander would be exonerated.

In the same year, the Senate Special Committee to Investigate the National Defense Program published its report on the nation's mobilization effort for the last war. Though the report did not get much publicity, the criticism leveled was harsh and it determined that the United States armed forces lacked a personnel selection system that rewarded "the alert, the intelligent, and the farsighted," and punished "the careless, the stupid, and the wasteful. Such a system is particularly essential in the higher echelons of the armed forces."[8]

Such brief public episodes followed rather self-serving accounts by American generals to explain their important contributions to the war effort and to pay old debts, but there were no other firestorms or further harsh critiques because after all, the Americans had won the war.[9]

A new controversy broke this silence when British Field Marshal Sir Bernard Law Montgomery published his memoirs in 1958, enhancing his own value and diminishing the leadership abilities of American generals.[10] The discussion remained largely to journalists and former generals because no military historian had dealt thoroughly and critically with the leadership of American commanders until noted military historian Russell Weigley published his still influential classic, *Eisenhower's Lieutenants*, in 1981.[11] He stated that caution on the side of the American leadership prolonged operations and that "more genuinely offensive-minded planning" would have helped in gaining objectives earlier.[12] Weigley noted that American commanders often complained about the lack of aggressiveness of their soldiers yet he never made explicit the connection with the lack of aggressive leadership in the U.S. Army. Troops fight the way they are led. The military historian observed correctly that when a commander showed ferociousness or wanted to put "unrelenting pressure" on the enemy he usually had to do so "despite every discouragement from his superiors."[13] To make matters worse, often "the cautious American generals expected equal caution from the enemy."[14] Weigley concluded that American generals relied primarily on superior material resources and that "a bolder generalship might have shortened the war."[15] The military historian had read widely through the papers of wartime leaders to come to this conclusion and his assessment is echoed by other American officers who decried the "lack of energetic command" of higher officers.[16]

Only one year later Martin van Creveld published his classic account of the German and American armies, comparing their *Fighting Power*.[17]

Van Creveld used for the time ingenious methods in his study and while some of his findings have been proven incorrect by recent research, much of it has stood the test of time. The author stated that "the American officer corps of World War II was less than mediocre."[18] He continued, saying that "those who did command at the front were, as the official history frankly admits and the casualty figures confirm, often guilty of bad leadership."[19] While quite a few of van Creveld's findings will be verified in this study, his statement that between the American officers "and their German opposite numbers there simply is no comparison possible" will be proven incorrect.[20]

In 1984, John Ellis published an account on the early part of the 1944 Allied campaign in Italy with devastating ratings for many British and American commanders conspicuously lacking the essentials for aggressive and effective wartime leadership.[21] Six years later he followed up with an account on the conduct of operations by the Allies of the whole war.[22] The title, *Brute Force*, hints at the content of the book. Ellis stated that the war "reveals the Allied commanders as being quite unable to adapt their tactics to the terrain in which they were fighting."[23] He generally noted "a tactical inferiority vis-à-vis the Germans" and that "even when all that was required was a modicum of speed and determination, to finish off a distinctly groggy opponent" the Allied commanders, and specifically the Americans, showed themselves as being "incapable" of doing so.[24]

At the end of the 1980s, Allan R. Millett and Williamson Murray edited a well-crafted three volume series on military effectiveness. The books are mostly of high quality and, in their majority, still sound today. However, some reveal that the education of American officers and its impact on the performance of the American officer corps has not been evaluated critically enough and has not been put into context.

Ronald Spector states in his article about the military effectiveness of the U.S. military in the interwar period that "the entry into the officer corps—largely through the service academies—was competitive and recruits were generally of high quality."[25] Two paragraphs further in the same article, the correct assertion is found that "the problem of officer quality in the army became acute in 1940 when U.S. rearmament and expansion of the army revealed that many regular officers were of questionable competence or physical condition for active wartime service or higher command." Because the majority of the officers in question successfully completed stints at the military academies and the schools at Fort Leavenworth, these statements clearly pose a contradiction. They demonstrate that faculties of the United States Military Academy at West Point and the Command and General Staff School at Fort Leavenworth consistently portray their teaching as excellent, yet the end product remained mediocre. This study will shed some light on the issue that has haunted the U.S. Army for decades.

In the last volume of the series, Allan R. Millet assesses the military effectiveness of the U.S. Army in the Second World War. To him, "the skill of the officers who organized, equipped, trained, and led" the American soldiers in battle is questionable.[26] The tactical doctrine—which had been largely developed and taught at the Command and General Staff School—proved "defective in several ways."[27] In Millet's opinion, "the American armed forces often compensated for their operational flaws," caused by a below average officer corps, "with logistical abundance."[28] He asserts that "army ground combat divisions depended on the advantage of numbers" and that attacks against the Germans were generally only successful if a 4:1 "local infantry superiority" was in place.[29]

Seven years later Richard Overy published his still influential *Why the Allies Won.*[30] It follows Ellis's basic outline and even uses some of his quotations to make certain points. Overy, however, wrote a more concise book. While the author states clearly that numerical superiority was not the only factor that brought victory to the Allies, he judges the "quality of their technology" as superior.[31] Surprisingly, he also lists the—widely disputed—fighting effectiveness of the allied forces as an important point. Overy indicates that it derived from the economic strength of the Allies.[32] Their leadership and command capabilities do not show up as remarkable. Instead, he remarks largely correctly that in Germany "the best military brains were at the battlefront, not in the rear."[33]

In his concise and influential group biography, Charles Kirkpatrick states that "the sum total" of the training and experience of the American generals in his study "was ordinary performance."[34] Kirkpatrick comments also on the rather erratic selection and promotion process in the U.S. Army of that time.[35] His findings are more positive in an article that was published the same year, but he maintains that the American military schools were "somewhat unimaginative" and obviously produced rather orthodox soldiers.[36]

Karl-Heinz Frieser points out in his *The Blitzkrieg Legend* that the Germans possessed a superior tactical—and often operational—leadership, but that ultimately "World War II, just like World War I, was decided not on the battlefields but in the factories."[37] In an analogy to Miguel Cervantes' *Don Quixote*, Frieser states that "the Panzer operations of the German blitzkrieg were much like jousting against the windmills of superior industrial potentials."[38]

While the other authors remain more cautious in their statements than Frieser, no one ranks the leadership and command abilities of the American officers as a decisive or even important factor in the war. Instead, there is ample criticism of their professional abilities.

Specialized studies like the one by Martin Blumenson are even blunter in their assessments.[39] He states that after the first clashes with the Germans in North Africa came "the shocking revelation of how ill-prepared our leaders were for combat and how poorly our system for producing war leaders had functioned."[40]

Apparently no systematic selection system in the U.S. Army existed for officer promotion, a fact that puzzled historians and even the officers themselves.[41] They were rather appointed to positions of responsibility because their abilities were personally known to those who appointed them—in contrast to superior abilities on paper, they were recommended by fellow officers who also knew them personally, or they had a very high-ranking mentor.[42] Often officers knew each other from their time at the United States Military Academy (USMA) at West Point where they, except for some of the wartime classes, stayed for four years and thus had the chance to get to know not only their classmates but also the members of the classes who preceded them and came after them. That a cadet will come to know his "comrades" at West Point quite intimately will be demonstrated in chapter 2 of this study.

All division commanders and the majority of G-3 operations officers of higher staffs of World War II had also attended the advanced military training at the schools at Fort Leavenworth, Kansas, which became after another one of many name changes in the early 1920s universally known as the Command and General Staff School (CGSS).[43]

Since the United States had doubtlessly won World War II and because most key positions had been taken by former Leavenworth graduates, it has been assumed, even by former commanders reflecting about the war, that the CGSS had been instrumental in providing the American officer corps with the tools to win the war.[44] Several excellent scholarly studies about the schools basically maintain this conclusion.[45] However, the presence of Leavenworth graduates in positions of command coupled with the U.S. victory does not automatically lead to the conclusion that the Leavenworth experience taught these men superior military expertise. Nor can we assume that the Leavenworth training developed the martial abilities vital for the winning of World War II.

Often overlooked in studies about the U.S. Army educational system was The Infantry School in Fort Benning, Georgia. The chapter on this school points out that it might have done more for the establishment of a certain proficiency in military matters than any other institution of military education in the United States.

This study sets out to examine the "command culture" of the United States Army officer corps and does so in a comparative context by incorporating the "command culture" of the German Army. This course seems to be especially appealing because the German military had since the American War of Independence been a fascinating organization for the American officers. The *Wehrmacht*—the German Army of World War II—but especially its officer corps, has been and remains today an object of the greatest interest, attraction, and even romanticizing by the American military and society alike.[46] The German officers were at the outset of World War II considered a formidable foe and they were respected and sometimes even feared by their American counterparts.

Scholars have argued that "culture consists of shared decision rules, recipes, standard operating procedures, and decision routines that impose a degree of order on individual and group conceptions."[47] Even more important is that "insofar as culture affects behavior, it does so by presenting limited options and by affecting how members of these cultures learn from interaction."[48] This study will work with these definitions but emphasizes that, though the officers examined here possessed a limited set of options as a result of their socialization and education, those options nevertheless were numerous.

The principles of command of an officer corps often reach far back into the past and they are part of the "corporate identity" of an army.[49] "Command culture" is in this study to be understood as how an officer considers himself to be in command, i.e., does he command as a visible person close to the action or rather through orders by his staff from his command post? It also means the way an officer tackles the turmoil and chaos of battle and war—whether he tries to make sense of it by the application of doctrine or rather utilizes the pandemonium to make bold moves. This study will therefore also deal with the question of whether the command culture of an officer corps emphasizes personal initiative or playing by the rules and regulations. Furthermore, the command culture refers to how command is understood by an officer, what its purpose and importance in war is.

Because the culture of command is taught by peers and—as indicated above—especially in military schools, this study will examine the educational system of the respective armies.[50] Both—the peers and the educational system—can be considered as the bearers of the culture of an army.[51]

Before an officer is educated, he has to be selected and commissioned and it will therefore be examined from which parts of the society young men came from in Germany and the United States and which path they had to follow to become commissioned and promoted to higher ranks.

The men of the sample used in this study succeeded as career officers and all belonged to the regular army. They were nearly exclusively members of the ground forces. Therefore, when the term "U.S. Army" is used, although it included at the time this study deals with branches such as the Air Corps, usually, but not always, the ground forces are meant.[52] The same is true for the use of the term *Reichswehr*, the German Army of the Weimar Republic between 1920 and 1934, and the *Wehrmacht*, its successor of 1935 to 1945.[53]

We will therefore follow largely the Eisenhowers, Pattons, Guderians, and von Mansteins, though the majority of the present sample did not gain such a prominence. The officers in this study achieved during World War II at least the rank of colonel or *Oberst* but most of them made general with several stars.[54] They were commissioned during or after 1901 but mainly between 1909 and 1925.

Because the American professional military education was far less structured than the German, the bulk of the American officers viewed here attended The Infantry School at Fort Benning, Georgia, and the Command and General Staff School at Fort Leavenworth, Kansas, or one of its predecessors, between 1902 and 1939, the majority between 1924 and 1939. Their German counterparts attended the *Kriegsakademie* or its substitute institutes between 1912 and 1938.

When examining the military schools, colleges, and academies, this study will not concern itself overly with the numbers of hours taught, the name changes of the schools, and when and why they occurred. The time the officers stayed there will also have little relevance. Though it has been discussed at length whether there should be one-, two-, or three-year courses at the advanced military schools, the practical fact is that the "how" and "why" in teaching is much more important than the "what" and "when." Everybody can remember a teacher from his school or university time who could inspire even when teaching topics generally perceived as dull and others who could ruin even the most interesting subject.

This is not a history of the advanced military schools in the United States and Germany because these studies already exist.[55] This study is rather an update of the existing works adding a different angle and a cultural component, which leads to surprising results. It points out who had access to the schools and which process he had to follow to continue. I am also concerned with the teaching philosophy of these schools, the didactics and pedagogies used, and the attitudes of the faculty because the main point will be to get hold of the command culture the schools instilled in their student officers. Though often following roughly a chronological order, sometimes I will depart from it to emphasize continuities or important events that cast their shadows forward.

The study will conclude its examination with the intermediate professional military education in both armies because by then the officers had formed their command culture. Though the visit to the Army War College or the Industrial College for the American officers or the attendance at the war games for higher German officers might have brought them benefits for their profession, it remains unlikely that at that time it altered their command culture.

The centrality of the "German military heritage" to the U.S. Army and the centuries-long relationship between the two militaries make the German Army ideal to incorporate into the study. Therefore, chapter 1 reviews the connections between both nations' armies before 1901 as well as some aspects of World War I. The chapter also points out the misperceptions visiting American officers got through their observation of German military institutions, maneuvers, and wars. Following 1901, the U.S. Army undertook major reforms after the German Army had been closely studied—and largely misunderstood. The scope of the study ends in 1940 with the United States seriously gearing up for war and the educational patterns used for decades dissolving. One year earlier, Germany experienced similar changes when it prepared to invade Poland.

Chapter 2 examines the United States Military Academy (USMA) at West Point and the way cadets were selected and educated at this institution. In the following text, the United States Military Academy usually appears as "West Point" or "the Academy" or its abbreviation, USMA. There will be no attempt to write a new history of this almost mystical cadet school because many already exist.[56] It will rather be studied which cultural mark the Academy left on the cadet, what he learned and how he learned. The selection process within the Academy will also be important as well as the selection of the faculty and the contribution it made to a professional command culture of the future officer. Since a few influential officers graduated from other military academies, mainly the Virginia Military Institute (VMI) in Lexington, Virginia, and The Citadel in Charleston, South Carolina, they will also briefly be examined in this chapter. Though the structure of both is very similar to that of West

Point, they are not official institutions of the U.S. Armed Forces.

To illustrate the frequency with which West Point graduates assumed command positions and to demonstrate the long-standing ties among them, throughout the text the graduation class of an individual will appear just behind his name at least once—thus, Dwight David Eisenhower, USMA 1915, or Mark Wayne Clark, USMA 1917.

Chapter 3 pits against these American institutes the German *Kadettenschulen* (cadet schools) in the form of the *Voranstalten* (preliminary institutes)—where boys could enter as early as the age of ten—and the *Hauptkadettenanstalt* (*HKA*, main cadet institution) in Berlin-Lichterfelde, which accepted boys at around fourteen. West Point generally accepted young men not younger than seventeen and not older than twenty-two.

The *Kadettenschulen* played a central role in the German military because numerous of the most prominent officers, like Heinz Guderian and Erich von Manstein, attended them for many years. Though former *Kadetten* respected and knew each other well, there existed no such mystical brotherhood among them as existed among the West Pointers. There are several reasons for that. Many of the *Kadetten* were processed through the numerous *Voranstalten* and when they reached the *Hauptkadettenanstalt*, they had several hundred classmates in their year in contrast to the usually just over a hundred to hundred and fifty at West Point. There will be therefore no graduate class numbers for the former *Kadetten*.

In addition, for a German officer belonging to the officer corps of his regiment was all-important and carried more weight than having graduated at a certain year from the *HKA*. Regiment comrades stuck together like glue and sometimes a clique of a certain regiment was even able to dominate the top ranks of the command structure of the German Army for a few years.[57]

Chapter 3 also briefly discusses the rather complicated commissioning procedure of a German *Fähnrich* (ensign) because, in contrast to the United States, most of them were not automatically commissioned to rank of *Leutnant* (second lieutenant) after successfully completing the cadet school. They first had to further prove their mettle as officer aspirants in a regiment and at a *Kriegsschule* before becoming members of the coveted German officer corps. There was of course no official Germany before 1871 and prior to this date Prussia and its military was a main point of interest for the Americans, but for better readability usually "Germany" is used.

Chapter 4 examines the intermediate advanced military education in the United States, specifically at the school at Leavenworth, which became more prominently known as Command and General Staff School (CGSS). Because of the several name changes of the school either the name Leavenworth school—though in fact there were several schools at this post—or CGSS is used throughout the text to avoid confusion.

In a less exhaustive way than the CGSS, I examine The Infantry School at Fort Benning, Georgia, particularly from 1927 to 1932 when George C. Marshall was assistant commandant and responsible for the curriculum and teaching at this school. This chapter will be used to highlight certain points about the American professional military education system and it will show how it could have been done for the whole U.S. Army.

On the German side, the famous *Kriegsakademie* is examined in the chapter following The Infantry School. Though the *Kriegsakademie* had to be abolished in 1919 by accord of the Versailles Treaty because it was considered a source for German militarism, it stayed in existence in a different form and in more or less secrecy and with the same teaching philosophy until it officially reopened in 1935. I will therefore often refer to the *Kriegsakademie* when in fact one of its substitute officer schools, which nevertheless taught nearly the same content in the interwar years, are meant.

Though many articles of the Versailles Treaty were violated by the Germans very quickly, none was as thoroughly "circumvented" as the ban of a General Staff officer's education and the General Staff "would survive under a series of disguises."[58] Because the majority of the German high-ranking commanders of the first three war years had been members of the German General Staff, the selection and education process for them will also be scrutinized.

Chapter 6 concludes the findings of this study but is also used as a crucible to point out other critical differences and commonalities between the two officer corps. It reveals cultural traits of the respective officer corps that have been emphasized or counterbalanced by the educational system. Some of these shaped the conduct of World War II. The chapter will also briefly review what historical cultural mark the U.S. Army's educational system has left on the officer corps today, and how that is reflected in today's wars.

ONE

Prelude: Military Relations between the United States and Germany and the Great General Staff Fantasy

"The German Army has been busy since the War, as it always was busy before the War, in developing new weapons or new applications of old ones, new tactics and new methods of training."[1]
—THOMAS BENTLEY MOTT, U.S. military attaché to France at the turn of the twentieth century

"We are indebted to the Germans for this system of teaching the art of war, now gradually working its way into our own Army."[2]
—ANNUAL REPORT OF THE COMMANDANT, U.S. Infantry and Cavalry School, 1906

It has been stated that "no other army in history has ever known its enemy as well as the American army knew the German army when the Americans crossed the Rhine River and began their final offensive."[3] While the U.S. Army might have known a lot, it understood little.

The German Army—and before that the Prussian—has been a source of inspiration and education and even a role model for the U.S. Army since it came into existence but especially since the successful wars of German unification.[4] However, because the Americans have misunderstood the German culture of war until the present day, the lessons drawn from it by the U.S. Army often were, and still are, flawed or not implemented. Warfare is so much based on culture, tradition, and history that it would have been hard anyway to put into practice the war-waging culture of one army in another but it becomes close to impossible when this culture is misinterpreted.[5]

The first close connection and experience the American Army had with the Prussian way of war was *Hauptmann* (Captain)—later *General*—Friedrich Wilhelm von Steuben, who was considered a second-rate officer in the Old Prussian Army and thus could be spared to advise about military subjects in a foreign country.[6] The assessment shows that even the professional soldier Frederick the Great was not flawless in his judgment about military matters, especially when it came to his officers. Von Steuben proved to be the right man for the job in the colonies and he did not really teach the Prussian way of war but altered it so much that it became something genuinely new.

Another Prussian in the colonial service—Captain John Ewald—noted not only the diligence with which his American comrades tackled the military literature but also that they often read translated Prussian treatises, especially Frederick the Great's instructions to his generals, which he had "found more than one hundred times" among the American officers.[7]

The Hessian soldiers "rented" by the British to help fight the revolutionaries came as Prussian clones, a fact well-known to von Steuben, though most likely not to the rest of the colonists. The Prussian Army in general was copied as much as possible in all aspects throughout Europe, but Hessia's armed force came as an aggravated case.[8] Hessia featured the highest ratio of soldiers to civilians in Europe; copied the regulations, manuals, uniform cuts, and drills of the Prussian Army; and was home to many "unhappy"—and often incompetent—former Prussian officers.[9] The Hessian soldiers were not mercenaries as is so frequently incorrectly claimed. Often conscripts and regular members of the Hessian Army, they do not fit a historical understanding of the definition of mercenaries or a modern one.[10]

During the War of Independence, the relations of the Americans with the already world-famous and legendary ruler of Prussia, Frederick the Great, remained excellent. After the good experiences with some formidable Prussian officers, it is therefore not surprising that the U.S. military looked to Prussia in military matters once in a while.

In the current scholarly literature, there is no hint of the notion that the United States Military Academy may have been founded after the role model of a Prussian cadet school.[11] But American officers at the turn of the twentieth century stated that West Point "was created upon a Prussian foundation."[12] In the next chapter, it will be discussed that West Point indeed showed resemblance to a—if distorted—Old Prussian *Kadettenschule* (cadet school).

American officers travelled relentlessly to the old continent to observe, make notes, and try to learn from the nearly constantly warring European armies. Except for the Napoleonic era and its aftermath and the brief World War I time, a main stop for them was usually Prussia or Germany.[13] Between the War of 1812 and the American Civil War alone, 105 American officers crossed the Atlantic for that purpose and some even stayed for several years.[14] The eagerness to adapt European ideas and the influx of different military cultures allegedly compelled General Philip Henry Sheridan, USMA 1853, to comment cynically that "every time they have war in Europe we adopt the cap of the winning side."[15] There is some truth in his statement because in 1881 the U.S. Army replaced its headgear, which was then leaning toward the French model, with the famous German *Pickelhaube*—the spiked helmet.[16] It was not only the caps though. The U.S. Army took an eager look at the manuals produced overseas and, of the military literature that appeared in Europe in 1859, "about half had been published first in German."[17]

When it came to battle tactics and army structure, the French Army still appeared to be more interesting to American officers in 1839. In this year, the American officer Lieutenant Philip Kearny visited especially the French cavalry branch and though he had a lot of praise, he noted the lack of discipline and cleanliness and surmised that "if he were to inspect German stables, he would find that they kept the buildings and the horses in perfect condition."[18] This cliché about the German military was obviously already well established in the first half of the nineteenth century.

During the American Civil War, officers and regiments of German origin were in high demand and generally much regarded. The battle tactics during that war derived from the Napoleonic wars and proved to be indecisive and caused an unnecessarily high number of casualties.[19] Prussian officers visiting and observing both warring sides during the campaigning were less than impressed by the amateurish conduct of a serious undertaking.[20] The information—or rumor—trickled down from the German

Great General Staff that the American Civil War armies were considered nothing more than armed mobs chasing each other. [21] The observation was later even attributed to the chief of the Great General Staff of the Prussian Army, Helmuth Karl Bernhard Graf von Moltke himself. General William Tecumseh Sherman, USMA 1840, asked by reporters on his trip to Europe in 1872 if he had asked Moltke about that statement, snapped angrily, "I did not ask him the question because I did not presume that he was such an ass to say that."[22]

The survey of the world's military forces published annually by the German Great General Staff would not contain the U.S. Armed Forces until 1896. That the U.S. Army was included at all might have been caused more by the awareness raised through the numerous visits of American officers than by the sense that the U.S. Army played any important role in the world at that time. Even in 1900, the U.S. Army "was still considered a joke" by many European powers.[23] The American military attaché in Russia reported in 1912 that among the Russian officer corps and his European attaché colleagues, there was the "universal belief that our Army is not worthy of serious consideration."[24]

That was also the opinion of the Great German General Staff. The German high-ranking officers' continuous historical underestimation of the U.S. military would cause the most serious consequences in two world wars.

Groundbreaking technical innovations like the famous *Zündnadelgewehr*—the needle rifle—were obviously not recognized as an important individual weapon system and largely overlooked by the American observers. The obsessive secrecy of the Prussians might have contributed to the failure of the U.S. observers to notice the rifle. It had been invented in 1841 and was introduced into the Prussian Army several years later. Only the elite *Füsilier* companies of the guards' regiments got it at first and had to turn it back into the armory after each practice. The visiting U.S. officers, however, did not have a clue over fifteen years and it is surprising that those observers from the land of Colt, Sharps, and Springfield showed so little interest in modern battlefield rifles. After the *Zündnadelgewehr* had made its second appearance in the Franco-Prussian War—three decades after its invention—an American observer finally noted that it was "capable of about the same rapidity of fire as our own breechloader."[25] However, he did correctly note the delicacy of the rifle.

For the American side, the Prussians became much more interesting than Napoleon ever was when the battle of Königgrätz was won decisively by the Prussian alliance in July 1866. Here the Prussians had, only one year after the American Civil War ended, accomplished what the Americans had struggled to do for four years—the rapid movement of several corps over a vast distance and their unification as an army at a specific location to fight a disciplined and decisive battle.[26] The success was even more astonishing considering the fact that Prussians had not been at war for nearly fifty years.[27]

Though two rather myopic American observers, Brevet Major General John Gross Barnard and Brevet Major General Horatio Gouverneur Wright, wrote "that we suffer nothing in comparison" to the Prussian Army, the impression of a more knowledgeable officer like Philip Henry Sheridan was different.[28] One of his observations would prove to be prophetic for the U.S. Army. Sheridan stated that "an imitation of the Prussian scheme in its details instead of in its spirit" would be a mistake.[29] The U.S. Army would make exactly this mistake when introducing reforms after the Prussian model.

Not only the U.S. Army but also most other high-ranking military observers worldwide incorrectly attributed the victory to the supposedly superior institution of the Prussian Great General Staff. In fact, though, it was rather due to the leadership and genius of the chief of the Great General Staff, Helmuth Karl Bernhard Graf von Moltke, and the professional training of the Prussian soldiers—officers and men alike. The so-often-hailed *Zündnadelgewehr* proved to be beneficial but not decisive during the battle.

In contrast to later versions of the Great German General Staff, it was said that under Moltke common sense ruled supreme.[30] That might well have been its greatest advantage.

In a later interview, Moltke laid the groundwork for the fame of a book that would become equally a curse and a boon for officers and military historians alike. When asked from which books he had profited the most and which would he consider the most important, he named as one

of them Carl von Clausewitz's *Vom Kriege*.[31] Clausewitz had been director of the *Kriegsschule*—the then Prussian War College—when Moltke
attended it as a junior officer from 1823 to 1826.[32] Though the position as director was publicly perceived as a prestigious position, it soon
frustrated the still young and dynamic Clausewitz because he had little
power to make changes to the curriculum of the institution.[33] It was later
renamed and became the equally famous *Kriegsakademie* (war academy),
which will be discussed in detail in chapter 3.

Vom Kriege (*On War*) was published a few years after the instructor's death in 1831 by his widow and then largely forgotten.[34] One reason for the unpopularity of the book was the fact that it was close to
unreadable in German—even by nineteenth-century standards. Whereas
Clausewitz was no doubt an intelligent officer and accomplished military
theorist, his abilities as a writer were nearly nonexistent. The first French
reviewers therefore judged the work to be "untranslatable."[35] Contemporary German reviewers noted that *Vom Kriege* "cannot be read, it has to
be studied."[36] One reason for the especially hard-to-digest *Vom Kriege* is
certainly that Clausewitz died without having more time to edit it. There
can be no question, however, that the Prussian general's thoughts were
basically complete on paper.[37] They just badly needed editing to enhance
readability. The other seven volumes—*Vom Kriege* consisting originally
of the first three—are a better read and deal with various campaigns especially from the Napoleonic Wars.[38] They are of great value because the
Prussian officer either was a participant or a close observer, or knew many
other officers who had taken part. These days, Clausewitz's intelligent
campaign analyses are unfortunately overshadowed by his philosophical
work. One of the troubles with current Clausewitz studies is that they
rarely connect the philosophical introduction he put forth in *Vom Kriege*
to his multi-volume campaign analysis.

Because of Clausewitz's problematic prose, the abridged and streamlined English editions of his work became much more popular—and are
still today—than Clausewitz's unabridged original.[39] That fact accounts
also for some misunderstandings in the interpretation of the Prussian
general's thoughts and philosophy.

A great number of American officers of our sample had read Clausewitz and recommended his work to their comrades and friends and he is regularly cited in lessons at the Command and General Staff School.[40] It has even been stated that "for the American military, *On War* is virtually a sacred text."[41]

After Moltke the Elder's statement about his book preferences, there was a brief Clausewitzian surge in Germany and to many Clausewitz was "the schoolmaster who won the battle of Königgrätz."[42] Yet the surge soon faltered. The book would never become mandatory reading in any of the German military schools or academies; thus, an important wider and independent philosophical view of things—Clausewitz was always considered a maverick in the Prussian military—was not taught to those who helped Hitler perpetrate World War II.[43] Only one German officer has stated that Clausewitz's work was *recommended* reading for the preparation to the *Wehrkreis-Prüfung* (defense district examination) of 1921.[44] The *Wehrkreis-Prüfung* will be dealt with in detail in a following chapter.

No matter its lack of popularity in German professional military circles at the beginning of the twentieth century, *Vom Kriege* will forever be connected to the victories of one of the most successful commanders in history.[45] Moltke the Elder soon came in conflict with Bismarck during the German wars of unification. The gifted strategist violated Clausewitz's dictum of the priority of political guidance during war and smoothly reinterpreted the military theorist, beating Bismarck on his own turf:

> *Policy uses war to achieve its aims. It influences decisively the beginning and the end of war, but in such a way as to increase or lower the aims during its course. Owing to this uncertainty, strategy can only go after the greatest possible achievement. In such a way, strategy helps policy best, for the latter's aim only, but acting completely independent on it.*[46]

Bismarck himself had never read *Vom Kriege*, which was one of the reasons for the friction between the politician and the great strategist.[47] After Moltke the Elder retired in 1888—at age eighty-eight—the German

Great General Staff never again showed even remotely the same performance. Instead, Moltke's successors tried to copy the personal appearance
and habits of the famous strategist while never attaining his wide education, leadership traits, and operational and strategic proficiency.

When it became apparent at the dawn of World War I that Russia
was the main player and not France—as the General Staff falsely pre-
dicted—*Kaiser* Wilhelm II asked Helmuth von Moltke the Younger, then
chief of staff, to alter the mobilization in the direction of the eastward
neighbor. The nephew of the great commander replied that this was impossible because alone "the paperwork would take a year."[48] Showing for once
that he had more brains that people gave him credit for, the Kaiser replied
in an icy voice, "Your uncle would have given me a different answer."[49]

The uncle was known as *"der große Schweiger"*—the great silent
man—because he communicated with his subordinates only in brief
sentences and never chatted idly. In 1855, Moltke had been adjutant to
the crown prince, who later became the Emperor Wilhelm I, and they
used to ride out together for hours in silence.[50] When it became necessary, however, Moltke proved to be an accomplished speaker in front of
the emperor or the *Reichstag*—the German Parliament. The emulation
of Moltke's introversion by his successors became so exaggerated that
their own staffs would no longer know about their chief's intention,
which inevitably flawed many of the operations in World War I, especially the fateful attack on Verdun in early 1916.[51]

Knowing the superiors' intentions, however, is a prerequisite for the
successful employment of the famous *Auftragstaktik*, a cornerstone of the
German military culture that will be more closely discussed later. Moltke
the Elder is one of the earliest proponents of this revolutionary concept.
As early as 1858 he remarked at the annual Great General Staff war
games, which were traditionally held in a different part of Germany every
year, that "as a rule an order should contain only what the subordinate
for the achievement of his goals cannot determine on his own."[52] Everything else was to be left to the commander on the spot.

After Germany defeated France in the war of 1870–71, the focus
of the American observers shifted completely from "marching equip-

ment for infantry, proper saddles for horses, and efficient field engineering techniques" of foreign armies to the General Staff and officers' education in Prussia.[53] The German military brain trust had supposedly again shown its superiority.

Fact-finding missions on the latter subjects by American officers produced two influential books: William Babcock Hazen's *The School and the Army in Germany and France* in 1872 and Emory Upton's *The Armies of Europe and Asia* in 1873.[54] Though they ignited some serious discussion inside and outside of the U.S. Army, no course of action was planned. There existed considerable agreement that something had to be done about the officers' education and planning abilities of the U.S. Army, but without an incentive, nothing changed. The catastrophic management of the Spanish-American War and the following Philippine Insurrection provided the necessary encouragement.[55] A bureau chief of the War Department, pestered relentlessly by then Assistant Secretary of the Navy Theodore Roosevelt to help raise his volunteer regiment of cavalry, exclaimed, "Oh, dear! I had this bureau running in such great shape and along came a war!"[56]

A year later, the situation for the field commanders had not improved at all and a colonel wrote with sardonic humor to the War Department after some paper pushers from that institution had harassed him repeatedly with requests for immediate action reports. The colonel replied, "I have just received two hundred soldiers who have never seen a horse, one hundred horses who have never seen a soldier, and six second lieutenants who have never seen either. I am taking the field tomorrow."[57]

The new Secretary of War Elihu Root pressed for reforms, though his competence was largely misjudged at the beginning. Theodore Roosevelt pointed out that having a lawyer run the War Department was "simply foolish—so foolish indeed that I can only regard it as an excuse" that President William McKinley "does not want a sweeping reform of the office."[58] While Roosevelt might be right with the first part of his allegation, he greatly underestimated Elihu Root personally. The future president of the United States soon changed his view on Root and later both men would become good friends. Roosevelt had nevertheless correctly assessed that President McKinley indeed had primarily in mind a proper administration of the Philippines rather than a sweeping reform of the army's educational and planning system.

Despite being a civilian, Root found the Commanding General of the Army, Major General Nelson Appleton Miles, and other senior officers at the War Department receptive to his nomination because the situation under his predecessor, Russell Alexander Alger, had been grave with both parties hardly on speaking terms. This catatonic situation was as much the fault of the civilian as the military side.[59] Elihu Root's ability to listen, therefore, might have been one of the key traits that gained him support in military circles, in addition to his work ethic, which was admired by all sides.

It is remarkable how an army as small the United States Army was at that time could entangle itself in such a vast and bloated bureaucracy. A contemporary observation about the officers serving at the War Department was made that should hold true for at least another fifty years and explains the difficulties that the United States had with fielding and maintaining an army in the Philippines and in other places. An insider concluded that "one half of it is capable of anything and the other half is capable of nothing."[60] The latter half always seemed to have the higher ranks, though.

Root, too, soon divided the officer corps into two parties, yet for different reasons. One consisted of the reform-minded officers and the other, those who still held on to the ways of the Civil War, despising any higher education as unsoldierly. The new secretary of war, though undoubtedly a highly intelligent man, was not an "original thinker."[61] He looked "in the direction of simplicity and effectiveness," both traits that were badly need in the Army.[62] He took the ideas from reports and books and relied as much on input from the civilian as from the military side. Most influential were books and reports written by American officers who went to Prussia on research and observation missions, specifically those who had returned recently and could be questioned personally by Root. The last of them would be Theodore Schwan, born in Germany, and now an officer in the U.S. Army. His account, *Report on the Organization of the*

German Army, though not as popular as Upton's work because of the latter's stellar reputation, became internally the definite account of the Prussian/German army organization and education.[63] According to an observer, Schwan's role in "lending a helping hand in the Adjutant General's Office in evolving a suitable staff system and system of military education for the army" was irreplaceable.[64]

All of the reports had a highly favorable, admiring, or even worshipful view on the Prussian military, but specifically its Great General Staff.[65] Those views expressed publicly proved to be "one of the principle obstacles to creating a General Staff."[66] It was for both sides equally easy to raise the idea of the supposed Prussianization or Germanization of the American military as a benefit or as a curse, as a model of effectiveness or a destructive element against democracy.[67] Major General John McAllister Schofield, USMA 1853, for example, acknowledged the fact that a strong German influence would be interjected into the U.S. Army with those reforms but he also remarked "we might Germanize a little with advantage."[68] Another—rather silly, but nevertheless stubborn—argument Root had to deal with was the allegation that the Union Army had won the Civil War without a General Staff and therefore would not need one in the future.[69]

Though senior officers of that time stated that "Root did not have a very clear idea of what he wanted," the course of action the secretary of war took proved that such allegations were incorrect.[70] The first and easiest step was to push through the bill for the creation of the Army War College to soften up the opposition, which Root succeeded in doing in 1900. A year later, he proposed the bill for the General Staff. The list of duties to be performed by this General Staff prepared for Congress to decide on was "drawn almost verbatim from Paul Bronsart von Schellendorf's *Duties of the [German] General Staff.*"[71]

To Root's great surprise, General Nelson Miles, who was supposed to be his ally, appeared before the Military Committee of the Senate and contradicted many of the earlier statements the Secretary of War had made in front of the same body. Root quickly marshaled "his Generals"— among them Adjutant General Henry C. Corbin—to repair the damage done by Miles, and the secretary continued extensive lobbying through-out the year until the "General Staff Bill" finally was ready for vote in 1903 and passed that same year.

While it has been correctly observed that the American General Staff was a product of a "combination of imitation and adaptation" of the Prussian Great General Staff, the latter was (a) not really understood and (b) not in all aspects superior.[72] The handbook "Command and Staff Principles" produced by the faculty of the Command and General Staff School at Fort Leavenworth in 1937 claims completely erroneously that the German General staff was really a "General's staff" with officers only performing "highly specialized duties."[73] German staff officers were—in their staff duties—anything but specialized but usually did extensive duty in most of the departments of the General Staff, like cartography and railroads. At the same time, however, the post-Moltke "Great" General Staff was not even able to produce integrated operations planning for all the arms of the *Wehrmacht*—*Luftwaffe*, *Reichsmarine*, and *Heer*. This is all the more surprising because the *Luftwaffe* generals at least originated, just like generals in the U.S. Army, from the ground forces. Therefore, it has been stated correctly that "the *Wehrmacht* never possessed a general staff in the true sense."[74]

At the time of Moltke the Elder, there was no air force other than a few balloons and Prussia/Germany possessed only a negligible navy until the megalomaniac Emperor Wilhelm II took over and authorized a fleet armament race with Great Britain. Culturally, the Prussians were a ground force and Moltke the Elder planned the operations of this force by incor-porating the newest technology, such as railroads and telephones. Moltke's successors proved to be completely incompetent in doing the same.

Before and after adoption by the U.S. Army of parts of the German system, there was much confusion about its authentic function and pur-pose.[75] General John McAuley Palmer, former operations officer (G-3) for the American Expeditionary Forces in World War I, stated correctly that "practically none of the generals at that time [before World War I], had any knowledge of the historic origins of the General Staff [...]."[76] This statement is just as true for the American generals of World War II.

Interviewed for the Office of the Chief of Military History, General Walter Krueger declared after World War II that "in contrast to the German Great General Staff our WDGS [War Department General Staff] was ineffective" and was "only a debating society."[77] "In Germany," Krueger continued erroneously, "the CS [Chief of Staff] was Chief of the General Staff only. Our CS is CS [also] to the Pres[ident]."[78] In fact, though, the chief of staff in Germany had historically the same function to the emperor or *Reichskanzler*. Krueger was head of the war plans division and thus knew the American institution inside and out but obviously had, despite being born in Germany, only a limited grasp of its German counterpart, like the majority of his comrades.[79]

There can be no doubt that an advanced planning organization is mandatory for the modern military, but it should not end up in a sort of dualism that creates the always neat but despised staffer and his "chairborne tactics" and the front officer who would, even in today's most modern U.S. Army, not be promoted with the ridiculous argument of "too much troop time."[80] The more or less scholarly works about the German General Staff are unfortunately often glorifying and lack a critical viewpoint.[81]

In theory, an officer should be rotated equally between troop and staff commands—even the members of the German Great General Staff. In practice, the system often produced high-ranking officers with vast power who had hardly ever commanded anything but a desk and had never, or only briefly, been in battle in World War I and thus were largely ignorant of the hardships and necessities of the frontlines or the realities of war in general.[82] When these officers were challenged, historic encounters occurred that would have been comical if they had not been connected to the deaths of hundreds of thousands of soldiers. During one of the many desperate situations of the *Wehrmacht* in August 1942, the chief of staff of the army, *Generaloberst* Franz Halder, asked Adolf Hitler to allow units of Army Group North to pull back. The dictator replied that he deemed it not feasible and that "we must hold out in the best interest of the troops."[83] Halder remarked angrily in return that "out there brave riflemen and lieutenants are falling in the thousands as senseless victims" because of Hitler's inflexibility.[84] That, however, caused the dictator to boil over and he screamed at his chief of staff: "What do you want, Herr Halder, you who only, and in the First World War too, sat on the same revolving stool, telling me about the troops, you, who have never once worn the black wound badge?!"[85] That outcry silenced the high-ranking officer completely because the dictator was right—not in regard to the strategy in question but in regard to Halder's past, whereas Hitler had fought as a volunteer with the rank of *Obergefreiter* in World War I where he was wounded. Hitler's bravery and popularity in World War I, however, was greatly exaggerated. He did not undertake the extremely hazardous duty of a company runner but that of a regimental messenger and was thus seen by his comrades as an *"Etappenschwein"*—a rear-area pig.[86] Yet in contrast, Halder had been in staff positions all his life and in the current German officer corps structure he was not a singularity.[87]

The U.S. War Department never made an attempt to study the German officer corps on a sociological structural basis. They would have found out that there were far fewer combat-experienced officers in high ranks than expected. Because of the constant pressure of some military attachés, the G-2 (intelligence) section finally created biographical data cards for German officers. The content of those cards ranged from abysmal to completely inaccurate. They are filled with unverified rumors, scuttlebutt, and hearsay. While it might be helpful to know if a German officer is a Nazi or not, the entry for *Generalfeldmarschall* Wilhelm Keitel says that he is "regarded as a dummy," that *Generalfeldmarschall* Siegmund Wilhelm List is "almost bored beyond endurance by his forced inactivity," that *Generalfeldmarschall* Walter Model is a *"Characterschwein"* (man with the character of a pig), *SS-Oberstgruppenführer* Sepp Dietrich was declared to be "an uneducated country yokel," and *Generalfeldmarschall* Gerd von Rundstedt was supposedly drunk most of the time.[88] Not only was all that data unverified and unconnected to possible military capabilities and decision-making, some was so outright wrong that the whole undertaking seemed completely ridiculous. The data card on *Generaloberst* Heinz Guderian states that the officer was so fanatical in his work that he had no private life and thus had remained a bachelor in contrast to most of his comrades. Guderian, however, had then been married for over twenty years and his two sons were both officers with the *Panzertruppen*.

While the background of the German officers was rarely studied by the U.S. Army, looking at selected campaigns was more popular. The fame of the Prussian/German Army and the intense study of its campaigns proved in some aspects highly beneficial for American officers who would fight the Germans in World War I over the same terrain they had examined so closely at home.[89] To the American officers, suddenly "nearly every village, city, and prominent terrain feature in the area was familiar."[90]

This fact cannot be overestimated in the absence of standardized maps for the Allies and quite often the lack of any maps at all. Thus the fame of the Prussian/German Army in past wars contributed to its downfall in another. After the defeat of the German Army, its reputation unsurprisingly did not remain completely intact. Many American officers would belittle the fighting power of the Germans, but were reminded— often to no avail—by one of the smartest officers the U.S. Army has ever produced, that the German soldiers of 1917 and 1918 were not the German soldiers of 1914.[91] George C. Marshall proved here once again that he usually saw things more clearly than his contemporaries.

Those who fought the Germans in World War I usually called them by their degrading war nicknames "Boche" or "Hun," invented by the French and British respectively, and would still use "Hun" during the next war for good reasons. General George Smith Patton, USMA 1909, used to write on the numerous pictures he took of dead German soldiers in World War II, "Good Hun."[92] Younger American officers, who had not been in World War I, called the Germans rather "Heinis," "Fritzes" or, like the enlisted men, "Krauts." "Heini" is a short form for the German Christian name "Heinrich," which was to the American soldiers as universal as "Fritz." "Kraut" is from the supposed German national favorite menu of *Sauerkraut und Bratwurst* (pickled sour cabbage and sausage). That, however, is rather a Bavarian treat, but when Americans think about Germany, they often mean Bavaria.

Among the American officer corps who fought in World War I, the more popular nickname was "Boche," which comes from the French "caboche" and describes a "hollowhead" as well as a "thickhead." The Germans acquired the other nickname, "Hun," from the British, after Emperor Wilhelm II's infamous *"Hunnenrede"* (Hun speech), which he delivered in

Bremerhaven on July 27, 1900, when sending off the *Ostasiatische Expeditionskorps* (East Asian Expeditionary Corps) to quell the Boxer Rebellion in China. The speech was—typically for Wilhelm II—full of martial splendor and gory exaggerations but even for him still a notch above the usual nonsense. He ordered the soldiers to give no quarter and take no prisoners and to make a name for themselves just as a thousand years ago the Huns under their King Etzel (Attila) did, which has made them mighty even in today's tradition. And in the same way, the soldiers should make the name "Germany" remembered in China for a thousand years so that no Chinaman will ever again dare to even squint at a German.[93]

Just like fourteen years and again thirty-nine years later in other parts of the world, the German soldiers in China would behave less than knightly when given carte blanche by their superiors to do so, which was obviously reason enough for the Allies to retain the old nickname for them in the next wars.

Perry L. Miles, then a captain in the U.S. Army in China, observed "that the Germans coming upon some small armed groups and dispersing them, killed Chinese soldiers and civilians promiscuously."[94] In hindsight, he added that "we had a preview of the ruthlessness of the German in war, which if remembered, should have tempered our surprise in the happenings of later wars."[95] The U.S. Army's memory proved to be short again.

Those American officers who travelled through Germany before and after World War I usually wrote very positively about Germany and the Germans. One of the most unlikely admirers was Dwight D. Eisenhower, who changed his opinion about the Germans several times in his life from one extreme to another. While travelling through Germany with his wife and his friends the Grubers, their travel diary noted on Monday September 2, 1929, as a result of a week in Germany, "we have been enthusiastic about Germany, the people as well as the beautiful landscapes. [...] We like Germany!"[96]

The same enthusiasm cannot be found with many of the officers detailed to occupy a part of Germany after World War I, in stark contrast to the occupation after World War II, where again the positive voices by far outweigh the negative. There are several possible explanations for that.

Whereas only a small enclave of Germany was occupied after the first war and thus only a limited experience was possible, American officers roamed freely in Germany after the Third Reich had crumbled. Another major difference can be detected in the attitude of the Germans themselves. They had been told their army had been undefeated after World War I, and they still were resentful because of the ongoing Versailles negotiations and the occupation.[97] After the Second World War, the Germans had every reason to be submissive and extremely friendly to the occupants for fear of persecution or any other repercussions they might receive because of the war and the Holocaust, and the "ordinary Germans" also needed to distinguish themselves from the "Nazis."[98] The schmoozing went so far that an American officer commented sarcastically "that each true German should be provided with a shiny halo."[99]

The decline of reputation for the German Army did not last too long, at least not at the American military schools. One reason might have been that so much material about Prussian and German battles was available; another, the late acknowledgement that the First World War against the Germans had indeed been a close thing. This led to the odd reality that the German operations were more discussed than those of the other Allies or of the Americans themselves. The Battle of Tannenberg, fought by the Germans in the last days of August 1914 and won against overwhelming Russian superiority, especially seemed to have fascinated American instructors and students alike. The results of the instructions and studies, however, were not always professionally useful, as will be demonstrated in the chapter about the Command and General Staff School.

American officers who used their language skills to translate French and especially German manuals into English received special credit. This happened particularly during the "boring" years when the U.S. Army was cut to pieces by budgetary means between the end of World War I and the rise of German military power in 1935. The more lively officers felt for the most part mentally unchallenged by the dull, routine work and thus picked out these translation projects. It meant an enormous amount of extra work but was rewarded with the gaining of knowledge and often publication and sometimes overseas travel.

Walter Krueger, born in Germany in 1881, but in 1922 a lieutenant colonel in the U.S. Army, translated a monstrous volume about the
German cavalry into English as well as a much more needed handbook on
regimental war games.[100] For his research on World War I, he was allowed
to travel to the Prussian Army Archives in Potsdam where the German
archivists rendered him every support.

Frequently, translated military manuals from France and Germany
were used as a basis for the American product and modified or even used
nearly unaltered by the U.S. Army.[101] Whereas it was common for officers with language skills to translate relevant military manuals, articles,
or books from other armed forces into their native language, it was most
uncommon that an army adopted them as frequently as the U.S. Army
did. The great advantage of such a procedure is of course the different
points of view and the "foreign input," which might lead to more flexible
procedures. A great disadvantage of such a procedure was that, just as
easily, it would lead to confusion and a contradiction of doctrines.[102]

A possible explanation for the U.S. Army's habit of using foreign
military manuals might have been a sense of insecurity about some soldierly—or scholarly—abilities. The officers of the U.S. Army could not,
or so it was thought, produce certain manuals on their own. If it happened, however, they were universally hailed.[103] A certain lack of trust of
American senior officers, especially in the abilities of the more junior officers, will be discussed in the following chapters.

By the influx of German manuals and articles and the continuous
teaching, dissecting, and refighting of Prussian and German battles, the
Germans regained their old position as an admired fighting force among
the officer corps of the U.S. Army.

After the conclusion of World War II and the defeat of Germany,
the assessment American officers made of their German counterparts had
a "tribal" quality. While there was universal consent among American officers that many German officers were Nazis and guilty accomplices in a war
of aggression or perpetrators of atrocities, those they worked with were generally excluded from all negative categories, while others were observed
with extreme suspicion The esteem in which a German officer was held

rose on the fact alone that he had a command of the English language. All those assessments of German officers show themselves to be without any foundation of fact and rather rest on an emotional basis.

One reason for the easy bonding of German and American officers shortly after World War II might have been that they had experienced similar problems during the interwar years. The fact had already been noted by Friedrich von Boetticher, a German General Staff officer, who undertook an extensive tour of the United States military installations and also civilian schools and universities in 1922–1923.[104] Both armies faced severe limitations in training and equipment and a general downsizing. The rationale on the American side was internal: primarily budget reasons but also the historical fear of a standing army and militarization—as funny as it sounds today. The Germans of course had to reorganize under the external pressures and limitations of the Versailles Treaty regulations.

Both armies had roughly the same size officer corps, but the U.S. Army was even smaller in numbers then the *Heer*—the German ground force. The latter numbered seven infantry and three cavalry divisions as prescribed by the Versailles Treaty.[105] In Germany, the general consensus about being defenseless and being treated unfairly after World War I led to an early agreement between the High Command of the *Reichswehr* and leading politicians to undermine the restrictions illegally. The *Reichswehr*, however, had not waited for this agreement but already started scheming. Even without political support, it is likely that the *Reichswehr* would have continued to violate the Versailles Treaty; they just would have acted more carefully. Adding the *Schwarze Reichswehr* and later the *Sturmabteilungen* (*SA*, assault units), the German ground forces by far exceeded the tiny U.S. Army ground forces. All those units were known as *Schwarze Reichswehr*, which were armed, not actually regular "line" units of the *Reichswehr* but more or less loosely controlled by the German military high command.[106] They included the *Freikorps*, short-term volunteers who were trained and phased out quickly against the regulations of the Versailles Treaty, border defense units, and various kinds of militia.[107] The only units organized by the *Wehrkreiskommando* III (defense district command) on a long-term basis were *Arbeitskommandos* (work units). For official pretense, they acted as construction units close to military installations but were uniformed and stationed in barracks. In 1923, they numbered 18,000 men—an additional full-fledged division but without the heavy weapons.[108]

The *Freikorps* alone, roaming around and warring in the East, numbered around 200,000 in 1919 when the official *Reichswehr* still had the same number of men.[109] That brought the available manpower to nearly the same as the old imperial regular army, though of course with a much lesser degree of coherence and a weaker command structure. The assertion, however, that at that time the *Freikorps* represented "probably the single most important power in Germany" is highly exaggerated.[110] "*Freikorps*" were units ranging in size from depleted companies to reinforced regiments; they had no uniform command structure and depended on the leadership and personality of the commander.[111] For some of them, the term "military desperadoes" might fit properly—men who were "unable or unwilling to demobilize psychologically."[112] Rarely were they able to act in concert with each other and only a few possessed heavy weapons larger then light field guns or trench mortars.

The U.S. Army had been so far reduced after World War I that its strength "seldom exceeded 135,000" during the 1920s and early 1930s.[113] At that time, it "may have been less ready to function as a fighting force than at any time in its history."[114] It is most likely that the German officers felt at that time the same about their army.

Officer promotions moved with a torturous snail's pace in both armies. In the U.S. Army, it took about thirteen years to become promoted from first lieutenant to captain and a man would remain in the latter rank for possibly seventeen years.[115] In the *Reichswehr*, an officer had to serve an average of fourteen years in the rank of *Oberleutnant* (first lieutenant) to become promoted *Hauptmann* (captain).[116] In the German Army, it was specifically hard to be selected for the rank of major, the *Majors-Ecke* (major's cliff) one of the traditionally steep steps to climb.

The German military had great hopes after World War I that the United States would become an ally and help in easing the sanctions planned by France, Great Britain, and Russia, despite the fact that Germans themselves had shown no restraint of any kind when imposing the "peace" of Brest-Litovsk on the Russians only a few years earlier. The German hopes were destroyed bitterly in what was perceived by them as another stab in the back when American politicians did not forcefully intervene against the Versailles Treaty. These ruptures in the otherwise cordial relations between the German and the American officer corps, however, were short-lived and returned to their former rather amiable state. While article 179 of the Versailles Treaty prohibited Germany from sending any military attachés or military emissaries to other nations, between 1922 and 1933 nearly thirty, mostly high-ranking, German officers, were welcomed in the United States.[117] What has been stated for the general relationship between the two nations can certainly be asserted for the military connection: "At the beginning of the 1930s, it could safely be said that no two major powers had fewer difficulties and worked better with each other than the United States and Germany."[118]

Several high-ranking German officers visited the United States Military Academy at West Point and were not overly impressed. Instead the visit to the Ford car factories became an "essential part of the officers' missions in the United States."[119] Technological interest ranked before everything else and the American mobilization capacities were correctly considered by the German officers as crucial for the U.S. Army's efforts in World War I. With this knowledge and the deep insight they got from their view of American industrial potential, it is all the more surprising that they were completely unable to grasp, even remotely, the industrial potential of the future enemy. A cultural barrier that ranked immaterial and rather spiritual abilities like willpower and creativity far above industrial capacity as decisive in war can partly be identified as the reason for that and will be discussed in the following chapters.

The Versailles Treaty had been a thorn in the side of the Germans, but for the military it resembled rather a log. For the German officers to undermine an international treaty that was so important and so closely monitored, much ingenuity was needed—and also criminal energy. Both traits would again be displayed during World War II by German officers who were then generals and field marshals. The "anything-goes-attitude," if backed by enough power or covered up properly, had become a general

motto for many officers and "weakened their moral fiber," even if that attitude was objectively recognized as wrong.[120]

For the American officers, who had always lived and acted in a
democracy, such actions were not possible or thought of. But their ingenuity and "outside-the-box-thinking" were likewise not challenged.

In Germany, young officers devised tank tactics based on trials
with trucks—and faced the wrath of their superiors and ridicule of their
comrades undaunted. In the United States, the only outdated tank unit
hardly ever drove cross-country or shot its weapons for fear of wear and
breakdown and the expense of costly shells. The success of the unit was
regularly measured by how many tanks and men showed up washed, polished, and "healthy" for the inspection by superiors but the restrictions
on fuel use made any longer driving difficult. In Germany, young officers risked their careers to promote new tactics and weapons, whereas in
the U.S. Army such actions were effectively subdued and the ghost of the
polished brown shoe army—and especially horse cavalry—prevailed.

The maverick spirit fostered in the *Reichswehr* would reap great benefits for the German Armed Forces but apparently died out when an officer reached a high position in the *Oberkommando des Heeres* (*OKH*)—the
High Command of the Army, the *Oberkommando der Wehrmacht*—the High
Command of the Armed Forces, or gained command of an army or army
group. An explanation for this stated "that ambitious officers when they
came in sight of promotion to the generals' list, would decide that they
would bottle up their thoughts and ideas, as a safety precaution, until they
reached the top and could put these ideas into practice. Unfortunately, the
usual result, after years of such self-repression for the sake of their ambi-
tion, was that when the bottle was eventually uncorked, the contents had
evaporated."[121] A less eloquent explanation will be offered in the concluding chapter. To come to this point, however, it is important to answer the
question of what made a young man choose the military profession in the
United States and in Germany and what were the first steps to his commission. This will be examined in the following two chapters.

When the U.S. Army decided that the Prussian/German Army should
be studied more closely because it had just won several wars, its officers

looked largely in the wrong places and through their own cultural glasses, which distorted reality. While every army needs a planning organization, the German General Staff was only that. It functioned without peer when led by Helmuth von Moltke the Elder but became nothing more than a paper-pushing bureaucracy under mediocre chiefs of staff and even hindered operations by constant infighting or sheer incompetence. One primary example is the Schlieffen Plan, devised by one of Moltke's successors, Alfred *Graf* von Schlieffen.[122] It would start the unfortunate history of go-for-broke operations planning in Germany that lasted until its devastating defeat in 1945. While Moltke always offered contingency war plans that were revised at least every two years, such a flexible and realistic approach was no longer upheld by his most prominent successor. Schlieffen was also the first chief of staff who staged the yearly *Kaisermanöver*—emperor's maneuvers—to impress the young monarch.[123] But in a staged maneuver with a predetermined outcome, the performance of the leaders and their units can no longer be properly assessed; it also undermines the trust of younger officers in their senior leadership.

The Schlieffen Plan devised for a future attack on France was written the same way his staged maneuvers used to run.[124] It was completely inflexible and the already moronic count had used units that did not exist and completely neglected logistics. The sorry state of affairs at the Great General Staff cannot be better described than with the fact that Schlieffen's successor, Moltke the Younger, adopted the plan with only slight changes and again without devising a Plan B. With over a hundred highly educated and tightly selected officers at their disposal chiefs of staff completely failed to make use of them.

If at all possible, Moltke's successor, Erich von Falkenhayn, showed in 1916 an even greater evidence of incompetence by no longer forwarding any strategic or operational planning but instead suggesting Germany bleed to death the forces of France in a place of his choosing—Verdun.[125] The French soldiers were, by the possible loss of this important fortress city, to be lured into a killing ground of great proportion. Because in Falkenhayn's mind, without possessing a shred of evidence for that belief, the Germans would always outfight the French and thus their casualties would be lower, ultimately ruining the French Army.[126] The whole "operations plan" backfired catastrophically.

During the interwar period, the German General Staff was not only unable to conduct joint planning but "virtually nothing was coordinated, neither financial nor economic nor political nor military factors."[127] In 1940—twenty-eight years after Schlieffen had submitted the last memorandum for his plan, and twenty-five years after it had proven futile— the Great General Staff led by *Generaloberst* Franz Halder forwarded basically the same plan for an attack on France with only slight modifications.[128] Not for the first time after Moltke the Elder's death and not for the last time did the German "Great" General Staff "display an utter lack of imagination."[129] In the light of the past and future performance of the Great General Staff and its senior leadership, the notion that the proposed amateurish plans comprised some sort of resistance against Hitler's aggressive plans is incomprehensible.[130] The dictator already had defied the generals with the foundation and expansion of the *Waffen-SS*, the *Anschluß*, or connection of Austria, and the annexation of Czechoslovakia and had them help him orchestrate an attack on Poland. Hitler's plans "were supported by a far reaching consensus" within the German military.[131] It is highly implausible that the generals would now sense success in opposition just by proposing a bad plan. After all, Germany was actually at war with France and thus battle had to be waged.

When an outstanding new proposal for the attack on France was forwarded by a trained General Staff officer, then *Generalmajor* (Major General) Erich von Manstein, chief of staff of *Heeresgruppe* (army group) A— to attack through the Ardennes forest and mountainous area to strategically and tactically surprise the enemy—the chief of staff and the senior officers around him stonewalled the plan with ridiculous arguments. Only through the machinations of two of Manstein's staff officers, *Oberst* (Colonel) Günther Blumentritt and *Major* Henning von Tresckow, was it possible to make the dictator aware of this plan. Tresckow had served with Rudolf Schmundt, who was now a colonel and Hitler's adjutant, in Infantry Regiment No. 9. Similar episodes during the war suggest the enormous importance of the connections among former regimental comrades for the decision-making of senior officers in the *Wehrmacht*, but there is not yet any study about it.[132]

Schmundt became convinced of the soundness of the plan after talking to von Manstein and began to scheme immediately. He got the "inspirational bright idea" to invite the newly promoted corps commanders who would attack France to a working breakfast with Hitler in Berlin.[133] Von Manstein was now among them because he had gotten command of a corps. In his memoirs, he portrayed himself—and his fellow officers followed his lead—a martyr for getting command of a corps instead of remaining chief of staff of an army group, blaming the whole episode on the chief of staff of the army, Franz Halder, who supposedly bore him ill will because of the memoranda von Manstein wrote. The fact is, however, that von Manstein was overdue for a unit command and there is no evidence of string-pulling by the chief of staff to get him reassigned, although it has to be conceded that the whole idea was well within Halder's narrow-minded capabilities.

After the working breakfast, von Manstein gained Hitler's ear and proposed his new plan, which was enthusiastically endorsed by the dictator. Termed *Fall Gelb* (case yellow) by the Germans and in later propaganda "Operation Sicklecut," it would be enormously successful and make military history. It would also remain the only successful decisive strategic German military plan since the days of Moltke the Elder. The episode shines a bright light on the lack of performance of the German General Staff in World War II. While *Fall Gelb* was invented by a trained German General Staff officer, the majority of the senior leadership—especially those members of the strategic planning section—opposed it and didn't even show enough self-confidence to have it discussed but rather covered it up.[134] The whole campaign became instead reality "by a fortunate convergence of a number of historical accidents" and not from the professionalism or inventiveness of the German General Staff.[135]

The further course of the war showed support for the suicidal attack on the Soviet Union by the Great General Staff while the *Wehrmacht* was still undertrained, underequipped, and undersupplied. Supposed military professionals on the General Staff made explicit statements that war against the Soviet Union "could be fought with existing equipment."[136] Any notion that the German senior staff officers mainly disagreed with Hitler on military matters has long since been banished into the land of legends.[137] It is obvious that the German Great General Staff after Moltke the Elder was neither a formidable organization nor decisive in winning wars because the Germans kept on losing.

Any organization is only as good as the leadership provided from the top. Structure may make up for a lot but—especially for a military organization—sound leadership is imperative. The "brain of an army" could easily become its tumor.[138] The American observing officers were so fixed on the Great General Staff fantasy that the more important and successful traits of the German officer corps escaped their attention. The American copy of the German Great General Staff, altered for their purposes, therefore suffered from a forest of red tape and infights among the bureau chiefs before George C. Marshall took over and provided the necessary leadership. The Americans did not even try to adapt the sophisticated selection, education, and commissioning process of officers existing in Germany, most likely because the faculties at West Point and Leavenworth had done such a successful whitewashing over decades, a fact that will be discussed in the next chapters.

Whatever professional military educational reforms followed, they were insular in character because the American military schools and academies did not communicate with each other, while in Germany one military school was the steppingstone for the other and they thus possessed interlinked curricula. The discussion about an ongoing revolution in command philosophy—the *Auftragstaktik*—completely escaped the attention of visiting American officers, as did other important traits that made the German officer corps the efficient group it was.

The sophisticated commissioning system of the Germans was noted but not implemented into the U.S. Army. Why that was the case and the differences between the American and German systems will be discussed in the next chapters.

PART ONE

The Selection and Commissioning of Officers

TWO

No "Brother Officers":
Cadets at the United States
Military Academy at West Point

> *"You can never be a 'brother officer' to him whom you once degraded. […]*
> *The discipline which makes the soldiers of a free country reliable in battle*
> *is not to be gained by harsh or tyrannical treatment."[1]*
> —MAJOR GENERAL JOHN MCALLISTER SCHOFIELD, USMA 1853

> *"The best way to extinguish a man is to send him to West Point."[2]*
> —DR. CHARLES E. WOODRUFF, Army Surgeon, 1922

Despite some "structural" similarities of both armies discussed in chapter 1, the route to becoming an officer differed dramatically in both nations. Young Germans who sought to become officers, either via a position in a military academy or in an existing regiment, pursued this goal with the intent of becoming regulars for a lifetime.[3] In contrast, the majority of young Americans who applied to West Point saw a military school or academy as a means to a free education unavailable in expensive private colleges. American adolescents, however, often became gradually overwhelmed by the martial spirit and at least tried to start a career in the military. More than 85 percent of the officers who had graduated from West Point in the years from 1900 to 1915 remained on active duty until their retirement.[4] The reason for staying that long in service, however, can not be attributed only to a martial spirit or a sense of duty; the occurrence of two world wars has to be taken into account.

Though only a minority of all American officers attended the United States Military Academy at West Point, they later constituted a majority in the highest ranks and the most important positions in the U.S. Army.

During World War I, West Point graduates made up a mere 1.5 percent of the whole officer corps yet comprised 74 percent of the 480 general officers.[5] Sixty-eight percent of all officers who reached the rank of permanent brigadier general or higher between 1898 and 1940 came from the Academy. For this reason, and that of a simple limitation of research possibilities, I will restrict the survey for the American side largely—but not exclusively—to officers who graduated from the military academies at West Point, New York, or the Virginia Military Institute (VMI), at Lexington, Virginia.

After the War of Independence and the turn of the nineteenth century, it was generally recognized that the U.S. Army had lacked and still lacked a professional officer corps with sufficient education. The United States Military Academy at West Point, founded in 1802, was intended particularly to equip the army with engineer officers.[6] There is no indication, though it is possible, that it drew its "main inspiration from Frederick the Great" and "was created as upon a Prussian Foundation."[7] If it was indeed inspired by Frederick, the Prussian king was—as usual by American officers—soundly misunderstood.[8]

Engineers were so important for the army because, during the War of Independence, fortifications and gun batteries devised and constructed by engineers with pure civilian or lacking military education had a rather "picturesque" appearance instead of being efficient and well sited.[9] This repeated incompetence produced numerous congressional fact-finding missions that sought to correct these glaring deficiencies. Claims that the "corps of engineers may well have been the ablest branch of the Continental Army" are therefore mistaken.[10] Consequently, the curriculum at the newly founded military academy, with an emphasis on mathematics and "technical science," is understandable, but when West Point became a general recruitment place for the whole army even well before the Civil War, curriculum requirements were not changed.[11] Officers required a more thorough understanding of warfare and leadership, which would have been badly needed during the Civil War but was not furnished to the cadets at West Point.

In 1900, an incredible 75 percent of a cadet's course work in the four years he attended West Point dealt with mathematics, the sciences, and engineering.[12] The academic board thwarted all proposals for mod-ifications of the old curriculum, such as introducing military history or modern infantry tactics, with the argument that the present one would build "mental discipline."[13] This "party line" persisted for more than a century and even appears in modern historiography.[14]

How to achieve mental discipline, however, provoked a lively debate among scholars at that time. Some voted for the use of the classics, others for physical sciences, and some for biology.[15] The whole idea comes across as a pseudoscience invented by old men to harness the minds of younger.

A senior professor at the Academy indirectly acknowledged this fact when he stated that "our academy stands practically alone among educa-tional institutions, civil or military, in retaining a considerable portion of its curriculum chiefly because of its value in mental discipline and devel-opment, and not at all for its utility."[16] Military history, a sine qua non for the education of officers, entered into the West Point curriculum as an independent discipline only in 1946.[17]

In 1919, the more modern-minded new superintendent of West Point, Douglas MacArthur, USMA 1903, fought another—largely unsuc-cessful—battle to reduce mathematics and natural sciences in favor of topics that would be more useful to a young officer in the U.S. Army. He had been ordered to become the new superintendent of the academy by the chief of staff of the army, General Peyton March, USMA 1888, with the words "West Point is forty years behind the times."[18]

Many of MacArthur's achievements would be undone after he left West Point. In particular, his struggle for curriculum changes was short-lived. MacArthur might have had an especially tough stand at the Acad-emy and with the academic board because most of those who had taught him as a cadet were still professors of the faculty. It has been correctly assumed that his "very presence must have been irritating to the oligar-chy of the permanent professors."[19] The thirty-nine-year-young general replaced a seventy-one- year-old superintendent who had been teaching at West Point for decades.

When the new superintendent asked the senior faculty to prepare suggestions for a streamlined curriculum because the cadets were already overburdened, the narrow-mindedness of the professors came clearly to the fore. They wanted the hours of their own discipline doubled and those of their colleagues quartered.[20] With such an attitude, any compromise or reform became impossible. An observer noted that in his whole experience he had never found a group "so powerful and deeply entrenched" as the senior faculty at West Point.[21]

Similar battles had been fought by MacArthur's predecessors and would be fought again by his successors. The senior professors and the underqualified instructors of the faculty, however, "could wear down or wait out" the superintendent, who would not stay as long as they would.[22] The term of a superintendent usually lasted four years while senior faculty served a lifetime.

Just overruling the professors was apparently not possible because the superintendent had only one voice among the senior members of the academic board. However, we are talking about an army institution and it should have been possible to change just about anything by executive orders.[23] The superintendent of the United States Naval Academy, Annapolis, Maryland, carried three votes. For a brief period in 1905 the superintendent of West Point was able to gain the additional votes, but like so many preferable reforms at the Academy, they were soon lost.

Because the senior faculty of West Point consisted either exclusively, or in the great majority, of former or current officers, it raises the issue of why the superintendent confronted so many problems in enforcing his orders.[24] It would have been one solution to the educational misery at the Academy to hire civilian teachers but—with a few exceptions—the senior faculty refrained from doing that to preserve the aura of a completely military-minded installation. In 1914 at least, it became custom to invite professors from civilian universities for lectures about twice a month.[25]

Knowing about the requirements West Point imposed on its cadets—especially in regard to the disciplines of mathematics and physics—alumni fathers often sent their sons to special preparatory schools, both to help them pass the entrance exam and to prepare them to survive the scholarly demands of West Point.[26] A failure to meet the demands of any one course would mean dismissal or the repetition of a year no matter how high the cadet scored in other areas.[27]

Though there have to be standards for a professional military education, it is evident that a cadet would need only limited mathematical skills during his future officer career. Instead, he would need infinite leadership abilities, or, in George Washington's words, the cadets should get at least passed on some of "the knowledge [...] acquired thro' the various stages of a long and arduous service."[28] The four years of engineering and mathematical training rarely played a role in the martial world of the cadet graduates and any skills in those sectors would often be forgotten because they were hardly ever used.[29] Leadership always trumped technical skills. Yet, these technical skills were weighted at West Point more heavily than leadership abilities, an obvious flaw in the system. A subcommittee appointed by MacArthur for assessing problems associated with the teachings of the stubborn professor of mathematics Charles P. Echols pointed to the deficiencies in the system and remarked that "too many good cadets had been discharged, and that mathematics accounted for a disproportionate part of these."[30]

Though there was explicitly a theme of character building at the Academy, in stark contrast to the German schools the Academy's professors "were not in full agreement on the best techniques for character development."[31] Obviously, character building was neglected in favor of subordination, extensive drill, and "mental disciplining."

The one-sided education eventually compelled even the twenty-sixth president of the United States, Theodore Roosevelt, to interfere. He declared that "mathematical training is a necessary thing for an engineer or an artilleryman, doubtless; but I esteem it to literally no importance for the cavalryman or infantryman. If tomorrow I had to choose officers from the regular army for important positions in the event of war, I should care no more for their mathematical training than for their knowledge of whist or chess."[32]

The contemporary superintendent of the Academy, Colonel Hugh Scott, and his senior faculty of that time replied with the warped logic that mathematical training was the means for the future officer to undertake "unhesitatingly the unfamiliar, and for going unerringly and indomitably after results whenever demanded by duty of any nature."[33]

No question exists that the president was correct and, indeed, the majority of West Point graduates who were later universally known as outstanding leaders finished the Academy with only mediocre scholarly records.[34] Apparently at least a statistical connection existed between good standing at the Academy and a successful military career, but the gaining of high rank does not guarantee an outstanding officer beneath the stars of the uniform.[35] The officer promotion system in the U.S. Armed Forces, especially the selection to the rank of general, has come under attack ever since World War II and the discussion has just recently intensified, for good reasons.[36]

Those who were accepted at West Point had a long way to go to reach the rank of general, yet graduates from the Academy were generally more successful than non-graduates. West Point accepted young men between seventeen and twenty-two, though with a little bit of faking and forgery a few gained entrance at an older or younger age.[37] The aspirants had to be at least five feet five when they were eighteen.[38]

The great majority of cadets gained entrance to West Point via a congressman's appointment.[39] Each congressman could select one young man from his district to West Point each year, with a total of two from the state.[40] The system insured, as a "democratic safeguard," that no political party or faction would be able to dominate the officer corps and that young men from all states had access to the Academy.[41]

There is rarely any preferential treatment noted in diaries and letters of former cadets. Congressmen usually decided after a competitive examination of their own design, at a school or before a Civil Service Board.[42] However, the numbers show that too many of the selectees did not even show up at West Point and thus lacked from the very beginning determination and steadfastness. In a little over a century, a staggering 2,316 candidates did not report after they had been selected.[43] During times when the army needed officers, notably during the years of 1914–1916, and the politicians did not nominate enough candidates, up to 65 percent entered West Point without any entrance examination.[44]

Entering the Academy seemed to have been the smallest problem; surviving it was much more difficult. This fact was well known to the new superintendent. MacArthur, then the youngest brigadier general in the army and highly decorated in the Philippine wars and World War I, changed West Point much for the better, especially for the plebes, by introducing the "MacArthur Plebe System."[45] For example, it denied any honors to those who did not actively take action against hazing. Merely not hazing or looking away was no longer sufficient.

He also wanted to change the whole cadet experience, which he described as "abnormally confining."[46] He correctly noted the paradox that West Point used "to boast about a cadet's truth and honesty" but did not "trust him to go out the gates of this medieval keep."[47] MacArthur experienced the confinement and hazing as a plebe in 1899. He had been "eagled," hanged from a stretcher, and was then forced to "shower" for twenty-two minutes, which is explained later in the text. The whole procedure left him unconscious and totally exhausted. In a common misunderstanding of the honor code among cadets, he first refused to testify against his tormentors in front of a congressional hearing. In front of a military court that explained to him the proper honorable behavior, he named the sadists who had hazed him.

The phenomenon of hazing will be discussed in this chapter in depth because the whole idea runs so contrary to all leadership principles in an army and yet it has always been to some extent a part of the American military academies.

The education at West Point lasted four years, of which the first year saw the greatest attrition rate because the new arrivals, called "plebes," were free game for the three older classes, the "yearlings," "cows," and "firsties" — the latter having the greatest power. At other military academies, the freshmen had different but equally degrading names. They were "rats" at the Virginia Military Institute (VMI) in Lexington, Virginia, and "knobs" at The Citadel in Charleston, South Carolina.

The name "Beast Barracks" aptly describes the first few weeks in which the plebes had to survive relentless harassment, insults, and aggravated physical training beyond any health recommendations. This procedure was called "hazing," and the severity of it depended on year and cadet company. It has been at all times a part of life at the American military academies.[48] The ordeal did not end after the weeks of the "Beast Barracks" but continued, usually less severely, throughout the "plebe year." Plebes remained at the mercy of the upperclassmen.

Some upperclassmen engaged in hazing only because it was "the system" and it was expected of them, while others thrived on sadism. A collection of potential hazing techniques reads like a supplement to the Marquis the Sade's writings. In reality, these techniques represented simply a compilation of what young males cornered in an extremely steep hierarchy can do to each other when unobserved and after a refinement of hazing techniques over many decades.

It is not yet clear when the hazing started in earnest at West Point—possibly after the American Civil War—but it may have been there since its foundation and just gained brutality.[49] Some claim that hazing appeared at the end of the reign of Sylvanus Thayer, USMA 1808, as superintendent of the Academy around the 1830s.[50] Thayer also issued the large set of confining rules for the cadets because he constantly had to combat poor discipline among the cadets.[51] Discipline, however, needs first and foremost leadership, and not regulations. The former can only be provided by example. It appears that many superintendents—"supes" in West Point lingo—were not exactly suited as role models for the cadets.[52] Hazing was allowed "to degenerate into a sadism" that was "aggravated by a tendency of 'old grads' and superintendents to side with the upperclassmen," as will be proven in the rest of the chapter.[53]

The number of dismissals because of bad treatment of plebes increased after the Civil War but that can hardly be viewed as a factor for judging the severity of hazing in any given period. Not only did this humiliating practice usually take place out of sight of officers who held the power to discipline upperclassmen, but nearly half of the dismissed cadets were later reinstated. Of the total of forty-one cadets dismissed or forced to resign from 1846 to 1909—a relatively small number given the many years and the magnitude of the problem—eighteen returned.[54] In the years when plebe hazing supposedly intensified, a much higher number of those dismissed were readmitted.[55] This clearly indicates a lack of will within the leadership of the Academy to deal decisively with the problem.

Though there are several titles about hazing at non-military colleges, there exists to my knowledge no scholarly work on the history of hazing at the Academy.[56] Hazing had unfortunately already been introduced into the very first American civilian colleges where students had to learn "through harsh punishments, the importance of hierarchy."[57] Perhaps John Adams's words that "in a society in which male adolescents find it increasingly difficult to discern what it means to be a man or how to become one, we should promote military service as a rite of passage to manhood" had been misunderstood by the military.[58] The idea of making a man seems to have vanished over time as the plebe cadets were even treated as "less than boys."[59] A harsher rite of passage prevailed and the hazing seemed to have increased in severity over time in the military schools, i.e., the hazing during the period viewed in this study—the graduating classes largely between 1909 and 1927—was less severe than in the 1960s or '70s.[60] This notion comes from a comparison of diaries, memoirs, and scholarly works. Even Dwight D. Eisenhower, USMA 1915, could afford to play pranks on the upperclassmen.[61] Benjamin Abbott "Monk" Dickson, USMA 1918, who was already as a teenager very critical towards the West Point educational system, reports to have experienced only "bracing," which is an exaggerated version of standing at attention.[62] The future extraordinary intelligence officer also observed that "the monotony of W[est] P[oint] is tedious."[63] Only two years after his graduation from the Academy, Dickson resigned his commission to enter a university because after what he had learned at West Point he believed himself to be "below par as to educational qualifications as compared with young men of my boyhood environment."[64]

Another indication for less severe hazing other than the experiences above is that at his time at the Academy, the guidelines against hazing were tightly defined. Similar to the regulations of a German *Kadettenschule*, which will be discussed in the next chapter, they left no room for interpretation.[65] Instead of defining hazing only in rather foggy phrases, a whole list of forbidden actions was added, which left the upperclassmen nearly no loopholes.

Dwight David "Ike" Eisenhower as a plebe (right) with his classmate Tommy Atkins (left) at West Point in the fall of 1911. Plebes were discouraged from smiling or laughing; otherwise the upperclassmen would punish them for it. (PHOTO BY BABE WEYAND, COURTESY DWIGHT D. EISENHOWER LIBRARY)

Benjamin Abbott "Monk" Dickson as a cadet at West Point. He was already as a teenager very aware of educational issues and his diary is a frank appraisal of his West Point experience. He looked down on hazing as childish and unsoldierly. Only two years after his graduation from the Academy, Dickson resigned his commission to enter a university because after what he had learned at West Point he believed himself to be "below par as to educational qualifications as compared with young men of my boyhood environment." (COURTESY U.S. MILITARY ACADEMY LIBRARY ARCHIVES)

At the tactical headquarters of First U.S. Army in Belgium, 1944. Major General William B. Kean (left), chief of staff, shows Lieutenant General Courtney H. Hodges (second left), the commander of First Army, the map positions in southern Germany. Watching are Brigadier General Truman C. Thorson (far right), the G-3 operations officer, and Brigadier General Charles E. Hart (second right), the chief artillery officer of First Army. The man in the middle with the mustache, nearly bored to death, is Colonel Monk Dickson, now the G-2 intelligence officer of First Army. He despised Kean for treating his staff like a yearling at West Point treated plebes and for portraying Dickson's insights into the German Army as his own accomplishments.

Dickson would predict nearly to the day the German offensive in December 1944, today known as the Battle of the Bulge. His now famous intelligence report no. 37 was suppressed because nobody wanted to hear about the Germans coming back when they were thought to have their backs against the wall. (PHOTO BY U.S. ARMY SIGNAL CORPS, COURTESY DWIGHT D. EISENHOWER LIBRARY)

Possible hazing scenarios included a range of imaginable physical exercises and abuses that usually only stopped when the plebe dropped or became unconscious. The severity of physical exercises could be aggravated, for example, by putting broken glass under the body of the plebe when he was forced relentlessly to do push-ups. Plebes got their hair glued with syrup and were tied to the ground near an anthill or were confined inside lockers for hours. They were forced to eat or drink so excessively that they vomited on each other.[66] Even regular meals could become "an exercise in targeted torture."[67] On occasion, plebes were deprived of food or water so that they would break down during physical exercises because of the resulting malnutrition or dehydration. When they got the "shower," plebes had to stand close to the wall with a glass pressed against it using the backs of their head and while wearing their woolen uniforms, the "plebe skin," and a heavy raincoat. The physical and mental stress and the lack of ventilation caused by the raincoat would render them soaking wet with sweat after a short time, thus "the shower," which caused rapid dehydration. If the glass fell to the ground, they had hell to pay but usually they had to stand until they passed out. The freshmen were so degraded that upperclassmen even urinated on them. In all American military academies, plebes had to act as servants for the upperclassmen by regulation and they were completely at the mercy of the upperclassmen, who could inflict cruelties on the plebes with boundless fantasy knowing full well that even minimal observation by superiors was absent.[68]

Hazing reached into other areas as well and even threatened the very important ranking of a military academy in athletic disciplines. Coaches of the athletic programs sometimes ordered upperclass teammates to protect the plebes who were physically and mentally exhausted from abuse and unable to train or compete in their sport for a long time. Given few upperclassmen on academy teams, such protection remained limited and teams would often lose some of the best freshmen players because of hazing-related resignations. The sudden loss of the best players baffled civilian coaches who had no clue what was going on in the American military academy and wondered why they suddenly lost their best cadre.[69]

Matthew Bunker Ridgway, USMA 1917, during World War II and the Korean War one of the most distinguished combat commanders of the U.S. Army, doubted the system and recounted that "there is many a night when a man, sore and bruised both physically and emotionally, doubts the wisdom of ever having entered West Point at all." His main reason for persisting was that his "father endured this thing, and thousands of other men went through it without breaking down. And if they did it, you can."[70] Only after the year of "personal harassment was over" did Ridgway begin to enjoy his life at West Point.[71]

Matthew B. Ridgway as a "firstie" in his last year at West Point. As a plebe, Ridgway was hazed severely and he doubted the system much because of that. His sole motivation to stay on was that his father had graduated from the Academy and Ridgway did not want to appear a lesser man than his father. (COURTESY U.S. ARMY MILITARY HISTORY INSTITUTE, CARLISLE BARRACKS, PENNSYLVANIA)

Ridgway, now a major general, commanding the famous 82nd Airborne Division during the invasion of Sicily in 1943. He was always well forward and is leaning here on the radio of his command Jeep pointing out to Master Sergeant Frank Morang the advance of his troops. Note the West Point graduation ring on his left hand. (PHOTO BY U.S. ARMY SIGNAL CORPS, COURTESY DWIGHT D. EISENHOWER LIBRARY)

Apparently the attempt was made once to let officers handle the hazing but this idea failed because they lacked the determination and stamina for abuse easily found in teenagers.[72]

Officially, authorities had repeatedly banned hazing throughout the existence of West Point, the last time in the early 1990s. Many hazing scandals have shaken "Hudson High," yet the savagery has persisted and demonstrates—maybe with the exception of the MacArthur years— that any real will never existed to stamp out this inhumane practice. It has been remarked on several times that the Corps of Cadets changed only when it wanted to.[73] Such a statement, however, casts a doubtful light on the leadership capabilities of the superintendents and the commandants of the Academy.

Hazing nearly cost the U.S. Army one of its very best officers. George C. Marshall, who attended the Virginia Military Institute (VMI) in Lexington, Virginia, was in his "rat" year so severely wounded by cruel hazing that it nearly ended his career before it had even begun.[74] He was forced to squat over the blade of an upright bayonet and after a time he fell because of exhaustion and cut his buttock severely.[75] This specifically dangerous hazing procedure was not uncommon at West Point either. The VMI, nicknamed "the West Point of the South," was founded and led for decades by Francis Henney Smith, USMA 1833, who allowed a hazing system basically identical to that of the Academy.[76] George S. Patton, who attended VMI as a "rat" in 1903 and a year later attended West Point as a "plebe," also noted that he had to "brace harder" at West Point and that the way they behaved toward plebes "will ruin the academy in a very few years."[77] Patton was found to be insufficient in mathematics and had to repeat his plebe year at the Academy.

The hazing system clearly undermined the "Duty—Honor—Country" motto that officially sustains the West Point spirit. Indeed, Major General John M. Schofield, superintendent of the Academy from 1876–1881, made it a matter of honor to "wholly eradicate" the hazing because it was "unbecoming of an officer and gentlemen."[78] Apparently, Schofield labored to no avail. Nearly a century later, cadets still "came away from plebe week with a distorted view of honor." Ironically, the very upperclassmen who

George Catlett Marshall as a first captain of "keydets" at the Virginia Military Institute. At VMI, Marshall had not been weighted down with an overload of mathematics and engineering but the system of hazing remained the same. Marshall was so badly wounded during a hazing incident that the United States nearly lost one of her best officers before he even was commissioned. (COURTESY GEORGE C. MARSHALL FOUNDATION, LEXINGTON, VIRGINIA)

taught plebes "honor" later brutalized them in the barracks "and they did not seem to be honorable men."[79] The cadets discovered "the truth about honor at West Point: in practice it is relative, not absolute, as they had been led to believe."[80]

Remarkably, nothing changed the next year because "many of the boys who suffered most grievously would turn into the cruelest guidon corporals, the most sadistic platoon leaders" when they became upperclassmen.[81]

Visiting alumni usually have done nothing to caution or restrain the cadets but instead fired them up to "put some teeth in the plebe system" and have told them how soft West Point had become and how hard and manly it was in their days.[82] For a good reason they carried the nickname DOGs—Disgruntled Old Grads—and together with the respective superintendents and the senior faculty they can be held responsible for the prevailing of the "plebe system" for nearly two centuries.[83]

In a complete historical misunderstanding, which is so common when American officers try to judge Prussian and German military culture and history, a faculty member observed that West Point discipline, "based on the hard, merciless system of Frederick [the Great], was too harsh for eighteen-year-olds."[84] Whereas the last part of the statement is undoubtedly true, the first statement is a complete misapprehension. Not only did the Old Prussian Army possess some of the most advanced and

George C. Marshall on the parade ground as a first captain in front of his company of "keydets." In the background to the right is one wing of the Virginia Military Institute. It was nicknamed "The West Point of the South" and even the architecture was similar to the United States Military Academy. [COURTESY GEORGE C. MARSHALL FOUNDATION, LEXINGTON, VIRGINIA]

The brass on the beaches. Supreme Commander Eisenhower (left front) and Chief of Staff Marshall (center, looking up) on the Normandy beach one week after the landings. Both men had gone a long way and were exceptions of the U.S. Army officer education system. (COURTESY GEORGE C. MARSHALL FOUNDATION, LEXINGTON, VIRGINIA)

modern regulations of its time, when it came to the handling of recruits, but physical punishment of officers or officer aspirants was forbidden by the king himself. For good reason the *Reglement vor die Königlich Preußische Infanterie*—the Royal Prussian Army Regulations—were copied by other armies throughout Europe.[85] If a regimental commander in the Old Prussian Army accepted too many *Junkers* as officer aspirants, sometimes they were inclined to haze each other to make the weaker leave and allow the remainder to advance upwards and become ensigns earlier. This procedure was called *ausbeißen*—biting out—and neither endorsed nor tolerated.[86] Frederick discouraged his commanders from accepting too many officers' aspirants.

There are topoi that are always repeated in the literature of those who successfully attended West Point and those who failed. There is always at least one especially outstanding bully, one sadist—sometimes teamed up with one or two goons—who is an upperclassman and even holds rank within the petty hierarchy of the cadet corps.[87] He and his helpers put the plebe and his friends into relentless misery day and night to break him. There are many who leave, close friends of great quality who could not or would not put up with the senseless system. And there is always the coach or tactical officer whose leadership qualities are so great that he reinstills some faith into the plebe and keeps him going throughout the cruel first year.[88] A tactical officer is supposed to supervise a cadet company. The emphasis here is on "supervise," not "command." In practice, the tactical officers remained "largely aloof."[89] Others were looked upon as "master ogre[s]" in a tower "harder to approach than a manager of a chain store."[90] Many closed their eyes before the cruelties perpetrated on the freshmen because as former West Pointers they agreed with the methods or simply did not dare take on the Corps of Cadets. Both reasons are in any case displays of bad leadership.

While many of those cadets whom the plebe got to know and began to admire would not make it, the bully, just like his sadistic friends, would graduate and become an officer in the United States Army, his honor—supposedly rock steady and hardened by the West Point system—and his ability to command already doubted by those who had suffered under him.[91] In regularly graduating men like these, another problem with the whole system becomes evident. Former graduates tend too often to disguise the problems in ambiguous language when they at least admit "that the Corps of Cadets had some rather fuzzy ideas on the meaning and utility of an honor code."[92] More compelling is the statement that "cadets often confused ethical honor with bravado."[93] That there is confusion about this important matter can certainly be agreed on.

While an abundance of literature exists about successful graduates, scholars have done virtually no research on those West Point lost, those who may have had the potential to become great officers but who would not put up with the dull and cruel system and the fact that they were treated like children, even "less than boys." James Maurice Gavin, USMA 1929, distinguished combat leader of the 82nd Airborne Division in World War II, suspected as much and opted for changes at the Academy after he returned from the war.[94]

Carl A. "Tooey" Spaatz, nearly quit during his first three weeks at West Point because of the senseless hazing.[95] Friends persuaded him to stay and he graduated in 1924. He became an expert in air warfare and Ike's staunch ally and one of his most valued commanders during World War II.

The few real diehards, who failed but whose taste for the army was not ruined at West Point, would enlist in the army and rise through the ranks, proving that they were officer material but not West Point or military academy material—two very different things, though supposed to be the same.[96] Douglas MacArthur is quoted as having said that "too many are thrust out of this institution who become successes in civil life or come back into the Army to do more credible work than some graduates."[97] Only fifteen years earlier, Chief of Staff General Franklin Bell voiced the same concerns in a letter. He feared that "the faculty at West Point [...] have a tendency to forget that West Point is maintained for the benefit of the Army, and not the Army for the benefit of West Point."[98] Bell's statement was no exaggeration. When the War Department ordered MacArthur's predecessor, Superintendent Colonel Samuel Escue Tillman, USMA 1869, to graduate the current classes early because of the great need for officers in World War I, he is reported to have said, "I don't understand why they are deliberately trying to destroy the Academy."[99] Other chiefs of staff decades later would make the same observation as their predecessor Bell. Creighton Williams Abrams, USMA 1939, voiced similar apprehension when he, some twenty-five years later, occupied the same position George C. Marshall had. Abrams "was concerned with West Point's isolation, that it did not resemble the real Army, and that its graduates were accordingly unprepared to deal with the professional environment in which they had to operate after graduation and commissioning."[100] Fifty years again had passed without noticeable change of heart at the Academy.

Numbers emphasize the problem: Of the 3,816 cadets who were separated from the Academy in the first century, only a fraction failed in tactics, the premier area of knowledge for an officer except leadership.[101] Major General Joseph P. Sanger, who made that discovery by pure number-crunching, pointed out correctly that "this might be considered an anomaly detrimental to the objects of the Academy as a military school.[102]

For the majority of those who left or were forced to leave, West Point had ruined any taste for the armed service at all—an unknown potential lost forever. Even of those who stayed, many harbored bitter feelings toward the army, because of the inhumane treatment they were forced to endure.[103]

There are many reasons given which try to make sense of the hazing system but as it is an "unofficial" practice, there is of course no official statement. The understanding prevailed that its purpose was "to reduce the individual to a subhuman status, susceptible to indoctrination, and to weed out those who lacked the necessary determination."[104] Other alumni showed an equal lack of comprehension and some mental confusion when they stated that the "severest discipline" and the suppression of personality was necessary so "the spirit of West Point" would not be "perverted through him"—the plebe.[105]

Why teaching and education has to be replaced with indoctrination and determination has to be tested with sadism instead of tough military training is unclear and it shows that there is no reasonable and intelligent explanation for the hazing system.

Creighton Abrams, one of the most outstanding combat leaders ever to wear the uniform of the U.S. Army, did his best as a cadet but years later was still annoyed remembering his treatment by the upperclassmen:

Creighton Williams Abrams as a West Point cadet. Abrams describes his plebe year as "a pretty brutal experience. The hazing was degrading and certainly not character building." He would become one of the most outstanding combat leaders ever to wear the uniform of the U.S. Army, leading from the front, taking part in the fighting with his own tank while already a lieutenant-colonel. Eventually he rose to four-star rank. (Courtesy U.S. Military Academy Library Archives)

Lieutenant-Colonel Creighton Abrams (left) and his close friend Major Cohen (right) celebrate another victory over the *Wehrmacht.* Creighton commanded the 37th Tank battalion and Cohen the 10th Armored Infantry Battalion, both part of the 4th Armored Division. Because of their close friendship and their high proficiency as officers and warriors, the units of both men worked together extraordinary effectively. The *Wehrmacht* propaganda called them "Roosevelt's highest paid butchers," certainly a high testimony for the ability of two mere battalion commanders. When the hospital in which Cohen stayed briefly was overrun by a *Waffen-SS* unit, Abrams was sure Cohen would be killed because he was Jewish. However, only a few days later Cohen was liberated by advancing U.S. Army units and the friends were united again. (COURTESY HAROLD COHEN COLLECTION)

"We plebes had to pick up things, and then set them right down, put on our coat, and then take it off, and I was punished if upperclassmen found paper in my wastebasket. Now, a wastebasket is a pretty simple functional thing, and that's where papers belong. How silly can one get?"[106] Abrams describes his plebe year as "a pretty brutal experience. The hazing was degrading and certainly not character building."[107]

So far it has been only discussed what hazing would do to the *average* cadet but woe betide the plebe who had the "wrong" religion, color, ethnicity, facial expression, a funny way of walking, or a noticeable accent and the upperclassmen decided he was unwanted in "their" corps for one of the mentioned reasons or an entirely different one. They could "get rid of any freshman they want if they are so inclined. They could run Samson and Hercules out [...] if they thought they didn't belong here."[108] They did so by giving the unwanted plebe an overdose of savage hazing, day and night ordeals, which would make him either leave because he could not take the brutality and stress anymore or because the strain made him unable to cope with the academic or athletic requirements and he would be dropped—or rather "separated" in the Academy's lingo. Only in the very rare cases when the rest of the plebes closed ranks behind him, took up some of his chores, and even tried to shield him from the upperclassmen's wrath—at the extremely high risk of becoming targets of aggravated hazing themselves—might the singled-out plebe prevail and last the first year.

People who would like to defend the system might argue that I mix up the "indoctrination process" during "Beast Barracks," "hazing," which is "officially" forbidden, and "harassment."[109] Assessed from a scholarly point of view, however, they are all the same. They just come in different camouflage, or to put it in the words of a former cadet and now successful writer: "The plebe system gave cruelty a good name, disguised sadism in the severe raiment of duty."[110]

Just as President Theodore Roosevelt later tried to interfere with the insufficient education at West Point, President Grover Cleveland attempted in 1896 to act against hazing by dismissing two upperclassmen from the Academy for harassing plebes.[111] His gesture was as much in vain as Roosevelt's. During numerous hazing scandals throughout West Point history, the public and the media addressed correctly the roots of the problem—a lack of leadership by the respective superintendents and the senior faculty.[112]

In the past few years, I have talked to numerous male and female officers from the classes between 1952 and 1996 and asked them about their experiences with the hazing system.[113] Not a single one gave a direct and frank account after my initial question. Other interviewers report the same experiences.[114] Some former and current officers refused to answer at all. Others needed to be persuaded gently. Evidently, those who went through the system—either as victims or as perpetrators, and as it has been shown many had been both—carried with them a sense of embarrassment and even shame. Remembrance becomes hard and sometimes even painful. For a psychiatrist, however, the reason is the immense stress connected to the memory rather than the shame.[115]

Usually, I was asked in return the defensive question, before I got any answer, "What is hazing anyway?" The answer to that was relatively easy in my own definition: Hazing in a military academy is any physical, psychological, or mental procedure that humiliates, insults, tortures, or injures a cadet and does not serve the direct purpose of modern military training.

The official definition of hazing by the Academy of the 1970s is "any authorized assumption of authority by one cadet over another cadet whereby the latter should suffer or be exposed to any cruelty, indignation, humiliation, hardship, or the oppression, deprivation, or abridgement of his legal rights."[116] It is obvious that this official definition provides a host of loopholes.[117] Over the centuries, the definition was changed numerous times, which shows the lack of clear thought given to the problem. The digression into the present was made because many of the graduates I look at in this study will most likely have carried the same burden.

At the same time the newcomers went through the hazing system, they had to master the artificially constructed and rigid rules of neat appearance and monastic withdrawal. Their only way to communicate with the "higher ranks" were—and are today—the four allowed phrases "Yes, Sir," "No, Sir," "No excuse, Sir," and "I do not understand, Sir."

In their bewildered and exhausted state, plebes were forced to memorize a mountain of senseless information, the so-called "plebe poop." One question was "How many lights in Cullum Hall?" The correct and relatively easy answer to this would be "340 lights, Sir." Things could become more tedious with "How many gallons in Lusk Reservoir?," for which the correct answer was "92.2 million gallons, Sir, when the water is flowing over the spillway."

Another possible question was "What is the definition of leather?," which had to be answered, "If the fresh skin of an animal, cleaned and divested of all hair, fat and other extraneous matter, be immersed in a dilute solution of tannic acid, a chemical combination ensues; the gelatinous tissue of the skin is converted into a non-putrescible substance, impervious to and insoluble in water; this, Sir, is leather."[118]

The answers had to be given exactly verbatim, otherwise some form of punishment was guaranteed. The "Sir" was directed to a boy only a few years older with no actual military merits whatsoever. The questions above are only examples; there was a whole booklet of them. The supposedly sense-making explanation for loading up a tired brain with useless information was that the cadets should train to memorize data quickly and flawlessly under stress. This would certainly be a useful ability for an officer, but there are doubtless other more pedagogic ways of learning to memorize data and the question remains why the plebes did not have to learn exclusively militarily useful information like tables of organization and equipment (TOEs) and the data of weapons systems. The cadets at West Point are still tortured with plebe poop today. A graduate from the class of 2000, leading a rifle platoon in the hills of Afghanistan, wished he had learned "the range of a howitzer or the number of minutes you could expect to shoot a machine gun before its barrel melted" instead of the "number of light bulbs at Cullum hall" or "the name of the four Army mules."[119]

West Point expected a fanatical neatness and order from the cadets and every mistake a cadet made, whether on his own or forced to make, would be punished officially with demerits or unofficially with an additional dose of hazing. Demerits could even be dished out by the first classmen.[120] That there often existed no real sense of leadership among them appears in the demerits given for "lingering too long in the bath" or "walking down the stairs in an unsoldierly manner."[121] It was even possible to get penalized when being "too early at the Riding Hall."[122]

Demerits in turn would be converted into penalty marches, called "punishment tours." The cadet would pace up and down the courtyard for many hours in full gear and in any weather, depending on the number of demerits "to march them off."

Not surprisingly, sons of officers and especially sons of former graduates of the Academy or their brothers had a little advantage over those who came from civilian life. Rarely was a son pressured by his father to go to West Point, because most fathers knew full well that their sons might not survive unless pulled through by their own motivation.[123] Also, knowing that certain disciplines were extremely demanding, they had often been sent to preparatory schools and thus usually came with a scholarly head start.[124] Their fathers or brothers had also provided them with insider information about the whole system and how best to survive it.[125] In addition, because their fathers or brothers had survived it, they possessed an enormous motivation not to back down, which would have made them lesser men in their own eyes. The army brats were instantly recognized by the upperclassmen because of their bearing and ability to adapt.[126]

Joe Lawton Collins, USMA 1917, later to become chief of staff of the army, had already gotten valuable advice from his brother, who graduated in 1907. He passed his experiences and encouragement on to his son, Jerry, when the latter became a plebe at West Point in 1943. Knowing well the greatest problem at the Academy, Collins urged his son: "Don't let the yearlings get you down."[127] "Yearlings" are sophomores in Academy lingo. They had been plebes the year before and now—having survived the plebe system and thus automatically gained power over the new arrivals—were ready to become their scourge.

In the West Point educational system, the cadets suffered not only because of the overload in mathematics and natural sciences but also because of the pedagogical and didactical backwardness of the teachers and their selection. Bidirectional teaching in communication with the cadets was unknown and after the lesson, each cadet would receive a little slip of paper with a task he had to perform in front of the class during the next lecture.[128] The cadet would present it, using predetermined fixed phrases and would be praised or chastened for it by the teacher.[129] A free discussion to raise questions or exchange ideas did not take place.[130] When a baffled cadet tried to gain clarification about a text, the instructor exclaimed, "I'm not here to answer questions, but to mark you."[131] A great part of the classroom work was taken up by just repeating what had been memorized and "the daily recitation in mathematics was, to most graduates, synonymous with West Point 'academics.'"[132] William H. Simpson, USMA 1909, "recalled that if one got

Joe Lawton Collins (left) and his classmate Henley Frier (right) as plebes at West Point in summer camp, 1913. In World War II, Collins gained the nickname "Lightning Joe" and his aggressiveness was rare among U.S. commanders. (Courtesy Dwight D. Eisenhower Library)

an incorrect answer, the instructor seldom explained the proper solution."[133] Even such important—and for future officers supposedly stimulating—topics like military history were just used to make the students parrot dates, names, and textbook contents.[134]

The selection of the teachers showed the same single-mindedness and inflexibility as the rest of the educational system at the Academy at that time. Former cadets detailed to West Point as teachers several years after they had graduated found themselves surprised to be ordered to teach a discipline in which they were not experts or even proficient.

In 1903, Perry L. Miles, USMA 1895, was ordered to West Point as an instructor of science, which included "chemistry, electricity, mineralology [sic] and geology."[135] He had, unsurprisingly, "not done any reading on any of these subjects [...] since graduation at the Point eight years before" and therefore would appear "embarrassingly handicapped."[136] Miles got away with an immediate transfer request because his regiment was shipping out to the Philippines and was short on officers. His "escape" did not leave a mark on his records. Years later, fellow officers in the same situation would not be able to get away so easily because the Corps of Cadets at West Point had grown and instructors were in direr need than ever.

Joe Lawton Collins noted being flabbergasted, when he appeared at West Point in August 1921, that he was assigned to the department of chemistry, to which discipline "he had scarcely given a thought since graduation."[137] He had studied three years of Latin and three years of French and during his occupational duty in Germany from 1919 to 1920 he had visited France several times and "had brushed up on French pronunciation" and thus expected to teach one of those languages.[138] He became instead a victim of the "antiquated system of selecting teachers at the Academy."[139] Collins does not note if he protested, but his classmate Matthew Bunker Ridgway, who found himself in a similar situation, complained. Like his comrade Collins, he would rise many years later to the position of army chief of staff. Ridgway maybe dared to resist only because he was already in a less than friendly mood. He not only thought his duty as instructor at West Point to be the "death knell of my military

An all-smiles-event in France, July 1944: Ike pins the oak leaves (2nd award) to the Distinguished Service Medal on Joe Lawton Collins's chest. In the middle is Major General Leonard Townsend Gerow, commanding general of V Corps and Ike's close friend. On the right, with the neat staffer's appearance, is William Benjamin Kean, chief of staff of First U.S. Army. Collins, now a major general, commanded the 25th Infantry Division in the Pacific. Because the U.S. Army had a great lack of aggressive commanders in the European Theater of Operations, Collins was rotated to Europe and given VII Corps, which often got the tough jobs. (Photo by U.S. Army Signal Corps, courtesy Dwight D. Eisenhower Library)

career"—and he was still a lieutenant then—but also badly wanted to
fight in Europe because the First World War was still raging.[140] In this
young lieutenant's case, the wish to go to Europe originated certainly not
solely from a desire to advance his career, but from a longing to fight.
Combat service officers looked down on the "coffee coolers" who stayed
behind in the United States during the war and the opinion was voiced
that "any officer who really wanted to get to the front could do so."[141]
Ridgway therefore felt special bitterness about the detail to West Point.

Ridgway considered himself able to teach English, and especially
Spanish, which he later translated on important occasions, but which
now was discontinued at the Academy. To his astonishment, he was
assigned as a French instructor and to a class that was well into its second year and thus more advanced then he was. Most likely only because
of the frustration about his personal situation, Ridgway dared to point
out to Colonel Cornelis deWitt Willcox, the head of the department of
modern languages at West Point and reportedly "the best French lin-
guist in the army" that he "didn't know enough French to order a scram-
bled egg in a French restaurant."[142]

Apparently Willcox was sufficiently happy with his own language
skills and didn't care much about advancing those of the cadets because
he answered Ridgway's reasonable argument only with "your classes start
tomorrow," before he turned away from the disillusioned young officer.[143]
Though the whole episode irked Ridgway greatly, it was fortunately not
the death knell to his career he had expected.

Unsurprisingly, most cadets who "successfully" finished a course during Willcox's reign and those of his successors had no command of the
foreign language they were supposed to have learned.[144] Already in 1899,
the Board of Visitors of the Academy had stated that now that the United
States was a world power "there is [...] an increasing necessity for an
acquaintance with modern languages. By this we do not mean a classroom
acquaintance, nor a stuttering, stammering acquaintance, but a practical
acquaintance that would enable a West Point graduate to make himself
understood."[145] Apparently this reasonable assessment remained completely unheeded by the senior faculty for languages even decades later.

The situation in other departments did not look different. On the occasion of the Academy's first centennial celebration and fifteen years before Ridgway's frustrating experiences, Harvard University President Charles Eliot noted publicly that the teaching at West Point was "uninfluenced by the great changes in educational methods."[146] Good instructors who were also popular with the cadets appeared to be so rare that they received special mention in memoirs of former graduates.[147]

Even in what was supposed to be one of the core courses at West Point—mathematics—the teaching quality seems to have been below average. Monk Dickson conceded that he was a slow learner in mathematics but obviously willing and wrote into his diary, "My present instructor Capt. Huntley is rotten + almost as ignorant as I which is damning indeed."[148] Dickson's observation is not surprising because Huntley was selected by one of the banes of West Point, Charles Patton Echols, USMA 1891, who himself utterly lacked any pedagogic or teaching abilities. Echols was a *prima* prima donna among many at the academic board and tended to fail many of the cadets in his courses when he was miffed by somebody. Echols "reigned" for 27 years at West Point and was described by a cadet as "one of the meanest men that draws the breath of life."[149]

Men like Echols and his colleagues on the faculty of the United States Military Academy seemed to have been much more interested in maintaining the status quo than in advancing the education of future officers. Instructors seemed to have been regarded as "interchangeable parts without reference to particular qualifications."[150] Unsurprisingly, in their reports, faculty peers would contradict themselves and put the blame for failures and problems elsewhere. Charles William Larned, USMA 1870, senior faculty member and professor of drawing, reported in 1904 that "it is entirely impossible to insure that the individual selected [as an instructor] shall possess in any fair degree of excellence the pedagogic quality. Indeed, as a matter of fact, many of the officers detailed for this duty possess it in a very limited degree."[151]

Not only did the selection of instructors show little motivation or common sense but it also violated standing orders of the superintendent that the selected "should be officers whose standing in the subject

The United States Military Academy at West Point, New York, from the air, sometime in the 1930s. The long building in the front is the riding hall, and the quadrangle in the middle is the cadet barracks. The imposing building above on the hill is the cadet chapel. Howard Serig wrote to his parents on a postcard in 1919, "Have arrived safely. There are a lot of fellows here. This place is not as beautiful as it looks on pictures. Howard." Serig made it and graduated in 1923. [COURTESY U.S. MILITARY ACADEMY LIBRARY ARCHIVES]

73

they are to teach [...] commend them for such detail" and they should
not be selected if they had been away from the Academy for more than
eight years.[152]

The senior faculty members not only had educated the junior officers, but also selected them themselves and they had the pick of most
young officers in the army. They also set their own standards for teaching and knowledge of the subject to be taught. For decades, they could
hire and fire at their own discretion and often the ability of an instructor was not their first consideration.[153]

They did, however, choose only West Pointers, which not only nar-
rowed their sample but also led to an "inbreeding" of the educational system, something that was also recognized by other regular officers.[154] The
inbreeding happened because of the standing orders of the superintendent.[155] Surprisingly, in this case the academic board chose not to rebel.

In 1935, West Point had an inbreeding rate of 97 percent of its
faculty, followed by the Naval Academy with an also high 73 percent. A
close third—not surprisingly—was the University of Notre Dame with
70 percent.[156] The average inbreeding rate of civilian colleges and universities in the United States was only 34 percent.[157]

Forty-five years after Ridgway's experiences and sixty years after
Eliot's remarks, the credentials of the faculty were still at a catastrophic
low. Instead of being proactive, encouraging dissertations, and attending pedagogy and didactics seminars, attempts were made to cover up
the sorry state of qualification of the teachers and instructors. In 1963,
Dean William W. Bessel suggested that the superintendent declare thirty
of the junior faculty as "graduate students" to artificially raise the number of postgraduate degrees.[158] At that time, of 341 faculty members
only 4 percent possessed a doctoral degree.[159] Fortunately, the superintendent abided by the code of honor and did not heed this suggestion.

The only highlight in that educational desert was the library at West
Point, which expanded considerably with the appointment of Edward S.
Holden as chief librarian in 1901. He tried to get "every important book
on a military subject published abroad, and substantially every military
book printed in America" since "cadets are confined to West Point during

West Point up close, showing the library (middle) and the east academic building (right). (COURTESY U.S. MILITARY ACADEMY LIBRARY ARCHIVES)

Reception day at West Point in 1905 in the courtyard of the quadrangle of the cadet barracks. Above is the cadet chapel. The plebes arrive and are immediately bothered by the firsties with salute training while still in line—the hazing would often start the very first day and intensify in the following weeks. George S. Patton had a year earlier transferred from the Virginia Military Institute and was now a yearling who would haze the newcomers. [COURTESY U.S. MILITARY ACADEMY LIBRARY ARCHIVES]

four years. It is the duty of the Library to enlarge their view of the world as far as books can do."[160]

As can be surmised, the little pure military training the cadets received was about as obsolete as the previously discussed education.[161] The greatest part of the time was wasted with excessive drilling and much riding, West Point being described as a "horsey institution."[162] These abilities would not be in demand in the First World War and even less in the Second. The shooting was done with outmoded rifles and the equipment used during the summer camps, where cadets saw at least a little bit of military training that tried to model reality, proved equally obsolete. In a travesty of soldiering, plebes were forced to clean and polish their rifle barrels so excessively that they became useless as instruments of war.[163] For live firing exercises, cadets used "normal" rifles because the polished ones had completely lost any accuracy and even become dangerous to the user. At the same time, "swimming instructions, dancing classes, and the two daily dress parades were as much part of summer camp as was the three-hour drill period in the morning."[164]

After four years of what was supposed to be a military education, the West Point graduate of the early 1900s "had not fired the rifle or revolver enough to meet the qualification standards of the Army, nor was he trained in the use of the Army's newer and larger pieces of weaponry and equipment."[165] Inconsequential improvements were that cadets finally had to be able to put up their own tents and tend to their horses, all chores that had previously been performed by enlisted men.[166]

Only when World War II had begun in earnest did the cadets gain access to new weapons and receive instructions in the use of modern firepower.[167] Although because of the new training the costs for educating cadets rose considerably, this was money well spent.[168]

In other aspects, the wartime changes were less favorable. Though the classes were understandably shortened and graduated earlier to supply the expanding wartime army with supposed officer material, "almost all subjects except those relating to engineering were cut out. Social sciences were abbreviated drastically and English was eliminated."[169] Everything was done to graduate the cadets with their Bachelor of Science degrees,

An examination in Ordnance and Gunnery of first-class (last year) cadets in 1908. The blond cadet at the left side of the door could be George S. Patton. Classes at West Point were larger than in the German *Hauptkadettenanstalt.* [Courtesy U.S. Military Academy Library Archives]

but little thought was given to their broader education, which already in peacetime had been severely lacking.

The question remains, what good did the four years do the young men for their future profession as officers? Though I could not find an official source explicitly saying so, the whole system was apparently invented with the thought of creating an "officer's class" or "caste" in the supposedly classless society of the United States of America.[170] My notion is supported by the fact that the possession of money was forbidden for the cadets and therefore the wealthy cadet had no advantage over his poor comrade.[171] Even bragging was out of the question.

When the class idea came up in a contemporary discussion, again the Prussian Army was incorrectly utilized to make a point. In a discussion about discipline in the journal New Republic in 1919, a writer pointed out that "it never entered his [the West Point second lieutenant's] head that the enlisted men under him were of the same flesh and blood."[172] In response, a reader replied that "West Point, or the Prussian idea of army caste and discipline is a peace time idea [...] to hold the men down while in idleness, repressive, harsh discipline and caste system are employed. [...] There is no test that I find of their ability sympathetically to understand the psychology of the common soldier, nor their power of wining the respect of their subordinates."[173] It rather seems that those who invented the system may have feared, after taking a look at the Prussian system and totally misunderstanding it, creating an officer corps of individuals.

During the West Point experience, the lowly educated son of a poor farmer in Alabama would become the same officer model as the son of a rich lawyer from Massachusetts. Therefore, equality—in the framework of white, Christian, Anglo-Saxon males—would be stressed, as well as manners and neatness. While at its creation in 1802 a worthwhile goal, the whole system failed to be modernized even remotely and would only change by pressure or force. Cadets would still, decades later, use the cynical phrase "West Point: 120 years of tradition unhampered by progress."[174]

The example of General George Smith Patton, Jr., USMA 1909, illustrates how ingrained this understanding of class still was. Patton dressed down his aide, Lieutenant Frank Graves, who was not a West Pointer, when the young officer carried the suitcases of his comrade, Lieutenant John S. D. Eisenhower, USMA 1944, the son of the Supreme Commander. In the general's view, this job had to be done by the driver.[175] This exaggerated understanding of an officer class was perceived by the enlisted men as a "caste-system" and it caused much bitterness among them.[176] In studies of social psychology about the U.S. Armed Forces of World War II, the gap between officers and enlisted men was described as a "yawning social chasm."[177] An acceptance of this "caste system" came easily to the cadets because they had few chances to question it and limited contact with the outside. After graduating from West Point, it was deeply ingrained in their character.

The majority of the cadets would be commissioned as second lieutenants, yet in their monastic exclusion, their contact with civilians and especially real soldiers—those they would command right away—was extremely restricted or nonexistent. Only the sons of former officers had experience with real soldiers, but they made up only about 20 percent of the cadets.[178] Their knowledge of hands-on military matters—unless they became engineers—was largely insufficient in respect of what weaponry or tactics they would encounter or use. As a result, after four years they were not only woefully unprepared for the next military assignment at hand but also felt that way. Often they tried to gloss over that feeling of unpreparedness with a display of arrogance, which in many cases had become synonymous with West Pointers. In other cases, they thought they were something special because they had survived the plebe regime of West Point. Some of those who carried this self-importance would lose it in the crucible of combat and advise their friends when they entered West Point, "Actually, the greatest failing we West Pointers have is looking down on others."[179]

Remembering his own shortcomings as a second lieutenant and elaborating about the future necessities for professional military education, Matthew Ridgway erroneously stated in his memoirs that "the Academy does not pretend to turn out finished Army officers."[180] Similar mistaken observations came from other alumni who, instead of promoting reform, tried to defend an illogical system when they stated that "the effort of the Academy is to produce the materials from which officers later will be made."[181]

In fact they were commissioned as second lieutenants—already officers and not officers to be made—and the majority would lead platoons or companies right away without having been given the proper knowledge to do so. In MacArthur's words, "they were thrust out into the world a man in age, but as experienced as high school boys."[182]

The cadets at West Point lived all the time under the strictest supervision and there was no other option to survive than to slavishly obey the jungle of rules. "The slightest deviation on the part of the individual" carried some sort of penalty and creative outside-the-box thinking was not only not learned but also discouraged.[183] There was a great danger in producing narrow-minded officers who simply did not dare do anything outside any doctrine or rule because they had been educated in an institution with "an almost total lack of opportunity for individual expression."[184]

The lack of preparedness and hands-on military knowledge of the Academy's graduates was at that time noted by other contemporaries. Dr. Charles R. Mann of the Committee on Education and Special Training in the General Staff noted in 1919 that, especially during World War I, "difficulties" had been experienced with respect to West Pointers' "resourcefulness, initiative, and adaptability to new ideas."[185] There were also considerable complaints about the lack of leadership capabilities and the humane treatment of men. This was also noted in a report to the secretary of war after World War I that "the fault lies in the first place with the Regular Line Officer."[186] Those, however, were to a great part trained at West Point.

One of George C. Marshall's greatest concerns had always been an adequate military education for his officers and he was maybe the person who can be credited with the greatest advances in this respect in the crucial time before World War II, but he was only one man and could only change so much. As a VMI graduate, he might have been biased when he noted an important distinction between West Point and his alma mater, but from a scholarly point of view, few of his criticisms hit home. Marshall

stated that one of the differences between the academies was the more balanced curriculum at VMI, which did not overburden the cadet with mathematics and the natural sciences but rather emphasized leadership abilities.

In a letter to his former commander, mentor, and friend, General
John J. Pershing, USMA 1886, Marshall reported in 1924 that Major
General Eli A. Helmick, USMA 1888, then Inspector General of the
Army, was concerned about the lack of leadership training the cadets received at West Point and observed correctly that "the matter has not been
given the consideration its importance merits.[187] Again the argument
was brought forward by the superintendent, Major General Fred Winchester
Sladen, USMA 1890, and his commandant, Colonel Merch Bradt Stewart,
USMA 1896, that the curriculum already was too overcrowded to imple-
ment regular leadership courses, which would be substituted by "talks" by
the commandant. That, however, satisfied neither Helmick nor Marshall.
They wanted a "carefully prepared course" in "how to handle young Americans [...,]; how to win their loyalty and secure their earnest and energetic cooperation; [....] how to inspire them in battle; and particularly,
how to maintain the offensive and aggressive spirit, despite fatigue, casualties and hostile resistance." Such a course did not materialize until
after World War II.

Surveys in social psychology among U.S. Army personnel showed a
catastrophic relationship between enlisted men and their officers. It was
one of the recommendations of the surveying scholars that cadets and
officer candidates "receive much more comprehensive instruction in command responsibility, personnel management, and human relations."[188]

With his characteristic frankness, Marshall summed up his assessment of leadership training at West Point: "Up to the present time I
think they have done little more than teach a cadet how to give commands and to look firm and inexorable, and this, I believe has been one
of the weaknesses of West Point. The cadet has largely had to find his
knowledge of leadership and command from what he has seen of the
disciplining of 'plebes' [...]. The results of this system showed themselves
in the handling of our National Army, where officers [...] failed to get
the most out of our young Americans, and too frequently aroused their

lasting animosity."[189] It would haunt the former cadets—but especially those whom they commanded—that they had learned to "deal with things and not with people."[190] Marshall's statement echoes the sentiments written down by Raymond B. Fosdick in a report to the secretary of war after World War I. Fosdick asserts that bad leadership by regular officers is "widespread" and has created lots of bitterness among the personnel of the American Expeditionary Forces.[191] Fosdick concludes correctly "that there must be something fundamentally wrong in our system of selecting and training officers."[192]

Something fundamentally wrong is not easy to adjust. Eleven years after Marshall's criticisms, the situation had not changed a bit. Marshall noted in a letter to Major General Edward Croft that "I was honestly horrified by the lack of development —if not a deterioration—in the young lieutenants who had reported directly from West Point."[193] One year later, Marshall even went so far to suggest to Major General Charles Kilbourne, superintendent of VMI since 1937, that once in a while West Point should get a VMI graduate as superintendent and vice versa, especially when outstanding leaders were available.[194] The shocked reply showed Marshall— again far ahead of his time—that he had nearly committed a sacrilegious act with his reasonable recommendation.

Even in 1976, a commission, like most of the numerous commissions before it, criticized the unbalanced power of the senior faculty and suggested that the Academy should make up its mind if it wanted "to train combat leaders" or "provide a fundamental education" for all basic branches of the army.[195]

The newly commissioned second lieutenants, before 1917 without any rank insignia on their uniforms, left the United States Military Academy with two distinct positive traits. Many of them were physically extremely fit and real sports nuts.[196] This would be an immeasurable advantage in the strenuous campaigning of World War II when they were not young men any more. They would also get the measurement of their peers during their long West Point time and would get to know the members of the classes above and below them and when later rank and position selections were to be made, there would be rarely any hesitancy.[197]

Those advantages, however, hardly justify an outdated educational system with a minimum of military instruction. In the next chapter, we will examine how the German *Kadetten* (cadets) fared on the other side of the ocean.

THREE

"To Learn How to Die": *Kadetten* in Germany

"You are here to learn how to die!"[1]
—COMMANDER OF A GERMAN *KADETTENSCHULE* TO NEW ARRIVALS

The pursuit of a free education via the military academies sharply distinguishes the American officers from their German counterparts. To become one of the emperor's, or the Weimar Republic's, finest, a young German usually had to come from one of the *"Offizier fähigen Schichten"*—officer-capable classes. In general, mid- to high-level officials, professors, the whole nobility, and current or former officers belonged to those strata, the sons of which filled the ranks of potential future military leaders. Those who lacked these privileged backgrounds yet held ambitions to become officers could pursue their goal through a "technical" arm, such as the artillery, which since the times of Frederick the Great traditionally welcomed common men of "low" birth. Frederick fully acknowledged that commoners as officers could show the same mettle as those of noble birth. He expected, however, the sons of nobility to have the additional motivation not to shame their family heritage, especially their fathers, something they learned from earliest childhood.[2] This incentive still lives in officers' families in modern times.[3]

In theory, the high commands of the army and navy attempted to recruit officers solely from the "capable classes." Still, the expansion of the armed forces outstripped the capacity of these classes to the rising demand for quality men. As a result, many of those who joined the officer corps came from the ranks of "commoners." For many in the upper strata, this practice steadily eroded the exacting "standards" that had insured the high levels of leadership in the German military.[4] A report of 1902 ominously claimed that in that year about half of the new officers came from "occupational circles" that in the past had rarely provided recruits.[5] The new chief of the army, Hans von Seeckt, did restore the old standards of "good breeding" over many other considerations after World War I.[6] In the late 1920s, almost 90 percent of the regular officers came from the *Offizier fähigen Schichten*, more than half from officer families, and 24 percent from the nobility.[7] The latter held a tight grip on the generals' ranks, 52 percent being nobles. On the eve of World War II, the extensive army expansion meant that fewer than half of the 24,000 officers belonged to the "officer-capable strata." Still, those from these prominent classes dominated the positions among the generals and the Great General Staff officers. The old "standards" for the regular officer corps in general finally evaporated in 1942; yet again, those from privileged families ruled the highest ranks of the corps and especially the General Staff.[8] Amazingly, officers with the same distinguished backgrounds appeared in the leadership ranks of the newly formed *Bundeswehr* of the Federal Republic of Germany in the early 1950s.

Despite the focus on social background in Germany, the average educational level of a young American officer aspirant ranked considerably below that of his German equivalent. Germany at the beginning of the twentieth century boasted one of the best educational systems in the world.[9] Many of the topics offered at West Point were already found in the entrance examinations of the German *Hauptkadettenanstalt*, as well as at the French military academy at St. Cyr.[10]

The young German officer aspirant had to possess an *Abitur* degree, or equivalent, which is the general qualification for university entrance in Germany. It asked for far more knowledge than an American senior high school would request at graduation.

In Prussia, however, the emphasis remained on "equivalent," because many high-ranking officers from the nobility feared being overrun by well-educated "butchers' sons."[11] This apprehension was unfounded because a certain education—as will be shown below—stood as just one criterion by which an officer aspirant would be judged and allowed to enter the coveted officer corps and by no means was it the most important. The remark rather shows the state of mind of some of the German high-ranking military leaders of nobility at that time.

In Germany, serious military education could start at a much earlier age, when the youngsters were sent to one of the famous *Kadettenschulen* (cadet schools). At the beginning of the twentieth century, they were spread all over Germany.[12] They were all called *Voranstalten* (preparatory academies), because they accepted boys as early as age ten. The most important, however, the *Hauptkadettenanstalt* (*HKA*), stood in Berlin-Lichterfelde and took teenagers at about the age of fourteen.[13] Only the *HKA* allowed graduation as an ensign or, in rare instances, even commissioning as a lieutenant.

The whole Corps of Cadets numbered 2,500, about half of them in the main facility in Berlin.[14] The high numbers reflect the demands of a conscript army ready to go to war at any minute and the whole number of cadets was thought to be 15 percent of the whole regular officer corps of the Prussian Army, which numbered 16,646 in 1890 and 22,112 in 1914.[15] At West Point, the average graduation numbers for the classes from 1911 to 1919 was 140, therefore, an average Corps of Cadets numbered 560, and it should be borne in mind that the *Kadettenschulen* were only one way to replenish the German officer corps.

As a suspected breeding ground for militarism all the *Kadettenschulen* were disbanded in 1920 in accord with the Versailles Treaty, but they are important to examine because many of the most notable German commanders graduated from these military schools.[16] Half of all German generals of 1914 and nearly 50 percent of all those who gained the rank of *Generalfeldmarschall* in World War II and originated from Prussia were graduates from the *Kadettenschulen*.[17] Interestingly, despite their great importance for the socialization of future officers, they have been largely ignored in the by now considerable literature and historiography of the German officer corps.[18]

Though military schools existed in the United States, too, they did not carry the same clout as the official *Kadettenschulen* in Germany. As early as the age of ten, boys would be send to the *Voranstalten* where they

The *Hauptkadettenanstalt* [*HKA*, main cadet facility] in Berlin-Lichterfelde. The photo is from between 1900 and 1910. The *HKA* was the home of about 1,250 cadets between fourteen and nineteen years of age. The high cupola in the middle is the church with the statue of the archangel Michael on top of it. In contrast to West Point, cadets graduating from the *HKA* were not automatically commissioned but first had to show their ability in a *Kriegsschule* [war school] and a regiment. [Courtesy U.S. Military Academy Library Archives]

88

would be introduced into the more rigid military life before being sent to the *Hauptkadettenanstalt* to graduate.

The question has been raised as to why there were *Voranstalten* at all and why cadets were not sent right away to the *Hauptkadettenanstalt*.[19] It shows simply the paramount importance the selection and education of future officers had in Germany. The *Voranstalten* gave parents, instructing officers, and the cadet himself ample time to decide if military life would be the best thing for the student and the military. Future leaders could also be identified early: "The subjective evaluation system of the Prussian Cadet Corps identified with impressive accuracy those who would be selected three years later in the HKA."[20] Yet, it always remained an option to have the son attend a civilian school until the age of fourteen or fifteen and then send him to the *HKA*.

The *Kadettenschulen* offered the same curriculum as a *Realgymnasium* and was regarded as such.[21] Basically, the *Realgymnasium* had omitted the dreaded old Greek language instruction and had reduced the hours for Latin. In contrast to the situation in the United States, the leadership of the *Kadettenschulen* and its faculty took an active part in the public modernizing debate. The recognition that the *Kadetten* already had a full schedule resulted in the consequence that if the curriculum had to be changed, it could not be done by simply adding more and more hours as was usually done at West Point. Within the modernization debate, concern for the *Überbürdung* (overburdening) of the *Kadetten* was shown. Unlike in the United States, the discussion was not stonewalled by selfish professors who wanted the hours of their discipline doubled and those of their colleagues quartered, as happened at West Point.[22] As a result, drawing lost six hours, natural sciences three, Latin three, and religion two.[23] Added were two hours in German, five in French, three in English, and four in geography. In addition, as early as 1890, the dreaded *Memorierstoff* (literally, stuff to memorize, meaning the recitations) had to be shortened to allow for more modern content during class.[24] Ten years before the board of visitors reminded the faculty of West Point to give the cadets a realistic acquaintance with languages that would enable a West Point graduate to make himself understood, it was decreed that the *Kadetten* "from the first hour on should receive encouragement and assistance for the practical use" of the foreign language.[25] The relatively high number of German officers who were able to communicate with their French and Anglo-American enemies, often to their astonishment, during both world wars shows that some success occurred in the language program. The *Kadetten* possessed a more progressive curriculum than a humanistic *Gymnasium* but were submitted to military discipline and drill and had many more sports and athletics lessons then a civilian school would provide.[26]

The reasons to send a son to these schools were threefold. The main motive for the parents of Erich von Manstein, for example, was to steer him as early as possible toward a military career and introduce him to military life because his genetic as well as his foster father had both attained the rank of general and his uncle was *Generalfeldmarschall* Paul von Hindenburg.[27] Anything else but a military career was unthinkable for him.

For officers in active service, who would be stationed in diverse places over the years, the main reason was to ensure a steady education for their sons and it might have been the primary reason for Heinz Guderian's father to choose for him the *Kadettenschule* because they were boarding schools and the child would remain in the same educational environment while the father rotated posts all over Germany.

The third reason to send their sons to these schools was for parents who had no military ancestors or martial roots but wanted for their son to become an officer and pave his way.[28] At the beginning of the twentieth century in Germany, the profession of officer can be considered as one of the most highly regarded occupations.[29]

Because of the tuition payment, however, the parents had to be well-off to send their sons to one of these military schools. There were free slots and fellowships available but they would be mainly distributed to sons whose fathers had distinguished themselves in the service or were active or retired officers in need.[30] Because of the latter, the schools functioned in a secondary purpose as "charitable institutions" since the days of Frederick the Great's father.[31]

Differences between the *Kadettenschule* and the United States Military Academy become immediately apparent. The youngsters were not treated as being "less than boys" but addressed with the respectful "*Sie*" instead of the "*Du*" reserved for lesser beings and children in civilian schools who were not friends. Even the emperor addressed them usually with "*Meine Herren.*"[32] The commanders and officers of the academies, however, recognized the youth of their cadets and were very lenient with punishment when they caught their flock at some pranks.[33] American officers visiting the cadet schools observed that the cadets could be successfully treated as pupils and as cadets as well, depending on the circumstances.[34] By the example of their superiors, the cadets had already learned to walk the fine line between duty and comradeship.

The *Kadetten* possessed five sets of uniforms, the oldest one for daily use, the fourth for church, the third for furlough, the second for parade, and the first and best was hardly ever used.[35] Though the *Kadetten* were responsible for having clean, orderly uniforms, many chores—like shoe polishing and bed making—were taken up by *Aufwärter* (higher level servants), who were usually retired enlisted soldiers, to leave time for studying and playing. The *Kadetten* were specifically told to treat them with dignity, which may well have had an impact on how they treated their soldiers when they became commissioned.[36] The teaching was done by civilian as well as military teachers and the former—as was custom at military academies—had usually a very low reputation with the *Kadetten* and the military personnel at the institute, whereas the latter were commonly held in high regard.[37]

As it had been custom in Prussian military service, cadets could circumvent the chain of command and talk directly to a higher superior officer to complain, which gave them a better chance against bullies if they dared to rat them out.[38] The cadets called that "*petzen*" or "*schustern*" and it might ruin the reputation of the complaining cadet.[39] Complaining about a mean superior toward a comrade, who had more clout and might be able to pull some strings, however, was not considered honorless and was often more successful.[40] Every new *Kadett* got a personal tutor called *Bärenführer* (bear leader) or *Amme* (wet nurse) to introduce the newcomer to the rules and discipline of the *Kadettenschule* and to protect him from the bullies. The whole system was invented to help the youngster cope and not to terrorize him. It began with the "wet nurse," went over to the room elder, and did not end with the commander of the school.

The better commanders would be accessible at all times for their pupils. That included the commander of the *Kadettenschule*. Senior officers would read the cadets poems or from books of Sir Walter Scott and James Fenimore Cooper or tell them war stories.[41] There was a direct line between *Kadetten* and commanders that was not interrupted by upperclassmen. At West Point, a cadet rarely ever met the superintendent in person other than from afar, "a custom from the Beginnings of the Academy."[42]

The *Erzieher*—usually *Leutnants* (second lieutenants) or sometimes *Oberleutnants* (first lieutenants)—were generally held in high regard by the cadets in contrast to the tactical officers at West Point who appear in the memoir literature and diaries with a mixed reputation.[43] The *Erzieher* taught classes and functioned as a link between the cadets and higher authority. They were therefore also regarded as comrades and not just as superiors in the view of the *Kadetten*.[44] The high command realized that the position of *Erzieher* was of the utmost importance and therefore the selection was demanding.

Whereas we encounter the same problems in the *Kadettenschulen* as in any other place where many male teenagers are put together—rough treatment and bullying—there existed no "Beast Barracks," denigrating "indoctrination system," or sanctioned hazing.[45] All who did harass the younger had to do so under peril of being punished by the military instructors and losing face in front of the Corps of Cadets.[46] Even a cadet company commander who gave a newcomer a rough introduction experienced immediately the wrath of one of the commander's comrades who did not fear speaking up in the face of such injustice and cowardice.[47] Many former cadets emphasize that in their time at the *Kadettenschule* they did not experience any form of hazing and in other classes any such acts had to be undertaken under the greatest secrecy lest the officers detect them and severely punish the perpetrators.[48] Whereas there are believable accounts of cruelties from the 1850s to the 1890s, any systematic hazing was rooted out at the end of the nineteenth and the beginning of the twentieth centuries. It is no coincidence that at this time the *Auftragstaktik*, which will

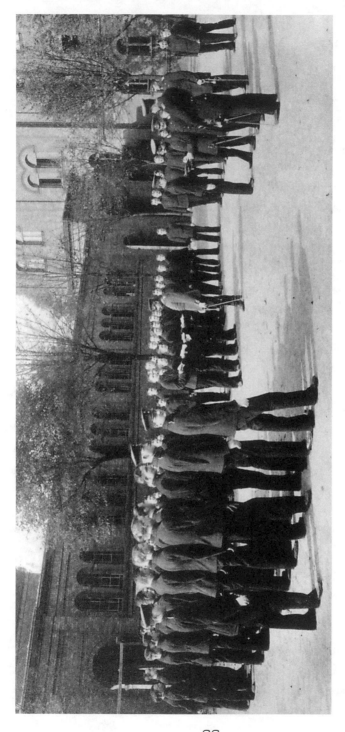

Noon muster of the 9th company of cadets in one of the corners of the huge courtyard of the *Hauptkadettenanstalt*. The atmosphere is much more relaxed compared to West Point. One reason is that all officers were present and thus bullying by upperclassmen impossible. The cadets could freely address the officers with problems or concerns. The officer in the middle controls the received mail. Cadets were not allowed to send or get mail from girlfriends. [COURTESY BUNDESARCHIV, PHOTO 146-2007-0134]

be discussed later, was adopted and other educational reforms introduced. The new picture of a more flexible, inventive, and creative officer appeared and any form of hazing contradicted the education of such an individual.

Though there are no numbers, judging from the memoirs of former cadets, boys who couldn't stand the military discipline in the cadet schools anymore and ran away were obviously uncommon. A cadet "deserting" from a school might ruin the career of his immediate superior and that of the school commander; it therefore seemed to have been a rarity.[49]

In great contrast to West Point, upperclassmen at the *Kadettenschule* did not automatically gain superiority or command capacity over the younger classes by virtue of just remaining in place.[50] The very few command positions as cadet company commander, NCO, *Stubenältester* (room elder), or *Aufsichtskadett* (supervising cadet) were highly coveted and easily lost. The whole Corps of Cadets was in addition to their normal companies, and school classes sorted into five *Sittenklassen* (moral classes).[51] Those who demonstrated exemplary behavior and good grades would advance in *Sittenklassen* while those who showed deficiencies in character or performance would drop. There were three main advantages to be gained, the most important being granted additional freedom and more of the highly regarded theater visits.[52] Cadets who had advanced to moral class one or two gained additional leave on weekends or even days off to visit relatives and would be allowed to go more often to the theater, which had rows of seats reserved just for the cadets.[53] The second advantage to be gained was respect. Because of their additional leave, cadets were considered more mature by their comrades as they were allowed to stroll through the city freely. Without advancing in the moral classes, any promotion was out of the question, which is the third reason to be motivated to advance. With the higher rank came a higher *Königliche Zulage* (king's allowance) as well.[54]

Dropping from a higher to a lower moral class obviously meant the reduction of freedom and the immediate loss of rank. The third class was considered the average class in which every cadet started; being in it meant regular leave. Being down at the bottom, a cadet would have to remain most of his time at the academy where he was even under surveillance

A geography class at the *Hauptkadettenanstalt* somewhere between 1900 and 1910. The class size in all German military schools and academies was much smaller than at their American counterparts. In addition the classes were often created with the abilities of the students in mind. Thus the faster learners were taught with others who did better while those students who needed a little bit more time were grouped with those of the same speed. Such advanced pedagogies were unheard of in American facilities. [Courtesy Bundesarchiv, Photo 146-2007-0133]

and his uniform carried a special mark.

Unlike West Point cadets, all German *Kadetten* were sorted into moral classes. The older cadets held no advantage here and a younger cadet could, with exemplary behavior, easily shame an upperclassman, whereas at the United States Military Academy, the younger cadets would at all times be at the mercy of the older ones. In Germany, a younger cadet could even gain superior rank over a cadet who had entered three years before him, which was another good reason not to haze the newcomers.[55] Correct behavior at a *Kadettenschule* did not mean the absence of punishment as at West Point, but the gaining of rewards, which were important for teenagers.[56] Thomas Bentley Mott, USMA 1886, notes his satisfaction about his promotions within the Corps of Cadets but states plainly, "no amount of glory can drive out the longing for youthful pleasures and a bit of freedom."[57] It was exactly this coveted freedom that could be gained at a German *Kadettenschulen* through proper behavior.

Another very obvious difference was that in Germany no one was afraid that the cadets were "corrupted" by civilian life during the visits of relatives, which were allowed on holidays and during the leave and days off they were granted. It has to be noted, though, that the German society at the beginning of the twentieth century was thoroughly "militarized" in contrast to the American population. In Germany, the military was looked upon as a role model in many aspects. The increase of militarization of the society in the early thirties was accompanied by a "wave of uniformization."[58] Military lingo and expressions were common, officials wore uniforms, and many large companies issued uniformlike attire to their employees as well. During a discussion about new uniforms for the *Wehrmacht* at the *Reichskanzlei* in 1935, Hitler's adjutant, Major Friedrich Hoßbach, remarked in jest "that the army should in the future wear civilian attire to be distinguishable" from the rest of the society.[59]

In one of the most democratic societies, the plebes at West Point were not trusted to leave the post at any time, but the German cadets— being five or more years younger than their American counterparts— were entrusted with regular leave and holidays. The admonishment that though they were not officers yet—most of them not even *Fahnenjunker* (officer-aspirant aspirants, ranking corporals)—they represented as individuals the honor of the cadet corps and this seemed to have worked better than any form of oppression.

Strangely, the trust that was shown usually to the *Kadetten* ended when they wrote letters home. The boys were usually treated as grown-ups but at all *Voranstalten* their letters were censored.[60] If anything was written in the letters the superiors did not like, they marked it on the original letter and wrote a statement on a separate page for the addressee.

The graduating and grading system was highly complicated. *Kadetten* got their marks for "character" and for their scholarly abilities. Thus, a young man who excelled in leadership but was weak on the scholarly side would be eligible for promotion or even promoted ahead of one with better grades in mathematics or French. It should not be forgotten, a former cadet wrote, that they were trained to become officers and not scholars or artists.[61]

Though the *wehrpsychologische Untersuchung*—the psychological and charakterologische assessment—of an officer candidate took place after he had left the *Kadettenanstalt* and attended the *Kriegsschule*, it makes more sense to discuss the matter of "character" here as the cadets were already judged on it during their time at the *Voranstalten*.[62] Foreign writers have repeatedly misunderstood the German idea of "character." It does not denote a list of character traits or habits such as *Pflichterfüllung* (duty), *Gehorsam* (obedience), *Ehrgefühl* (sense of honor), *Selbstständigkeit* (self-reliance), *Sparsamkeit* (frugality), *Wahrheitsliebe* (love of truth), *Sauberkeit* (cleanliness), *Ordnungsliebe* (orderliness and comradeship).[63] As pointed out earlier, it is also not connected to noble birth or love for the kaiser.[64] It rather describes how things are done by the candidate, his bearing under certain circumstances. The superiors at the cadet schools would, just like the *Wehrmacht* psychologist, look for the individual character traits a cadet or candidate possessed and how these could be useful for his career as an officer.[65] They did not look for a "standard officer person" but for an individual who was able to use his personal character traits in an officerlike manner and for accomplishments in war and battle.[66] Paramount among the capabilities were *Willenskraft*—willpower—which covered the will to become a role model of an officer, the will to succeed in any given task, the will to force a tactical decision, the will to speak his mind, and the will to remain steady under pressure.[67] *Verantwortungsbewußtsein*—sense of responsibility—covered another area and meant being aware of his responsibilities toward the officer corps and the *Wehrmacht* in his deeds and to have the bearing of an officer at all times in all situations. It meant also the very important sense of responsibility towards his men, walking the fine line between being a hard-ass superior in a crisis situation and taking care of his men like a father would his sons, in short, being a comrade. Last but not least, it meant the responsibility of learning his trade and excelling in his area of expertise. Finally, the candidate had to display a *kämpferisches Wesen*—a fighting spirit, going against any odds, possessing a longing for battle and to lead up front, not afraid to die if necessary.[68]

While the German officer corps was, just like its American counterpart, predominantly Protestant, religious faith played no role in the official character building. In the U.S. Army, it became a cornerstone.[69] While in Germany religious topics rarely showed up in the officer's education, the new character-building theme of the U.S. Army was directly linked to religious faith.

In Germany, showing character and leading by example were synonymous. The necessity of leading up front generally—but especially in a war of movement—was a credo taught to the boys at the *Kadettenschule*. Even the ten-year-old *Kadetten* were told right away by the commandant of their *Kadettenschule* that they were there to learn how to die and this attitude of dying heroically on the battlefield was deeply rooted in the German officer corps.[70]

When the little *Kadett* Ernst von Salomon asked his older brother, then fifteen years of age, what would be the nicest thing that he could imagine happening to him he got the answer: "The most wonderful thing would be to croak as a twenty year old Lieutenant in a ditch in front of Paris."[71]

The answer by an old officer to the news of his eldest son having died after great suffering from wounds received at the battle of St. Privat during the Franco-Prussian war has correctly been described as "characteristic": "Youth is very much to be envied. There is no more beautiful way for an officer to die."[72]

German generals and occasionally even field marshals would show up at the frontline and exert leadership at the most crucial points. In the U.S. Army, GIs were surprised to see a division commander on the frontline and they rarely even knew their battalion commander because he didn't show up.[73] An example is an American veteran combat division surveyed at the beginning of 1944. About half of the soldiers felt unprepared to return to combat. Eighty percent of those "said that their company officers had no interest in their personal welfare."[74] Even longtime surveys on the attitudes of GIs toward their officers showed that usually only a minority thought that "officers take interest in men" or that they went through the same their men did.[75] Those, however, were exactly the traits a soldier, no matter his nationality, looked for in his commanding officer.[76] German soldiers when writing home often praised their officers, something that rarely happened in the U.S. Army.[77]

American observers before the war failed to recognize upfront leadership as a decisive peculiarity of German combat excellence.[78] German units often were provided with leadership in the most desperate and crucial situations, which enabled them to either attack or defend against heavy odds. The fact would be noted during the course of World War II—by then far too late—by American intelligence officers of all levels. One report deals under a chapter titled "German Officers" with the "father and son" relationship of officers and men in the *Wehrmacht* and the high leadership capabilities of junior officers.[79] In 1944, it was no rarity that a *Leutnant* or *Oberleutnant* (second or first lieutenant) often was the company commander and single remaining officer in his unit. Still, the depleted unit fought with efficiency and ferocity.

Being an example—especially in battle and even if it means dying—is one of the key features of leadership and was constantly emphasized in German officer training. The number of *Wehrmacht* officers killed in action is therefore extraordinarily high, especially when compared to in the U.S. Army. The numbers are even more astonishing when comparing the numbers of the general officers who died in battle. The highest-ranking casualty of the U.S. Army was Lieutenant General Simon Bolivar Buckner, Jr., USMA 1908, who was killed by Japanese shrapnel during the Battle of Okinawa. The second highest-ranking, Lieutenant

General Lesley McNair, was killed by an American bomb during Operation Cobra. Both were posthumously promoted to four-star generals.

About twenty U.S. Army generals lost their lives during combat throughout World War II, the numbers for the Army Air Corps included.[80] The latter makes up about 50 percent of the casualties. Only thirty-four were wounded and that includes officers from the Marine Corps. Though the German numbers suffer from exaggerated counting and problematic statistical methodology, it is certain that with about 220 *Heer* (ground forces) and *Luftwaffe* generals, more than ten times as many German officers died in combat than American during the same time.[81] Of the warring parties, only the Red Army officer corps had a nearly equal number of generals killed in combat, but it is questionable if the high number resulted from leading up front.[82]

When they showed up at the front, U.S. generals repeatedly received commendations or awards for being there, displaying "calmness on the way to the front" or sometimes even under fire but the "valor" displayed would rank as negligible in the *Wehrmacht*.[83] In the German Army, it was considered the job of an officer to show courage in combat; "mere bravery, however exceptional, was not enough" to gain a decoration for valor.[84]

Some American general officers who shared that opinion unsuccessfully tried to return their decorations because they embarrassed them.[85] When Douglas MacArthur in World War I observed the attack of his unit closely and came under heavy shellfire, his aide tried to pull him to cover by force. MacArthur broke his grip and informed him that "the finest thing that could happen to the morale of the AEF would be to have a general officer bumped off."[86]

It is safe to say that if the casualties of field-grade ranks, from major to colonel, would be compared, the numbers of German officers fallen in combat would be even higher than the number of fallen U.S. Army officers.[87]

When trying to find a good cover photo for this book, I searched numerous online databases and picture books of World War II browsing through thousands of war photos. While it was no problem to find a German officer commanding in battle, it was close to impossible to find an

American. Even in photos that show soldiers resting or just gathering casually, on the German side an officer is most of the time at least within the picture. In a group of GIs, the highest-ranking soldier is usually an NCO.

In stark disparity to the American GI who often never even saw his higher commanders in war, it is not uncommon that a German *Landser* still remembers the names and features of his officers even after forty or fifty years.[88] It is also not uncommon that a German regimental commander was to be found in the foxhole with his soldiers shooting a rifle or throwing grenades.[89] After the officer promotion reforms in 1942, it was decreed that a colonel could only be promoted to major general after one year of frontline service.[90]

General Wilhelm Ritter von Thoma, who took over the Africa Corps from Erwin Rommel, had been wounded twenty times when he came into captivity in 1942. Characteristically, he was captured while leading an assault on a ridge.[91] German generals with badges showing that they had personally destroyed tanks with grenades, mines, or satchel charges or who had earned other close combat badges were no rarity. The notion that the education of German officers was lacking because they were not taught classes on "battlefield lethality" or "protective countermeasures" reinforces my earlier statement that the German war culture has been little understood in the United States despite the enormous amount of literature on the topic.[92] It was the place of a German officer—no matter the rank—to die in front of his men, fighting with them if necessary, and it was exactly this knowledge that inspired the German soldiers in desperate situations. They were literally led in battle and not managed from behind. German officers themselves assert that "the fundamentals of our successes are based on the fact that the officer exposes himself more than the enlisted men."[93] The high casualties of German officers are "natural" because they legitimate the credibility of leadership.[94] The German basic manual for leadership, *Truppenführung*, states that even a corps commanders was supposed to be in "personal touch" with his divisions while the division commander's place "is with his troops."[95]

Whereas the American GI was as willing and able as any soldier of the warring parties in World War II, he often lacked the proper leadership to excel.[96] For this reason the average U.S. Army officer was not held in high regard by his soldiers.[97] Most often, the GIs did not even know their battalion or regimental commander because he was nowhere to be seen.[98] Yet the American rifleman was looking for exactly the same leadership the German officer corps was providing. It is apparent that "far too many officers had soft jobs in the rear, far too few commanded at the front."[99]

In a survey, when American veteran infantrymen were asked to characterize "one of the best combat soldiers," they would point out an officer who "was always with his men in combat and led by personal example."[100] That, however, was apparently rare enough because three-fourths of the enlisted men agreed "that most officers are more interested in getting promoted than in doing a good job."[101] One of the rare American general officers who would tell his troops, "I will never promise you anything but a wet ball on a muddy field, but I will be there for you," and actually keep his promise would inevitably be adored by his troops.[102]

Exceptions regarding the esteem of the enlisted men were the second and first lieutenants leading combat units, who seemed because of their youth like little puppies to the often older troops.[103] By the very nature of their command, the junior officers always stood in the midst of battle and were repeatedly the first to die.

For the very same reason of frontline leadership, the U.S. airborne troops are an exception.[104] Here colonels and even major generals would jump with their troops into combat and many of them had been together with their units—just as in Germany—since basic training. The differences in attitude between the paratrooper generals and the "normal" generals would become most apparent during the Battle of the Bulge. Matthew B. Ridgway, who had as commanding general jumped with the famed 82nd Airborne Division behind enemy lines at D-Day and took over the XVIII Airborne Corps defending a part of the Ardennes in December 1944, was appalled by the lack of leadership of his subordinate units and stated in the presence of many of the commanders in question that there was a "failure of all commanders, from the division commander on down, to influence the action by applying a strong and positive leadership."[105] The situation at the Italian front did not look much different and the lack of aggressiveness and leadership was equally decried.[106]

Whereas the U.S. Army fielded only a comparatively few divisions and corps and often enough found for those commanders of at least average capability, the problem was grave with the leadership of the regiments.[107] From Kasserine to Normandy and the Ardennes, regimental commanders crumbled in great numbers under the pressure of combat and lack of physical fitness but, above all, lack of ability, leadership skills, and aggressiveness.[108] In one of these crises, Matthew Ridgway, then commander of XVIII Airborne Corps phrased it decisively: "My crying need is for high-type leadership [...] some good regimental commander material that can step up right in and take a hold of a shaky regiment and make something out of it in a minimum of time."[109] Many of the regimental commanders, however, graduated from Leavenworth, a school that had the word "command" in its very name, yet did not teach leadership properly, a fact that will be discussed in detail in the next chapter.[110]

The American senior commanders got in their own way to create a more efficient officer corps. They were generally extremely reluctant to relieve and reclassify unfit officers, a problem that had already appeared in peacetime.[111] A reclassification, for which the U.S. Army possessed a specific form, usually meant the relocation of the officer to an unimportant command, his demotion down at least one rank, and an early phasing out of the army. It therefore happened that officers unfit for command were relieved for dubious reasons to get them out of their own division and then they started to rotate from unit to unit.[112] The War Department was not made aware of their unfitness, unless finally a consequent commander like Matthew B. Ridgway axed them. Sometimes senior officers were sent home or even promoted after they had failed in battle.[113] The Prussian and German armies traditionally acted harshly and consequently when an officer proved unfit for command.[114]

The whole *charakterologische* assessment of the *Wehrmacht* intended to weed out those who supposedly lacked the mettle of an officer was not based on modern scholarly principles and it was interlaced with racist beliefs. Mostly retired officers "guided" civilian psychologists, who had in turn often served in the army before. However, in stark contrast to the U.S. Army, in the *Wehrmacht* there was a consensus on what an officer's character, traits, and abilities had to be and how the candidates were to be selected. For example, those cadets who attained leadership positions in the *Voranstalten* would gain them again when moving up to the *Hauptkadettenanstalt* and later as officers would get excellent assessments in leadership abilities.[115] A great consistency in the officer aspirants' education and selection has to be noted.

After the completion of the *Obersekunda*—the eleventh class—every cadet would take the *Fähnrichsexamen* (ensign exam).[116] It asked for a general knowledge in all kinds of topics, such as languages, geography, mathematics, geometry, and history, as well as basic military-related questions. It can be considered as a light version of the *Abitur*, which is usually done after the thirteenth class and represents in Germany the general degree for admission to a university.[117] If successfully passed, the cadet would become a *charakterisierter Portepee-Fähnrich*.[118] The new status allowed him to wear the ensign uniform and ranked him just above a sergeant. Everybody recognized him now as a serious officer aspirant, but he had no command authority until a regimental commander granted him the *Seitengewehr* (dagger, but actually bayonet) and make him *patentierter Fähnrich*, also called a *Degen-Fähnrich* (dagger ensign, or rather rapier ensign). Technically "dagger ensigns" still ranked below sergeant majors but carried so much clout that they often would take command of units in wartime when superior officers were killed. At the beginning of World War I, the *Hauptkadettenanstalt* graduated those sixteen and older immediately at least as *patentierte Fähnriche*. Thus seventeen-year-old lieutenants were no rarity. The usual age for this rank, however, would be nineteen.

Those who had the right connections or were daring enough would step into a regiment as *charakterisierter Portepee-Fähnrich*, just after the exam, and hope to gain some time on the others by getting promoted early. The von Mansteins, von Stülpnagels, and von Bocks, for example, would enter one of the highly coveted guard regiments, whereas the Heinricis, Hopeners, and Hoths had to make do with regular regiments.[119]

The *Kadetten* from nobility had another unfair advantage over their common comrades. In the winter most of them were selected for page duty at the emperor's court. This coveted favor seemed to be even more unjust because, for the cadets of nobility, their standing in moral or school class did not matter at all.[120] The number of "noble" cadets, however, declined steadily from 46.7 percent in 1895 to 23.1 percent in 1918.[121] Their upbringing and distinguished positions as page no matter their merits sometimes led to the creation of a nobility clique within the *Kadettenschule*. The superiors and cadets from a common background thought to break that up immediately with all means at their disposal.[122]

Access to a *Fähnrich* position in a guard regiment was not only tightly monitored but also connections were needed as well as a lot of extra money for the opulent parade uniforms. An aspirant had to be able to prove the possession of a considerable amount of money, which left out the majority of regular ensigns anyway.

However, many would be sent to a *Kriegsschule* (war school) first, before any advancement in the regiment, and thus remain for another eight months to one and a half years in their rank. At the *Kriegsschule*, the flexible German military educational system again went to work when the officer aspirants were put in different classes according to their previous training and the assessments of their superiors.[123] Though the day at the war schools started at around 0600 hours (6 a.m.), the lessons were only held between 0800 hours (8 a.m.) and 1500 hours (3 p.m.) with a lunch break in between. The faculty taught all relevant military disciplines from army organization to personal marksmanship.

The candidates got their free afternoon for a purpose. Again their character was assessed by the instructors of the school and their classmates. Woe betide the *Fähnrich* who would drink, gamble, pick a fight, attend a political rally, get into a romantic relationship, or show any other sign of behavior considered unbecoming an officer while attending the *Kriegsschule*. It was explicitly the mission of the schools to "groom the moral strength" of the officer candidates even before instructing them in pure military topics.[124] The importance of assessing an officer candidate off duty as well as on duty is emphasized in nearly every psychological pamphlet of the German Army.[125]

Those who stayed at the *Kadettenschule* would finish after the *Oberprima* (thirteenth class) and gain a degree equivalent to the *Abitur*, despite the fact that in the last two years the military subjects taught would by far outweigh

Fahnenjunker [officer aspirants] at the *Kriegsschule* [war school] in Dresden in 1935 during machinegun training. German *Kadetten* and officer aspirants underwent extensive small-arms weapons training and had to show great proficiency with all infantry weapons and their tactics before even a thought was given to commissioning them as officers. [COURTESY BUNDESARCHIV, PHOTO, 183-R43502, PHOTOGRAPHER WEGNER]

the "regular" school disciplines.[126] However, the final exams were held in front of a civilian committee in accord with the same standards as a civilian *Abiturprüfung*.[127] Very good cadets would be promoted to the rank of lieutenant and exceptional cadets were granted a backdating of their *Rangdienstalter* (time in grade or rank) gaining them a great advantage over those who had left earlier. Doing well at the *Kadettenschule* therefore could bring long-term advantages for a later career, a fact well known to the cadets.[128]

Civil War hero and military reformer General Emory Upton, USMA 1861, noted after his tour through Europe that the entire mathematics curriculum of the *Hauptkadettenanstalt* would be taught at the United States Military Academy in one year.[129] This observation shows remarkably well the narrow focus of a former West Pointer and the misunderstandings about an officer education.

In both the German and the American military academies, the cadets would be submitted to a harsh, hierarchical discipline. The German *Kadetten* nearly all use the words *hart* (hard) and *einseitig* (one-sided) to describe their experiences at the military schools,[130] the latter despite the fact that they were taught basically the same content as civilian pupils, which shows how remarkably backwater the West Point education was in contrast.

The greatest problem for the cadets in Germany and in the United States, however, seemed to have been rather the sadistic upperclassmen or ranking cadets.[131] The bullies had a much greater problem succeeding in the German institutions because there existed no immature and questionable indoctrination system, and hazing was consequently forbidden at all times by the commanders of the *Kadettenschulen* and older cadets were tasked with proactively discouraging and ending any hazing.[132] Upperclassmen might try to assume positions of authority over the younger ones but were not granted these automatically under the German system. They had to prove their maturity and leadership abilities or otherwise would lose rank, face, or drop in moral classes. "*Schinder*," called "Flamers" at West Point—those who were unnecessarily hard on the younger ones— violated a cornerstone of German military culture and effectiveness—the *Kameradschaft* (comradeship)—and thus might find themselves despised by the Corps of Cadets.[133]

Erich von Manstein admits that *schleifen* (aggravated physical military training) was no rarity in his class.[134] At the same time, he gained the physical strength during his cadet years—he was an extremely fragile boy— to get at least a "limited eligibility for military service,"[135] although there is the possibility of pressure by his high-ranking military relatives to let him pass anyway.[136]

The *Kadettenanstalt* provided their students with the same equipment that was currently used in the emperor's army, unlike the obsolete equipment used at West Point. All classes at the German academies did bayonet fighting and the older classes were regularly detailed to active units for training.[137] At least during World War I, regular company-size attack exercises—commanded by cadets—were no rarity in a *Kadettenschule*.[138]

In Germany, a sophisticated grading and promotion system put equal weight on the "character" of a cadet and his scholarly abilities.[139] Even a total lack of the latter and failing final exams would not prevent a graduation by *Kaiser's Gnade*—"the mercy of the Emperor"—when the cadet was considered an able leader.[140] The emperor used his mercy about a thousand times between the years 1902 and 1912 because the Imperial Army would not want to lose possible outstanding officers who just had a weakness in mathematics.[141] For those advancing to higher classes despite lacking scholarly skills, the term on the graduating paper carried the Latin phrase *propter barbaram*—"close to being uneducated."

The so-called *Paukerärsche* (crammer asses), who had excellent grades but could not hack it at athletics, were despised by the other *Kadetten*.[142] If, however, someone excelled as a scholar as well as an athlete, his position within the Corps of Cadets became "untouchable and unshakable," no matter how young he was.[143] *Kadetten* who were weak scholars had a greater chance of succeeding because they would not only be helped by their friends but also by a tutoring system that was in place through their room elder, who was responsible for the knowledge of the cadets under his command.[144]

The *Kadett* learned also by the example of his superiors at the *Kadettenschule* that he had to lead by example too, which may be illustrated by a little case in point. In military academies all over the world, the *Kostümfest*—literally translated "costume party" but called "clothing formation" in West Point lingo—was a common punishment for a whole unit of cadets.[145] The cadet company commander would call out the set of uniforms that had to be worn and the time the cadets had to change, which was usually only a few minutes. The cadets would race up the stairs to their rooms and put on their uniforms, race down to the parade ground, and stand in formation. After a short look at the quality of dress, the unit commander would call out the next uniform and the race to the rooms would begin anew until either enough punishment was dished out or the whole formation was perfectly dressed. Whereas at West Point the unit commander would idly await the racing cadets, at a *Kadettenschule* the unit commander was expected to change with the *Kadetten* and show them in how little time he could appear perfectly dressed for every single set of uniforms he called out.[146]

In contrast to the graduates of West Point, only a small minority of *Kadetten* would be promoted to officers in Germany after finishing the academy and they had to show an exceptional performance, both in scholarly and in leadership abilities. All the others first had to show that they could hack it in real life before becoming lieutenants and they would remain officer aspirants for some time.

The *Kadettenschulen* were anything but role models for an educational system, but they were much more suited for the education of future officers than the United States Military Academy. The point here is to compare the American and the German systems and look at the advantages and disadvantages of the respective cadet training facilities and not to hail one as a preferable organization for general youth education.

It should be kept in mind that a military academy is not for everyone, especially not for boys whose parents send them there to be straightened out.[147] The facilities would be equally horrifying for "*Muttersöhnchen*" (literally "mothers' little sons," meaning those who still needed their mothers' undivided attention, maybe best translated as "milquetoasts") and those who were "tender and cuddly."[148] However, a boy longing to attend the *Kadettenschule* was no rarity at this time in Germany.[149]

None of the former cadets in Germany is without criticism of the *Kadettenschulen*, which also shows a marked difference to West Point alumni, who tend to glorify their experience.[150] On the rare occasion an alumni—even a successful one—dared criticizing the Academy, his work was ridiculed and other former graduates made sure in letters to fellow officers that his book should not be touched, instead of reflecting on its content.[151]

The Americans had overtaken the Germans on the right side and thoroughly "Prussianized" their military academies in a way that the Prussians were known for only in clichés. It produced hidebound second lieutenants with an extremely one-sided and narrow education, which was in many aspects not even military. The results were usually officers who longed for doctrine, conformity, order, and neatness, all of which would be of hindrance in the chaos of war and battle. There was no mechanism to catch and keep those who showed prospects as leaders but failed in engineering or mathematics. Only the personal determination of the "separated" would keep them for the army when they entered as enlisted men.

While the German system suffered from an unjust preselection—those of "low" birth had greater difficulties entering the officer corps than others—it offered a sophisticated selection mechanism for those who made it. A German *Kadett* had to constantly prove his ability as a future leader even when he was only a teenager. He learned early on that seniority would not determine his place in the Corps of Cadets or the officer corps. Younger German *Kadetten* could overtake upperclassmen and become their superiors if they showed the proper performance. That was one of the greatest advantages of the German system. At West Point, the four-year system was set in stone. Conformity helped more to survive than leadership. The latter, however, was paramount at a *Kadettenschule*. Not only was hazing expressly forbidden at German *Kadettenschulen*, it had no chance of surviving because the system of promotion and the example of the commanders prevented it. An upperclassman would have to go easy on a new *Kadett* because he might be his subordinate in one or two years. Commissioned officers were constantly present during the daily life of the *Kadetten* and education was not left in the hands of those who had just suffered the year before at the hands of the upperclassmen. That is a travesty of leadership training, which endured at West Point for centuries.

The cadet schools were forbidden in accord with the Versailles Treaty because the Allied powers surmised they were a breeding ground for militarism. After Hitler came to power, his fanatical bodyguard the *Waffen-SS "Leibstandarte Adolf Hitler"* took over the former *Hauptkadettenanstalt* as their barracks. The unit would during the war amass a nearly unparalleled record of atrocities and war crimes including the Malmedy massacre. The picture shows the dictator reviewing the *Leibstandarte* on December 17, 1935, in the courtyard of the former *Hauptkadettenanstalt*. On his far right is the commander Josef "Sepp" Dietrich. [COURTESY BUNDESARCHIV, PHOTO 102-17311]

Officers at a German *Kadettenschule* were revered figures who could be approached and talked to. Many former *Kadetten* wrote that they had an intimate talk with the commander of the *Kadettenschule*. The superintendent and his commandant appear in the literature of former cadets at West Point as distant figures and even tactical officers talked to cadets only when the latter messed up. Communication between the officers and the cadets was handled through the writing of notes—bureaucracy at its best and leadership at its lowest.

Having survived the four years entitled an American cadet to an officer's commission. The young American lieutenants suffered therefore from a lack of self-confidence when they got their first command because they had not received a proper education in military matters and leadership. Mathematics and yelling at plebes proved to be completely insufficient preparation for the real daily military life. Many were saved by an old NCO or an understanding colonel.

A *Kadett* finishing a German school was far ahead of any of his American comrades even though he was several years younger. His formal education resembled that of a civilian his age and he possessed the tactical and leadership knowledge to lead a company. Yet he was just a *Fähnrich* in rank and would not be commissioned until he proved his ability over and over again. Two stints at a regiment and one at a *Kriegsschule* would decide if he was to be commissioned. Real life was the deciding factor and not the artificial life at an academy.

However, as an ensign or second lieutenant just begins his military career, let us further compare the advanced professional military education in Germany and the United States.

PART TWO

Intermediate Advanced Education and Promotion

The Importance of Doctrine and How to Manage: The American Command and General Staff School and the Overlooked Infantry School

"A career officer is going to school as long as he lives."[1]
—General Matthew Bunker Ridgway

Another cornerstone of the American professional military education system was founded by General William Tecumseh Sherman, USMA 1840, in May 1881 at Fort Leavenworth, Kansas. Then known as "School of Application for the Infantry and Cavalry," it went—even in later years—through several name changes, which proves the point that it "initially lacked a clearly defined purpose."[2] The problem of lacking a definite educational task would haunt the school even decades later.[3]

From the outset, the school ran into several problems that tainted its reputation. Though the U.S. Army had the greatest demand for officers with knowledge of professional staff work, the majority of students Leavenworth school admitted at first were lieutenants. Officers with this rank, however, were supposed to command a platoon, while the school was supposed to teach staff procedures for higher units.

Because of the low level of instruction, the requested reading out loud, and recitations the institution became known as the "kindergarten."[4] Graduates, especially those who attained honors, were teased and ridiculed by their comrades for years after completing the school, because it was thought that they had not accomplished much.[5]

Alarmed by the low reputation, everybody from Sherman downward who had an interest in the school tried to improve it. Several commandants showed the wisdom to ask their staff and instructors for suggestions. In the following years Leavenworth improved, but every step away from a kindergarten can be termed a success and does not mark automatically an excellent advanced military school. It was rather within the wake of reforms of the whole army promotion system at the beginning of the 1890s, initiated by General John M. Schofield, that commandants of Leavenworth took more vigorous actions, for example, by minimizing the daily recitations.[6] They had given a Leavenworth class the appearance of a middle school and the class's didactical value came close to zero. The hard-to-remove belief of the students, however, remained "that the closer one adhered to the words of the text the better his marks were likely to be."[7] That there was much truth in that belief will be demonstrated below.

For U.S. Army standards, rather visionary senior instructors Arthur L. Wagner and Eben Swift helped raising the overall teaching level, but also introduced serious flaws.[8] Wagner had travelled to Germany to visit Prussian schools and was no doubt influenced by that experience.[9] However, when finally the applicatory method was introduced to the students he had to admit, "It was well known and practiced for more than thirty years when we took it up."[10] Under the applicatory method the student was requested to actually use—apply—what he had learned before in theoretical lessons, instead of memorizing and reciting only textbook knowledge and regulations over and over.[11] When the applicatory method reached its high point at Leavenworth, it had already been phased out at the German war academy and replaced by extensive role-playing and war games.[12]

Put into perspective, the advances at Leavenworth can therefore be considered only relative. Unsurprisingly, just like at West Point, the didactics fell as far behind as the content of the teachings. Despite the rapid changes in weaponry and the forms of battle, "the reformers at Fort Leavenworth remained surprisingly ambivalent and at times even hostile to technical knowledge and technological solutions."[13]

Eben Swift allowed his students to war-game, which was common in German military schools at all levels. Like so many other examples from German military institutions, this one was watered down for American purposes. Whereas in Germany students "fought" through a whole engagement, including sudden changes of assignments and tactical surprises, the American students' task would end after the main forces had made contact.[14] This, however, seemed to have been common practice in the U.S. Army of those days and even the Army War College operated in such an unimaginative and inflexible way.[15] The faculty at Leavenworth did nothing to change this unfortunate procedure.[16] Only in the year 1939 would a continuous series of theoretical engagements be fought by the students.[17]

In Swift's opinion, modern weaponry made the outcome of the battle predictable after the units were positioned. Not only did this attitude fail to challenge his students mentally but it became also "an excuse to ignore complex problems."[18] Only in the 1930s would multifaceted war games be introduced, but here again they were highly choreographed without any surprises involved.[19] Tactical studies in German books were considered "too ambitious for the typical American officer" and as a consequence "simplified" for the American officer students.[20] It seemed, and this assessment is true for the first decades of the schools, that the instructors simply continuously underestimated the intellectual capacity of their students.

Following the conclusion of the Spanish-American War, the school reopened in 1902, having now acquired the nickname "Bell's Folly" after one of its strongest supporters, General J. Franklin Bell, USMA 1878, who became commandant of the school a year after the reopening.[21] Usually lieutenants and a few majors attended the school, which was supposed to especially teach staff procedures.[22] Interbranch rivalry in particular put obstacles in the way of that goal for many years and resulted in a "narrow curriculum."[23] Military history, which has to be considered an essential part of any officer's education, played a small role in the teaching "while much time was given to elementary subjects that should have been common knowledge to any officer of several years experience."[24]

This decision was basically confirmed in 1919 when Assistant Commandant W. K. Taylor decided that "in the interest of fairness" the courses were tailored to suit the weakest student.[25] This example shows, and there will be further proof in the following, that didactical flexibility was not at all at home at Leavenworth. At the German *Kriegsakademie*, just as at the war schools for ensigns before, officers would be detailed into classes according to their individual abilities and branches, which enabled each student to gain his personal maximum at each school. The fundamentals would not slow down and bore the brighter students. Unqualified students would not make it to the *Kriegsakademie* anyway because of the demanding entrance examination, which will be discussed in the next chapter.

Apparently the basics at Leavenworth took up so much time that current wars were neglected outright, a problem that would haunt the school until 1940. Perry Lester Miles had just successfully completed the Leavenworth schools when he went to Europe to command a unit in World War I. He observed that the teachings had been "oblivious of the lessons the combatants in Europe were learning in the trenches, and [...] nothing authentic had been furnished to us."[26] As usual the instructors at Leavenworth "sought to be teachers before they themselves had learned the crucial lessons of the battlefield."[27] It has therefore been correctly observed that "clearly the AEF learned to fight by fighting, not because of Pershing's insistence on 'open warfare' or because the prewar Leavenworth had expounded the proper tactical doctrine."[28]

After World War I, some restructuring occurred and the school received a new name in 1922: Command and General Staff School (CGSS). In the brief period from 1919 to 1923, the classes lasted two years, one year in a regular course, called "School of the Line," and one year in an advanced course called "General Staff School." Those who did better in the "School of the Line" would be allowed to stay for the second year.[29]

According to the annual report of the director of the year 1920, the School of the Line was supposed to teach "First, organization, second, tactics, techniques and capabilities of the different arms, separate and in combination; third, tactical principles, decisions, plans and orders and their application; fourth, supply principles and their application to the division; fifth, the duties and functions of the commander and the general staff of a division; sixth, details of troop leading within the division."[30] It

Grant Hall, the main academic building of the Command and General Staff School at Fort Leavenworth, Kansas, in 1939. (Courtesy U.S. Army, Combined Arms Research Library)

The picture is labeled a war game but it looks rather like a map exercise that was so common at the Command and General Staff School. [Courtesy U.S. Army, Combined Arms Research Library]

is surprising that the so-important factor of leadership would be last in importance at an advanced military school. The curriculum, however, mirrored this strange weighting of priorities.

The persons responsible seem to have overlooked completely the fact that even a well-functioning staff has to be led properly. Leadership can be considered one of the most important traits of an officer because it is needed everywhere.[31] Senior officers therefore cautioned "that high marks at the Command and General Staff School and War College should not be a measure of capacity for high command. If history is worth considering, it points to the fact that most commanders did not excel in theory. They were successful because they were highly practical."[32]

It is apparent that, even shortly before the next world war and after decades of operation, the Fort Leavenworth schools had anything but an undisputed good reputation.[33] Though the curriculum of the CGSS "emphasized the command process involving interaction between commanders and general staff officers," in practice such was apparently rarely the case.[34]

Below it will be shown that the majority of topics at Leavenworth were taught highly theoretically and it "seems that the school believed that those bright enough to finish the Leavenworth program possessed what was needed to be good commanders."[35] A comparison of war records, however, does not support such a notion.[36]

As late as 1939, a student survey showed that the subjects taught with the least effectiveness "were command, troop leading, mechanized units and tanks, aviation and supply and logistics"—exactly the topics whose knowledge an officer would need for World War II.[37] Though the student officers's complaints in these surveys were not about the instructions in intelligence gathering, evaluation, and dissemination, the war proved that there were also serious deficiencies in the instructions of that topic. With his typical harsh bluntness, Walter Bedell Smith, the chief of staff of the highest Allied command authority in World War II, remarked to his friend Lucian K. Truscott, "The fact is, Lucian, that our greatest shortage when we got into this fracas was in high level planning and high level intelligence work. Our G-2 [intelligence] has always been a collection of broken down military attachés and our service school simply did not know how to tell us to do real planning."[38] Smith had been a graduate of the CGSS.

Bruce C. Clarke, USMA 1925, noted that the G-2 course at the CGSS tended to teach the intelligence to present "too many 'Essential Elements of Information' […] instead of the few which were really essential" and that the intelligence people always looked "for just one more indicator before making a recommendation or report" and thus delayed the decision-making process of the commander.[39]

To Paul M. Robinett, one of the few professionals in the field who in the view of his comrades knew "more about G-2 work than anyone in the army," the lack of proficiency in the instruction of that important field had already been apparent during peacetime.[40] He relentlessly lobbied for "the augmentation of intelligence instruction at Leavenworth," but his advice remained unheard by the faculty of the CGSS.[41] The professional correctly saw the deficiency not only in the extent of the topic but especially in the didactics, and because the faculty of the professional schools would not listen, he wrote to one of his comrades that "I cannot urge too strongly that you consider the possibility of making your course more practical—getting away from the old conference type of instruction which is common to all of our schools."[42]

In the typical eyewashing manner of the faculty of Leavenworth, however, the publication for instructors stated in 1939 under the chapter title "'Training for the G-2'": "It is believed that the present methods are excellent. … "[43]

In the years after World War I, a mass of officers from the mobilization had to be schooled, the so-called hump, clogging the schools and promotion pipelines. To get a picture of the bottleneck: There were 5,960 regular army officers in April 1917, a number that rose to 203,786 at the end of World War I.[44] All of those did of course not remain in the service and all were also not eligible for the CGSS, but the magnitude of the problem is apparent. For several years, the CGSS ran only one-year classes, which were again shortened to ten-week courses during the next world war. The two-year classes were reintroduced from 1929 to 1936. The rank structure of those attending the CGSS had now changed: 61 percent of the students held the rank of captain while 37 percent were majors and some years later the best part held the rank of major.[45] Soldiers in these ranks appear to be far better suited for instruction in staff work for divisions and corps than the formerly taught lieutenants, but in the German Army the thought prevailed that one cannot start early enough with advanced professional military education; thus, in German war games lieutenants would command divisions. Those who attended the *Kriegsakademie* therefore carried in the majority the rank of *Leutnant* (2nd lieutenant) or *Oberleutnant* (1st lieutenant). In later years, they were promoted to *Hauptmann* (captain) while still at the war academy.

At the CGSS, the initial competition that allowed only excellent students to stay the second year in an advanced course was nearly reversed in the years of the hump. Only those who failed completely would be eliminated after the first year. The rest were allowed to stay the duration of the two-year course. Commandants of the CGSS had long fought for a regular two-year course because they were of the opinion that the content necessary could not be taught in one year. This, however, seems to be an overly long estimate for the teaching of proper brigade and division staff procedures. The long time was rather needed because of bulky, meticulous, and textbook- and doctrine-oriented teaching. George C. Marshall, arguably one of the foremost experts in professional military education in the army at that time, was of the opinion that with the proper didactics the contents necessary could be taught at the CGSS in four and a half months.[46]

Supposedly attendance at the next higher-level schools, like the Army War College (AWC) and the later established Industrial College, was only possible when the officer had attended the CGSS. In real life, however, others made it without running through all the schools.[47] The notion that only consecutive attendance at the schools named would punch the tickets necessary to advance in rank drove many officers to pester their superiors relentlessly to get assigned to the schools.[48] The institutions, however, were not universally held in high regard, especially by the older war veterans who were now regimental or division commanders. In their minds, they had beaten the mighty Imperial German Army and therefore knew enough about warfare without the introduction of new doctrines. They preferred a well-run unit instead of having some smart officers with fancy new school ideas.[49] It thus happened quite frequently that an officer was detailed to the school who could be spared at the regiment because he didn't carry his weight—or was even considered the "regimental idiot."[50] Even that is not an exaggeration because there is at least one instance recorded when a mentally ill person was selected to attend the CGSS.[51]

Incredibly, the same selection problems persisted twenty years later.[52] Therefore, exactly some of those attended schools who should not have, like "some Old Man's aide, adjutant, or favourite staff officer."[53] This conservative approach to education prevailed in the highest ranks. Then Major Bradford Grethen Chynoweth, USMA 1912, noted about then Army Chief of Staff (1926–1930) Charles P. Summerall, USMA 1892, that "like many others of that era, [. . .] he was not devoting himself to anticipating the changes that would occur in a future war. He had had his war."[54] Chynoweth was considered by many to be a "great brain" but his maverick ideas about education and tank doctrine and his frank statements in front of superiors got him repeatedly into trouble.[55] He ended up in the Philippines at the beginning of World War II, was captured by the Japanese, and had to endure the inhumanity of a Japanese prison camp for many years. Chynoweth and his experiences with narrow-minded, old-fashioned officers is no singularity. It is therefore not surprising that officers who wanted to attend Leavenworth had to follow a rather non-transparent and conservative procedure.

The selection of officers for the Leavenworth schools by their superiors posed a problem in itself and not only for the reasons stated above—that they were detailed to the school to get rid of them or the superiors were merely too old-fashioned to understand the value of an advanced military school. Able officers could simply be overlooked when they did not possess the ability to shine properly. Others were so valuable that the superior would simply deny their request to attend the school, thinking more about their regiment than the career or education of their subordinate. Even with the agreement of or selection by the regimental commander, the ultimate decision rested with the branch chiefs. Often personal influence and cunning paperwork helped officers to attend the CGSS rather than a proper and fair selection process.[56]

For those dedicated to attending the CGSS, whether because of the genuine desire to expand their minds or purely to get their ticket punched for promotion, the nontransparent and every-few-years-changing selection criteria made it even harder to get there. General age limits, age-in-rank limits, and efficiency rating requirements changed over the years so that even people who were proficient in all matters of the army, like George C. Marshall, were occasionally fooled on who was eligible for Leavenworth and who was not.[57] He had to remark that "The annual contest for a place at Leavenworth is growing more strenuous each year."[58] In the same year a young officer complained to Marshall that "it seems to require quite a battle these days to get on either the Leavenworth or War College lists."[59] Others thought it to be a "silly sort of way to run an army."[60]

The frustration in these statements is evident and derives not only from the nontransparent selection criteria but also because the young officers were always dependent on someone else. In Germany, every eligible officer could take the entrance exam for the *Kriegsakademie*, a procedure that will be discussed in the next chapter. Though the commandants of the American schools frequently recommended and requested an entrance examination because of the low quality of students sent by the branch chiefs, their advice was never followed.[61]

When the American officers had finally made it to the CGSS, the deficiencies of the school became immediately apparent to the students. It was no rarity that an instructor was less qualified to teach a subject than the students present, even in a special field. The situation changed after World War I when veterans of the AEF achieved an "absolute dominance" in the faculty of the CGSS and even in the mid-1930s they still made up about a third of the instructors.[62] Now they at least possessed some modern war experience. However, with those officers as teachers, the attitude also became more prevalent that everything that was significant in military matters had happened in the war to end all wars and little would change in the future. Though the faculty became busy rewriting doctrine, neither the manuals they produced nor their teaching matched the necessities of modern war as it was to come. A memorandum from 1919 states in the typical boastful Leavenworth faculty lingo that "the tactical principles and doctrines heretofore recognized and taught at the Leavenworth Schools have been tested in the European War and have been found to be as sound today as heretofore."[63] Such a statement really deserves the label "eyewash." Consequently, those students with combat experience from World War I who tried to apply some of the lessons they had learned from trench warfare to map problems would be graded down because according to the then-commandant of the school, Colonel Hugh A. Drum, "open warfare doctrine was a sounder tactical solution."[64] In fact, the American Expeditionary Forces had never before experienced more than a quarter of a million battle casualties in fewer than two hundred combat days.[65] Training for World War I along existing doctrine "produced infantry willing to be killed in straight-ahead attacks because it knew no better."[66]

There is no evidence that the instructor veterans of the AEF were selected because of their teaching skills or because of proficiency in a certain field. Apparently, although they must have had different individual experiences, they nevertheless bent all to the Leavenworth doctrine. The statements about a special capability of the faculty came usually from the faculty members themselves, the commandant, or the assistant commandant of the CGSS—but rarely from former students. The latter rather described the instructors as having a "dull manner of instruction" and lessons being filled with "mind-numbing detail" and "stereotyped" teaching.[67]

Former faculty members would return to the CGSS for another stint as teachers, as assistant commandants, or commandants and thus make sure that little would be changed and nothing would be questioned. The CGSS followed the same unfortunate policy in teacher selection as the United States Military Academy—only former graduates were selected. The same "inbreeding" that occurred at West Point befell the advanced military school. Any influence of mavericks or fresh, outside-the-box thinking became close to impossible.

There are indeed hardly any complimentary accounts about the teaching abilities of the inflexible instructors at Leavenworth. The lessons were known to be arduous, boring, and complicated. Because of that, the commandants badly needed two years to go through all the material. The problem was homemade and the bulky way of instructing appeared as a constant concern for those who criticized the way of teaching at the CGSS. The majority of the student officers claimed in their autobiographies and letters that they had to work very hard to get through at Leavenworth.[68] There were always a few officers in a class who had to be "relieved on account of sickness."[69] Because of the horror accounts, the reputation of the Leavenworth school suffered again. Dwight D. Eisenhower, recently graduated from the school, was prompted to write an article about it to help polish the tarnished image.[70] While supposed to be a public relations article, the shortcomings of the school can be read between the lines. Even though it was a featured article, Eisenhower wrote it anonymously and covered himself from all sides in case some senior officer disagreed and would endanger his career. While Ike generally was held in high regard within the army, the article was one reason why he got the reputation of a "brownnoser" in some circles.

The reasons for the high workload at Leavenworth were real and manifold. The general instructions an American officer received in his regiment were very limited. Regimental commanders tended "to rely on the service schools for the education of their officers" and they therefore often lacked any advanced military knowledge before attending the school.[71] The "garrison schools" were supposed to be a cornerstone of the Elihu Root reforms but were badly neglected in the U.S. Army whose personnel was already short an education.[72] The example of Creighton Abrams, whom we got to know in the chapter on West Point, is no singularity. Between his graduation from the U.S. Military Academy in 1936 and the beginning of World War II, "the sum total of schooling he had received" was "a two-day orientation on provisions of the National Defense Act of 1920 and one week in the 7th Cavalry horseshoer's school."[73] Therefore, the majority of officers arrived with a great lack of expertise and education at the CGSS. Grown-up captains and majors were forced to write examinations on drill regulations at the CGSS, a topic that every German ensign knew in his sleep.[74]

Another reason for the hard work was the ponderous way of instruction and the formal way of teaching, which required the memorizing of much textbook material, procedures, and regulations, which suppressed any creativity and made necessary committing to memory a certain formal writing style. In contrast to their German counterparts, the only way American officers could prepare themselves was to request privately advice from former graduates. George S. Patton wrote his young friend Floyd S. Parks, who had been on his staff in Hawaii and was now detailed to attend the CGSS, that "high marks at Leavenworth depend more on TECHNIQUE than on INTELLIGENCE. While I was there I copied in long hand one order every night. The purpose of this practice is to make the correct writing of orders automatic."[75] What Patton really thought about Leavenworth becomes even clearer in his actions than in his words. After graduating, he would for years ask the school for its tactical problems to work them out for himself, but he would never request the school solution.[76]

George C. Marshall concurs completely with Patton when he remarks that "practically all the tactical instruction I have seen in the Army has been ninety percent technique, and ten percent tactics."[77] Marshall remembered from his time at Leavenworth that "in those days we were required to write out in long-hand a lengthy estimate of the situation, which occupied about two hours."[78] Little had changed decades later because Marshall had "talked to a number of recent Leavenworth students, and I find quite a few of them feel that two and three hour periods on some of the subjects in the afternoon could have been effectively handled in an hour."[79]

In Germany, information about how to be selected for the *Kriegsakademie* and what to expect there was readily available publicly. In addition, it was customary in a regiment that officers who had been through the entrance examination or even attended the *Kriegsakademie* would expose their comrades to the same learning material that they had to handle during the examination and their time at the war academy. Educating their younger comrades had always been an integral part of being a German officer.

Despite the fact that all were officers in the same army and that they quite often shared the same rank, there existed a steep hierarchy at the

CGSS between instructors and student officers that hardly loosened up even after hours. During a round of golf with student officers, faculty members might "unbend a little, but never forget that they were 'The School.'"[80] Others noted that a master-student relationship existed at the school.[81]

In a 1939 student officer questionnaire, about 50 percent claimed that the "contact opportunities" between students and the faculty were "insufficient."[82] It can be imagined how bad it must have been twenty years earlier. Such a gap between instructors and students in no way encourages discussions, questioning, or critique and it seems that this is how it was intended to be. The commandants obviously had an interest in pushing a standard level of normed procedures and causes of actions into the heads of the students rather than making them independent thinkers and decisionmakers. It was, however, exactly the latter who were needed as commanders in the modern mobile and mechanized warfare of the twentieth century. Instead they were trained to conduct a "methodical battle," something that did not even exist in Napoleon's times.[83]

Another major problem the newly arrived officers experienced at the CGSS was the theoretical and academic approach, very different from the hands-on, practical teaching they were accustomed to at The Infantry School if they had attended it before. Most of the time they dealt with classroom map problems and procedures and in the early days it was not unlikely that the instructor had less practical and wartime experience— even in his special teaching topic—than the students present.

Bruce C. Clarke, USMA 1925, was so humiliated by an instructor at the CGSS that the experience still riled him forty years later and he wrote an article about it. He attended the last regular class in 1940. At this time, the faculty of CGSS finally offered map-maneuvers that stretched over several days. Clarke, then a captain, commanded a whole division of the "blue force" in the exercise with an attached tank company. He gave the orders to his infantry battalions to achieve a breakthrough on a narrow front to enable the tank company to pass through and directly attack the headquarters of the whole "red force" located in a city in the enemy's rear area. Clarke's course of action caused "much consternation in the school."[84] The map exercise ended a day earlier than planned because the ingenious officer had taken the enemy's headquarters. Clarke was "severely criticized" for his commands and told that he had "misused his tanks" because they were "never sent into towns" and never acted without the protection of the infantry.[85] An infantry colonel who led the exercise inferred that because Clarke was an engineer he would not understand such things. The flabbergasted and frustrated captain received the dreaded "unsatisfactory" for his performance as division commander. If it had not been for the war, that assessment would have ensured the ruination of Clarke's career. But three years later he found himself leading Combat Command A (CCA) of the 4th Armored Division as part of Patton's Third Army. He ordered his 37th Tank Battalion to perform basically the same action as during the map maneuver at Leavenworth. The battalion was commanded by the already famous Creighton Abrams, whom we know from preceding chapters and who had suffered so much as a plebe at West Point.[86] Just as in the map maneuver, the battalion broke into the town located in the rear area and overran the German headquarters responsible for coordinating the defense of the region. Clarke became a four-star general and commanded U.S. Army Forces Europe. He retired in 1962, considered an expert in leadership and armored warfare. His career, which was nearly destroyed by inept instructors at Leavenworth, was saved by the war. Still bitter about his experience at the school decades later, he sent the article to several of his friends with handwritten remarks like "this is how Leavenworth teaching in 1940 was preparing its graduates to defeat the Panzer armies of Hitler."[87] His treatment by the head instructors he called "inexcusable" and he noted that the infantry colonel who humiliated him so much commanded a regiment in France in 1944 but retired at that rank.

The theoretic approach and its dangers were addressed in a memorandum by George C. Marshall, who stated that "Training in larger problems is rarely done because the Leavenworth system is too ponderous and as a rule it only deals with some distant affair, like a Gettysburg map."[88] Such an approach was not satisfactory because there was after all "a world of open country accessible to everybody."[89] Marshall called for some ingenuity and creativity that was clearly lacking in the teachings at Leavenworth.

The important difference between indoor map exercises and doing the same lesson in the countryside cannot be overemphasized. Officers who solve map problem after map problem will gain the false confidence of thinking that the map will reveal to them all that they need to know. In war, they will stay in headquarters instead of being outside and seeing the troops and the conditions at the frontlines, which are of course totally different from what the map and incoming dispatches are able to reveal.[90] In a real crisis, the appropriate map will usually not be at hand.[91] Even during large-scale maneuvers on American soil, detailed maps were not available to officers who participated.[92]

Map exercises, map maneuvers, and map problems, however, constituted "seventy percent of the total instruction time" at the CGSS.[93] The Leavenworth schools conditioned their officers to get a "staff officers attitude," which was already noted by contemporaries and forced the then assistant commandant Colonel Hugh Drum to publish a—rather unconvincing—defense in his annual report.[94] Changes to the curriculum to more emphasize real-life command decisions, however, were in "in reality, more cosmetic than actual."[95]

True to the unfortunate U.S. Army culture of that time, the "school solution" was again held up at the Leavenworth schools as the sole example for a correct approach to and result of every exercise.[96] Treating student officers, who often had vast experience of their own, like middle school children led to cynicism among the officers. One of them created a poem stating their opinion clearly:

> *Here lie the bones of Lieutenant Jones*
> *A product of this institution*
> *In his very first fight*
> *He went out like a light*
> *By using the School Solution!*[97]

Though it has been maintained that the students sometimes participated in the creation of the school solution, there is no such instance recorded in the memoirs or letters of former students where they actually made a difference.[98] Indeed, even an officer student research paper dealing with the instruction methods at the CGSS in 1936 is highly critical regarding the emphasis on the school solution.[99] The author was not the only one to request "more freedom of thought."[100]

Under a new grading system, which had changed and would again change several times, a student had to "hit the approved solution" to gain the coveted "E" for "Excellence."[101] Any use of inventiveness that deviated from the school doctrine endangered the student's performance and he might get an "S" for "Satisfactory" or even the hated "U" for "Unsatisfactory." Evidently, "the overall effect was to discourage initiative."[102]

The rigid and rather surreal atmosphere is best described in an incident related to us by Joe Collins, whom we got to know in chapter 2 during his unhappy detail as instructor at West Point. When Collins attended Leavenworth, it had happened "several times" that the then commandant, Major General Stuart Heintzelman, USMA 1899, sat in the classroom and disagreed openly with the "school solution" of the instructor.[103] Heintzelman would apologize to the instructor, tell the class his own solution, but "would caution us to follow the instructor's guidance in any subsequent test problem" or otherwise the students might receive an "unsatisfactory." Just as Chynoweth had noted before, Collins remarked that "most of us students followed his advice, and played the instructor's game, often with tongue in cheek."[104] Announcements about a supposedly flexible handling of possible solutions and statements like "the function of the school is not to disseminate dogma, but to teach its students to think" come again largely from the faculty and proved to be incorrect in real life.[105] The latter proclamation is from Heintzelman himself and in apparent contradiction to the advice he had given his students in the classroom. Inconsistencies like these show clearly that the greatest care has to be taken when statements of faculty are viewed in assessing the performance of the school. Even in the biased feature article Eisenhower wrote about the "Leavenworth Course," he advised against disagreeing or arguing with the instructors.[106] Any encouragement to make the students think cannot be observed.

In addition to attending lectures and classes and solving map problems, a student was required to prepare and present an individual research paper, which could also be organized with a teammate or a group of fellow student officers (then termed group research papers). The whole teaching and curriculum structure reminds one of a civilian college in the countryside with a high ivory tower.

Not surprisingly, the operations of the Imperial German Army and especially the Battles of Tannenberg and Gumbinnen were often centers of interest for students and faculty. Though a memorandum from the faculty had stated in 1919 that "the German textbooks heretofore utilized cannot be employed for psychological reasons," this rather funny statement was forgotten ten years later and the German wars and armies became popular again.[107]

Translated German Field Regulations and treatises of war and tactics by German officers were mainly used as teaching material in the 1930s as they had been used before. The way they were used shows also how little they were understood. The majority of the American officers viewed in this study attended the CGSC in the early to mid-1930s. During this time—more than ten years after the Great War—there appear hardly any lectures or individual research papers that dealt with the current *Reichswehr*.[108] Instead, World War I was replayed again and again on the basis of the literature of old German officers.[109]

Neither the students nor the instructors possessed any training in source evaluation and they were greatly limited in the amount of intelligence they could gather for their papers. Nevertheless, some of their studies were made available to the G-2 section of the War Department, which shows how desperately the U.S. Army of that time hungered for input, an input, however, which was most often just filed away, instead of reflected on.

An example for the result of one of these group research papers is Major M. B. Ridgway, "Operations of the German Eighth Army from End of Battle of Gumbinnen through the Battle of Tannenberg (Dramatization)," Individual Research Paper No. 88, 1935, CGSS. We already got to know Matthew Ridgway through his experiences at West Point, where he had suffered as a plebe and where he had later feared for his career when he was ordered to teach French to cadets despite knowing little of that language. The teaching assignment had not been the death knell to his career but after six years at West Point, where the fitness buff was also manager of athletics, Ridgway served as a company commander in the 15th Infantry in China. The regiment was then commanded by Lieutenant Colonel George C. Marshall. Ridgway "ditched" his participation in the Olympics pentathlon team to honor a request from one of his most revered superiors, Major General Frank R. McCoy, to assist on the Bolivian-Paraguayan Conciliation Commission. From 1934–1935 he attended the CGSS where he created, together with a host of fellow officers, the above-mentioned "group research paper," which judging by the other papers' titles, doesn't sound too bad.[110]

However, Ridgway retained a copy of it in his papers. What is called a "dramatization" in CGSS lingo is nothing but a theater play of monumental size, played out in a prologue, four acts, and a synopsis, and performed over the length of three days. From the humorous notes and the whole setting, it is apparent that all participants had a lot of fun preparing, staging, and performing the play. The military value, however, came close to nil. The play ended with the conclusion that the battle was brought about victoriously "by that unmeasurable intangible yet vital force, THE WILL OF PAUL VON HINDENBURG, THE COMMANDER."[111] It is highly unlikely that the whole work was conceived as a comedy because it would have been an enormous waste of time and the faculty of the CGSS was known for its lack of humor.[112] Other individual and group research papers were of equally low value in regard of source evaluation and military significance.

The grading system at the CGSS confused many students and showed a low didactic understanding. Instead of having clear-cut grades with distinguishable levels, students were rated into the second digits after the decimal.[113] George C. Marshall received the highest score of 100 after solving a map problem when he was a student at Leavenworth, while Second Lieutenant Fay W. Brabson, with a grade of 95.17, ranked forty-seventh.[114] The grading system not only feigned excellence where there was none, but it also left the student with the greatest insecurity about his personal performance as long as the assistant commandant or a department head had no word with him explaining in plain English his accomplishments or lack thereof.[115] Officers with many years of expertise and experience in military matters often resented being graded like "a graduate student."[116]

The Leavenworth school overtook the *Kriegsakademie* in the first two decades of the twentieth century when it came to racist lectures. That seems to be rather consequential because cadets at West Point had already been exposed to racist thoughts through their directed reading.[117] At Leavenworth, it was not uncommon that former generals or even captains could present their twisted worldviews to a whole class on a regular basis.[118] Captain LeRoy Eltinge, USMA 1896, a senior instructor at the Department of Military Arts at Leavenworth for five years, was able to cover with his little booklet "Psychology of War" pretty much every possible racist and sexist base. The booklet was the source for his lectures, used for many years at Leavenworth, and printed in several editions. To invoke higher authority, he states in the first footnote that "the material in these lectures is not original," but all his racist ramblings come without citations.[119] He begins his chapter "Psychology of Races" by offering his insights about the superiority of the "pure Anglo-Saxon."[120] He goes on to state that Negroes "think with a different kind of brain" and because of that "we will not be able to get the best out of him as a soldier."[121] Jews, in Eltinge's mind, "despise hard physical work" and they do "not have the qualities of a good soldier."[122] In his appendix, "Causes of War," Eltinge reemphasizes his racist assertions and then goes on to justify slavery and asks the student officers how they would feel if their daughters or sisters married a black, yellow, or red man.[123] With even more insight, he assures the listeners that the mind of the Chinaman "ceased to develop at an early age" and that two sure signs of a civilization that uses more than it produced are "increased influence of women in politics" and "sterility among women of the upper class."[124] Racist lectures would be even more common at the Army War College (AWC).[125] It is therefore "likely that these theories became part of the mental equipment of our [the U.S.] higher ranking officers."[126] It would be an exaggeration, however, to put the blame for raising racist beliefs and sentiments on the American officer's education alone. There is no doubt that they existed to a certain degree in American society and there is evidence that many officers—especially those born in the South—were raised with them.[127] The military educational system of that time, however, "reinforced" these beliefs instead of countering them.[128] Racist ramblings and remarks are still to be found in the autobiographies of former generals even long after World War II where American soldiers of color had proven their fighting capabilities over and over again beyond any doubt.[129] And they had done that for that matter already in the past wars of the United States.

There is no question that racism also ran rampant in the German officer corps of that time.[130] The point that I wanted to make, however, is that until the 1930s such indoctrination was not part of the German officer's education at official army schools and that it is surprising—considering the number of complaints about the short time available to educate the officers at all the American military schools—that even an hour was wasted with "ideological" lectures delivered by a mere captain.

While in the following chapter about the *Kriegsakademie*, U.S. Army officers will be cited who attended German military schools, now German officers who experienced or observed the American military education system should be heard. The Leavenworth school and West Point were generally held in little regard by visiting German officers while the U.S. Army War College, especially the Army Industrial College, had a better reputation. The latter was founded in 1924 and taught to develop "logical thought in the problems involved in industrial mobilization."[131] Part of the course was extensive tours of production plants and factories with lectures by chief engineers and leading managers.

Generalleutnant Werner von Blomberg, who would ten years later become war minister and lead the German Army on a catastrophic path towards National Socialism, noted in the late twenties after a visit to the American military educational institutions that Leavenworth taught *Papierwissenschaft*—paper knowledge—to its student officers and that there was "lack of the appliance of modern tactics."[132] Blomberg's assessment carries special weight because he had been *Chef der Heeresausbildungsabteilung*—chief of the army's educational department—for many years and he had not only visited the United States but also other countries and was thus able to compare. He concluded, however, that "despite my reservations" about the quality of the school a General Staff officer should be send to Leavenworth to establish a connection with the Americans and ultimately gain access to the Industrial College. The detail to Leavenworth was a means to an end—to finally gain entrance to the coveted Industrial College. Indeed, *Hauptmann* Hans von Greiffenberg did show up at the CGSS fewer than two years later. Obviously disappointed by the school and not able to gain access to the Industrial College or the War College, he never graduated from Leavenworth. His short stint at the CGSS, however, would have far-reaching consequences more than a decade later.[133] One of Greiffenberg's classmates at the CGSS was Paul M. Robinett, who would become chief of the Special Studies Division, a major section of the Office of the Chief of Military History, responsible for writing the history of the U.S. Army in World War II. Because of their friendship, Greiffenberg would relent to Robinett's requests for assistance in presenting the "German side" of the war in the official U.S. Army history, the so-called Green Books. Greiffenberg had been a subordinate of Franz Halder, former chief of staff of the German Army, and in turn was "instrumental in securing his chief's cooperation in the historical program."[134] Halder's central position as head of the control group for the thousands of studies that were prepared by German officers for the U.S. Army assured that a "purified" picture of the *Wehrmacht* officer corps would reach the history books and prevail for decades.[135]

Another school that was more important for the U.S. Army officer corps than any other institution of professional military education was rarely in the focus of German observers—The Infantry School in Fort Benning, Georgia.[136] The American second lieutenants, who were then about four to six years older than their German counterparts, left West Point to command their platoons—or even companies—without deeper knowledge of tactics and the efficiency of the weapons in the inventory of the U.S. Army.[137] Without the help of seasoned NCOs, they would excel in spit-and-polish operations but not much else. Only years later did many get the opportunity to attend the then best military school in the

United States—The Infantry School. Even before George C. Marshall took over as assistant commandant with full responsibility for the curriculum, the school was highly beneficial for the younger and even older officers attending it and, though it was supposed to be a steppingstone to the Command and General Staff School, it had become in fact superior to it.[138] Correctly labelled "the heart and the brain of the infantry," no other school taught the desperately needed hands-on knowledge of infantry weapons and tactics on a company, battalion, and regimental level.[139] Attending officers, however, were still four to eight years behind their German counterparts in experience. Experience is here defined as knowledge of operations, tactics, and weaponry in modern wars.

Yet highly doctrinal material, masses of paperwork, school solutions, and the superiority of the instructor, no matter his qualifications, were daily experiences for the students, just as at the CGSS.[140] Map exercises instead of field problems and several page-long written orders for simple troop movements clogged the teaching, caused an "inexcusable waste of time," and dulled the senses of the officers.[141] Map and battle problems for the students were, just like at Leavenworth, "too minutely structured, leaving far too little to the students' imagination and initiative."[142] Even when it came to the infantry weapons, they were used with "great inefficiency."[143]

Help, however, was on the way in the person of George C. Marshall, who was determined to set right the wrongs he had experienced when a woefully unprofessional U.S. officer corps went to war in Europe, causing an unparalleled number of American casualties in only nineteen months of war. In his view—and it can be stated now that he made a historically correct assessment—the inadequacy of many American officers came from their advanced ages, inflexibility of mind, and lack of modern and practical training.[144] Marshall was especially keen regarding the physical capabilities of a commander because "in my experience in the war— and I saw about 27 of 29 divisions in battle—there were more failures, more crushed careers of officers of considerable rank that grew out of physical exhaustion than by reason of any other one cause."[145]

Marshall's time came, when in November 1927 he was appointed assistant commandant of The Infantry School and head of the academic

The Officers' Quarters at Fort Benning in 1925. Benning, like many army posts at that time, was not exactly famous for its commodities and the spouses of the officers especially had to put up with a lot. Extensive reconstruction in the 1930s improved the situation at the school and the post. [Reprinted with permission from Fort Benning, by Kenneth H. Thomas Jr., Charleston, South Carolina: Arcadia Publishing, 2003.]

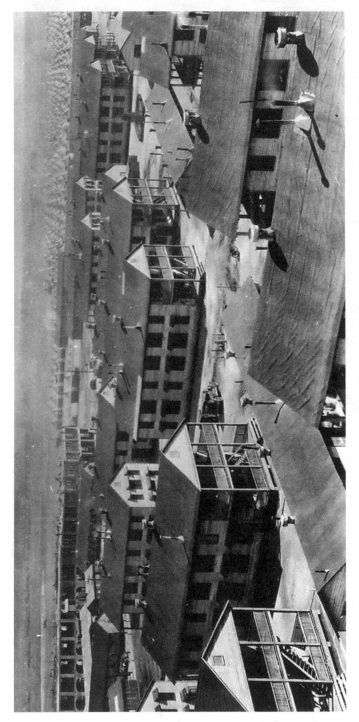

A view of part of the Fort Benning post, here the area where the 29th Infantry was housed. In the background to the left, the beginning of the badly needed reconstruction that started around 1925. Many of the troops were still living in tents (upper right). [COURTESY NATIONAL INFANTRY MUSEUM, FORT BENNING, GEORGIA]

department. His term, lasting until November 1932, has been aptly named the "Benning Renaissance."[146] The school was in 1927 only nine years old, having been founded after the shortcomings of American officers in infantry tactics had become obvious in World War I.

Sometimes one man's tragedy is another's good fortune. Marshall was known as a hard worker anyway but, because his first wife had died shortly before, he cut himself even less slack to get his mind away from his grief. At his "most restless moment" he received the new assignment and plunged into work with more vigor than ever before.[147] Marshall would streamline the whole teaching procedures of The Infantry School and "Germanize" them. He undertook, in his own words, "an almost complete revamping of the instruction" and raised it to new levels.[148] Instructors were hired or fired because of their teaching abilities, all were required to speak without reading from notes or papers, and field exercises often replaced map problems.[149] It might be "demanded peremptorily" of every student to hold an extemporaneous three-minute presentation on a current event and "this kept the wise student on his toes."[150] From now on, the instructions were run on a "realistic and practical basis."[151] Much more importantly, Marshall tried to instill and foster a free spirit in the young officers: to question, to speak out, and to go their own ways when necessary. There can be little doubt that the whole heretical undertaking was only possible because the current commandant of the school, Brigadier General Campbell King, was a good friend of Marshall.

Marshall's endeavors for his fellow officers continued after hours. At his quarters, Major Gilbert Cook, who would become a corps commander under Patton, handed out books "on psychology, sociology, or military history to read and discuss."[152] Marshall had realized, and tried to demonstrate to his flock, that reading is one of the most important acts of an officer.

It is clear from his papers that Marshall had planned to improve the officer's education for a long time and had his very own ideas. When he commanded the 15th Infantry in China, he had to deal with a young officer who "had stood first at Benning" and "was no fool" but "had been taught an absurd system."[153]

Marshall received specific input for his reforms from a German war veteran and exchange student to The Infantry School. *Hauptmann* (Captain) Adolf von Schell stayed in Marshall's house and came as close to a friend as a foreigner could get to the enigmatic Marshall. Schell, officially a student officer, was because of his vast battle experience in World War I and his personality soon invited to lecture.[154] The smart leadership and faculty at Benning soon realized that Schell "had far more to teach to us than we had to teach him."[155] Partly out of those lectures, the German officer made a book, which became popular within the U.S. Army.[156] While the German officer gained an excellent reputation in teaching, the faculty of The Infantry School followed suit with a book project of its own in a similar mold and one of Schell's war stories was implemented, telling the tale of an infantry unit in severe weather finding shelter in a barn, which was, however, pretty close to the impact of heavy artillery shells.[157] The officer ordered the company barber to give him a shave and a haircut, calming his troops with his example. The little book from The Infantry School received great praise in German military journals and was ultimately translated and distributed in Germany.[158] The book featured war stories and, at the end of each, a lessons-learned section. Because Erwin Rommel's book *Infanterie greift an!*, which was published only two years after the German translation of the American book, followed a very similar structure, it is possible that the future Desert Fox had taken it as an example for the publication of his own military experiences with tactics lessons at the end of each chapter.[159]

The American officers who got to know Schell followed his fast-rising career in the *Wehrmacht* before and during the war with interest and fascination. The German officer became a highly praised teacher at the *Kriegsakademie* and published another book.[160] Lieutenant Colonel Truman Smith, on the faculty of The Infantry School when Marshall was assistant commandant and Schell a student officer, was now, in 1938, military attaché in Germany. He reported to Marshall that "Hitler today appointed Adolph von Schell Czar of the complete German automotive industry [...] I happen to know that at the time Hitler wished to make him a Major General but that Schell feared jealousy in the officer corps and declined the same, taking a simple promotion to Colonel. […] I am personally of the opinion that you had at Benning in 1931 the future commander in chief of the German army. […] You may be interested to know that von Schell, in return for the kindness shown him at Benning, has given me every break in the world here. We know probably more of the Tank Corps, than any other attaché […]."[161]

In his grateful and modest reply to Marshall's letter of congratulation, Schell confirmed that he had indeed turned down the promotion to major general. He further explained about his rise that he "had the occasion to tell Mr. Hitler of some necessities—and there I was."[162]

The German officer, however, made in his new function as Inspector of Army Motorization an enemy who proved equally ruthless on the battlefield as in the arena of bureaucratic infights—Heinz Guderian. Guderian felt that everything that even remotely had to do with wheels or tracks had to be subordinated to the effort to create more *Panzer-divisions*.[163] Because Guderian held the title of General Inspector for the Fast Troops, conflicts were nearly automatic. Such overlapping designations or job descriptions were a characteristic of the "Third Reich's" bureaucratic inner workings.[164] The ensuing frictions greatly hindered the German war effort. Von Schell tried to oust Guderian to a position of no responsibility. But even though he had the backing of *Generalmajor* Friedrich Fromm, who was largely responsible for the army rearmament efforts and who was then in bureaucratic infights with Wilhelm Keitel, Guderian prevailed. Schell nevertheless implemented a plan that bore his name—the *Schell-Plan*—and simplified motor and vehicle production in Germany to an astonishing degree. It is entirely possible that he got some of his ideas from a tour through U.S. military installations in 1937 where he commented freely to his American guests on weapons and tactics. He basically gave the Americans the gist of the whole German *Panzer* tactics.[165] The information, however, was obviously not used by his American hosts.

Back in Germany, Schell gained some respite when Guderian led units in Poland, France, and the initial stages of the attack against Russia, but when the *Panzergeneral* was relieved and returned as General Inspector of

The faculty of The Infantry School for the years 1930–1931. Among the illustrious band is Harold Roe Bull (14, background middle), who would become Eisenhower's operations officer in World War II; Walter Bedell Smith (32, outside left), who would become Ike's chief of staff; Truman Smith (48, center), who would become military attaché in Berlin for many years and with his reports and connections influence German-American military relations until 1957; Joe Lawton Collins (53, outside left below W. B. Smith), famously aggressive commander of VII Corps in World War II; Joseph Warren Stilwell (65, center), one of the few true mavericks in the U.S. Army who made general's rank; George Catlett Marshall (66), the mentor of them all, who hated photo shoots; and Omar Nelson Bradley, Ike's trusted friend and commander of 12th Army Group in World War II. The Infantry School, more than any other educational institution of the army, contributed to the professionalism of the officer corps. (COURTESY GEORGE C. MARSHALL FOUNDATION, LEXINGTON, VIRGINIA)

144

Major General Adolf von Schell, who as a mere captain had taught Marshall "much that was highly important to my profession" when the German officer was detailed to The Infantry School. The Americans were fascinated by Schell's teaching abilities, which were no rarity among German officers. The picture shows Schell in March 1940. After only two years in his position as head of the German motor transportation effort, the 14-to-16 hour workdays and the bureaucratic infighting with Heinz Guderian had taken its toll. Von Schell's formerly glossy black hair had gone gray and receded and his features had become gaunt. (COURTESY BUNDESARCHIV, PHOTO 146-1994-031-08, PHOTOGRAPHER HEINRICH HOFFMANN)

the Armored Troops, he took the gauntlet up again. On January 1, 1943, von Schell got command of the new, to-be-raised 25th *Panzerdivision*—in Norway and as a *Generalleutnant*.[166] That can be considered a clear demotion because a division was commanded by a lower ranking *Generalmajor*—a *Generalleutnant* usually ranked a corps—and the major theater of war was on the eastern front. Schell's enemies were successful in staining his reputation somehow because he remained in the same rank until the end of the war, which was also highly unusual.

After the war, Marshall was alerted that Schell might be delivered to the Soviets and tried as a war criminal. Characteristically, Marshall never admitted it, but it is likely that he intervened on behalf of Schell, who was eventually set free. The facts can be pretty well reconstructed from the correspondence in the Marshall papers.[167]

Marshall, never one to deny another man credit, acknowledged in a letter to Schell that the German officer had brought him "much that was highly important to my profession.[168] The Infantry School introduced in teaching what had been common at all German military schools—the element of surprise. After a seventeen-mile cross-country ride, Marshall ordered the participating student officers to draw a map of the covered terrain to help them "think on their feet," which can be considered a price-less ability for any officer.[169] Matthew Ridgway tells the tale of similar sur-prising episodes he experienced at The Infantry School and which could have been taken from the classroom of the *Kriegsakademie*: "Many a time, in Infantry School, I had been given such a problem. A map would be thrust before me. 'You are here,' I was told. 'The enemy is here. The tactical situation is thus and so (it was always bad). Your battalion commander has been killed. You are now in command. What do you do?'"[170]

Marshall had given standing orders "that any student's solution to a problem that differed markedly from the 'approved' solution, yet made sense, would be published to the class."[171] His attitude towards the in-structors and the "school solution" could not be more different from the attitude of the commandant at Leavenworth. In a tactics class that was observed by Marshall from the back of the room, a young maverick 1st lieutenant by the name of Charles T. "Buck" Lanham, USMA 1924, dis-agreed with the "school solution" and offered his own, which in turn was denigrated by the instructor. Marshall stepped in, "briefly demolished" the instructor's solution and then praised Lanham's version.[172] The learning environment shows a world of difference to the highly choreographed map problems and *Kriegsspiele* at the Command and General Staff School.[173]

It is evident from the papers of the officers that the years at this school had a defining impact on their life. It resulted not only from the modernized curriculum, didactics, and realistic training, but also from the sage advice they received from George C. Marshall in personal and pro-fessional matters. He created a lasting legacy in the hearts and minds of his students, The Infantry School, and the U.S. Army. In stark contrast to Leavenworth, whose reputation is mixed at best, The Infantry School "received the most lavish praise from its graduates."[174]

Nearly ten years after Marshall had departed, The Infantry School still stood out among the army's professional military education facili-ties. A qualified observer noted that The Infantry School "keeps abreast of the times, is intensive and strenuous, and is turning out fine junior leaders."[175] Students praised the school in equal terms.[176] To them, "it was obvious that instructors at Benning had been selected with greater care than at West Point."[177] The latter followed the same basic system as the CGSS.

In the words of the usually overcritical John A. Heintges, "The Infantry School was perfection."[178] His comrade Buck Lanham, who was so critical about the CGSS, describes his experience at Benning as "an electric current that coursed through that place for people who had anything to offer."[179] Bearing West Point and Leavenworth in mind, it is obvious that a positive tradition in teaching and didactics can be upheld the same way as a negative tradition.

The Infantry School appears here in much briefer fashion than the Command and General Staff School to make certain points:

When senior U.S. Army commanders praised the school system of the U.S. Army, they may well have had in mind The Infantry School instead of the Command and General Staff School. The abilities U.S. Army commanders gained they had obviously been taught at The Infantry School during and after Marshall's reign rather than at any time during their stint at the CGSS. The level of command—regiment, division, or corps—seems much less relevant than the command culture in this respect. Marshall hit the nail on the head when he noted that "you give a good leader very little and he will succeed; you give mediocrity a great deal and they will fail. That is illustrated everywhere I turn. [...] It depends on leadership."[180] Those who attended The Infantry School before the CGSS were able to comment on the great differences between the schools and the correctness of Marshall's principles.

Because the majority of the U.S. Army senior commanders of World War II passed through the Leavenworth school, it has been assumed that this school was instrumental in shaping their abilities. However, 150 future generals attended The Infantry School and fifty more were members of the faculty.[181] Here, only Marshall's time at the school is counted and because Benning obviously kept its quality, there are more to add to the above numbers.[182]

In the next chapter, it will be examined how the "Germanized" Infantry School and the Command and General Staff School fared compared to "the real thing"—the German *Kriegsakademie*.

FIVE

The Importance of the Attack and How to Lead: The German *Kriegsakademie*

> *"One can do in war only what one has learned in peace."*[1]
> —HAUPTMANN (LATER GENERALLEUTNANT) ADOLF VON SCHELL

As a supposed threat to Europe, the German Great General Staff was forbidden by the Versailles Treaty, as was the education of General Staff officers. But, with a little ingenuity, the Germans just renamed the General Staff into *Truppenamt* (troop office), whose section T4 dealt with the education of the General Staff officers. The staff officers themselves were in turn just renamed *Führergehilfen* (leader assistants). That fooled the Inter-Allied Control Commission for a few years. No regulation of the Versailles Treaty was more thoroughly "circumvented" than that of the abolition of the General Staff and education and selection of its officers.[2] The fact that they were undertaking illegal activities was well known to the majority of the German officers.[3] Though the whole extent was not recognized by the visiting American officers, they knew the Versailles Treaty was violated before their eyes. The American acting military attaché, Major Allen Kimberley, hit the mark when he stated in 1924 that Germany's brains were far from being disarmed.[4] In fact, observers noted that the Germans had "converted their entire army into a single, far more efficient school."[5]

The mission of the advanced German military educational system remained the same as had been formulated during the reform of the *Kriegsakademie* in the middle of the nineteenth century: "The purpose of the *Kriegsakademie*, which has the character of a military university, is to enhance the general scholarly spirit of the armed forces ... ."[6]

Though the philosophy of professional military education remained the same, it was occasionally more improvised because of the necessity for secrecy.[7] That, however, was apparently not always taken too seriously by German officers. When in 1928 the American military attaché Colonel Arthur L. Conger pestered the German High Command relentlessly to let him attend an officer's school, he was allowed to visit the 3rd Division's school, which had then taken over some of the responsibilities of the *Truppenamt* T4. Conger gained permission to see "absolutely everything without reservation" but was asked to tell "no one that he had visited the school" or to even "admit knowledge that such a school existed."[8] The attendance of the American officer was perhaps only possible because the German military considered him "an open, straight soldier and an honest friend of Germany."[9] Incidentally, nearly twenty years earlier, Conger had been a student of Hans Delbrück, the latter now considered the founder of the discipline of modern military history, when he had lectured at Berlin University.[10]

The episode at the officers' school, however, is also one of many examples of the excellent relationship between the German Army and the visiting American officers. Conger obviously gave his word because he was allowed to attend a war game and the school, but he violated the trust of the German officers and wrote a detailed report for the War Department in Washington.[11]

The American military attaché noted that the instructions began with basic tactics and moved over to strategy using the Königgrätz campaign of 1866 as a basis. He observed also that the atmosphere in the class was "pleasantly relaxed."[12] Similar observations would be made when looking at the classes of the then re-established *Kriegsakademie*. The difference in the classes at the Command and General Staff School, with its stiff middle-school atmosphere, is apparent.

There were other dissimilarities between the schools as well. As already stated, basically every German officer who was eligible by rank and age or service—usually a lieutenant with at least five years in his rank—and able to pass the *Wehrkreis-Prüfung* (defense district examination) with the necessary score could be accepted. The letter of recommendation from his regimental commander, however, would count nearly as much as his score at the examination.[13] There were officers with high scores gained at the *Wehrkreis-Prüfung* who would not be detailed to the *Kriegsakademie* because of "character deficits."[14]

An error in the system was that of course only a certain number could attend the *Kriegsakademie* and thus a certain percentage would be failed by competitive examination.[15] The others had to try again and might lose a year or more, if their superiors would allow them another attempt. Generally, an officer who had failed once would get at least another shot.

It was possible, however, that one year would have a lot of outstanding officers who would be failed because there were so many who produced excellent results during the examination, and another year might have more mediocre officers of whom many would pass just because the competition was mediocre. The German system, however, was much better than the American because the army got a greater selection and the younger officers were not completely at the mercy of their direct superiors. The examinations were entirely anonymous and only when an outstanding result was achieved would the numbered file be sent back to the defense district command to obtain the regimental commander's efficiency report for the officer in question.

The *Wehrkreis-Prüfung* did not ask for sophisticated or arcane knowledge but for a sound understanding of military matters. A logical line of thought and the ability to express it counted as much as the portrayal of brilliance.[16] The examination was not only used by German senior officers to determine if a junior officer was able but also to get the opinion of a younger generation on current military matters.[17]

Like all other matters dealing with the German officer corps, the *Wehrkreis-Prüfung* was a transparent procedure. The military questions of the previous year were published with a solution and—true to the German military culture—the point was emphasized in every foreword that the printed solution was not to be regarded as a *Patentlösung* (patent solution) but just the result the officers who worked for the publication thought to be best.[18] For the manifold not-directly-military-related tasks, the little booklets did not offer any solutions. To find answers for the exam sections on history and athletics, for example, the young officer had to find other means to prepare himself.

A regular *Wehrkreis-Prüfung* consisted of several sections worked in several consecutive days, the whole examination process lasting up to a week.[19] The doubtless most important part of the whole examination lay in the first section, *angewandte Taktik* (applied tactics). The candidate received a detailed tactical situation of a unit, usually of regimental size with some attached units to make it more interesting, and typically also a map. He had to understand the situation and write down the necessary orders as concisely and precisely as possible. Brilliance and creativity was always looked for in the German system but both traits were not necessary to get an exceptional score. It is important to point out that not even congruence with the grading officer's solution was important. Exemplary solutions "were extremely well thought through," the orders were "clearly stated," or "clear judgement" was shown. Also "fresh ideas but clear considerations" were important and, again and again, "audacity" and "decisiveness."[20]

A regimental order for all parts of the hypothetical unit was not allowed to exceed one page, which was about a fifth of the length of a U.S. Army order for the same unit, and the German officers complained that they were still too long and detailed.[21]

It should also be kept in mind that those who took the exam were in the majority lieutenants. It was expected that they would be able to command a reinforced regiment in all its respects, a job that was usually accomplished by a colonel about fifteen years their senior. If the tactical situation was perilous and there would have been no time in reality to issue orders on paper, the applicant had to write down the brief verbal orders he would issue in that case.

The time given was usually between two and three hours, after which the young officers would get a new situation with the same unit, which typically had evolved out of the initial contact with the enemy forces. The third part would be another evolved tactical situation. The examination was clearly designed to find out if the applicant had only been lucky in the former parts or if he really was made of the right stuff and if his mind worked as flexibly in attack as it did in defense or retreat. It should also be mentioned that the applicants had to deal with the modern equipment that was available in the armies of those days even if the *Reichswehr* did not then possess it because of the restrictions the Versailles Treaty imposed.[22] A great deal of imagination and creativity, as well as sound knowledge of modern weaponry and its capabilities, was therefore required by the applicant. The mental challenge for a mere lieutenant is apparent. The units—either enemy or friendly—generally included as early as 1924 airplanes and tanks.[23] Out of necessity, the applicant had also to deal with sizeable contingents of cavalry because the *Reichswehr* was forced by the Versailles Treaty to retain three cavalry divisions. The fact that in these exams, as well as in war games, German officers still had to deal with the cavalry and cavalry tactics were emphasized was erroneously often interpreted as clinging to outdated units by old noble cavalry officers. However, because the *Reichswehr* was forced to maintain those three cavalry divisions, the High Command thought to make the best of it. The early abolition of the cavalry arm only a few years after the *Wehrmacht* came into being demonstrates the true estimate most German officers had of the efficiency of cavalry on modern battlefields. Though the *Wehrmacht* possessed its share of traditionalists, as well as over-aged and narrow-minded officers, they were not able to hamper modern developments decisively as happened in the United States.[24] The U.S. Army had the archconservative and horse-crazy chief of cavalry, Major General John K. Herr, and his counterpart in the infantry, the only remotely less inflexible chief of infantry, Major General Stephen O. Fuqua.[25]

The next task of the *Wehrkreis-Prüfung* dealt with *formale Taktik* (formal tactics), which usually emphasized marching and logistics. The applicant had again to understand the tactical situation of his regiment and write the orders for a river crossing or a movement to a certain point or the orders for supplying a unit.

The section *Feldkunde* (fieldcraft) dealt specifically with map-reading abilities and the use of terrain. The applicant had to describe certain features of a map and assess it in regard to the tactical situation given. Often he was required to mark on the map where he would place his units and why.

After this task, usually *Bewaffnung* und *Ausrüsting* (armament and equipment) had to be worked on, but the *Wehrkreis-Prüfung* of 1924 featured an additional section *Pionierdienst für alle Waffen* (engineering for all branches), which would be retained for all examinations in later years.[26] In this instance, the applicant was put into the shoes of the commander of the Infantry Regiment No. 1 and had orders to cross a river to attack the enemy right away. Especially important for this task was to select the right spot for the crossing, to have the engineers and the right equipment at hand, and to give them the right orders. Obviously, a cadet and future officer does not have to be drowned in mathematics and engineering to be able to solve a task like this, even on a regimental level. The sections of the *Wehrkreis-Prüfung* dealing with physics, chemistry, and mathematics had only to be worked by officers of the technical branches.[27]

The following armament and equipment task might well be one of the most unusual because the junior officer was most of the time asked for his personal view and judgment. It shows that the German High Command not only valued the opinion of even its most junior officers but that creativity was also requested. This was also a section for which preparation was hardly possible. As has been portrayed earlier, officers who had been through the *Wehrkreis-Prüfung* would usually teach their younger comrades how to deal with it and there was a whole industry of *Repetitorien* (revision courses) in Germany where junior officers—just like lawyers for their bar exam—would be taught over and over again the mettle of their profession for lots of money. Such a *Repetitorium*, however, would not help when an officer was just being asked his opinion and to logically argue for it. The officers of different branches got different questions. Cavalry officers, for example, were asked in the *Wehrkreis-Prüfung* of 1924, "What are the technical means of communication of a cavalry regiment? Are they sufficient in mobile warfare? Offer recommendations for improvements."[28] Officers of the *Kraftfahrtruppe* (motorized troops) were asked in the *Wehrkreis-*

Prüfung of 1921 if the new *Feldwagen* 95 (field car) was sufficient as a military vehicle and if it should be recommended for all branches.[29]

After the purely military sections, the applicants were also tested on their *Allgemeinbildung* (general or public knowledge). The *Wehrkreis-Prüfung* of 1921 still offered a selection of historical topics to choose from, but this practice was not retained in further examinations. Instead the section *Staatsbürgerkunde* (civics, or literally citizens' knowledge) was added, which for example asked in 1929 for applicants to describe and compare the law of the *Reich* according to the old and the new constitutions.[30] In all following defense district examinations' sections of *Staatsbürgerkunde*, the officer was always asked for his knowledge about aspects of the constitution and as the applicant never knew which question exactly would be asked, he had to be well versed in constitutional law. Telling was the question for the examination in the year of 1931, not far from the disaster to happen only two years later: "How is the idea of the rule of the people realized in the constitution?"[31]

Not all sections of the *Wehrkreis-Prüfung* were of equal importance; instead, they had different multipliers.[32] The questions about tactics had the highest multiplier of four, while *Staatsbürgerkunde* had one of two. However, because of the tough competition at the examination, an officer could not afford to mismanage even a single low-scoring task—could be worth eighteen points—and therefore had to be proficient in the constitutional law of Imperial Germany as well as of that of the Weimar Republic. Any postwar claims that high-ranking German officers didn't know the legal implications of Adolf Hitler's interior policies can therefore not be taken seriously.

The *Wirtschaftsgeographie* (economic geography) that followed nearly always asked a question connected to iron, coal, or waterways. Because of the narrow focus, the preparation for this section seems to have been the easiest.

The tasks in the history section could deal with the past of all Europe, so the young officer had therefore to be well grounded in this subject too. The *Wehrkreis-Prüfung* of 1924 asked the reasons for the rapid growth of Turkey after World War I.[33] In 1931, the officers had to write about the meaning of the eastern German borders after the Versailles Treaty and its dangers for Germany—quite an easy question for every officer, even without any preparation.[34]

In the mathematics section, which came next, officers who were destined to follow a technical branch usually had to solve an equation or a task in advanced geometry. The questions for physics could be related to weaponry like ballistics but were, like the tasks in chemistry, in the format that students in a German *Realgymnasium* would get when examined for their advanced degrees.

Officers could prove their language skills in a variety of ways and the ability to choose from several languages in this section remained. French and English were considered the easiest, and the test required translating two to three sentences from French or English into German and five to seven sentences in the reverse.[35] The selection of Russian and Polish made it necessary to transform seven sentences into German. Occasionally, Japanese and Czech showed up but that was an exception.

Last but not least, from 1924 on came the section *Leibesübung* (athletics) in which the applicant was examined theoretically as well as practically. This task was the one least liked by some officers because they felt after their experience with training troops on the platoon and company level for years, it was "unnecessary."[36]

First, each applicant had to present his *Freischwimmer* (independent swimmer) badge, which represented the lowest-ranking swimming emblem for adults in Germany, affirming the athlete possessed the ability to swim for fifteen minutes in deep water and jump once from a height of one meter. Those possessing the badge could automatically add five points to their score. Those not having it would receive no points and were not exempted from the question in the year of 1929 when the officer had to explain how he would teach the soldiers of his company to swim—even if he could obviously not swim properly himself.[37] In the following year, applicants had to elaborate on how to impress the thought of close-quarter combat on their soldier during athletics and weapons training.[38]

For a decade, the first practical part of the athletics section consisted, properly for a military examination, of hand-grenade throwing, where only the throwing distance was measured. Those able to hurl the grenade for forty-five meters would be considered "good" and gain seven points. Ten meters more was considered outstanding and the officer could add nine points to his score, the highest available. Fewer than fifteen meters was considered insufficient and worth only one point.

In the broad-jumping contest, "good" officers reached between four meters fifty and four meters seventy, adding seven points, whereas more than five meters was considered an outstanding achievement and fewer than three meters fifty insufficient, gaining nine and one points respectively. The expectations for the distance were lowered over the years. In 1924, the officer had to jump between thirty and sixty centimeters more to get into the next higher category.[39]

The applicants were requested to run three thousand meters, once in the field and once on a dirt track. On the latter, every time above fifteen minutes gained only one point and better than eleven minutes forty seconds would achieve the coveted "outstanding," adding nine points. The speed increments consisted of only thirty seconds intervals; thus, one minute faster would gain two points. The expectations for the field track were about thirty seconds slower to gain the respective points.

Several standard exercises on the high bar, parallel bars, and the vaulting horse followed. In these, all the former *Kadetten* would excel because they had trained on this equipment for years. In the 1930s, the practical, rather military exercises expected at the *Wehrkreis-Prüfung* were converted into the civilian standards of the *Deutsche Sportbehörde* (German sports agency).[40] I was unable to find an explanation for this new procedure but a strong possibility is that at that time more officers were needed because of the expansion of the German Army and therefore the athletic examination was outsourced to civilian authorities because of the high number of applicants.

In 1935, after all the restrictions from the Versailles Treaty were shed and the "new" *Wehrmacht* came into being, little would change about the selection for the advanced schools.[41] The eligibility for officers who could take the *Wehrkreis-Prüfung* changed now to *Oberleutnants* (first lieutenants) with about eight years of service. In the rapidly expanding *Wehrmacht*,

The new building of the famous *Kriegsakademie* [war academy] in the *Kruppstraße*, Berlin-Moabit, in March 1938. In contrast to the old opulent model of the pre-World War I architecture, it is built in the simple Nazi-era style for military buildings. (COURTESY BUNDESARCHIV, PHOTO 183-H03527)

higher staff officers were needed desperately. This requirement showed in the tactical tasks of the *Wehrkreis-Prüfung*, which now demanded the command of one reinforced division instead of the reinforced regiment of previous years.[42] All tasks of the examination became mandatory and there were no more choices except for the translation of languages. Official preparatory courses were now installed, which started about six months before the examination.[43] The number of officers eligible rose, but the quota of officers who were selected to attend the next higher course, or now the officially reinstated *Kriegsakademie*, remained very rigid with about 10 to 20 percent of all applicants accepted.[44] The problem with those numbers is that they derive exclusively from the writings of former General Staff officers and they have been generalized in the literature. Comparing the eight statements or studies—which are more or less detailed and emphasize different points—it becomes obvious that no single year in the selection of the officers remained the same but was highly individual in the number of officers selected and their social backgrounds, the washout quota, and the questions asked. This observation is even truer for the years at the *Kriegsakademie*, which will be discussed below. A good example are the examinations of the years 1934 and 1935 which—in the eyes of the Great General Staff—overrepresented applicants from *Wehrkreis VII*, which largely incorporates Bavaria. The General Staff thought about "tweaking" the next examination to stop a "Bavarian invasion" of the General Staff.[45] Because in the next years the quota from *Wehrkreis VII* normalized, there was no recorded interference. It is possible, however, that the quota normalized because of interference but it was not recorded anywhere.

It is apparent that the *Wehrkreis-Prüfung* represented a very thorough examination of the applicant. The test embodied an integral part of the German officers' education because the candidates had to start preparing for it years in advance and had to be proficient in a variety of areas, but tactics remained paramount in importance. Superiors and fellow officers anticipated that those who were in an advanced state of preparation and those who had been through the test would teach their younger comrades thoroughly. Thereby they would not only display the comradeship expected from a German officer but also gain more teaching experience.

The triple burden of excelling in everyday regimental duty, advancing personal knowledge, and teaching younger comrades put a tremendous strain on the officers.[46] The ability to teach enlisted men as well as fellow officers was considered a fundamental part of being a German officer. American officers visiting German military schools noted that "the German officer aspirant is trained to be constantly on the alert and to be able to express his thoughts logically and distinctly before a group of subordinates, equals or superiors."[47]

The importance of the preparation for the *Wehrkreis-Prüfung* has been underestimated or completely neglected in the historiography dealing with the education of the German officer corps. A German officer, if he wanted to rise, had to be constantly on his toes and advance his knowledge in between attendance at schools. Therefore a *Fähnrich* had better

The animated atmosphere of a high-level war game at the new *Kriegsakademie* on November 4, 1935. This was the first class in the new building that had just been completed. Civilian officials from the foreign ministry were often invited to give everything a realistic touch. German officers loved nothing more than war games for a mental challenge, the more complicated the better. In contrast to the games at the U.S. Command and General Staff School, the German war games were not scripted, were loaded with surprises, and played until one side was completely defeated. Sometimes they lasted several days. (Courtesy Bundesarchiv, photo 108-2007-0703-502)

have done his homework before he went to the *Kriegsschule,* a *Leutnant* before he even went to the *Wehrkreis-Prüfung,* and an *Oberst* when he was selected for the higher level war games. This "high sense of duty and responsibility" toward learning and preparation was noted by American officers visiting German schools.[48] The rather laissez-faire treatment of learning at the *Kadettenschulen* had done the German officers no harm because there they had already been taught the high sense of duty. Even in wartime, American officers showed up late for a briefing.[49] Such behavior has never been reported from German officers.

Lack of ability or preparation of a German officer would be immediately noted by his comrades and the leaders of the courses or schools. The German officers could not remain in a cocoonlike state for years as did their American counterparts, who often "had almost lost the habit of study," and then shift into overdrive only when the order to attend the Command and General Staff School arrived.[50] Consequently, because of his preparation, the average German officer did not feel himself overburdened when he began to study at the coveted *Kriegsakademie* or the officer schools that preceded it. [51]

Another marked difference between the United States and Germany lay in the selection of the teachers and commandants for the schools. Only war veterans with extensive experience were detailed to the army schools or the *Kriegsakademie* and they had to have a demonstrated aptitude for teaching.[52] The officers were usually selected at the annual *Lehrerreisen*—teacher journeys—where representatives of the army personnel office and higher commanders would evaluate them. They were also called to give a trial lecture.

So as not to get them *truppenfremd*—alienated from the troops— and so they would receive new input from the real military life, the stints as teachers lasted usually only three years, the same time a student officer would remain at the school. There also existed no rule that only former graduates were accepted as teachers, though the majority may have been. Before they returned to the *Kriegsakademie* as teachers, however, they had gathered experience in reality and made up their own mind about military matters.

It has been repeatedly noted by German officers that the practice of the American military schools of exclusively making former students into instructors, often without giving them the chance to gain a different set of know-how in real units inevitably led to a "narrow experience horizon."[53]

While student officers at Leavenworth were taught by a multitude of instructors who all slavishly adhered to the school's doctrine, the most important figure for the German officers was their carefully selected *Hörsaalleiter* (lecture-room leader) who taught tactics and was "given the greatest freedom in his treatment of any subject."[54] He would also write the efficiency reports for the student officers after the conclusion of the course.

In Germany it was not a matter of availability, feasibility, and convenience as at the CGSS, but a matter of the highest importance for the German High Command to get experts and veterans for the instruction of their officers. Despite the high expectations and tight selection, the German army had no shortage of outstanding instructors even for their advanced military schools.[55] Therefore, young German officers would be taught by Erwin Rommel in tactics and Heinz Guderian in motor transportation procedures. Both were *the* experts in their field. After the campaign against Poland, distinguished regimental and division commanders would be rotated to command the *Wehrmacht* schools and the same happened after the campaign against France when the heads of the schools went back to the battlefield.

The instructors understood themselves as the comrades of their students. The best chance of success for an instructor was not to be a *Pauker* (crammer) but to remember his own time as a student at military schools.[56] Judging from the testimonies of student officers, they succeeded extremely well. While it is rare to find praise for the instructors at the CGSS, the praise for the teachers at the German institutions is nearly universal and comes from visiting foreign officers of several nations as well as from the Germans.

The *Kriegsakademie* was, in the words of its commandant "not a school but a university."[57] It was unthinkable to examine the officer students on drill regulations as happened at Leavenworth.[58] An officer who attended the German war academy observed "that the officer who is detailed to the

Kriegsakademie is a very acute student" and would not take low-quality instruction by any of the teachers without speaking up.[59]

There existed no air of superiority at the German schools because of rank or experience, and instructors would play sports with their students, go along on ski tours, or just meet after school for a beer and a discussion.[60] Social gatherings and parties on an equal footing were common and considered an integral part of the stint at the school because the officers could be observed in a different environment than the classroom.[61]

In the tradition of the *Kriegsakademie*, the instructors could be officially ridiculed in the so-called *Bierzeitung* (beer newspaper), a satiric periodical created by the student officers.[62] There existed a rough equivalent at the CGSS—called "The Horseshoe"—but it was not half as merciless as the German version. At the American school, funny or satirical attempts were generally discouraged by the faculty, who were perceived as stiff and humorless.[63]

As comrades, German officers were able to walk the fine line between the two roles of student and instructor without establishing blind obedience, still remaining vigilant in classroom discussions and during war games and retaining the proper respect for each other.[64] In the *Abschlusszeitung*—the final satiric periodical—published after the successful conclusion of the course at the *Kriegsakademie*, the students would report their final assessment of their instructors. The witty judgements printed here, again cloaked in satiric language, portray nevertheless a very clear picture of the instructors' character.[65]

Not all went well, however, after the official reopening of the *Kriegsakademie* in 1935. The three-year course shrank soon to two years and to free even more time and get more bodies, the new chief of staff of the army, *Generaloberst* Ludwig Beck, ordered that the lectures in tactics—which had been predominant—were to be more focused on staff procedures for the division *Ia*—the operations officer.[66] What seemed like a big change, however, had little effect in practice because of the great amount of tactical knowledge the German officer had received thus far and would get in the future. Because the *Ia* was the first staff officer and responsible for operations plans, he would have to deal mainly in tactics and command anyway. Despite some curriculum modifications, tactics and military history remained, in hours and teaching emphasis, the most important lectures for a German officer.[67]

However, the officers who appeared a few years after the *Wehrmacht's* expansion seemed slightly less well rounded than their predecessors but that observation is based only on a few remarks of older officers and may rather show a generational conflict.[68] In 1936, the American military attaché Major Truman Smith reported that the group of officers he observed this year was "far from being the uniquely homogenous and intelligent officer corps of *Reichswehr* days."[69]

In addition, the Nazi-minded war minister, *Generaloberst* Werner von Blomberg, issued a decree in 1936 that within the framework of the education at the *Kriegsakademie* there was to be "national political education."[70] He thought that the officer corps could only maintain its position of leadership "when the national socialist world view as a complete mindset in personal spiritual property and inner conviction" became part of the officer.[71] The order was most likely drafted without any intervention on the part of Adolf Hitler because Blomberg was well known for his "national socialist alacrity" and a host of Nazi-friendly orders came from the war minister's pen.[72] It is equally important to note, however, that he was not opposed in his fanaticism by other high-ranking officers. To the time- and battle-tested abilities of German officers, the Nazis within the officer corps added quasi-religious requests that were already part of the occult twilight of National Socialism. The mixture would not bode well.

There is no record that the curriculum at the *Kriegsakademie* actually changed in regard to the war minster's decree but because we know details only from the accounts of former officers and they have good reason not to remember, there is no final conclusion on this. However, any national socialist education could only have taken place in the form of additional lectures by civilians in the afternoon. The impact on officer education as a whole would be limited. The environment at the *Kriegsakademie* remained largely unchanged; there was only more haste because of having one year less available. It has been claimed that from 1937 onward, the education at the *Kriegsakademie* had become "restrictive."[73] Some officers echo that complaint but for different reasons. While the historian regrets the cutting of topics that would help with a broader education, officers complained that they could no longer "operate" and were not taught in depth that so-important area between strategy and tactics anymore. Despite the well-known cuts, the flair and the basics at the *Kriegsakademie* as well as the comradeship remained by all accounts intact.

The atmosphere of mutual understanding—everybody could learn something from his comrades—was supported by the fact that there was no "school solution" at the *Kriegsakademie*. Every student's solution would be discussed and criticized the same way as the instructor's solution. Because at the German institution exercises ran through various phases, "the solution of one of the students was quite often taken as point of departure" for the next stage.[74] This method of teaching supported the real notion that there are no perfect solutions in war. Things would constantly go wrong or break down, intelligence would be faulty, the enemy would behave unpredictably, a company would get lost, etc. Therefore flexibility of mind is the most important thing to teach an officer—that he would be able to make do, no matter the situation, that he would be able to command unruffled amid the turmoil and chaos of war, which would in itself calm the situation. He would "command into the uncertain," but command he would.[75]

The classes and exercises at the *Kriegsakademie* sought to teach that lesson to their students as well as possible. When the officers had prepared a whole day for their position in a war game, the instructor might declare one of them dead by a bomb or shell and all positions were reassigned and the students had to improvise immediately. The so-called *Führerausfall*—leader fatality—was an infamous part of the teaching at all German military schools and kept the students constantly on their toes. Creativity was not only important in setting up the war game by the instructor but it had also to be displayed by the student officer to survive it.[76]

In another case, students would get a large set of intelligence reports and notes before a tactical situation became a war game and had to decide under pressure which were reliable, phony, or had jumped from the scared mind of an eighteen-year-old private.[77]

It was also common to have the officers decide if the *Auftrag* (mission) they had gotten from their superior was still valid after new intelligence and events were rapidly introduced.[78] The exercise assumed the officer was out of contact with higher headquarters and had now to decide whether to follow the original order or create an entirely new mission for himself and his unit because the circumstances had changed. It shows clearly that initiative and decisiveness were hallmarks of the education of a German officer.

Except in summer, there was a war game or tactical situation held outside every week. Every year ended with a journey of the whole class to a more distant place somewhere in Germany to conduct an extensive war game. Three months of every year, the student officers were ordered to a *Waffenkommando* (weapons command) to get to know a different branch, i.e., infantry officers would go to the artillery and cavalry officers to the infantry, etc. In the expanding army of the late 1930s, this valuable time became severely shortened.[79] During the large fall maneuvers, the officers went back to their units so that they would not lose any practical abilities.

The end of the *Kriegsakademie* course was the all-important eight- to fourteen-day-long *Abschlussreise*—final journey. The class would travel to an unknown location in Germany and indulge in an extensive war game that completely simulated a real battle, including rapid movements of the command post, the simulated temporary death of participants and days lasting from 0630 (6:30 a.m.) to 0100 hours (1:00 a.m.) the next morning.[80] The *Abschlussreise* would strain the officer students to the last but would give everybody the chance to excel.

The German military culture put—in contrast to the American— a high value on young officers. Junior officers were already highly regarded because they were per se members of the coveted German officer corps, and they could at any time appear at court, something hard to accomplish even for high-ranking civilians.[81] German senior officers realized that these young men might in war suddenly be charged with commanding a company or even a battalion in a vital position when their superiors had fallen and they would command with a high degree of independence because of the *Auftragstaktik*. American junior officers were treated rather as know-nothings and more of a liability than an asset until they had reached a certain rank or were unavoidably put into an important position. The lack of appreciation started with the hazing of future officers at West Point and continued with being treated like first-graders at Leavenworth. An American senior officer wrote in 1883 in a military magazine that "the profession of arms has always been one of great labor for those at the head of armies, and one of partial indolence for subalterns and the rank and file."[82] Though the author of the statement expected this attitude to change, it apparently never did.

During wartime or in large-scale maneuvers, young American officers were able to show their worth and it happened that lieutenants became logistics officers of an armored corps or occupied other important positions but after the emergency was over they reverted to their old rank or a reduced rank and were treated according to their low position. Because of the high opinion the German Army had of its junior officers, their personal views were valued and their disagreement was tolerated or even encouraged. German junior officers were regularly asked for their opinions and they would criticize the outcome of a large maneuver with several divisions before the attending general had the floor. The American army culture in contrast has historically had a great problem with dissenters and mavericks and just speaking one's mind to a superior officer, disagreeing with or criticizing him could easily break a career.[83] The famous social-psychological study of Samuel Stouffer about the U.S. Army in World War II describes the existing ambience as "rewarding of conformity and the suppression of initiative."[84] Stouffer and his colleagues proved that "conformity to the officially approved military mores" was one consideration for the promotion of an officer and "those officers who were conformists "were the most likely to have been promoted."[85] In addition, 60 percent of the officers and 80 percent of the enlisted men thought it was more important for promotion "*who* you know" then "*what* you know."[86]

As a young officer, Dwight D. Eisenhower wrote an article favoring mechanization of the cavalry.[87] The article displeased the chief of infantry greatly and Ike was commanded not only to cease such heretical activities but also to publicly reverse his opinion. He was threatened with a court-martial.[88] His superiors expected a fellow officer to become a sycophant. Ike's comrade, and later close friend, Henry Harley "Hap" Arnold, USMA 1907, lobbied for reforms of the air arm with an article of his own six years after Eisenhower and nearly got court-martialed.[89]

The same basic situation happened in Germany when young Heinz Guderian wrote in favor of mechanization and tanks. *Generaloberst* Ludwig Beck—the chief of staff of the army—looked in disfavor upon young Heinz and went to the publishers and editors of the military magazines to have them reject Guderian's treatises. That course of action was rarely successful and Guderian was never threatened with nor did a stall of his career happen.

The German and Prussian officer corps are the officer corps with the greatest culture of disobedience—with maybe the exception of the French. The stories and events that kept alive the virtue requiring an officer— even in war—to disobey an order "when justified by honor and circumstances" were corporate cultural knowledge within the Prussian and German officer corps and it is therefore important to recount them here.[90]

The Mark Brandenburg was the core region of Prussia even before Prussia became a kingdom. The Great Elector Friedrich Wilhelm still struggled in 1675 with remnants of the mercenaries who had belonged to the Swedish Army during the Thirty Years War. They still held several cities demanding contributions and marauding the countryside. The Great Elector was not master in his own country. At his disposal he had only a few regiments of mostly veteran soldiers. Because his whole army was still outnumbered by a single mercenary force that controlled the city of Rathenow, the only chance for a victory was a surprise attack. The Great Elector's dragoons charged the city at night—one of the very few night attacks in early modern times—and forced the mercenaries out of the city. They retreated in disarray and it was no doubt their plan to reach the next city, occupy, and fortify it. The Great Elector's force could only follow directly behind them at first light and, because there was only one route, it was impossible to overtake them or use a shortcut. The commander of the vanguard was Friedrich II, Prince of Hessen-Homburg, who had explicit orders from the Great Elector not to engage the enemy unless the Great Elector—who was with the main force, thus founding the long-standing Prussian tradition of having the ruler present in the field—gave the order. Fields for battle, however, were few in Brandenburg because the soil was sandy or swampy or both. In the morning mist of June 18, 1675, the Prince of Homburg detected a suitable battlefield near the town of Fehrbellin and with his cavalry vanguard attacked the mercenary forces against orders.[91] While the battle is well documented, the reasons for the prince attacking never came to light. Some say he was just a glory hound, yet the city of Ruppin, which was just around the corner, could have been taken and fortified by the mercenaries if they were allowed to do so. Dislodging them with the inferior Brandenburg forces would have been close to impossible. Throwing them out with another night attack was out of the question because it would no longer be a surprise.

The battle was extremely difficult because the prince possessed only cavalry against the mercenaries' combined forces.[92] He got bloodied badly until the Great Elector arrived with his forces and went immediately into battle. It was still a close victory for the Brandenburg forces and it was the beginning of independence for the state.

The grand-grandson of the Great Elector, Frederick the Great, had to put up with the same disobedience from his officers. During the Seven Years War, at the first clash with Russian forces during the battle of Zorndorf, August 25, 1758, the situation was desperate. Frederick the Great had to ride into the midst of battle and grab the flag of a broken regiment, steadying it with that action. The fifty-squadron-strong cavalry under the youngest Prussian general, Friedrich Wilhelm von Seydlitz, had been uncommitted so far. A *Flügel-Adjutant* (wing adjutant) showed up and told Seydlitz that the king thought it wise to attack with the cavalry now.[93] Seydlitz replied that it was not yet time. Once more the *Flügel-Adjutant* appeared. This time the king's order was more urgent and less courteous, but unwavering, Seydlitz gave the same reply. When the *Flügel-Adjutant* showed up the next time, he told the young cavalry general that the king would have his head if he did not attack immediately. Seydlitz answered, "Tell the King that after the battle my head is at his disposal, but meanwhile I will make use of it."[94] Seydlitz attacked at a time of his choosing and saved the day—the first to give him credit for that was Frederick the Great himself.

Three years later, in the same war, an even more famous act of disobedience occurred. Fredrick the Great, still furious about the looting of his castle at Charlottenburg, ordered *Oberst* Johann Friedrich Adolf von der Marwitz, the commander of one of Prussia's most prestigious heavy cavalry regiments, the *Kürassier-Regiment Nr. 10 Gens D'Armes,* to loot in turn the castle Hubertusburg of the Elector of Saxonia who was allied with Prussia's adversaries. The old noble von der Marwitz was appalled and answered the king that this was an order appropriate for one of the king's *Freibataillone* (free battalions) but not for one of the king's oldest and most exalted cavalry regiments. *Freibataillone* were only raised during wartime and given to freelancing officers. They and their units were held in contempt by any line officer and regiment. Von der Marwitz resigned on the spot and the castle was indeed looted by the *Freibataillon* Quintus Icillus. Von der Marwitz was later recalled but not as a regimental commander and he reached the rank of major general. When he died in 1781, a relative created the famous inscription for his tombstone: "He saw Frederick's heroic times and fought with him in all his wars. He chose disgrace when obedience brought no honor."[95] Incidentally, a memorial for him stands close to the battlefield of Fehrbellin.

The Prussian Army, lacking the leadership of Frederick the Great, was beaten by the Napoleonic army in 1806 at the twin battles of Jena and Auerstedt. The Prussians were forced to ally with Napoleon and offer him troops for his megalomaniac adventures into Russia. *Generalleutnant* Johann David Ludwig Graf Yorck von Wartenburg commanded a Prussian corps that lost contact with the French main forces during the catastrophic retreat.[96] On his own initiative and without consulting King Friedrich Wilhelm II of Prussia, he signed the Convention of Tauroggen on December 30, 1812, with the Russians, effectively ending the "alliance" with France and paving the way for war against the French despot. The Prussian king initially sentenced the Prussian officer to death but after the official breakup with Napoleon showered him with decorations and rewards. Despite the fact that Yorck von Wartenburg was raised in East

Prussia as the son of a Prussian company commander, he was known as a difficult and headstrong officer and even once lost his commission as a young lieutenant.

The widespread army reforms during and after the Napoleonic wars did nothing to eradicate the tradition of disobedience in the Prussian officers corps. In the fateful *Dreikaiserjahr* (the three-emperor year) of 1888, the immensely popular Emperor Wilhelm I died and was succeeded by his son Friedrich III, who fell victim to throat cancer the same year and was in turn succeeded by his problematic son, Wilhelm II. Friedrich III, though, had enough time to make military history. During a high level war game, he gave a young major of the Great General Staff an order to test his abilities. Following the order would bring the young officer into a perilous situation. When the major unhesitatingly relayed the order, a general stopped the officer and reminded him: "His Majesty has made you a Major of the General Staff so that you know when to disobey an order."

Even in July 1938 *Generaloberst* Ludwig Beck, then chief of staff of the German Army, reminded his comrades that "military obedience has a limit where knowledge, conscience, and a sense of responsibility forbid the execution of a command."[97] Beck resigned shortly thereafter in protest of Hitler's aggressive policies. He was involved in the plot against the dictator and got the chance from a comrade to commit suicide to escape the humiliating experience in front of the *Volksgerichtshof*.

It was not by accident that the phrase *führen unter der Hand* (leadership behind the superior's back) originated from the German and not any other army.[98] All those examples were collective cultural knowledge within the Prussian officer corps, recounted and retold countless times in an abundance of variations during official lectures, in the officer's mess, or in correspondence between comrades. The independence that was expected from a German officer and that was part of the tradition of the German officer corps could always attain the character of disobedience, a fact that was also recognized and acknowledged.[99]

The mind of the Prussian or German officer was generally anything but set in stone. During his professional military education, doctrine played a far less important role for German officers than it did for their

American counterparts, a circumstance that has been misperceived in the U.S. military and Anglo-American historiography because a variety of books exist that deal with the supposed "doctrine" of the German Army.[100] In fact, the word *Doktrin* hardly shows up at all in German Army manuals, training papers, or the letters and diaries of German officers. For them, doctrine was discerned as an artificial guideline that could be violated anytime, even by junior officers, when the situation demanded it.[101] Because there were no school solutions, there could be no fixed doctrine that would solve battlefield problems.[102] For the American officers in turn, it proved to be hard to deviate from learned doctrine. Only heavy casualties, some time, and tough resistance would persuade American commanders to go their own way against the Germans. Even when operational flaws, based on unsound doctrine, became obvious, corrections were not quickly at hand because officers feared that "the shock of change might be more severe than the cost of pursuing a second-best but known operational doctrine."[103]

The only one ever to violate the German military cultural dictum of "no school solution" was Erich von Manstein. In the early thirties, he held the position of *Chef der Ersten Operationsabteilung*, basically an assistant to the *Chef der Heeresleitung*, which in turn was nothing but a term for the *Oberbefehlshaber des Heeres*, *Generaloberst* Kurt Freiherr von Hammerstein-Equord.[104] "Young" von Manstein was already so impressed by himself that he tried to force his own solution onto his comrades after the war games for the higher commanders. This caused considerable frustration because Manstein was dealing with seasoned officers, many of them older and more senior than he was. Hammerstein-Equord, like Manstein, came from the clique of the 3rd Infantry Guards Regiment, which then dominated a good part of the *Truppenamt*, and was so fond of him that he gave him a free hand, not even checking on the final discussion papers his assistant prepared.[105] Manstein could thus make and break careers during that time. The same would happen several years later when Manstein supervised the war games of the *I. Armeekorps* (1st army corps).[106] Unsurprisingly, his rigid attitude carried over to World War II. There is no question that he possessed above-average strategic planning abilities but his personal lead-

ership skills ranked low. Though he himself demanded freedom of action
at all times from his superiors, he kept his own subordinates on a tight
leash despite the remoteness of his headquarters.[107]

The whole German professional military educational system paved
the way for the famous *Auftragstaktik*. The entire concept is inappropri-
ately translated in American English into "mission-type orders." The British equivalent is hardly better: "directive control."[108] In other languages
an appropriate translation is equally elusive.[109]

Often *Auftragstaktik* is misunderstood as a technique to issue orders,
while in fact it is a command philosophy.[110] The basic concept of *Auftragstaktik* means that there is direction by the superior but no tight control. "Task tactics," or "mission tactics," may be a closer but still insufficient
translation.[111] The best version seems to be "mission-oriented command
system," which better emphasizes the principle of command within the
philosophy, but the whole school of thought might best be illustrated by
an example.[112]

In a hypothetical case, an American company commander would get
the order to attack and secure a certain village. He would be told to use
first platoon to flank the village and third platoon to attempt a frontal
assault. Four tanks would be attached to his company to support the
frontal assault, which would be the main effort. After several hours, the
company succeeded and the commander radioed back for further orders.

A German company commander would get the order to secure the
village by 1600 hours, period. Before the attack he would ensure that
"even a *Grenadier* knew what was expected of him during the attack."[113]
If his platoon commander and sergeant fell, the enlisted man had to
take over. The American soldiers longed for the same information but
were not provided with it. That they "did not get enough chance to learn
the 'reason why' of orders" proved to be one of the GIs' foremost problems with army authority.[114]

The German company commander might put the allocated tanks on
the heights adjacent to the village to provide covering fire or might drive
them around the settlement to block the escape of the village defenders.
He might take the village by frontal assault, infiltration, or pincer attack—

whatever he saw fit the situation best. After he secured the village, he would pursue the remnants of the defenders and push forward with those of his elements who would not be immediately needed because he knew the over-all idea of his superior was to attack and, within the idea of *Auftragstaktik*, all his actions were covered by the simple order to take the village at 1600 hours. Because of his training, a German officer simply did not "not require detailed instruction."[115]

One of the best examples are the words of *Oberst* Kurt Zeitzler, then chief of staff of *Panzergruppe* Kleist, shortly before the attack on France in 1940 to the subordinated commanders of the fast troops and their staff officers:

"Gentlemen, I demand that your divisions completely cross the German borders, completely cross the Belgian borders and completely cross the River Meuse. I don't care how you do it, that's completely up to you."[116] In contrast, the orders for the American Forces to land in North Africa were the size of a Sears Roebuck catalog.[117]

Generalleutnant Heinz Guderian, commander of the *XIX Panzerkorps*, which was subordinated to *Panzergruppe* Kleist, gave an even more famous order to his units in the spirit of *Auftragstaktik* when he told them they all had a "ticket to the last station," meaning the respective towns on the French coast.[118] How they got there was entirely up to them.

Even after studying the Prussian and German armies for decades, the U.S. military showed "difficulty interpreting" the concept of *Auftragstaktik* and most officers would not come closer to it even when they attended the next higher military education institute.[119] Only a very few American commanders, such as George C. Marshall, George S. Patton, Matthew B. Ridgway, and Terry de la Mesa Allen, understood the concept even though it had never been taught to them in American military schools.[120]

This was all the more surprising because of the detailed reports the War Department received from the American officers who attended the *Kriegsakademie*. All of those men went through the full program of the German war school and nothing, except the mobilization plans, was barred from them.[121] The most prominent, because of his later assignments and rank, Albert C. Wedemeyer, claimed in his memoirs that he received his "real education as a strategist" at the *Kriegsakademie* but this claim has been doubted for good reasons because there were no explicitly strategic courses at this school.[122] Wedemeyer, however, correctly points out that he acquired "a deeper and broader understanding of international affairs" because many of the war games at the *Kriegsakademie* would be introduced by the development of a political crisis or the lecture of an official from the foreign ministry.[123]

Though it has been stated correctly that both the CGSS and the *Kriegsakademie* "required the application of principles to solving concrete problems," this was the lowest level of commonalities between the two schools because the principles themselves proved to be totally different.[124] At Leavenworth, the principle of doctrine reigned, whereas it was the principle of creativity at the *Kriegsakademie*. The supposed "stressed similarities" between the schools are negligible, at least in the detailed reports written by Captains Hartness and Wedemeyer; instead, the differences are emphasized.[125] It should be borne in mind that in the unfortunate U.S. Army culture of that time both officers had to fear the stalling of their careers if they criticized the CGSS too much. A copy of each of their reports about the advantages of the German school was sent to the CGSS but obviously not read by the staff and faculty.[126]

As major differences, Hartness and Wedemeyer pointed out the desirability of entrance examinations because those who reached the *Kriegsakademie* had already proven themselves as "outstanding individuals." As another great advantage, the American officers noted that their German counterparts were exchanged to different branches to gain experience, "a most salutary measure, one which we could well adopt." Furthermore, they emphasized the outstanding quality of the teachers several times and remarked that every problem is treated as a "troop leading problem."[127]

The captains praised the practical teaching and the way an actual war situation was portrayed and discussed in contrast to "a detached, contemplative solution" that "may function as a proper product but not as a life and blood proposition."[128] The critique of the Leavenworth school solution can be clearly read between the lines. But later in the report, the formulation is even more decisive: "Since no two tactical situations are identical, no schematic solution can be formed which may be applied now and later to difficult problems [...] In the discussion of the problem no 'approved' solution is offered, since every problem will have several satisfactory or workable solutions."[129] There can be no question that the two American officers preferred by far the German *Kriegsakademie* as an institution for advanced professional military education.

While the Americans had copied the institution from the Germans—a place for intermediate advanced professional military education—they had completely failed to fill it with the spirit of their role model. An American officer often did not even know how to become eligible for the Command and General Staff School even if he wanted to go. The school itself was known rather for its reputation as a ticket puncher than for its teaching excellence.

For German officers, where to go and what to know was transparent from the moment they became members of the officer corps. Because they knew that they could only go places when they showed the proper diligence and knowledge, they studied all their lives and thus were not overwhelmed with the exams they had to pass or the courses at the *Kriegsakademie*. Their American counterparts had often forgotten how to study when they finally made it to the CGSS. Brushing up on all that explains the many accounts of exhaustion at Leavenworth, much more than a tough course. Another aspect accounting for the stress at the school is the fact that a student had to hit on the "school solution" if he wanted a good grade. Therefore, even the most clever and tactically gifted officer was in a constant state of insecurity because he never knew what solution the instructor came up with. It is no rarity that the students were ahead of their instructors at Leavenworth. This fact was not taken into account nor acknowledged by the faculty. Instead of making use of the brains of experienced student officers, instructors treated them like middle-school pupils.

Such conduct towards fellow officers was anathema in the German Army. The single *Hörsaalleiter* who taught the greatest course load of tactics and military history to a class during their years had to act as a comrade or he would lose face with the class. The *Hörsaalleiter* taught after 1933 under a dictatorship yet was completely free in how he expressed himself and instructed. American instructors teaching in a democracy were constantly restrained in what they were allowed to instruct. The restrictions, however, did not come from the government but from the U.S. Army. The so-well-known stereotypes often don't fit after a historical reevaluation.

The *Hörsaalleiter* was often only one rank and a few years older than the officers he taught. They had been carefully selected not only for their character but also for their teaching abilities. The latter hardly ever shows up in a discussion of the Leavenworth faculty.

Civilian terms were often used to describe the atmosphere in the two different schools and they can be used as a further comparison. While the CGSS can be seen as middle school that should enable the "average" officer to pass somehow, the *Kriegsakademie* resembles the doctoral student colloquium of an elite university. Students expressed themselves freely and the instructor was aware that he could learn from them as well. Officers at the *Kriegsakademie* resembled a carefully selected lot and many were experts in their fields. At the CGSS, however, there were many capable officers too, but their expertise was summarily dismissed by the faculty of the school.

The greatest failure of the American institution was the "school solution," which was common in all American military installations and teachings except for The Infantry School. The officers were presented with only one right way to handle things. Such a teaching methodology has no place in a professional officer's education and it cannot be defended. It makes grown up-officers into yokels and the results were predictable. Mediocre officers relied entirely on doctrine because they knew no other way. Outstanding officers had a hard time to shake it up and become creative. The consequence was a lack of leadership, unimaginative problem solving against an imaginative enemy, and a slow and methodical approach to warfare.

At the *Kriegsakademie*, every problem was approached through troop leadership. How to command units in a situation had paramount importance, just as it would in war. Staff procedures were of secondary importance. Any solution was discussed as if it were the *Hörsaalleiter*'s solution.

That gave all the officers present a multiple number of possible actions in any war situation even remotely resembling that of the classroom problem. There is no place in war for doctrine because it harnesses the mind of an officer. The German officer left the *Kriegsakademie* with leadership capabilities and as an excellent tactician. Those were the areas where the German officer corps excelled and that is the reason the German Army was such a formidable enemy. The post-war literature of the German General Staff officers portraying themselves as strategic geniuses is pure fiction.

In the minds of the American officers who attended the *Kriegsakademie*, there can be no question which was by far the superior school. Many years after passing successfully through the CGSS, the next steppingstone for American officers was the Army War College (AWC), which taught the deployment of the largest units in a rather academic atmosphere. Attendance at this college—usually filled with students at the rank of lieutenant colonel or colonel—would partly decide if they would ever make it to the lowest general rank of brigadier general. The lucky ones would be able to attend the Industrial College, which brought them in close contact with the American industrial war machine. Leading industrialists lectured on the problems and costs of armament production and high-ranking officers would be able to visit factories that produced military equipment.

There existed no such institutions on the German side. German officers regularly attended higher-level command exercises and war games, travelled to historic or possible battlefields and discussed them, and constantly had their performance evaluated. At these exercises, they also heard lectures from state officials and higher commanders.

Though officers of both nations would gain valuable theoretical knowledge in their respective higher professional education, it can be surmised that they were already "coined" as officers individually in a way the exercises or colleges would not change and that their command culture had been set at an earlier stage through their early and intermediate professional military education.

PART THREE

Conclusions

SIX

Education, Culture, and Consequences

"If, in order to succeed in an enterprise, I were obliged to choose between 50 deer commanded by a lion or 50 lions commanded by a deer, I should consider myself more certain of success with the first group than with the second."[1]
—SAINT VINCENT DE PAUL

"Rules are for fools."[2]
—*GENERALOBERST* KURT FREIHERR VON HAMMERSTEIN-EQUORD,
commander in chief of the *Reichswehr*, 1930–1934

After the overwhelmingly successful wars of German unification, the U.S. Army switched its focus completely from the French to the victorious Prussian/German Army. The American officers also changed their priorities from matters of equipment and weaponry to the supposedly war-winning institution of the Great General Staff. They got it all wrong.

Though it is evident that an army needs a top planning institution, such an organization does not guarantee success or superiority. Even when staffed with professionally trained officers, it will show only average performance—or even harm the war effort—if there is not outstanding leadership in the highest positions. It is no coincidence that two of the greatest chiefs of staff ever, Moltke the Elder and George C. Marshall, were lauded for a trait they shared—common sense.

The German Great General Staff saw a steady steep decline in performance after its founder and mentor, Moltke the Elder, retired. His successors tried in vain to emulate the habits and outward appearance of the great old man but failed miserably in their basic tasks—to provide leadership, strategic planning skills, and sound advice for the head of state—until the whole organization collapsed in the apocalyptic defeat of a two-front-war, which every sane staff officer would have thought to prevent with all his might.

While so focused on the supposedly mighty planning organization, the observing American officers missed the small things that counted for much more in the German excellence in war. A sophisticated and nearly scientific officer education system was in place, focusing primarily on command, tactics, and leadership abilities. The German officer procurement and training system was of paramount importance to the army and worked under totally different premises then the American system.

Whereas in the United States the officer was one cog among others in the huge machine, one member of the vast team, in Germany the officer was considered the switch to the machine or its whole power source. Accordingly, the utmost care was taken in selecting officers and no costs were too high or challenges too great. Indeed, during several army expansions in the history of Prussia and Germany, it was argued correctly that it was better to have a smaller army well led than more manpower but a mediocre officer corps.[3] During the rise of mass armies and the supposedly increasing importance of deployment speed over tactical and strategical flexibility, the Germans were forced to make amendments when they expanded their army, but the heritage and idea of the officer remained the same until 1942.[4]

Paradoxically, young Germans grew up in a highly authoritarian society but would go through an advanced and nearly "liberal" professional military educational system. Already at the *Kadettenschule*, rewards were used instead of punishment to get performance from the youngsters and these rewards—freedom, privileges, and entertainment—appealed directly to a teenager's mind.

The reverse was true for young Americans aspiring to become officers. They would grow up in a society that would grant them the greatest freedom in the world—as long as they were white—but they would submit to an extremely harsh and narrow-minded military educational system when they decided to become cadets and attend a military academy. No American cadet had a chance to escape the four-year system whose hierarchy was set in stone and whose "greatest failing was in the area of practical leadership development among the upper classes. Like its counterpart in the preceding period, it cloaked the weak upperclassman with an authority which he neither merited nor knew how to use."[5]

Those who survived the insults, humiliations, and sometimes outright torture of the first year would automatically become superiors to the younger cadets entering the academy after them and so on. At the *Kadettenschulen* by the beginning of the twentieth century, the hazing had by all accounts been eradicated because it ruined the cornerstone of German officership—the officer as role model and comrade. In addition, the famous *Auftragstaktik* had been introduced into the army and, to employ it efficiently, independent thinking and individual responsibility had to be fostered in a new officer type. The permitting or tolerance of hazing would have been counterproductive to these goals.

The important connection between the introduction of *Auftragstaktik* and the educational reforms for officers' training in the Prussian/German Army has so far been overlooked in historiography. The visiting American officers completely missed the ongoing discussions in Germany about the revolutionary concept of *Auftragstaktik*, which manifested itself officially in the field manual of 1888.[6] First called by a host of different names, *Auftragstaktik* established itself in the last decade of the nineteenth century precisely when the most important mission of American officers was to study the German military system. The *Auftragstaktik* became an "essential factor" in the tactical superiority of the German Army.[7]

Kadetten showing exemplary behavior would be promoted over the heads of upperclassmen, effectively demonstrating that individual performance was king and not "the system."[8] A lack of knowledge in engineering or other scholarly disciplines would not prevent a *Kadett* from being allowed to take the *Fähnrichsexamen* or to become an officer if he consistently displayed strong leadership capabilities and—above all—determination. An uncountable number of possibly excellent officers would be "separated" from West Point because they could not take the overdose of mathematics, while in Germany a *Kadett* would be pulled through if he showed all the other characteristics of officer material. All the reports by visiting foreign officers that noted exemplary work ethics displayed by German officers of all grades proved that the system of the *Kadettenschule* did the German officers no harm in this respect.[9]

At the very end of a student's time at the *Hauptkadettenanstalt* (*HKA*), the whole German system became complicated and highly selective, granting those who exceeded expectations a backdating in rank if they should become officers. Only a very few outstanding individuals were commissioned outright as lieutenants when finishing the *HKA*. The visiting American general Emory Upton noted largely correctly that "Prussia—alone of the major military powers—did not commission its cadets immediately upon graduation from its military schools."[10] Unfortunately, the U.S. Army never followed up on this observation. A future officer can never be assessed properly in the sterile atmosphere of a military academy, but should first show his mettle in a regiment where he has to lead real enlisted men.

Instead of being commissioned, the *Kadetten* would either go to war school—*Kriegsschule*—or step directly into a regiment and then attend war school. Those who had applied as or were selected to be engineers or artillerists would now receive extra training for these branches, including a heavy load of mathematics.[11] The aspirants for the other branches were not so burdened, in contrast to American cadets, who all suffered the outdated curriculum at West Point no matter their branch.

In any case, the *Fähnriche* had to prove themselves again and again before becoming commissioned. Finally, the regimental commander would decide—usually after a conversation with all the officers of the regiment— if the young aspirant finally had proven worthy to become an officer. The real life was the test for the German officer aspirant, not the artificial atmosphere of an enclosed military academy.

Instead of the training with obsolete equipment at a U.S. military academy, *Kadetten* used the same hardware that was used in the regular army.[12] When they became *Fähnriche*, it was expected that they would be able to handle the weapons better than the troops. If they did not already have those skills from their training at the *Kadettenschule*, the regimental commander would make sure they soon acquired them.

In the U.S. Army, just the opposite happened and George C. Marshall had to assert that "I thoroughly agree with the Chief of Infantry as to the too strong tendency of regimental commanders to rely on the service schools for the education of their officers."[13] And the service schools in turn did not do a good job.

The *Kadettenschulen* were by no means a role model for youth education. Their main fault was that they accepted boys at a far too young age, a flaw already discussed at that time.[14] The military wanted to give the parents and the boy ample time to check out if the youngster was suited for an officer career. However, if the boy detected that he was ill suited for the harsh environment, harm had often already been done.

For the military, the *Kadettenschulen* were suited exclusively for the purpose of raising future officers although parents sometimes abused them by sending their son there to straighten him out when they were incapable of doing so themselves. A boy with no aspiration to become an officer, suffered and complained the most because his entire teenage life seemed like a constant punishment tour.

Another great flaw of the German system was that the officer corps selected its offspring still in large part from the "officer-capable strata." Thus many who could have made excellent officers were rejected or had fewer opportunities because of their social background. This tendency, however, had been slowly eroding over the centuries and the number of officers who came from formerly undesirable strata increased steadily as did the level of education of junior officers.

The Imperial Army, *Reichswehr*, and *Wehrmacht* largely got the officers they wanted. There are not remotely as many complaints by senior officers about officer aspirants in any of the German armies as in the U.S. Army. Rather the contrary is the case—junior officers had a high reputation among the German senior leadership.

In contrast to the *Kadettenschulen*, the American military academies largely treated their cadets more like factory products than individuals. A certain standard was expected of them—a standard that was extremely antiquated—and after meeting this standard they would after four years be commissioned as 2nd lieutenants, never having commanded any real troops although now they were immediately expected to do so. The same attitude of officers as factory products would be demonstrated when they attended the Command and General Staff School at Fort Leavenworth.

For American cadets during their time at the Academy, there was no left or right but only a narrow path to follow with no room at all for individualism. Discipline was enforced, but not taught.[15] Therefore, misunderstandings about discipline and leadership were perpetuated throughout the years. When another attempt was made in 1976 to curb hazing, upperclassmen complained that they had "no leadership tools if they could not deprive plebes of food or use verbal abuse."[16] It is apparent that there existed a historically grown, alarming misunderstanding about the very nature of leadership within the Corps of Cadets at the United States Military Academy.

Consequently, the number of those successful officers who enjoyed their time at West Point was exceedingly slim. Claims like "I have never met any man who said he had enjoyed his cadet days at West Point" are not uncommon from more critical alumni.[17] "Monotony" is one of the words that most often appears when describing the experience, in contrast to the "diversified" daily life at the *Hauptkadettenanstalt*.[18]

Though scholarly abilities were of secondary importance for the German officer-aspirant selection at the *Kadettenschulen*, especially the *HKA*, the schools' faculties sported the same qualifications and tried to attract the same type of teachers as a civilian *Realgymnasium* or *Gymnasium*.[19] The scholarly and didactic qualifications of the West Point faculty were ridiculously low in comparison and remained so—long after the Pattons and Eisenhowers had graduated—for at least another fifty years. Any changes made can only be described as cosmetic.[20]

Despite the fact that there existed no research and no battle accounts on the connection between "mental-disciplining" and the ability to lead troops, this strange teaching philosophy was upheld for decades even after war veterans returned to West Point as instructors, commandants, or superintendents who should have known better.[21] Weird statements like "the habit of exact thought which has been developed by mathematical training and the subsequent applications of its principles to mechanics, ordnance and engineering, constitute the main asset of the master of military organization" were accepted again and again by the president of the United States, the secretary of war, and the War Department, despite all experience in previous wars—especially the recent Spanish-American War and Philippine Insurrection—demonstrating the contrary.[22]

Finally, a young German with the proper abilities could become, even under peacetime conditions, a *Fähnrich* at the age of seventeen and a lieutenant at the age of eighteen or nineteen, thus giving them a head start over their American counterparts, who under the same conditions would have to be at least twenty-one, and usually older.[23]

The U.S. Army had, when putting its own cadet education into effect, overtaken even the Prussians on the far right. American cadets experienced in the twentieth century what a Prussian cadet had to endure perhaps a century earlier. The reasons were twofold: First, American cadet education was molded after a Prussian model that has been misunderstood and has also been mixed with American ideas, such as that of a four-year-school system, for example.

Second, though the times changed and the *Kadettenschulen* changed with them, in many aspects the American academies remained largely the same. The blame can be put mainly on the shoulders of the senior faculty, the lack of leadership provided by several superintendents, and visiting alumni who preferred to "put teeth" back into the plebe system instead of providing modern means of education and leadership for their followers in the long, gray line.[24] In Germany, the military took a proactive stand in all public discussions about education and implemented new ideas into the *Kadettenschulen*.

The U.S. Army of these days did not have good officers because of West Point but in spite of it. During these first decades of the twentieth century, the Academy "presents the spectacle of a monstrous waste of youthful enthusiasm."[25] Biographers of generals who graduated from the Academy and a psychiatrist analyzing the system have pointed out that their "subjects" learned little from West Point but, because of their upbringing in solid families already had formed personalities that gave them the means to survive the harsh military academy regime without doing them intellectual harm.[26] One of Ike's biographers, for example, stated that the future supreme commander's "basic attitudes and beliefs were already set; four years on the dedicated Plain could do nothing to change them."[27]

About Creighton Abrams, it was noted that his values and personal traits were fully congruent with the West Point ideals but that it seemed likely "that he brought most of those values with him when he entered as a cadet rather than learning them during his years at the Military Academy."[28]

The author's reading of numerous diaries and personal letters of officers confirms this finding. Role models in leadership and personality for the officers were their parents, a senior officer they found later along their way who acted as a mentor, or even an old NCO who taught them the ropes.[29] The influence of a tactical officer at West Point is a rarity, in great contrast to the German equivalent at the *Kadettenschule*— the *Erzieher*—who were held in high regard by the cadets, who usually looked with equal admiration at the other officers of the schools.[30]

Even after a study that accurately describes the devastating educational system at West Point, former alumni try to smooth over the results with unscholarly statements like "the sense of group unity and esprit that comes from a common struggle in the face of difficulty bound the cadets together through a lifetime of service. This esprit was a foundation block for much of the Army unity and efficiency in two world wars."[31]

From a sociological perspective, there is no question that a common struggle forms a bond between individuals. However, it does not have to be formed by suffering hazing and an overload of mathematics. There is no evidence for an "Army unity" or special "efficiency" in World War II because of West Pointers in the U.S. Army. They have proven themselves to be as good and as bad as other officers who were trained in other facilities or who were even battlefield-promoted.[32]

The existence of a "West Point clique" in the army has been denied by former graduates and nongraduates alike. Indeed, there is no such circle to be found in the papers of the generals. However, the officers of my sample were either West Pointers themselves or largely successful in their careers and, thus, had no reason to be critical towards this aspect.

Nevertheless, when an officer was to be selected for a higher command and the superior was a West Pointer, he was inclined to select a person whom he knew very well because the stakes were so high.[33] The likelihood that he would select another West Pointer from around the four years he attended the Academy was therefore high. He may also have chosen an officer whom he became closely acquainted with during his stay as student or instructor at another school.

The founding of what would later be known as the Command and General Staff School shows the same misunderstandings by the U.S. officers that their other actions had revealed when observing the German system of educating officers. Whereas it has been demonstrated that the basic contents of the curriculum of the CGSS and the *Kriegsakademie* were similar, the teaching philosophies and didactics were completely different.[34] The U.S. Army copied the institution but failed to recreate the spirit, just as General Sherman had warned.

In the further course of their professional military education, American officers encountered a largely academic and theoretical environment. On the plus side, those who hardly ever took up a book now were forced to do so. The minus side, however, weighed more heavily. The mixed blessing of the CGSS is best described with its impact on the officers who served in the American Expeditionary Forces (AEF). Even while World War I was raging in earnest with fighting taking place in vast trench lines and fortifications, no lectures in Leavenworth took up the new lessons learned from a static war of attrition but instead continued to emphasize waging "open warfare." The results were increased and unnecessary casualties. In contrast, Leavenworth graduates filled important staff assignments and did satisfactory work in this capacity. However, because of their often vain attitude toward the field commanders, they occasionally gained nicknames like "pampered pets" and friction among Leavenworth graduates and other officers was common.[35] In World War I, "none of the army or corps commanders had attended Leavenworth, and of the fifty-seven officers who commanded the twenty-six divisions committed to combat, only seven were graduates"; the staffs of these units, however, were often led by Leavenworth graduates.[36]

In defense of the Command and General Staff School, it has been stated repeatedly that "Leavenworth gave the Army a common, professional language and a shared military value system" as well as "common assumptions."[37] These, however, are basic traits of a military school and not especially noteworthy achievements. To constantly emphasize uniformity in judgment in a military school—as was done at Leavenworth—sooner or later stifles original and creative thinking. The latter is, for an officer, of paramount importance in war. There is a great danger—as George S. Patton has put it—that "no one is thinking if everyone is thinking alike."[38] A military school has to teach more than uniformity—it has to teach excellence.

At Fort Leavenworth, school solutions were always the norm. Ineffective courses were led by instructors who sometimes lacked knowledge of their fields and usually failed in didactics and pedagogics. Though an empirical study is still out on that, before World War I, and in the late 1930s especially, "surplus" officers who could be spared or were not welcome anywhere else seemed to have gotten instructor positions—with predictable effects. Doctrine and hierarchy reigned to such an extent that student officers were occasionally even insulted when they did not put forward the "proper" solution. It seems in general not to have been a good idea to challenge the instructors at Leavenworth in any way if an officer student wanted to leave the school with a respectable grade. Just as at West Point, the motto was "cooperate and graduate" instead of "question and challenge."[39] This was not a learning atmosphere for adults at all, especially not for officers who had by then considerable professional experience of their own to offer.

When the value of a school is assessed, the performance of its students must be examined. The performance of Leavenworth graduates in World War II is so uneven that a positive impact of the teachings of the school cannot be demonstrated and, in fact, should be doubted. In addition, there is no difference between the performance of one- and two-year graduates, and "distinguished graduates of Leavenworth did not perform in command significantly better than their peers who graduated without distinction."[40] Those observations are not only true for the command but also for the staff performance of the graduates.

At the *Kriegsakademie*, experts in their fields, who were usually *also* war veterans *and* had displayed an aptitude for instructing, taught their courses on a *primus inter pares* basis. An instructor position showed the high value in which the German Army held the selected officer.[41] Thus, the students were taught tactics by Erwin Rommel and motorized transportation by Heinz Guderian—or in earlier times even by Carl von Clausewitz. All three officers were considered mavericks by their peers, yet they were free to teach their ideas at the *Kriegsakademie* without any restrictions imposed. During the course of war games and map problems, students would be asked to take over in a certain situation; thus, they would *command* a virtual battalion of infantry or a virtual *Abteilung* of trucks in contrast to the academic course of action at the CGSS where many of the solutions had to be forwarded in long formal writing.

Whenever solutions for map problems and war games were discussed at the *Kriegsakademie*, the instructor understood himself to be a comrade among others. Not only did this attitude help everybody to express himself freely, but in addition to the absence of school solutions one important thing would be ingrained in the minds of the officers—there are no optimal solutions in war. War is too much chaos and turmoil, too much lack of intelligence and communication so that there never could be something like an optimal "chairborne" school solution.[42] Instead, the solutions of all students were discussed, just like the solution of the instructor. This gave the whole class an enormous set of possible options to draw from in the future if they ever found themselves in a situation even remotely resembling that of the problem presented by the instructor. At the same time, they learned that decisiveness and creativity ranked before the long, elaborate construction of a supposedly optimal solution. The latter describes exactly how the operations of American commanders were usually conducted in World War II.

It has often been noted that attendees of the *Kriegsakademie* did not find the course work especially hard and that there was much spare time for the officers. The latter is due to the fact that, just as at the *Kriegsschule*, the officers' conduct during their free time was observed. In regard to the toughness of the course work, it should not be forgotten that those who attended this esteemed institution had already been several times preselected.

For decades, the Leavenworth school had a mixed reputation at best and because of that many officers did not attend it. They thought it more effective to further their careers by making a good impression in their regiments instead of wasting two years at a questionable institution. It was through the mouth-to-mouth propaganda of renowned senior officers—and former Leavenworth graduates—that the school gained prominence and prestige rather than through its own performance. Even then, attendance at the school was often seen as a ticket to be punched for promotion more than an opportunity to gain essential knowledge and broaden one's professional horizon. Up until World War II, who was eligible for the schools and how to gain admission was unclear to many officers because the rules were changed frequently and remained nontransparent to the average U.S. Army officer.

In Germany, the procedures on how to go to the *Wehrkreis-Prüfung*—the exam that might open the doors to the famous *Kriegsakademie*—could be found in every civilian and military library and the military exam questions of the preceding year were officially published continuously. Before World War I, every officer who wanted to try out had to be given at least one chance by his regimental commander. When the *Reichswehr* decided to secretly build up its General Staff again after the Versailles Treaty was signed, every officer had to take the exam at least once because the High Command wisely determined that a greater sample from which to select would be beneficial. Despite common belief, an excellent grade at the *Wehrkreis-Prüfung* did not alone guarantee access to the *Kriegsakademie*. The character assessment of the regimental commander weighed just as much.

Completely overlooked in historiography has been the fact that the *Wehrkreis-Prüfung* and preparation for it were an integral part of the German officer's education even though only a small minority would make it to the *Kriegsakademie* and even fewer of those would be selected for the Great General Staff. Preparation for the exam and what they learned at the war academy made them more valuable officers. They already had made a professional leap by preparing for the *Kriegsakademie* and not just by attending it. Officers were only allowed to take the *Wehrkreis-Prüfung* if they had a reasonable chance of making good grades; anything else would have brought disgrace to the regiment.

The *Kriegsakademie* has been misunderstood in historiography as a "*Generalstabsschule*" or a "General Staff School." This was not at all the case because only about 15 percent of the graduates would end up in the General Staff. The *Kriegsakademie* was a war university, which had the mission of raising the general level of professional military education in the officer corps and, by all accounts, it succeeded in that task.

The way of a future German officer was the path of constant preparation and selection. In the *Voranstalten*, the *Kadett* had to show his mettle to finally be sent to the *Hauptkadettenanstalt*. At the *HKA*, he had to display leadership abilities to stay on course and prepare for the *Fähnrichsexamen*. If he aimed high, he would need special preparation to gain entry into the coveted *Selecta* class whose successful completion would grant him a backdating in grade. Immediately afterward, he had to be fully prepared not to make any mistakes in the regiment's daily life and, while struggling with this, also gain the necessary knowledge to excel at the *Kriegsschule*, to which he would be sent shortly. His performance at the *Kriegsschule* would partly determine his commissioning as *Leutnant* (second lieutenant). After that, he had to show in everyday duty that he was worthy of getting the endorsement of his regimental commander for attending the *Wehrkreis-Prüfung*. After two to three more years, the young officers had to begin preparation for the *Wehrkreis-Prüfung*, a preparation that lasted well over one—usually about one and a half—years. The whole German officer education system was an integrated structure with concerted steppingstones from one to the other. In stark contrast to the sophisticated German educational system, every American military education institution vegetated in its insular existence and there was no clear vision what the "end product" was supposed to be.[43]

The only highlight of the U.S. Army's educational system in the first decades of the twentieth century was the Infantry School and then only when George C. Marshall was its assistant commander. The officers were systematically exposed to command problems in the field in addition to getting to know the real weaponry of the U.S. Army—now that they were captains and majors. They constantly had to learn to shorten their orders, lectures, and presentations until they reached the economy of words and time common in the German Army and Marshall emphasized realism wherever he could: "What appears satisfactory on paper too frequently we find quite impracticable in actual operations. Organization and planning, based too largely on theoretical grounds, result in cumbersome organizations, too large staffs and too lengthy and complicated orders."[44]

It was Marshall's declared goal to assimilate the U.S. command culture and training as much as possible "under our system of government" to the German role model.[45] Because of his thorough and diligent study of the German Army, the assessment is most likely correct that "by 1945 the U.S. Army Chief of Staff George C. Marshall may have known the German army better than Hitler did."[46]

The Marshall-Benning experience cannot be overemphasized. Many years later, in letters and even in their memoirs, officers describe the different atmosphere of this school and remember the sage advice of George C. Marshall. Marshall had systematically studied the Germans and their educational system and tried to employ whatever he could at The Infantry School. He had no problem taking advice from German officers detailed to the school. Marshall had been credited before with many achievements that secured the victory of the Allies in World War II and this study confirms the enormous amount of positive and decisive influence that he exerted as a multiplicator for professionalism, education, and common sense in the U.S. Army.[47]

But Marshall was only one man and could only do so much. He repeatedly became entangled in the vast bureaucracy of the army and the War Department, which became—just after the Germans and the Japanese— the greatest enemy of the American fighting soldier in World War II. When the chief of staff encountered a bureaucratic roadblock, he "spoke his mind as only he can do," which often enough cleared the channels.[48]

The U.S. Army's professional military educational system produced for World War II an average officer who knew the basics of his trade in theory because he had run through a number of schools that had taught him that. He generally longed for doctrine and prepared solutions and tried to "manage" rather than command. In stark contrast to the German Army, mavericks were not sought or fostered. Brilliant American officers who were ahead of their time were often instead either phased out to a position where no promotion was possible or even court-martialled for their heretical ideas. Before George C. Marshall became chief of staff, U.S. Army officers were actively discouraged from thinking outside the box.

The German system was constantly looking out for the next Friedrich Wilhelm von Seydlitz, Gerhard von Scharnhorst, or Helmuth von Moltke and had active procedures in place to get hold of them instead of discouraging their development. The system failed often, just as on the American side, when selections to the highest ranks were made. There are indications that the same is true for the British and French side, but that merits another study.

The American officer schools largely taught war on the basis of fixed examples, school solutions, and especially doctrine. They communicated to the student that the solution of a problem was to be found in a pre-developed doctrine or a manual and not in battle leadership, which required going out to the frontlines, making a personal assessment, and even throwing everything learned overboard because it did not fit the learned solutions and then attacking in an unusual and creative way.

If the most important verb and the most important noun should be found for the U.S. Army and the *Wehrmacht*, according to the vast number of manuals, regulations, letters, diaries, and autobiographies I have read, they would be "manage" and "doctrine" for the U.S. Army and *führen* (lead) and *Angriff* (attack) for the *Wehrmacht*. Such a comparison alone points out a fundamentally different approach to warfare and leadership.

Rarely did student officers go outside during their classes at Leavenworth. Map problems replaced the command of a virtual unit outdoors. Paper engagements in exercises were only "fought" until the instructor had made his point and introduced the school solution. The whole procedure created officers with a staff attitude who thought that maps would reveal the important information and who would not be at the frontlines to command and to lead.[49] This fact had been noted by senior commanders but never corrected: "When the 'General Staff School' became a 'Command and Staff' school, I had serious misgivings. I feared that the same principle of academic eligibility would be applied to command and staffs assignments. Apparently this has taken place ... ."[50] The few maverick officers left in the army agreed with that apprehension and decried the "all-too prevalent U.S. Army custom of *staff command*" that apparently had been taught at the service schools.[51]

In a memorandum on this subject, George C. Marshall emphasized that," vital qualifications for a general officer are leadership, force, and vigor. Ordinary training, experience, and education cannot compensate for these and the officers who possess them must be singled out and advanced regardless of other considerations."[52] The memorandum is dated December 1, 1942, and just as he had foreseen top-level leadership became a constant problem in World War II for the U.S. Army.

Finding outstanding leaders for key positions in the U.S. Army in wartime seemed not to have been an easy task. In the letters and memoirs of the commanders often only a very few individuals are discussed as having the necessary capabilities for a certain position.[53] Especially hard-hitting combat leaders were considered rare and those few who possessed leadership abilities and aggressiveness found themselves again and again in tight spots, commanding units for landings or breakouts or rescue missions. Joe Lawton Collins was considered such an individual and was even rotated back from the Pacific theater to the European theater of war because his capabilities were badly needed and apparently neither to be found in officers currently fighting in Europe nor in those not yet deployed and waiting in the United States. The problem, however, was neither new nor surprising because in the big 1941 maneuvers on U.S. soil a "massive failure in leadership and general military confidence" had already occurred.[54]

Though age still played a role, it should not be exaggerated because once in a while a grizzled old regimental commander showed more stamina, toughness, and leadership than his much younger comrades but he might be relieved because of the unfortunate general age limits imposed in the U.S. Army.[55] The radical age limits for certain ranks were imposed by Marshall and Lesley McNair to rapidly get rid of the "dead wood" in the officer corps but could cost the U.S. Army a few good fighters.[56] How successful their measures were is displayed by the—not totally serious—exclamation of Major General Lloyd R. Fredendall when he saw the new staff of the II Corps he commanded: "By God, I am going to war surrounded by children."[57]

Because of the overemphasis on management in the U.S. Army in contrast to battle leadership, able commanders often found themselves in staff positions, whereas there was a want for them in combat commands "There are loads of good combat leaders pushing papers and I say this with all due personal modesty," remarked Walter B. Smith, who always wanted a combat command dearly but was so good at paper pushing that he could not get away from desk jobs.[58] Thomas Troy Handy, VMI 1914, who was perhaps even more admired among his comrades than "Beadle" Smith and who had to stay at the War Department during the whole of the fighting found in his fitness report this formulation: "Washington deprived him [of] opportunity f[or]/f[ie]ld com[man]d, would have no hesitancy assigning him to most difficult type com[man]d position, peace or war."[59] The efficiency report was written by Dwight D. Eisenhower, who most likely could have called Handy to command a division or corps if he had wanted to.[60]

Equally interesting is the difference between the handling of staff positions in both armies. In the U.S. Army, even division commanders were allowed to select or bring along their former staff but the *Wehrmacht* normally granted this favor only to army and army group commanders. Below that level they were considered equally competent.[61] It shows also that personal relations were less important than in the U.S. Army. Comradeship ranked before possible teamwork advantages because certain officers were better liked.

Not all the maladies of the American military educational system are the fault of the U.S. Army's senior leadership, though most of the burden of responsibility falls squarely on their shoulders. Some cultural traits that gave the Germans an advantage were impossible to imitate or copy or, if it had been possible, it might not have been desirable to emulate them.

The Germans did of course have the great "advantage" of possessing a militarized society.[62] Like Sudoku for people today were the enormously popular tactical problems printed in biweekly and monthly military magazines in the 1920s and 1930s for German males of all ages. They became a regular hobby.[63] The first chapter of those magazines would portray some heroic action from the Franco-Prussian or the First World War. In the second chapter, a small map was printed with units marked on it and a tactical situation described, ranging in scale from sections to companies, but usually staying at the non-commissioned officer level to avoid the exalted area of officer responsibilities. The person who sent in to the magazine's editor the best command solution for the problem would be named in the next issue and his solution would also be published there.

In Germany, the honor of belonging to the officer corps was considered so great that the payment for the subaltern ranks had been traditionally neglected since Frederick the Great's times—a German lieutenant earned only one-fifth of what his American counterpart would get at the beginning of the twentieth century although his social obligations were much higher.[64] In their autobiographies, nearly all American generals complain about their precarious financial situations when they were junior- or field-grade officers. Those complaints have to be seen in a relative perspective because their German counterparts were always worse off, even without a world financial crisis.

In stark contrast to the Germans, American society either feared a regular army or did not even know that it existed.[65] While the reputation of the U.S. officer corps was considerable among the elite—they shared the same social background—the common population had a widely different view.[66] In some regions of the country, soldiers were so despised that they were not permitted to enter restaurants or inns, which forced Congress in 1911 to take action and impose a fee of five hundred dollars upon those who discriminated against soldiers.[67] American observers noted the excellent relationship between the military and the civilian population in Germany, even just seven years after World War I, which had definitely dealt a blow to the reputation of German officers.[68]

German senior commanders and politicians alike had successfully spread the tale of the *Dolchstoßlegende* (literally, "dagger-thrust legend," generally translated as "stab-in-the-back legend"), which proclaimed that the German military had won the battles in the field but the war was lost by weak-willed civilians, communists, and social democrats on the home front who failed to provide for the soldier or even sabotaged the war effort. The story was readily and enthusiastically believed by many Germans. Therefore, the military, especially the officer corps, had nearly regained its former exalted status only shortly after the Great War.

In the United States, the military remained "covered." American military buildings in the era before the Pentagon had a "wholly civil character."[69] American officers serving in Washington in the interwar period all wore civilian suits, so a gathering of the highest American commanders looked more like a meeting of businessmen than of professional soldiers.[70] Only after they were massively ridiculed by the press for going around "posing as suburban taxpayers" did George C. Marshall issue the order to appear from now on in uniform for work until further notice.[71] In contrast, German subaltern officers were forbidden to ever wear anything but uniforms and German generals often did not even possess any civilian attire at all during their entire lives until the end of World War II.[72]

Interestingly—and another paradox—it was American officers who had a much harder time dealing with their fellow citizens in the Civilian Conservation Corps (CCC) camps or when training raw recruits during World War I or in the expanding army at the end of the 1930s.[73] The idea of class had taken root in the American officer corps and the secluded existence of officers in army posts had not helped in enabling them to communicate with ordinary civilians or raw conscripts. Those who retired after a long career at an army post had concerns about their ability to get along with civilians at all.[74] This is all the more surprising because the whole idea of the American regular army was that of being a nucleus for an expanding mass force in wartime where, consequently, the regular army officers were supposed to be the instructors and instructors must be able to communicate with their fellow citizens who were now recruits. Teaching, however, was not taught in the U.S. Army. Because of that, officers tried to "dodge" lectures and suffered "acute stage fright" and even fear when they were called to instruct.[75]

An American officer with considerable experience in that matter noted that "nobody can expect all army officers to be born teachers. A few are; but the rest ought to be given an early chance to learn."[76] Only a very few got that chance and many of them instead thought teaching ability was demonstrated by three years of yelling at plebes at West Point. In the German Army, it was stressed on the highest level that "the officer is a teacher and a leader" and he was trained to excel in both, even

A conference of the Chief of Staff (Marshall, sitting between the flags) with his Army and Corps Area commanders on November 30, 1939, held in the War Department general council room. U.S. high-ranking officers generally served in civilian suits at the War Department until the press needled them that they "go around posing as suburban taxpayers." From then on, Marshall ordered them to appear in uniform. In Germany subaltern officers were not allowed to wear anything but uniforms and generals often didn't possess a single civilian suit until until after the war. [COURTESY GEORGE C. MARSHALL FOUNDATION, LEXINGTON, VIRGINIA]

when he was still an officer aspirant.[77] Because of that, hazing at the German *Kadettenschulen* had largely disappeared because it explicitly contradicted this mission.

At the CCC camps, in addition to supervising the work—military drill was not allowed until 1942—the regular army officers would train 60,000 reserve officers.[78] Frequently, regular army officers had to be rotated from the camps back to their posts because their "authoritarian behaviour" was resented by the young civilians. The reserve officers got along much better with the young volunteers.[79]

From then on, it would be remarked in the American officer efficiency reports whether the assessed officer was "suited for duty with civilian components."[80] Possibly, the whole CCC program had a "salutary effect on the Army as a whole."[81] Those who were able to successfully handle the civilians at the CCC camps often found themselves detailed to National Guard units to instruct them and had a hard time getting back into regular army outfits because their ability was so much in demand.[82]

A contemporary said about George C. Marshall, "He had a feeling for civilians that few Army officers [...] have had. [...] He didn't have to adjust to civilians—they were a natural part of his environment. [...] I think he regarded civilians and military as part of a whole."[83] That officers in those days were singled out for their ability to interact with civilians shows that a majority of the U.S. Army officer corps did not possess that skill. For the instructors of a future citizen conscript army, that can be considered a grave deficiency.

The question remains: when the selection, promotion, and especially schooling system of the U.S. Army in those days was so flawed, why were there still daring, able, and aggressive commanders who knew how to lead their men and had outstanding successes? The answer was in part given by Forrest Pogue, the biographer of George C. Marshall, who stated correctly that "the officer of an earlier era had to train himself. And for this he needed a belief in himself, an intense desire to know, the capacity to grow, the trait of self-discipline, and a compulsion to excel in his chosen field."[84] Many of these traits originated from a solid upbringing rather than from any army education. "The intense desire to grow" manifested itself in avid readership. Rather than relying on the medio-cre education the U.S. Army offered, "talented, gifted officers could and did see to their own professional educations."[85] Outstanding officers con-sumed great quantities of books of all types but especially about military history, a topic that can be considered a sine qua non for every officer but that was neglected during their professional military education. From their book order lists, book inventories, discussion of various books in their correspondence, and existing former officers' libraries, a direct connec-tion between outstanding officership and avid readership can be drawn. The papers and/or biographies of Walter Krueger, Matthew B. Ridgway, Lucian K. Truscott, George C. Marshall, Joe Lawton Collins, Dwight D. Eisenhower, and George S. Patton, for example, contain this evidence.

The question has to be raised, if the German officer's education was so successful at selecting men with "character" and the ability to speak up and there was a tradition of disobeying orders if they were harmful, incorrect, or illegal, how was the immense amount of collaboration and support for the Nazi regime waging a war of extermination possible?

The answer puts an even heavier burden on the German officer corps than current scholarship has already cast upon it.[86] Junior officers who had been taught that the battlefield was constantly changing, that every war was a new war with new means to be fought, and who were not brought up within a democratic society that set boundaries for a certain behavior would far more easily accept the orders that would cause a bar-barization of warfare on the Eastern Front. This was especially true when these orders were invented, condoned, or endorsed by high-ranking offi-cers. The responsibility, therefore, falls squarely on the backs of many of the *Wehrmacht*'s senior officers. This study clearly points out that that every German officer had a choice—more so than officers in other armies. Not only did there exist a centuries-old tradition of disobedience and speak-ing one's mind to a superior, but that was also taught in the schools.

The officers who went along with the dictator's criminal policies were senior, high-ranking officers whose personal aims were in many cases so congruent with Hitler's. Chief culprits among them were *Generalfeld-marschall* Werner von Blomberg, the war minister; *Generaloberst* Werner Freiherr von Fritsch, the commander in chief of the army; and *General-*

oberst Walther von Brauchitsch, his successor. They were the first to replace the matter-of-fact statements about what a German officer had to be with proclamations that had a weird, near-religious twist to them.[87] Those proclamations read rather like church dogma than the guidelines for an officer. Faith in the Nazi regime was to rank higher than common sense. The infusion of highly ideologically charged content into rather technocratic-minded cultural content became one of the reasons for the downfall of the German officer corps.[88] The senior officers' examples proved overwhelmingly successful. More than 40 percent of the young officer candidates between 1939 and 1945 were party members.[89]

German senior officers in the rank of *Generaloberst* and *Generalfeldmarschall* readily accepted an extra payment from Adolf Hitler, which doubled their regular salary and has been largely construed correctly as "bribes."[90] Most of the officers did not want to see it that way because, just like the knights of old and the nobility of Frederick the Great, they thought they were due a reward for their outstanding service. However, the rewards that had come to their supposed predecessors had come in public and not from the secret bank account of a dictator. Once more, the German senior officers showed themselves indulging in "selective realities."[91]

In addition to the ideological complications, there were homemade military difficulties. It was the chief of staff of the army, *Generaloberst* Franz Halder, who took away the German field commanders' traditional right to lead by *Auftragstaktik* long before Hitler considered such a course. The man who complained the most about the dictator taking away the officer's freedom of action was in this case actually his role model who showed him the ropes.

The other main reason for the defeat of the *Wehrmacht* is the sheer boundless arrogance of its officer corps. Being for so long the most famous and prominent group in a nation and admired by their countrymen and international observers alike left pathological marks. The result became "a persistent tendency of most German Generals to underestimate the size and the quality of the opposing forces."[92]

All those immense flaws of the *Wehrmacht* senior officers counterbalanced the excellence in command, tactics, and leadership German officers displayed in World War II. The latter explains why the German

Army was such an outstanding fighting force on the tactical level but still unable to win the war.

It is high time that the *Reichswehr* officer corps receives a scholarly revaluation. Scholarship usually still repeats the statements of former German officers that only the best of the best were taken into the small *Reichswehr* officer corps of four thousand after the Versailles Treaty had reduced it to this number.[93] There is zero historical evidence for such a conclusion. Specifically, the performance of the *Wehrmacht's* highest-ranking officers in World War II speaks against such a successful selection process. The fact is that with *Generaloberst* Hans von Seeckt's new selection criteria a 150-year-old evolution of the German officer corps was broken. Before the *Reichswehr*, there was a steady increase of commoners as well as a steady increase of officers from parts of the society whose young men had before been considered non-officer-capable.[94] They proved the point that the father did not determine the son's military abilities. Historically, it was also combat-experienced officers who commanded most of Prussia's units.

Seeckt's selection reversed the former natural evolution and dramatically increased the percentage of the officers from the nobility and from the old officer-capable strata as well as officers from the Great General Staff. Many had never even held a regimental command, which was historically considered a milestone in personal demonstration of leadership for an officer's development.[95] It was those officers who gained the highest ranks in the *Wehrmacht* and it was they who got along with Hitler's criminal policies more often than not. While in World War I, combat commanders were often leaders of the large units, but in World War II such units were often commanded by staff officers with limited combat experience and only a faint idea of what an ordinary private had to go through.

While a few Rommels were selected, many slots of the small *Reichswehr* officer corps went to the von Wedels, von Stülpnagels, or von Mansteins who had a tradition of serving in the Prussian or German armed forces going back hundreds of year, and any notion of a civilian occupation was to them completely incomprehensible. It is, therefore, until a scholarly study proves otherwise, my hypothesis that the officer corps of the *Reichswehr* was often selected through personal, family, and old regimental connections rather than through true superior performance.[96] Prosopographical evidence suggests that many army and army group commanders of the *Wehrmacht* lacked sufficient combat experience and were thus unable to relate to the sufferings of the men on the frontlines.[97]

The strength of the *Wehrmacht* officer corps laid in the creativity, leadership capabilities, and tactical finesse of officers who commanded anything from platoons to corps. They had been taught to be innovative and inventive, to disregard doctrine when desirable, to surprise the enemy whenever possible, and to live and survive in the chaos of war. They were taught to welcome that chaos and use it against the enemy instead of making sense of it with a "school solution" or a preconceived doctrine. German officers were able to fire off oral orders an instant after a short tactical deliberation employing the *Auftragstaktik*, trusting their subordinate commanders to carry out those orders with minimal interference. They would go forward with their troops into battle to observe the fighting and go into combat themselves if necessary—from lieutenant to major general. Those abilities were the power of the German officer corps that enabled them to hold out for so long, inflict catastrophic casualties on their enemies, and made them the terror of Europe. The list of abilities, however, also shows clearly their limitations. Even the sharpest set of claws needs a brain to guide it. Without superior strategy direction, numerous battles can be won, but no wars.

Above the corps level and in the higher staffs, excellence was no longer common. In fact, the German Army and army group commanders were desperately waiting for the military guidance of the *"Führer"* after the situation on the Eastern Front turned into a nightmare. This observation points out the fact that the selection to the highest ranks in Germany—*General, Generaloberst*, and *Generalfeldmarschall*—was as flawed as the selection to the highest ranks in the United States. The newest essays commenting on the current generals in the U.S. Army seem also to be correct from a historical perspective.[98] It was often opportunism, the ability to assimilate with the current leadership, and having the right connections that made generals. That seems to have been true for the U.S. Army of World War II as well as for the *Wehrmacht*.

While the U.S. Army's officer education as a whole, but specifically at the Command and General Staff College, has taken enormous leaps, important beneficial lessons from the German officer education have either been misunderstood or have not been incorporated because of ignorance or cultural reasons. The selection process is not tough enough and a culture of the "no major left behind" dynamic will not help making the right officers.[99] Sophisticated computers, satellites, the Blue Force Tracker system, and flying drones with cameras seemingly allow a high commander sitting in his air-conditioned bunker in Doha to supposedly understand what is happening on the road to Baghdad or the streets of Fallujah. This, however, is not the case at all. The presence of the commander, on the ground, is irreplaceable for sound decision-making, no matter how many stars he carries. Or, in the words of an American regimental commander in World War I, "For a commander there can be no substitute equal to his own eyes."[100]

A case in point is the conduct of Operation Iraqi Freedom (OIF). It shows that the U.S. Army has learned a lot but still has shortcomings in vital areas. It is still very officer heavy, especially in the highest ranks. Just as in World War II, "there is a feeling in the field that there are too many generals at desks and not enough with troops."[101] More officers, especially more generals, mean more friction and usually a cumbersome chain of command. However, as demonstrated by the Germans countless times, quick decisions in war are essential. To conduct an operation in Iraq, an American brigade commander had to ask his division commander, who in turn had to ask his corps commander, who was usually in Kuwait, and then had to ask the Coalition Forces Land Component Commander (CFLCC), who had to ask the theater commander, who was usually in Doha. The U.S. Army still does not trust an officer with more than twenty years of experience to independently command his brigade. The distrust is a historical cultural problem and prevails even though there has never been a U.S. officer corps even remotely resistant to civilian directions.

In the current example, Major General Buford C. "Buff" Blount III, the commanding general of the 3rd Infantry division had devised a plan against breaking the stalemate in front of Baghdad in what were the last days of the city under Saddam Hussein's command. Nobody knew it then. The current doomsday setting of the U.S. Army prescribed a costly urban warfare scenario in which the U.S. Army had to forfeit much of its superior technology and firepower. The latter had become major part of the American military thinking since World War I.[102]

Blount devised an armored strike into urban terrain against U.S. Army doctrine and against V Corps plans. The latter were created in Kuwait without contact with the battlefield and considered too timid by the commander of the distinguished division that had earned the title of honor "The Rock of the Marne" in World War I. The first strike—called a *Thunder Run*—was undertaken by the Rogue Battalion of the 2nd "The Spartan" Brigade. It was conceived to get the lay of the land, which was the four-lane-highway network of a part of Baghdad, and to surprise the enemy and keep him off balance. It had to be sold to V Corps as an opening of supply lines between two objectives the 3rd currently held.[103]

When the Rogue Battalion's commander, Lieutenant Colonel Eric Schwartz, got the orders from his superior, the Spartans' commander, Colonel David Perkins, to attack inside Baghdad, his flabbergasted response was, "Are you fucking crazy ... Sir?"[104] While this could be construed as a rare American officer speaking up against his superior, it was most likely a comment motivated by a sudden rush of fear. It also shows how uncommon bold and decisive strikes are for too many American officers.

Perkins sensed the wavering of his battalion commander and decided on the spot to accompany him. During the Thunder Run on April 5, 2003, the enemy came so close to him that he thought, "if the brigade commander is taking out enemy with his nine millimeter, we're in serious trouble."[105] Similar feelings crossed the mind of the Rogue Battalion's operations officer, Major Michael Donovan, when the enemy closed on the column: "Holy shit, I'm the S-3 and I'm shooting dudes with a rifle!"[106]

While both officers showed great courage, it is apparent that leading up front is for American officers of a certain rank still in no way considered normal.

The first Thunder Run was considered a great success by the leaders of "The Rock of the Marne," but those who had been far away in Doha and Kuwait, the U.S. Army top leaders and the media, were unconvinced. Blount and Perkins, undeterred, nevertheless planned a massive armor intrusion into the city with the whole Spartan Brigade. This time, they intended to stay. However, first, V Corps had to be convinced of the wisdom of the operation and that proved to be the hardest part. Just like sixty years before in World War II, a U.S. Army unit commander had to fight for aggressive action "despite every discouragement from his superiors."[107] In the best U.S. Army cultural fashion, V Corps had watched the Thunder Run through the eyes of a UAV (unmanned aerial vehicle) and thought it knew what was going on.[108] UAVs were in constant short supply for combat operations because they were used by higher staffs to take a convenient look at what was supposedly going on in Iraq.

Discouragement followed on the spot when Blount presented his plan for the massive intrusion and the occupation of parts of the governmental district of Baghdad to V Corps. Despite the recommendation from the commander who was on the front line and had more than thirty years of army service under his belt, V Corps deemed the operation too risky. The second Thunder Run was downgraded to another armored reconnaissance mission. While the division commander relented to V Corps orders, the brigade commander chose to create a misunderstanding and went ahead with the plan—a true Prussian course of action.[109]

On April 7, the whole Spartan Brigade suddenly turned downtown to the astonishment of V Corps, which was watching the event conveniently on the Blue Force Tracker system, a computer system that requested the location of key units by GPS and projected them on a digital map as blue spots. An argument arose between the captain responsible for the system and the civilian contractor about whether it showed false data.[110] Because nobody from V Corps was on the spot, nobody

could verify it. A forward element of V Corps rested at the airport in an
"assault command post," though who they would want to assault is a mystery that only a higher staff entity might be able to explain.[111] When the
verification from the division commander got through to V Corps that
the Spartan Brigade had seized its objective downtown, they agreed to
let Perkins stay, though this time he had difficulties convincing even the
hard-charging Blount. Recalling the unit would have been a major publicity failure. Later, Blount headed where he belonged, downtown to the
lead elements of the Spartan Brigade.[112] During the very day of the attack,
it became clear that it had broken the backbone of the Iraqi resistance.
There would be much more fighting in the days to come, but the regime
was crushed.

The episode shows a command culture that has only gradually
evolved from the days of World War II. While the technical knowledge
of today's U.S. Army officers is far superior to that of their predecessors, their leadership capabilities are not. There are exceptions as some
of the aggressive officers of the 3rd Infantry Division have demonstrated.
Before the second Thunder Run, Perkins outlined for his officers which
decisions were his to make and which ones they could make. That is as
close as the U.S. Army has ever come to *Auftragstaktik*, but Perkins has
proven to be an exceptional officer. This most effective and democratic
of all command philosophies has, 120 years after its invention, been
studied but not yet understood nor yet found a home in the armed forces
of the most democratic of all nations.[113]

Likewise, the U.S. Army is still short of senior officers who "don't
mind being in the middle of a fire fight."[114] While many can, it feels alien
to them because in their military education, leading up front is obviously not emphasized.

Even though the U.S. Army has shrunk so much in recent years, the
officer selection process seems not to be tough enough. The eyewitness
accounts and analysis of the operations in recent wars show too many
inefficient or even incompetent officers. That something is wrong with
the selection and promotion system becomes evident when officers are
not promoted because of "too much troop time" and when a U.S. Army

senior command supports a stop-loss policy instead of fighting against it with all its might.

Doctrine still reigns in the U.S. Army, before common sense and creativity.[115] As a earlier study pointed out, "American officers treated doctrine like dogma" and this attitude is apparently still prevalent.[116] The heavy reliance of the U.S. Army on doctrine has historically caused nothing but setbacks because new developments on the battlefield are always faster than the creation of new doctrine to combat them. What happened during World War I happened during World War II, Vietnam, the Iraq Wars, and now the War on Terror. The officers wanted to prepare for the new war, "but resources and doctrine remained rooted firmly in the former."[117]

Commanders are often discouraged by their superiors when proposing bold and aggressive actions that violate doctrine and that is true on all levels. "School solutions" and computer diagnosis of future battle events lead to exclamations that would be comical if the setting were not a war. Lieutenant General Scott Wallace, commanding General of V Corps, told reporters of the *New York Times* and the *Washington Post* that "the enemy we're fighting is a bit different than the one we war-gamed against […]."[118] Completely forgetting Moltke's old dictum that no plan survives contact with the enemy, Wallace was even so shaken by the resistance of the paramilitary forces that he had earlier suggested waiting for weeks before pressing the attack until the 4th Infantry Division was deployed.[119]

The sharpest and most devastating weapon the U.S. Army could possess today in the War against Terror is not a new computer system, a sophisticated unmanned aerial vehicle, or a smart artillery shell; it is rather a carefully selected, aggressive hard-core battalion or brigade commander who was exposed to a large dose of military history, is trusted by his superiors to conduct his own operations, and oversees them wherever the bullets fly.

The last words belong to Matthew B. Ridgway, who has escorted us through many chapters of this study. He said them when he took command during the Battle of the Bulge, when American units had crumbled and were fleeing in front of the attacking German spearheads in December 1944. The same words could have been spoken in a German *Kriegs-schule* ten or twenty years earlier:

> *Then I talked a little about leadership. I told them their soldier forebears would turn over in their graves if they heard some of the stories I had heard about the behavior of some of our troop leaders in combat. The job of a commander was to be up where the crisis of action was taking place. In time of battle, I wanted division commanders to be up with their forward battalions, and I wanted corps commanders up with the regiment that was in the hottest action. If they had paper work to do, they could do it at night. By day their place was up there where the shooting was going on.*
>
> *The power and the prestige of America was at stake out here, I told them, and it was going to take guns and guts to save ourselves from defeat. I'd see to it they got the guns. The rest was up to them, to their character, their competence as soldiers, their calmness, their judgment, and their courage.*[120]

Author's Afterword[1]

My book deals nearly exclusively with the time from 1901 to the end of World War II. However, because I have studied the U.S. Army—and especially its officer corps—throughout its existence, I could not avoid making observations that stretch into the closer past or even the present.

This work is very closely based on my Ph.D. dissertation that was submitted at the University of Utah in 2010. At the defense of the manuscript, the notion came up that a historical work dealing with the officer corps of two such important armies should read rather like the report of a friendly soccer match. Every team should be able to get some goals and no one should look too bad. That, however, is not my understanding of a scholarly work. The U.S. Army officer's education of that time looks so bad because it was. The interpretation is certainly mine but the facts speak clearly. It is possible that such a book could have only been written by a foreigner because of the many "sacred cows" that exist within the U.S. Army.

While it has been suggested that I was biased toward the German Army because I am German, that completely misses the point because I have a lifelong fascination with the U.S. Army—past and present. I also owe it a great debt. It was the GIs who ensured that I could grow up in free-dom in West Germany and not under a regime of oppression like my bro-thers and sisters in the East.

Two times a year the small town in which I grew up was, to the great unhappiness of most German inhabitants but to the great delight of me, the exercising area for major maneuvers. The American soldiers, who have historically the best record of all forces stationed in foreign countries, always talked to the eager German kid, often grateful that someone would listen to their problems, of which there were many. One of them was the lack of appreciation for their presence by the Germans. That was a sad fact. The Germans wanted the protection, but no hassle.

The enthusiastic German kid was shown all the equipment an Amer-ican soldier was allowed to handle, from the amazing 1911 handgun to M-60 tanks to the Bell Cobra attack helicopter and it was a hands on-experience because I was allowed to touch all that stuff. The soldiers had a remarkable trust in me and it was never violated. A pilot grabbed me by the waist and hoisted me into the gunner's seat of a Bell Cobra attack helicopter and pointed to the large bright red handle for the emergency canopy ejector: "Just don't touch that." That was certainly an hour in heaven for me while I played with the myriad of levers, switches, and buttons—but of course not with the bright red handle.

Sitting under the camo webbings of a Chaparral AA tank on top of a hill, I was taught to play draw poker while we used matchsticks for the gambling. Repeatedly, I was the center of betting because the soldiers who knew me better by then rested assured that I knew everything about the U.S. Army equipment from memory. When the taunt came, "Hey Joe, I bet you two bucks that that little German kid knows the muzzle velocity of the M-60's main gun," great laughter would follow after I unfailingly delivered the correct data, grinning so hard that my ears would jump and the two bucks changed owners.

At night I would crawl into one of the many camps that lit up the night in the dense Hessian forests to trade the Licher Beer most coveted by the GI for one of the most highly prized possessions among male Ger-man teens at that time—combat rations. In the pre-globalized world of my youth, American peanut butter, coffee, and chocolate were hard to come by and the owner of several C-rations could even trade amazing toys for the food. Though I was a poor kid, I usually ate the C-rations instead of trading them in because to me that stuff tasted just fabulous.

The whole undertaking of obtaining the prized possessions, however, was dangerous indeed because it was strictly forbidden to bring the soldiers beer. One of my friends had been caught by an officer, his beer confiscated, and he was spanked by that very same officer in the camp. To me, in contrast to my friends, the insignia on the uniforms were not arcane knowledge but a rank hierarchy with a purpose and I knew that sergeants were safe but that it was better to crawl a long way around an officer in the night—but only when it came to the trading beer.

My connection with the U.S. Army was never entirely severed because I kept studying it, first as an enthusiastic amateur and later as a professional historian. In German academic military history, the U.S. Army barely shows up. I therefore travelled to the United States to visit battlefields and military installations and by now many soldiers—past, present, any rank—are counted among my longtime friends.

In 2005, I had the great privilege of being selected as a member of the West Point Summer Seminar in Military History. I was treated with the greatest hospitality and courtesy and had an amazing and unforgettable time. I also had the chance to observe the United States Military Academy firsthand. There can be no question that the teaching—at least in history—is not at all comparable with the time that I look at in my book. In my six weeks there, I did not see a single bad teacher and quite a few good ones and even some outstanding instructors. Much more important, they were all dedicated and motivated.

There were, however, many other things to observe. One of them was that there is still—to phrase it diplomatically—great room for improvement in the leadership training and especially the treatment of the plebes.

I am very grateful to the people of the history department of West Point for the invitation and my great time there and it would be unkind of me if I would put up a "dog-and-pony-show" just because of that gratitude.

West Point has always been one of the sacred cows of the U.S. Army and it has done neither of them any good. Officers are such an essential, extremely important component of the armed forces that every tradition, every ritual and convention of their selection and education, has to be put on the testing range once in a while and changed if it does not contribute to excellence or has even become a burden. Alumni should lead that movement of constant change instead of trying to drag West Point back into medieval times. The U.S. Army has to relearn that outstanding personnel are essential for every war and not just high-technology gadgets.[2]

West Point is a magical place and needs to remain as a source of officers for the U.S. Army. While the academic instruction appeared sound to me, there are other aspects of the cadet training that would need reexamination.

For nearly two decades, I was an instructor in several disciplines of sports. Never did I have the policy of glossing over the mistakes of my students for some soul massage after a tournament. They were all dear to me but it wouldn't help them if I patted their backs and told them how great they were when they didn't make the top places or didn't give everything they had. It is the same for my favorite subject—the U.S. Army. I would not repay my debt if I just glossed over the problems I saw and looked at everything through rose-colored glasses. History is by its very nature a harsh profession.

The basic American GI of today—if such a person exists—is unchanged from the days of my childhood. He is one of the best ambassadors the United States will ever get and in the great majority acts and fights with great courage for what he thinks is a good cause. He will even hang on and do his duty when his own senior leadership enacts an unjust stop-loss policy against him.

He—and now also she—deserves only the very best officers that can be selected and educated. Such a selection necessarily has to be harsher than in any other profession because an officer should be a multiplier of excellence but also can be one of incompetence—the latter often costs lives.

Historically, the U.S. Army senior leadership has had occasionally a tendency to present dog-and-pony shows or to "polish" data instead of taking a critical look at its internal system. Giant snafus, scandals, or a rising casualty count often provided necessary wakeup calls. I sincerely hope that my book will make a modest contribution for reflection before the next snafu occurs.

Officers' Rank Index

Reichswehr/Wehrmacht	U.S. Army
Generalfeldmarschall Was, until Hitler made it one, never a regular army rank, was title of honor, became in WWII rank of army group commanders	Field marshal, not used in U.S. Army
Generaloberst, commands an army or an army group	General of the Army, Five Stars, commands an army group or a theater of war
General, commands an army	General, Four Stars, commands an army
Generalleutnant, commands a division but usually a corps	Lieutenant General, Three Stars, commands a corps
Generalmajor, commands a division	Major General, Two Stars, commands a division
No equivalent in German Army	Brigadier General, One Star, commands a brigade but is usually assistant division commander. *There is no equivalent in the German Army.* This fact is constantly misinterpreted in historiography making the BG incorrectly the equivalent of a German *Generalmajor*.
Oberst, commands a regiment, or is corps staff officer	Colonel, commands a regiment
Oberstleutnant, commands a battalion	Lieutenant Colonel, commands a battalion
Major, division staff officer, can also command a battalion	Major, regimental and division staff officer
Hauptmann, commands a company	Captain, commands a company
Oberleutnant, commands a platoon or a company	First Lieutenant, commands a platoon
Leutnant	Second Lieutenant, commands a platoon

Reichswehr/Wehrmacht	U.S. Army
"Degen"-Fähnrich, literally Rapier-Ensign, the *"Degen"* not part of the rank, distinguished uniform from *charakterisierter Fähnrich*, ranks in the regiment just below Master Sergeant, officer aspirant, treated as a future officer	Ensign, not used in U.S. Army
Charakterisierter Fähnrich Rank of honor, usually bestowed upon cadets or *Fahnenjunker* who passed the *Fähnrichsexamen*, but have not yet earned enough real-life recognition, officer aspirant, ranking above a Sergeant, treated as a future officer	Ensign, not used in U.S. Army
Fahnenjunker No equivalent in the U.S. Army, officer aspirant, ranking Corporal, treated as a future officer	Not used in U.S. Army

Endnotes

Introduction

1. Cited in Russell Frank Weigley, *Eisenhower's Lieutenants: The Campaign of France and Germany, 1944–1945* (Bloomington: Indiana University Press, 1981), xix.
2. This correspondence can be found in the Dwight D. Eisenhower and Walter B. Smith papers at the Dwight D. Eisenhower Library in Abilene, Kansas.
3. Walter Bedell Smith, *Eisenhower's Six Great Decisions: Europe, 1944–1945* (New York: Longmans, 1956), 532.
4. Harry C. Butcher, *My Three Years with Eisenhower: The Personal Diary of Captain Harry C. Butcher, USNR, Naval Aide to General Eisenhower, 1942 to 1945* (New York: Simon & Schuster, 1946).
5. The original manuscript of the book without the omissions is still available at the Eisenhower Library and has unfortunately never been published in its unedited form: *Harry Butcher Diaries Series*, Dwight D. Eisenhower Pre-Presidential Papers, Box 165+166, Dwight D. Eisenhower Library, Abilene, Kansas.

6. George S. Patton and Paul D. Harkins, *War as I Knew It* (Boston: Houghton Mifflin, 1995). The book was first published in 1947. Ladislas Farago, *The Last Days of Patton* (New York: McGraw-Hill, 1981).

7. Dwight D. Eisenhower, *Crusade in Europe* (Garden City, New York: Doubleday, 1947; reprint, 1948).

8. Keith E. Eiler, *Mobilizing America: Robert P. Patterson and the War Effort, 1940–1945* (Ithaca, New York: Cornell University Press, 1997), 459–450.

9. Clark's own account, for example, fits exactly that description: Mark W. Clark, *Calculated Risk* (New York: Harper & Brothers, 1950).

10. Bernard Law Montgomery of Alamein, *The Memoirs of Field Marshal Montgomery* (Barnsley: Pen & Sword, 2005).

11. Weigley, *Eisenhower's Lieutenants*. The military historian was inspired by an earlier work, Douglas Southall Freeman, *Lee's Lieutenants: A Study in Command* (New York: Scribner, 1942).

12. Weigley, *Eisenhower's Lieutenants*, 432.

13. Ibid., 589, 594.

14. Ibid., 433.

15. Ibid., 729.

16. *Letter from Paul M. Robinett to his father J. H. Robinett*, February 26, 1943, Paul M. Robinett Papers, Box 10, Folder General Military Correspondence, January–May 1943, B-10/F-8, George C. Marshall Library, Lexington, Virginia.

17. Martin van Creveld, *Fighting Power: German and U.S. Army Performance, 1939–1945*, Contributions in Military History (Westport, Connecticut: Greenwood, 1982).

18. Ibid., 168.

19. Ibid., 168.

20. Ibid., 168.

21. John Ellis, *Cassino: The Hollow Victory* (New York: McGraw-Hill, 1984).

22. John Ellis, *Brute Force: Allied Strategy and Tactics in the Second World War* (New York: Viking, 1990).

23. Ibid., 331.

24. Ibid., 532, 534.

25. Ronald Spector, "The Military Effectiveness of the U.S. Armed Forces, 1919–1939," in *Military Effectiveness: The Interwar Period*, ed. Allan Reed Millett and Williamson Murray (Boston: Allen & Unwin, 1988), 76.

26. Allan Reed Millett, "The United States Armed Forces in the Second World War," in *Military Effectiveness: The Second World War*, ed. Allan Reed Millett and Williamson Murray (Boston: Allen & Unwin, 1988), 76.

27. Ibid., 77.

28. Ibid., 74.

29. Ibid., 61.

30. Richard Overy, *Why the Allies Won* (New York City: Norton, 1995). There are numerous errors in Overy's book: Dwight D. Eisenhower was not born in "Abiline," Kansas, but in Denison, Texas. He was raised in *Abilene*, Kansas (p. 144). Ike could not have been promoted to the Pentagon three weeks after Pearl Harbor because the Pentagon was not finished before 1943 (p. 261). Overy states that "Axis forces did little to alter the basic pattern of their military organization and operational practice, or to reform and modernize the way they made war" (p. 318). This sentence is—at least in respect to the *Wehrmacht*—completely erroneous. The structure of the German divisions, the officer corps, as well as the operational way to wage war had changed greatly from 1939 to 1945. "It is inconceivable that a Marshall or an Eisenhower, with no combat experience between them, could have won supreme command in either the German or Japanese war effort." (Ibid.) That is a comparison of apples and oranges. Marshall was chief of staff of the army and comparable officers on the German side—like Franz Halder—had even less combat and command experience than Marshall. There were other German army and army group commanders who had little or no combat experience, like Albert Kesselring and Friedrich Paulus, both field marshals. It is methodologically problematic for

both Ellis's and Overy's book that for the German side they largely rely on post-war writings of German officers.

31. Ibid., 318.

32. Ibid., 325.

33. Ibid., 318.

34. Charles E. Kirkpatrick, "'The Very Model of a Modern Major General': Background of World War II American Generals in V Corps," in *The U.S. Army and World War II: Selected Papers from the Army's Commemorative Conferences*, ed. Judith L. Bellafaire (Washington, D.C.: Center of Military History, U.S. Army, 1998), 272.

35. Ibid., 270–274.

36. Charles E. Kirkpatrick, "Orthodox Soldiers: U.S. Army Formal School and Junior Officers between the Wars," in *Forging the Sword: Selecting, Educating, and Training Cadets and Junior Officers in the Modern World*, ed. Elliot V. Converse (Chicago: Imprint Publications, 1998), 107.

37. Karl-Heinz Frieser, *The Blitzkrieg Legend: The 1940 Campaign in the West* (Annapolis, Maryland: Naval Institute Press, 2005), 351. The German original is from 1995.

38. Ibid., 353.

39. Martin Blumenson, "America's World War II Leaders in Europe: Some Thoughts," *Parameters* 19 (1989). Blumenson is, like Weigley, especially qualified for such assessments. He saw service in World War II, was a U.S. Army historian, published the Patton papers, and wrote numerous works on the U.S. Army or individual officers.

40. Ibid., 3.

41. Kirkpatrick, "'The Very Model of a Modern Major General'," 273; Blumenson, "America's World War II Leaders," 13; Hugh M. Exton and Frederick Bernays Wiener, "What is a General?," *Army* 8, no. 6 (1958).

42. Robert H. Berlin, *U.S. Army World War II Corps Commanders: A Composite Biography* (Fort Leavenworth, Kansas: U.S. Army Command and General Staff College, 1989), 13.

43. After the last name change, it is now the Command and General Staff College.

44. Ernest N. Harmon, Milton MacKaye, and William Ross MacKaye, *Combat Commander: Autobiography of a Soldier* (Englewood Cliffs, New Jersey: Prentice-Hall, 1970), 49.

45. Timothy K. Nenninger, *The Leavenworth Schools and the Old Army: Education, Professionalism, and the Officer Corps of the United States Army, 1881–1918* (Westport, Connecticut: Greenwood, 1978); Timothy K. Nenninger, "Leavenworth and Its Critics: The U.S. Army Command and General Staff School, 1920–1940," *Journal of Military History* 58, no. 2 (1994); Philip Carlton Cockrell, "Brown Shoes and Mortar Boards: U.S. Army Officer Professional Education at the Command and General Staff School, Fort Leavenworth, Kansas, 1919–1940" (Ph.D. diss., University of South Carolina, 1991); Peter J. Schifferle, "Anticipating Armageddon: The Leavenworth Schools and U.S. Army Military Effectiveness 1919 to 1945" (Ph.D. diss., University of Kansas, 2002).

46. Michaela Hönicke Moore, "American Interpretations of National Socialism, 1933–1945," in *The Impact of Nazism: New Perspectives on the Third Reich and Its Legacy*, eds. Alan E. Steinweis and Daniel E. Rogers (Lincoln: University of Nebraska Press, 2003); Ronald Smelser and Edward J. Davies, *The Myth of the Eastern Front: The Nazi-Soviet War in American Popular Culture* (New York: Cambridge University Press, 2007); Ronald Smelser, "The Myth of the Clean Wehrmacht in Cold War America," in *Lessons and Legacies VIII: From Generation to Generation*, ed. Doris L. Bergen (Evanston, Illinois: Northwestern University Press, 2008).

47. Alistair Finlan, "How Does a Military Organization Regenerate its Culture?," in *The Falklands Conflict Twenty Years On: Lessons for the Future*, eds. Stephen Badsey, Rob Havers, and Mark Grove (London: Cass, 2005), 194. Finlan cites Alistair Ian Johnston, *Cultural Realism: Strategic Culture and Grand Strategy in Chinese History*. Princeton, New Jersey: Princeton University Press, 1995.

48. Ibid.

49. Friedhelm Klein, "Aspekte militärischen Führungsdenkens in Geschichte und Gegenwart," in *Führungsdenken in europäischen und*

nordamerikanischen Streitkräften im 19. und 20. Jahrhundert, ed. Gerhard P. Groß (Hamburg: Mittler, 2001), 12.

50. William D. O'Neill, *Transformation and the Officer Corps: Analysis in the Historical Context of the U.S. and Japan between the World Wars* (Alexandria, Virginia: CNA, 2005), 98.

51. Wolfram Wette, *The Wehrmacht: History, Myth, Reality* (Cambridge, Massachusetts: Harvard University Press, 2006), 176–177.

52. The Army Air Corps became a component of the army in July 1926. Its political and military power increased in manifold ways over the years and it was reconstituted and renamed Army Air Forces in June 1941.

53. Throughout the text most of the time the original German word is set in italics with a translation in parentheses just behind it at least once after appearing for the first time.

54. For a comparison of the ranks in the U.S. Army and the German Armed Forces, see the table at the end of the book.

55. On Germany, for example, see Hansgeorg Model, *Der deutsche Generalstabsoffizier: Seine Auswahl und Ausbildung in Reichswehr, Wehrmacht und Bundeswehr* (Frankfurt a. M.: Bernard & Graefe, 1968); Steven Errol Clemente, „"Mit Gott! Für König und Kaiser!" A Critical Analysis of the Making of the Prussian Officer, 1860–1914" (Ph.D. diss., University of Oklahoma, 1989). On the United States, for example, see Nenninger, *The Leavenworth Schools and the Old Army*; Boyd L. Dastrup, *The U.S. Army Command and General Staff College: A Centennial History* (Manhattan, Kansas: Sunflower University Press, 1982).

56. To name just a few: Stephen E. Ambrose, *Duty, Honor, Country: A History of West Point* (Baltimore: Johns Hopkins Press, 1966); Theodore J. Crackel, *The Illustrated History of West Point* (New York: H. N. Abrams, 1991); Theodore J. Crackel, *West Point: A Bicentennial History* (Lawrence,: University Press of Kansas, 2002); Lance A. Betros, ed. *West Point: Two Centuries and Beyond* (Abilene, Texas: McWhiney Foundation Press, 2004).

57. Waldemar Erfurth, *Die Geschichte des deutschen Generalstabes von 1918 bis 1945*, 2nd ed., Studien und Dokumente zur Geschichte

des Zweiten Weltkrieges (Göttingen: Musterschmidt, 1957), 112–113.

58. Peter J. Schifferle, "The Prussian and American General Staffs: An Analysis of Cross-Cultural Imitation, Innovation and Adaption" (M.A. thesis, University of North Carolina at Chapel Hill, 1981), 30; Erfurth, *Die Geschichte des deutschen Generalstabes von 1918 bis 1945*, 127.

ONE Prelude: Military Relations between the United States and Germany and the Great General Staff Fantasy

1. Thomas Bentley Mott, *Twenty Years as Military Attaché* (New York: Oxford University Press, 1937), 29.

2. Annual Report of the Commandant, U.S. Infantry and Cavalry School, U.S. Signal School and Staff College for the School Year ending August 31, 1906 (Washington, D.C.: U.S. Government Printing Office, 1907), 67. Cited in Cockrell, "Brown Shoes and Mortar Boards," 36.

3. Stephen E. Ambrose, foreword to *Handbook on German Military Forces*, edited by U.S. War Department (Baton Rouge: Louisiana State University Press, 1990), iii. The original was published in March 1945.

4. Don Higginbotham, "Military Education before West Point," in *Thomas Jefferson's Military Academy: Founding West Point*, ed. Robert M. S. McDonald (Charlottesville: University of Virginia, 2004), 24; Clemente, "Making of the Prussian Officer," 10.

5. An exhaustive treatment of war and culture is found in John Keegan, *Die Kultur des Krieges* (Berlin: Rowohlt, 1995); John A. Lynn, *Battle: A History of Combat and Culture* (Boulder, Colorado: Westview Press, 2003); Martin van Creveld, *The Culture of War* (New York: Presidio, 2008). For the U.S. Army culture, of special importance is the visionary article, Murray, Williamson, "Does Military Culture Matter?" in *America the Vulnerable: Our Military Problems and How to Fix Them*, edited by John H. Lehman and Harvey Sicherman (Philadelphia: Foreign Policy Research Institute, 1999), 134–151.

6. The most recent research about the Prussian way of war and the Prussian military culture is found in Sascha Möbius, *Mehr Angst vor dem Offizier als vor dem Feind? Eine mentalitätsgeschichtliche Studie zur preußischen Taktik im Siebenjährigen Krieg* (Saarbrücken: VDM, 2007); Sascha Möbius, *Mehr Angst vor dem Offizier als vor dem Feind? Eine mentalitätsgeschichtliche Studie zur preußischen Taktik im Siebenjährigen Krieg* (Saarbrücken: VDM, 2007); Jörg Muth, *Flucht aus dem militärischen Alltag: Ursachen und individuelle Ausprägung der Desertion in der Armee Friedrichs des Großen* (Freiburg i. Br.: Rombach, 2003).

7. Higginbotham, "Military Education before West Point," 35.

8. Muth, *Flucht aus dem militärischen Alltag*, 28.

9. Rudolph Wilhelm von Kaltenborn, *Briefe eines alten Preußischen Officiers*, 2 vols., vol. 1 (Braunschweig: Biblio, 1790; reprint, 1972), ix.

10. For a recent definition of what makes a mercenary, see United Nations Legal Document A/RES/44/34, 72nd plenary meeting, 4 December 1989, at http://www.un.org/documents/ga/res/44/a44r034.htm.

11. Betros, ed. *West Point*, Robert M. S. McDonald, ed. *Thomas Jefferson's Military Academy: Founding West Point* (Charlottesville: University of Virginia, 2004).

12. Mott, *Twenty Years*, 29.

13. See also the diligent compilation in Thomas S. Grodecki, "[U.S.] Military Observers 1815–1975," (Washington, D.C.: Center of Military History, 1989).

14. Peter D. Skirbunt, "Prologue to Reform: The 'Germanization' of the United States Army, 1865–1898" (Ph.D. diss., Ohio State University, 1983), 19.

15. Mott, *Twenty Years*, 117–118.

16. Jay Luvaas, "The Influence of the German Wars of Unification on the United States," in *On the Road to Total War: The American Civil War and the German Wars of Unification, 1861–1871*, eds. Stig Förster and Jörg Nagler (Washington, D.C.: German Historical Institute, 1997), 598.

17. Clemente, "Making of the Prussian Officer," 32.

18. Skirbunt, "Prologue to Reform," 26–27. The attributes "neat," "tidy," and "clean" for German soldiers and facilities show up repeatedly in reports of American officers. Kearny went in the same year to Algiers and fought to the astonishment of his hosts on their side. Seven years later, he lost an arm in the U.S. war against Mexico, again leading a cavalry charge. He died in 1862 during a reconnaissance mission as a Union major general, highly respected by friend and foe.

19. Donald Allendorf, *Long Road to Liberty: The Odyssey of a German Regiment in the Yankee Army: The 15th Missouri Volunteer Infantry.* (Kent, Ohio: Kent State University Press, 2006). For a different point of view, see Christian B. Keller, "Anti-German Sentiment in the Union Army: A Study in Wartime Prejudice" (paper presented at the Annual Society for Military History Conference, Ogden, Utah, April 17–19, 2008).

I appreciate the author's time to share his thoughts with me on the topic.

20. Russell Frank Weigley, *The American Way of War: A History of the United States Military Strategy and Policy* (London: Macmillan, 1973), 195; Skirbunt, "Prologue to Reform," 2, 41–44.

21. Luvaas, "The Influence of the German Wars of Unification," 605.

22. Ibid., 605.

23. Mott, *Twenty Years*, 18.

24. Edward M. Coffman, *The Regulars: The American Army, 1898–1941* (Cambridge, Massachusetts: Belknap Press, 2004), 203.

25. William Babcock Hazen, *The School and the Army in Germany and France* (New York: Harper & Brothers, 1872), 86–87.

26. Luvaas, "The Influence of the German Wars of Unification," 597–598.

27. Manfred Görtemaker, "Helmuth von Moltke und das Führungsdenken im 19. Jahrhundert," in *Führungsdenken in europäischen und nordamerikanischen Streitkräften im 19. und 20. Jahrhundert*, ed. Gerhard P. Groß (Hamburg: Mittler, 2001), 19.

28. Skirbunt, "Prologue to Reform," 57.

29. Luvaas, "The Influence of the German Wars of Unification," 605.

30. Herbert Blank, "Die Halbgötter: Geschichte, Gestalt und Ende des Generalstabes," *Nordwestdeutsche Hefte* 4 (1947): 13. "Common sense" (*gesunder Menschenverstand*) as one of Moltke's main leadership traits shows up quite often in assessments at different times. See also Stig Förster, "The Prussian Triangle of Leadership in the Face of a People's War: A Reassessment of the Conflict between Bismarck and Moltke, 1870–1871," in *On the Road to Total War: The American Civil War and the German Wars of Unification, 1861–1871*, eds. Stig Förster and Jörg Nagler (Washington, D.C.: German Historical Institute, 1997), 125. Förster's term is "matter-of-factness."

31. Carl-Gero von Ilsemann, "Das operative Denken des Älteren Moltke," in *Operatives Denken und Handeln in deutschen Streitkräften im 19. und 20. Jahrhundert*, ed. Günther Roth (Herford: Mittler, 1988), 42.

32. Görtemaker, "Helmuth von Moltke und das Führungsdenken im 19. Jahrhundert," 27. It is still disputed if Clausewitz taught and he and Moltke met in person. Clausewitz had an earlier stint as instructor in 1810 and taught guerilla warfare, general staff duties, artillery tactics, and the art of field fortifications.

33. Ulrich Marwedel, *Carl von Clausewitz: Persönlichkeit und Wirkungsgeschichte seines Werkes bis 1918*, Militärgeschichtliche Studien 25 (Boppard a. R.: Boldt, 1978), 53–55.

34. Carl von Clausewitz, *Vom Kriege*, reprint from the original ed. (Augsburg: Weltbild, 1990).

35. Marwedel, *Carl von Clausewitz*, 209, 232.

36. Ibid., 109.

37. Jon Tetsuo Sumida, *Decoding Clausewitz: A New Approach to "On War"* (Lawrence: University Press of Kansas, 2008), xiv–xv, 1–2.

38. Only an article Clausewitz wrote in 1817 about his mentor and best friend, Gerhard von Scharnhorst, after the latter died, received praise for the writing because it came obviously from the heart. The Prussian historian Leopold Ranke published the article after Clausewitz's death.

39. In 1943, the United States Military Academy issued a small reader, "Jomini, Clausewitz and Schlieffen," wrapping them all in one within 96 pages. It was republished in 1945, 1948, 1951, 1964, and 1967: Robert A. Doughty and Theodore J. Crackel, "The History of History at West Point," in *West Point: Two Centuries and Beyond*, ed. Lance A. Betros (Abilene, Texas: McWhiney Foundation Press, 2004), 409, 431. Today there are countless shortened or abridged English translations of *Vom Kriege* on the market but not a single definitive edition.

40. *Letter from Paul M. Robinett to Ben W. Goldberg, University of Missouri, October 18, 1939*, Paul M. Robinett Papers, Folder General Military Correspondence, January–December 1939, B-10/F-15, George C. Marshall Library, Lexington, Virginia; Richard Carl Brown, *Social Attitudes of American Generals, 1898–1940* (New York: Arno Press, 1979), 299; I. B. Holley, Jr., "Training and Educating Pre-World War I United States Army Officers," in *Forging the Sword: Selecting, Educating, and Training Cadets and Junior Officers in the Modern World*, ed. Elliot V. Converse (Chicago: Imprint Publications, 1998), 27.

41. Sumida, *Decoding Clausewitz*, xii.

42. Arden Bucholz, *Delbrück's Modern Military History* (Lincoln: University of Nebraska Press, 1997), 54.

43. Model, *Generalstabsoffizier*, 36. See also the interviews conducted by Liddell Hart with German generals during their captivity: Basil Henry Liddell Hart, *Jetzt dürfen sie reden: Hitlers Generale berichten* (Stuttgart et al.: Stuttgarter Verlag, 1950), 358.

44. See the statement of General Erich Brandenberger cited in Othmar Hackl, ed. *Generalstab, Generalstabsdienst und Generalstabsausbildung in der Reichswehr und Wehrmacht 1919–1945*, Studien deutscher Generale und Gneralstabsoffiziere in der Historical Division der U.S. Army in Europa 1946–1961 (Osnabrück: Biblio, 1999), 208.

45. Marwedel, Carl von Clausewitz, 118–119, 129, 213.

46. Förster, "The Prussian Triangle of Leadership," 135. More of Moltke's violations of Clausewitz's principles are found in Wilhelm Deist,

"Remarks on the Preconditions to Waging War in Prussia-Germany, 1866–71," in *On the Road to Total War: The American Civil War and the German Wars of Unification, 1861–1871*, eds. Stig Förster and Jörg Nagler (Washington, D.C.: German Historical Institute, 1997), 325.

47. Marwedel, *Carl von Clausewitz*, 177.

48. John Keegan, *The First World War* (New York: Knopf, 1999), 69.

49. Barbara W. Tuchman, *The Guns of August* (New York: MacMillan, 1962), 80. I appreciate that my student Mandi Meredith pointed out to me the location of this quote.

50. Delbrück about Moltke, cited in Bucholz, *Delbrück's Modern Military History*, 71.

51. Alistair Horne, *The Price of Glory* (New York: Penguin, 1993), 33–40.

52. Lothar Burchardt, "Operatives Denken und Planen von Schlieffen bis zum Beginn des Ersten Weltkrieges," in *Operatives Denken und Handeln in deutschen Streitkräften im 19. und 20. Jahrhundert*, ed. Günther Roth (Herford: Mittler, 1988), 23. Interestingly, there are only two monographies that deal with the *Auftragstaktik*, both written by German officers: Dirk W. Oetting, *Auftragstaktik: Geschichte und Gegenwart einer Führungskonzeption* (Frankfurt a. M.: Report, 1993) and Stephan Leistenschneider, *Auftragstaktik im preußisch-deutschen Heer 1871 bis 1914* (Hamburg: Mittler, 2002). Both, however, point out different developments of the *Auftragstaktik*.

53. Schifferle, "The Prussian and American General Staffs," 46.

54. Hazen, *The School and the Army in Germany and France*: Emory Upton, *The Armies of Europe and Asia* (London: Griffin & Co., 1878) (British version). Babcock graduated from West Point in 1855, Upton in 1861. Upton's work was more influential because of the fame he had gained in the American Civil War.

55. James L. Abrahamson, *America Arms for a New Century: The Making of a Great Military Power* (New York: Free Press, 1981), 66–68.

56. Coffman, *The Regulars*, 5.

57. "Faith—It Moveth Mountains" (article draft), John E. Dahlquist Papers, Box 2, Folder Correspondence 1953–1956, 13, U.S. Army Military History Institute, Carlisle, Pennsylvania.

58. Theodore Roosevelt to Henry Cabot Lodge, 21 July 1899, cited in L. Michael Allsep, Jr., "New Forms for Dominance: How a Corporate Lawyer Created the American Military Establishment" (Ph.D. diss., University of North Carolina at Chapel Hill, 2008), 170–171. I greatly appreciate that my friend and colleague Michael let me have the manuscript of his excellent dissertation and that he pointed out relevant source material to me.

59. Russell Frank Weigley, "The Elihu Root Reforms and the Progressive Era," in *Command and Commanders in Modern Military History: The Proceedings of the Second Military History Symposium, U.S. Air Force Academy, 2–3 May 1968*, ed. William E. Geffen (Washington, D.C.: Office of Air Force History, 1971), 15.

60. Allsep, "New Forms for Dominance," 201.

61. Ibid., 264.

62. Coffman, *The Regulars*, 142.

63. Theodore Schwan, *Report on the Organization of the German Army* (Washington, D.C.: U.S. Government Printing Office, 1894).

64. Schifferle, "The Prussian and American General Staffs," 69.

65. Weigley, "The Elihu Root Reforms," 18.

66. Allsep, "New Forms for Dominance," 297–298.

67. This playing of both sides of the coin would continue over seven decades, again at the discussions about the German rearmament and from the armed forces reforms under presidents Harry S. Truman and Dwight D. Eisenhower to the change to an all-volunteer U.S. Army in the early 1970s: Andrew J. Birtle, *Rearming the Phoenix: U.S. Military Assistance to the Federal Republic of Germany, 1950–1960*, Modern American history (New York: Garland, 1991), 259, 277; Michael J. Hogan, *A Cross of Iron: Harry S. Truman and the Origins of the National Security State, 1945–1954* (Cambridge: Cambridge University Press, 1998), 34–36, 43, 64, 149.

68. Schifferle, "The Prussian and American General Staffs," 79.

69. *Interview with Major General Dennis E. Nolan, Nov. 14, 1947, OCMH (Office of the Chief of Military History) Collection*, Box 2, U.S. Army Military History Institute, Carlisle, Pennsylvania.

70. *Interview with General Peyton C. March, Oct. 13, 1947, OCMH (Office of the Chief of Military History) Collection,* Box 2, U.S. Army Military History Institute, Carlisle, Pennsylvania.

71. Weigley, "The Elihu Root Reforms," 18.

72. Schifferle, "The Prussian and American General Staffs," 128.

73. Cited in Cockrell, "Brown Shoes and Mortar Boards," 184.

74. Manfred Messerschmidt, "German Military Effectiveness between 1919 and 1939," in *Military Effectiveness: The Interwar Period,* eds. Allan Reed Millett and Williamson Murray (Boston: Allen & Unwin, 1988), 223.

75. Weigley, "The Elihu Root Reforms," 18; Coffman, *The Regulars,* 185.

76. *Letter from John McAuley Palmer to George A. Lynch, May, 25, 1938,* George C. Marshall Papers, Box 4, Folder Vancouver Barracks Correspondence, General, May 20–23, 1938, George C. Marshall Library, Lexington, Virginia.

77. *Interview by Harold Dean Cater with General Walter Krueger regarding the German and U.S. General Staff, March 18, 1948, OCMH (Office of the Chief of Military History) Collection,* Box 2, U.S. Army Military History Institute, Carlisle, Pennsylvania.

78. Ibid.

79. There are numerous other different and erroneous opinions by American senior officers in regard to the German General Staff in the collection of Office of the Chief of Military History, Box 2, U.S. Army Military History Institute, Carlisle, Pennsylvania.

80. The term "chairborne tactics" is borrowed from the man who commanded the Royal Marine 42 Commandos during the Falklands War and later published his own account of the events: Nick Vaux, *Take That Hill! Royal Marines in the Falklands War* (Washington, D.C.: Pergamon, 1986), 115. Martin Stanton, *Somalia on $5 a Day: A Soldier's Story* (New York: Ballantine, 2001), 295. The different worlds and attitudes of staff and frontline officer is nowhere better portrayed than in the unforgettable novel by Anton Myrer, *Once an Eagle* (New York: HarperTorch, 2001).

81. Spenser Wilkinson, *The Brain of an Army* (Westminster: A. Constable, 1890; reprint, 1895); Walter Görlitz, *Der deutsche Gener-*

alstab: Geschichte und Gestalt, 2nd ed. (Frankfurt a. M.: Frankfurter Hefte, 1953); Trevor Nevitt Dupuy, *A Genius for War: The German Army and General Staff, 1807–1945* (Englewood Cliffs, New Jersey: Prentice-Hall, 1977).

82. For the German side, for example, *Generalfeldmarschall* Fedor von Bock, Commander of *Heeresgruppe Mitte*; *Generaloberst* Friedrich Fromm, Chief of Rearmament and the Replacement Army; *Generaloberst* Franz Halder, Chief of Staff of the Army; *Generalfeldmarschall* Albert Kesselring, *Oberbefehlshaber West*; *Generalfeldmarschall* Friedrich Paulus, Commander of Sixth Army. (Named are their last ranks and commands).

83. Geoffrey P. Megargee, *Inside Hitler's High Command*, Modern War Studies (Lawrence: University Press of Kansas, 2000), 180.

84. Ibid., 180.

85. Ibid., 180–181.

86. The new and very enlightening evidence is in Thomas Weber, *Hitler's First War: Adolf Hitler, the Men of the List Regiment, and the First World War* (London: Oxford University Press, 2010).

87. The rank of *Obergefreiter* is usually incorrectly translated into corporal. While a corporal is an NCO, an *Obergefreiter* is not. Corporals lead squads or fire teams. That is in the German army the job of a *Hauptgefreiter*, one rank above *Obergefreiter*, and still not an NCO position. Hitler's rank is therefore best translated as private 1st class. While Hitler's courage in World War I is not in question, his leadership capabilities were continuously ranked so low that he never achieved NCO status.

88. *"Who's Who" Datacards on German Military, Civilian and Political Personalities 1925–1949*, RG 165, Records of the War Dept. General and Special Staffs, Office of the Director of Intelligence (G 2), 1906–1949, Box 3, National Archives II, College Park, Maryland. The cards are sorted by rank and in alphabetical order. There are ten thousands of them down to the rank of major.

89. Forrest C. Pogue, *George C. Marshall: Education of a General, 1880–1939*, 3 vols. (New York: Viking Press, 1963), 1:101.

90. Nenninger, *The Leavenworth Schools and the Old Army*, 141.

91. George C. Marshall, "Profiting by War Experiences," *Infantry Journal* 18 (1921): 36–37.

92. Kevin Hymel, ed. *Patton's Photographs: War as He Saw It*, 1st ed. (Washington, D.C.: Potomac Books, 2006), 33. Later also "Good German" or just "G.G." Decades after the Patton papers were deposited at the Library of Congress and numerous scholars had them examined to write voluminous biographies about the famous commander, Hymel found the photographs Patton had taken during the war with his personal camera.

93. For the full speech, see Bernd Sösemann, "Die sogenannte Hunnenrede Wilhelms II: Textkritische und interpretatorische Bemerkungen zur Ansprache des Kaisers vom 27. Juli 1900 in Bremerhaven," *Historische Zeitschrift* 222 (1976): 342–358.

94. Perry L. Miles, *Fallen Leaves: Memories of an Old Soldier* (Berkeley, California: Wuerth, 1961), 132. A German account from the war shows that Miles was not exaggerating: Georg Hillebrecht and Andreas Eckl, "*Man wird wohl später sich schämen müssen, in China gewesen zu sein.*" *Tagebuchaufzeichnungen des Assistenzarztes Dr. Georg Hillebrecht aus dem Boxerkrieg 1900–1902* (Essen: Eckl, 2006).

95. Miles, *Fallen Leaves*, 132.

96. *The [Travel] Diary of William R. Gruber [and Dwight D. Eisenhower]*, Dwight D. Eisenhower Papers, Box 22, Dwight D. Eisenhower Library, Abilene, Kansas.

97. Joe Lawton Collins, *Lightning Joe: An Autobiography* (Baton Rouge: Louisiana State University Press, 1979), 27, 37.

98. There are several cartoons and anecdotes in American service magazines of 1945 about the sudden high demand of brief English lessons from the English teachers in German villages and cities, who before that had been so much despised. The most popular phrases, according to those satiric accounts, were "I have never been a Nazi" and "I have relatives in Minnesota."

99. George F. Hofmann, *Through Mobility We Conquer: The Mechanization of U.S. Cavalry* (Lexington: University of Kentucky Press, 2006), 443.

100. *Correspondence regarding Walter Krueger's translation projects and re-search travels*, Walter Krueger Papers, Box 1, West Point Library Special Archives Collection, West Point, New York.

101. Cockrell, "Brown Shoes and Mortar Boards," 40. The basis for the American Field Service Regulations of 1910 came from German sources. The same is true for the later version of the Field Manual 100—5. See also, van Creveld, *Fighting Power*, 38–40.

102. Spector, "The Military Effectiveness of the U.S. Armed Forces, 1919–1939," 90.

103. Charles T. Lanham, ed. *Infantry in Battle* (Washington, D.C: Infantry Journal, 1934). The book was produced at The Infantry School when George C. Marshall was assistant commandant. It was well made didactically and gained great praise, even internationally. For more on it, see chapter 4.

104. Paul Fröhlich, "Der vergessene Partner": Die militärische Zusammenarbeit der Reichswehr mit der U.S. Army 1918–1933" (Master's thesis, University of Potsdam, 2008), 38.

105. Erich von Manstein, *Aus einem Soldatenleben 1887–1939* (Bonn: Athenäum, 1958), 73.

106. William Mulligan, *The Creation of the Modern German Army: General Walther Reinhardt and the Weimar Republic, 1914–1930* (New York: Berghahn, 2005), 150–151. A guesstimate for the number of members in all paramilitary organizations in the Weimar Republic is found in James M. Diehl, *Paramilitary Politics in Weimar Germany* (Bloomington: Indiana University Press, 1977), 293–297. The numbers, however, originate only from a very small source base.

107. Jun Nakata, *Der Grenz- und Landesschutz in der Weimarer Republik 1918 bis 1933: Die geheime Aufrüstung und die deutsche Gesellschaft* (Freiburg i. Br.: Rombach, 2002), 168–169. I appreciate it that Jürgen Förster pointed this work out to me.

108. Ibid., 171.

109. Diehl, *Paramilitary Politics in Weimar Germany*, 30.

110. Ibid., 42.

111. A vivid and glorifying description of such a unit by one of its members is found in Ernst von Salomon, *Die Geächteten* (Berlin: Rowohlt, 1930).

112. Diehl, *Paramilitary Politics in Weimar Germany*, 18.

113. Spector, "The Military Effectiveness of the U.S. Armed Forces, 1919–1939," 71.

114. Ibid., 70.

115. Ibid., 77.

116. Clemente, "Making of the Prussian Officer," 290.

117. Fröhlich, "'Der vergessene Partner.' Die militärische Zusammenarbeit der Reichswehr mit der U.S. Army 1918–1933," 3.

118. Gerhard L. Weinberg, "From Confrontation to Cooperation: Germany and the United States, 1933–1945," in *America and the Germans: An Assessment of a Three-Hundred-Year History*, eds. Frank Trommler and Joseph McVeigh (Philadelphia: University of Pennsylvania Press, 1985), 45.

119. Fröhlich, "'Der vergessene Partner.' Die militärische Zusammenarbeit der Reichswehr mit der U.S. Army 1918–1933," 25.

120. Harold J. Gordon, Jr., *The Reichswehr and the German Republic, 1919–1926* (Princeton, New Jersey: Princeton University Press, 1957), 191.

121. Basil Henry Liddell Hart, *Why Don't We Learn from History?* (New York: Hawthorn, 1971), 29.

122. The newest research is found in Hans Ehlert, Michael Epkenhans, and Gerhard P. Groß, eds., *Der Schlieffenplan: Analysen und Dokumente*, Zeitalter der Weltkriege, Bd. 2 (Paderborn: Schöningh 2006). Outdated but still to the point is Gerhard Ritter, *The Schlieffen Plan: Critique of a Myth* (New York: Praeger, 1958). An unsatisfactory reappraisal, thoroughly defeated in Ehlert, Epkenhans, and Groß is Terence Zuber, *Inventing the Schlieffen Plan: German War Planning, 1871–1914* (Oxford: Oxford University Press, 2002).

123. Burchardt, "Operatives Denken und Planen von Schlieffen bis zum Beginn des Ersten Weltkrieges," 60.

124. Holger Afflerbach, *Falkenhayn: Politisches Denken und Handeln im Kaiserreich* (München: Oldenbourg, 1994). In this example, offi-

cers of the Schlieffen School used to make their maneuver plans without regard for the physical capacities of man or horse.

125. Horne, *The Price of Glory*, 36.

126. Robert T. Foley, *German Strategy and the Path to Verdun: Erich von Falkenhayn and the Development of Attrition, 1870–1916* (Cambridge: Cambridge University Press, 2005). Foley unsuccessfully tries to defend Falkenhayn's reasoning. I appreciate it that Gerhard Weinberg pointed this book out to me.

127. Messerschmidt, "German Military Effectiveness between 1919 and 1939," 225.

128. Johann Adolf Graf von Kielmansegg, "Bemerkungen zum Referat von Hauptmann Dr. Frieser aus der Sicht eines Zeitzeugen," in *Operatives Denken und Handeln in deutschen Streitkräften im 19. und 20. Jahrhundert*, ed. Günther Roth (Herford: Mittler, 1988), 150.

129. Frieser, *The Blitzkrieg Legend*, 61.

130. Ibid., 62. Frieser suggests that possibility.

131. Wette, *The Wehrmacht*, 2–3.

132. Bernhard R. Kroener, *Generaloberst Friedrich Fromm: Der starke Mann im Heimatkriegsgebiet; Eine Biographie* (Paderborn: Schöningh, 2005), 450–455.

133. Frieser, *The Blitzkrieg Legend*, 67.

134. Ibid., 60.

135. Jürgen E. Förster, "The Dynamics of *Volksgemeinschaft*: The Effectiveness of the German Military Establishment," in *Military Effectiveness: The Second World War*, eds. Allan Reed Millett and Williamson Murray (Boston: Allen & Unwin, 1988), 193.

136. Ibid., 195.

137. Megargee, *Inside Hitler's High Command*.

138. Wilkinson, *The Brain of an Army*. The book has been highly influential in glorifying the German General Staff in the world.

TWO No "Brother Officers": Cadets at the United States Military Academy at West Point

1. Schofield was superintendent of the United States Military Academy from 1876 to 1881. Disgusted with the atrocities and hazing

at the academy, he addressed the Corps of Cadets, on August 11, 1879. His well-chosen words, however, were in vain as the hazing even increased in later years. It is one of the paradoxes of history that upperclassmen at West Point have required plebes to memorize some of Schofields's words as part of the "plebe poop," obviously without properly understanding and appreciating them.

2. Charles E. Woodruff, "The Nervous Exhaustion due to West Point Training," *American Medicine* 1, no. 12 (1922): 558.

3. The *Kadetten* memoirs and the Wehrmacht's officers' autobiographies are in total agreement here.

4. Roger H. Nye, "The United States Military Academy in an Era of Educational Reform, 1900–1925" (Ph.D. diss., Columbia University, 1968), 145. The title of the study is not well chosen. A great part of it deals with the expansion of the Corps of Cadets and the athletic program at West Point. Most of the primary sources are West Point internal or official papers and regulations. Notably absent are the voices of cadets. The study, however, becomes dense and relevant in its second part. Nye, USMA 1946, fails, like many former Academy graduates, to be truly critical when it comes to his alma mater. The author taught at West Point from 1954 to 1957 and from 1961 to 1970 as an instructor at the department of social science. He then switched to the department of history where he worked as the deputy department head until 1975. I appreciate it that Edward M. Coffman pointed that information out to me. Compare Nye's excellent work: Roger H. Nye, *The Patton Mind: The Professional Development of an Extraordinary Leader* (Garden City Park, New York: Avery, 1993).

5. Harold E. Raugh, Jr., "Command on the Western Front: Perspectives of American Officers," *Stand To!* 18 (Dec. 1986): 12.

6. Edward S. Holden, "The Library of the United States Military Academy, 1777–1906," *Army and Navy Life* (June 1906). Holden, USMA 1870, the former senior librarian at West Point, places the establishment of "the Military Academy at the Army" at West Point at 1781. According to Holden, the order came from George Washington.

7. Mott, *Twenty Years*, 29.

8. Hofmann, *Through Mobility We Conquer*, 45. Here a Marine Corps officer is cited who compares Frederick's style of war with the tactics used in World War I.

9. This fact was brought to my attention during a staff ride to the fortifications around the United States Military Academy at the West Point Summer Seminar in Military History 2005, which I had the privilege to attend. The problems with the fortifications and civilian-minded engineers, as well as the interaction with the members of the fact-finding missions, was brought to light during role-playing on the basis of original contemporary sources. Current and former officers of the West Point Academy and members of the seminar filled the ranks of the re-enactors. It was military history at its best. My grateful appreciation goes to the History Department of the United States Military Academy for the invitation and to all who made the seminar the success that it was.

10. Higginbotham, "Military Education before West Point," 39.

11. It has been suggested that West Point was also founded to be sure that republican-minded officers would populate the army, though it would go too far to discuss that here in depth. However, neither the selection process nor the curriculum of the academy supports this notion. McDonald, ed. *Thomas Jefferson's Military Academy: Founding West Point*. See especially the chapters written by Crackel and Samet. The many West Pointers of southern origin who left the army to fight for the rebels also indicate that the Academy at least failed in its education in this respect, but it is rather likely that the republican education was never there. See James L. Morrison, "The Struggle between Sectionalism and Nationalism at Ante-Bellum West Point, 1830–1861," in *The Military and Society: A Collection of Essays*, ed. Peter Karsten (New York: Garland, 1998).

12. Nye, "Era of Educational Reform," 39. See the appendix of Nye's study for details about class schedules and curriculum.

13. William B. Skelton, *An American Profession of Arms: The Army Officer Corps, 1784–1861* (Lawrence: University Press of Kansas, 1992), 399.

14. Robert S. Norris, "Leslie R. Groves, West Point and the Atomic Bomb," in *West Point: Two Centuries and Beyond*, ed. Lance A. Betros (Abilene, Texas: McWhiney Foundation Press, 2004), 107.

15. Nye, "Era of Educational Reform," 30. See chapter one of Nye's study for a discussion of the teaching of "mental discipline."

16. Ibid., 35. Emphasis in the original.

17. There were, however, "considerations" of selected battles of the Second Punic War, the Seven Years War, the Napoleonic War, and the American Civil War: Doughty and Crackel, "History at West Point," 399. Roger Nye claims in his study that military history as a discipline was introduced in the early 1920s but in his appendix where he lists the courses, the topic is not to be found. See Nye, "Era of Educational Reform," 344, 380.

18. Douglas MacArthur, *Reminiscences* (New York: McGraw-Hill, 1964), 70. Interestingly, MacArthur's account of his time as superintendent is fewer than seven pages out of 426 of his autobiography.

19. Coffman, *The Regulars*, 226.

20. Nye, "Era of Educational Reform," 271.

21. William Addleman Ganoe, *MacArthur Close-Up: Much Then and Some Now* (New York: Vantage, 1962), 35.

22. Donald B. Connelly, "The Rocky Road to Reform: John M. Schofield at West Point, 1876–1881," in *West Point: Two Centuries and Beyond*, ed. Lance A. Betros (Abilene, Texas: McWhiney Foundation Press, 2004), 173. See, for the same struggle decades later, Brian McAllister Linn, "Challenge and Change: West Point and the Cold War," in *West Point: Two Centuries and Beyond*, ed. Lance A. Betros (Abilene, Texas: McWhiney Foundation Press, 2004), 223–226.

23. A different opinion is found in Nye, "Era of Educational Reform," 65. The author's arguments, however, are not convincing because, in other cases, the secretary of war or the president of the United States himself changed the situation by their orders.

24. Mott, *Twenty Years*, 37.

25. *Annual Report of the Superintendent of the United States Military Academy*, (West Point, New York: USMA Press, 1914), 39. The report lists pretty much everything that was going on at West Point down

to the number of bad teeth filled by the dentist. It is a supreme example of U.S. Army bureaucracy.

26. Clark, *Calculated Risk*, 24.

27. Bradford Grethen Chynoweth, *Bellamy Park: Memoirs* (Hicksville, New York: Exposition Press, 1975), 50.

28. Elizabeth D. Samet, "Great Men and Embryo-Caesars: John Adams, Thomas Jefferson, and the Figure in Arms," in *Thomas Jefferson's Military Academy: Founding West Point*, ed. Robert M. S. McDonald (Charlottesville: University of Virginia, 2004), 85.

29. Ewing E. Booth, *My Observations and Experiences in the United States Army* (Los Angeles: n.p., 1944), 94. Booth was a member of the staff class of 1904 of the Leavenworth school, soon to become an instructor at this facility. When ordered to design and build a bridge he turned to at least two of his comrades who were West Point graduates. They were unable to help. Booth, commissioned from the ranks, got the job done nevertheless. See also Brown, *Social Attitudes*, 371.

30. Nye, "Era of Educational Reform," 321–322. The numbers were even published by a critical officer: Joseph P. Sanger, "The West Point Military Academy—Shall Its Curriculum Be Changed as a Necessary Preparation for War?," *Journal of Military Institution* 60 (1917): 128.

31. Nye, "Era of Educational Reform," 19.

32. Patricia B. Genung, "Teaching Foreign Languages at West Point," in *West Point: Two Centuries and Beyond*, ed. Lance A. Betros (Abilene, Texas: McWhiney Foundation Press, 2004), 517.

33. Ibid. Differently cited as a letter from the General Committee of Revision of Courses, made up of West Point senior faculty members in Nye, "Era of Educational Reform," 233.

34. Richard C. U'Ren, *Ivory Fortress: A Psychiatrist Looks at West Point* (Indianapolis: Bobbs-Merrill, 1974), 134–137. The author worked as a psychiatrist at West Point from 1970–1972. His book stands out as a very balanced and careful account amid the piles of glorifying or damning literature about the United States Military Academy. For evidence on the same point, see also the biographical sketches

of George S. Patton, Henry H. Arnold, and Creighton Abrams, all with mediocre scholarly records at the Academy, but all considered outstanding leaders, in Betros, ed. West Point. The Army chief of staff did research on the subject and came to the same conclusion in *Some Reflections on the Subject of Leadership: Speech by General Maxwell D. Taylor before the Corps of Cadets of The Citadel, January 21, 1956*, James A. Van Fleet Papers, Box 19, Folder Correspondence General, Taylor, Maxwell D., 1955–1959, George. C. Marshall Library, Lexington, Virginia.

35. Cited in Norris, "Leslie R. Groves," 120. The evidence about a connection between class standing and the later achievement of high rank was prepared by a West Pointer.

36. H. R. McMaster, *Dereliction of Duty: Lyndon Johnson, Robert McNamara, the Joint Chiefs of Staff, and the Lies That Led to Vietnam* (New York: HarperCollins, 1997). McMaster sparked a discussion with his book, criticizing heavily the top armed forces leadership of that time. Despite a Ph.D. in history and an outstanding combat record in *Desert Storm* and *Operation Iraqi Freedom*, he was recently passed over twice for selection to brigadier general, which in turn opened the discussion of whether the selection process to the rank of general is today not as faulty as it was during the Vietnam Era: Paul Yingling, "A Failure in Generalship," *Armed Forces Journal* (May 2007). Fred Kaplan, "Challenging the Generals," *New York Times Magazine*, August 26, 2007.

37. Chynoweth, *Bellamy Park*, 55; Dik Alan Daso, "Henry H. Arnold at West Point, 1903–1907," in *West Point: Two Centuries and Beyond*, ed. Lance A. Betros (Abilene, Texas: McWhiney Foundation Press, 2004), 76.

38. *Regulations for the United States Military Academy* (Washington, D.C.: U.S. Government Printing Office, 1916), 24.

39. The details are found in Sanger, "The West Point Military Academy," 123–124. Sanger was a major general with 50 years in the U.S. Army. He won his commission in 1861 in the First Michigan Infantry and later gained a lieutenancy in the regular army. As a major, he accompanied Emory Upton during his tour of military

schools and academies of Europe and thus possessed an excessive knowledge of military education systems. His article is highly critical towards West Point. The changes he proposed would have resulted in changing the Academy into a German *Kriegsschule*.

40. *Official Register of the Officers and Cadets of the U.S. Military Academy* (West Point, New York: USMA Press, 1905), 33.

41. Holley, "Training and Educating Pre-World War I United States Army Officers," 27.

42. Chynoweth, *Bellamy Park*, 53.

43. Sanger, "The West Point Military Academy," 128.

44. Nye, "Era of Educational Reform," 98. A detailed overview of the knowledge required to pass successfully the entrance examination to the United States Military Academy can be found in *Official Register of the Officers and Cadets of the U.S. Military* Academy, 33–40.

45. The MacArthur reforms are found in detail in Nye, "Era of Educational Reform," 302–320. The things undone follow in the next chapter. See also Ganoe, *MacArthur Close-Up*. Ganoe was MacArthur's chief of staff at West Point. His account and the one of Major General Robert M. Danford, who was MacArthur's commandant of cadets are the only "close-ups" that exist from MacArthur's time as superintendent. Ganoe is a convert from the "old" West Point circus to the new MacArthur methods and clearly worships the young "supe." He is, however, extraordinarily frank in describing his own change of mind.

46. William E. Simons, ed. *Professional Military Education in the United States: A Historical Dictionary* (Westport, Connecticut: Greenwood, 2000), 181.

47. Ganoe, *MacArthur Close-Up*, 113.

48. John S. D. Eisenhower, *Strictly Personal* (New York: Doubleday, 1974), 37.

49. William Skelton suggested that hazing might have increased after the Civil War: "Old Army" Lecture, West Point Summer Seminar in Military History, June 7, 2005, author's notes; Walter Scott Dillard, "The United States Military Academy, 1865–1900: The Uncertain Years" (Ph.D. diss., University of Washington, 1972), 292.

Dillard, USMA 1961, is in agreement. He served as an instructor at the department of history of West Point from 1969–1972.

50. Dillard, 90–92.

51. Crackel, *West Point: A Bicentennial History*, 86–88.

52. Ibid. for brief characterizations of the superintendents.

53. Leslie Anders, *Gentle Knight: The Life and Times of Major General Edwin Forrest Harding* (Kent, Ohio: Kent State University Press, 1985), 3. The author also surmises that the "absence of a well-rounded intramural athletic program" was a reason for sadistic hazing. However, when such a program later existed, hazing did not decrease. I appreciate it that Edward Coffman pointed this book out to me.

54. David R. Alexander III, "Hazing: The Formative Years," (research paper submitted to the faculty of the United States Military Academy, History Department, West Point, New York, 1994), 19.

55. Ibid., 18. From 1850–1859, 28.5 percent; from 1860–65, 7.6 percent; from 1866–1869, 22.2 percent; and from 1870–79, 44.8 percent.

56. Philip W. Leon, *Bullies and Cowards: The West Point Hazing Scandal, 1898–1901*, Contributions in Military Studies (Westport, Conneticut: Greenwood Press, 2000). Leon deals only with this single incident. It is disputed among reviewers if the author, a former senior advisor to the superintendent at West Point from 1987 to 1990, has assessed the scandal critically enough. See also Dillard, "The Uncertain Years," 89–95, 292–340. Dillard offers an overview of hazing for the first century of the Academy's existence. He has drawn from cadets' diaries stored at the West Point Library's Special Collections and Archives. A tour de force through the origins of hazing but only on a limited source basis is found in Alexander, "Hazing: The Formative Years."

57. Gordon S. Wood, *The Radicalism of the American Revolution* (New York: Knopf, 1992), 21; Dillard, "The Uncertain Years," 89–91. The author also sees the roots of hazing at civilian learning institutions. For his study, he investigated several civilian colleges and universities.

58. Samet, "Great Men," 91.

59. Pat Conroy, *The Lords of Discipline* (Toronto: Bantam, 1982), 62.

60. Pat Conroy, *My Losing Season* (New York: Doubleday, 2002). Conroy thinks the reason for increased hazing was the Korean War where allegedly American soldiers did not withstand the Communist torturing well enough. The chief culprit responsible for aggravating the ghastly plebe system at The Citadel, where Conroy studied, was Mark Wayne Clark, USMA 1917, who was a superintendent at The Citadel for twelve years after his retirement from the army. Clark had already shown lack of judgment and leadership during World War II.

61. David Ralph Hughes, *Ike at West Point* (Poughkeepsie, New York: Wayne Co., 1958), 4.

62. *Monk Dickson West Point Diary*, Benjamin Abbott Dickson Papers, Box 1, Folder Dickson Family Papers, West Point Library Special Archives, West Point, New York. The entry is from somewhere in the first half of September 1917. As G-2 of First Army, Dickson would become famous for predicting the German counterattack in the Ardennes, known as the "The Battle of the Bulge." His legendary G-2 Intelligence Estimate No. 37 of December 10, 1944, was suppressed by his superiors who didn't want pessimistic accounts to be submitted when a supposedly beaten *Wehrmacht* was thought to be on the run. The consequences were catastrophic when the German forces attacked only six days after Dickson had submitted his estimate.

63. Ibid., 1, entry from September 18, 1917.

64. *Letter from Benjamin Abbot Dickson to the Commanding General Philippine Department*, May 8, 1920, Monk Dickson Papers, Box 2, West Point Library Special Archives, West Point, New York.

65. *Regulations for the United States Military Academy*, 48–50; Klaus Schmitz, *Militärische Jugenderziehung: Preußische Kadettenhäuser und Nationalpolitische Erziehungsanstalten zwischen 1807 und 1936* (Köln: Böhlau, 1997), 137.

66. Craig M. Mullaney, *The Unforgiving Minute: A Soldier's Education* (New York: Penguin, 2009), 39. Like so many other hazing techniques,

timeless fun for the upperclassmen. Mullaney, USMA 2000, suffered that in his plebe year. See part one of his book for more details
on recent hazing and education at West Point. I appreciate it that
Edward Coffman pointed this book out to me.

67. Ibid., 20.

68. For all kinds of hazing accounts from authors who attended military academies, see Jamie Mardis, *Memos of a West Point Cadet* (New
York: McKay, 1976); Red Reeder, West Point Plebe (Boston: Little,
Brown & Company, 1955). Russell Potter "Red" Reeder, USMA
1926, "studied" at West Point not for four but six years because for
him athletics always came before other scholarly obligations and
consequently he had to repeat classes. He earned the Distinguished
Service Cross in the Normandy while commanding the 12th Infantry and was so badly wounded that he lost a leg. In 1946, General
Maxwell D. Taylor, then superintendent of West Point and formerly
distinguished commander of the 101st Airborne Division, authorized Reeder to establish the much-needed Leadership Center at
the Academy. Reeder continued close contact with West Point after
his retirement and is responsible for bringing together the Audie
Murphy Collection for the West Point Library's Special Archives.
Conroy, *Discipline*. Pat Conroy graduated from the military academy The Citadel, Charleston, South Carolina, in 1967. He states
in the author's foreword of his acclaimed novel that "he interviewed
men from West Point, Annapolis, the Air Force Academy, VMI
[Virginia Military Institute], The Citadel, and dozens of military
schools [...]. There is a sameness to all these schools; yet each is
unique and has its own fiercely protected identity. It is the military school as it has evolved in America [...]" See also his autobio-
graphic account for an even more detailed description of hazing
in Conroy, *My Losing Season*. What is basically the same in all the
American military academies is indeed the hazing system.

69. Conroy, *My Losing Season*, 123.

70. Matthew B. Ridgway, *Soldier: The Memoirs of Matthew B. Ridgway*
(New York: Harper & Brothers, 1956), 23.

71. Ibid., 23.

72. Reeder, *West Point Plebe*, 77.

73. Alexander, "Hazing: The Formative Years," 16.

74. Larry I. Bland and Sharon R. Ritenour, eds., *The Papers of George Catlett Marshall: "The Soldierly Spirit,"* December 1880–June 1939, 6 vols., (Baltimore: Johns Hopkins University Press,1981), 1:9.

75. Pogue, *Education of a General*, 44.

76. Ibid., 64. Amazingly military academies built in the image of West Point came rather as clones than as copies. The cadets of these institutions suffered from the same narrowmindedness, the same brutal hazing, and the same lack of a modern and educated faculty. See the account from the Philippine Military Academy in Alfred W. McCoy, "'Same Banana': Hazing and Honor at the Philippine Military Academy," in *The Military and Society: A Collection of Essays*, ed. Peter Karsten (New York: Garland, 1998), 101–103.

77. Carlo D'Este, "General George S. Patton, Jr., at West Point, 1904–1909," in *West Point: Two Centuries and Beyond*, ed. Lance A. Betros (Abilene, Texas: McWhiney Foundation Press, 2004), 60–61.

78. Connelly, "Rocky Road," 175.

79. Conroy, *Discipline*, 73.

80. U'Ren, *Ivory Fortress*, 97.

81. Conroy, *Discipline*, 66–67, 162.

82. Reeder, *West Point Plebe*, 245.

83. Trese A. LaCamera, "Hazing: A Tradition too Deep to Abolish," (research paper submitted to the faculty of the United States Military Academy, History Department, West Point, New York: 1995), 12–13. LaCamera states that "hazing still continues to be an issue into the 1990s." Ganoe, *MacArthur Close-Up*, 106.

84. Nye, "Era of Educational Reform," 145.

85. Muth, *Flucht aus dem militärischen Alltag*, 25. In the years when Frederick had become old and disgruntled, it happened that he told a regimental commander in a private letter to "*fuchtel*" an "insolent" ensign. "*Fuchteln*" is a spanking with the flat side of a saber's blade. However, the standing orders in the Old Prussian Army

were that there ought to be no physical punishment for officers. Frederick's reign has been named for a good reason a "Kingdom of Contradictions": Theodor Schieder, *Friedrich der Große: Ein Königtum der Widersprüche* (Frankfurt a. M.: Propyläen, 1983).

86. Muth, *Flucht aus dem militärischen Alltag*, 92–93.
87. Conroy, *Discipline*, 96.
88. Reeder, *West Point Plebe*, 63.
89. Eisenhower, *Strictly Personal*, 49–50.
90. Ganoe, *MacArthur Close-Up*, 120.
91. Conroy, *Discipline*, 96; Reeder, *West Point Plebe*, 73, 122.
92. Nye, "Era of Educational Reform," 163.
93. Dillard, "The Uncertain Years," 79.
94. Linn, "Challenge and Change," 234.
95. Richard G. Davies, *Carl A. Spaatz and the Air War in Europe* (Washington, D.C.: Center for Air Force History, 1993), 4.
96. Chynoweth, *Bellamy Park*, 50. Another example is Lewis B. "Chesty" Puller who left VMI during his rat year and enlisted as a private in the Marine Corps. He became the most highly decorated Marine in the history of the Corps and retired with the rank of lieutenant general.
97. Ganoe, *MacArthur Close-Up*, 116.
98. Nye, "Era of Educational Reform," 260.
99. Ganoe, *MacArthur Close-Up*, 15. Tillman repeatedly averted attempts to modernize the curriculum at West Point. For him, chemistry and geology were the most important topics for a future officer to learn.
100. Lewis Sorley, "Principled Leadership: Creighton Williams Abrams, Class of 1936," in West Point: Two Centuries and Beyond, ed. Lance A. Betros (Abilene, Texas: McWhiney Foundation Press, 2004), 124.
101. Sanger, "The West Point Military Academy," 121–122, 127–129.
102. Ibid., 128.
103. Of the class of 1971, 30 percent stated that "the unhappy experience" during Beast Barracks made them "decide against an army career." U'Ren, *Ivory Fortress*, 28.

104. Eisenhower, *Strictly Personal*, 36; Ganoe, *MacArthur Close-Up*, 124.

105. Norris, "Leslie R. Groves," 37. The words were written decades after his retirement by former Brigadier General William W. Ford, who was a plebe in 1918. Not surprisingly, he just repeated what he was told by one of the Academy's faculty who speaks of "contaminating impurities": Charles W. Larned, "West Point and Higher Education," *Army and Navy Life and The United Service* 8, no. 12 (1906): 18. Colonel Charles William Larned, USMA 1870, became an enemy of the football program that was installed at West Point at the time and was known to be an advocate of an outdated educational system and to write "polished" reports and articles, *The Genius of West Point*, etc., about the academy. He was a senior professor of drawing at West Point and stayed there as a teacher for 35 years. The considerable influence senior faculty like him were able to wield becomes evident.

106. Sorley, "Leadership," 123.

107. Ibid.

108. Conroy, *Discipline*, 33.

109. In 1988, faculty at the USMA tried to "curb" the use of the word "hazing." Alexander, "Hazing: The Formative Years," 2.

110. Conroy, *Discipline*, 172.

111. Nye, "Era of Educational Reform," 147.

112. Ganoe, *MacArthur Close-Up*, 36.; Nye, "Era of Educational Reform," 148–172. Several cases of hazing, scandals, and attempted punishment and disciplining can be found here, including the extraordinarily weak excuse of the author that the Academy was too short on staff to observe the cadets properly.

113. Since 1976, West Point was forced to accept female cadets by presidential directive. Their bad treatment and hazing is another sad story, which, however, cannot be discussed here. For a summary of the horrible behavior the female cadets had to endure, see Lance Janda, "The Crucible of Duty: West Point, Women, and Social Change," in *West Point: Two Centuries and Beyond*, ed. Lance A. Betros (Abilene, Texas: McWhiney Foundation Press, 2004), 353–355. The whole

story is in: Lance Janda, *Stronger than Custom: West Point and the Admission of Women* (Westport, Conneticut: Praeger, 2002). It is evident that in those years quite a few male cadets would be commissioned as officers, who sure were no gentlemen. An interesting historical view of a tactical officer, USMA 1985, judging the Academy's efforts nearly twenty years later, is provided in Dave Jones, "Assessing the Effectiveness of "Project Athena": The 1976 Admission of Women to West Point" (research paper submitted to the faculty of the United States Military Academy, History Department, West Point, New York, 1995). For recent developments, see D'Ann Campbell, "The Spirit Run and Football Cordon: A Case Study of Female Cadets at the U.S. Military Academy," in *Forging the Sword: Selecting, Educating, and Training Cadets and Junior Officers in the Modern World*, ed. Elliot V. Converse (Chicago: Imprint Publications, 1998). The other military academies discussed so far, VMI and The Citadel, behaved even more embarrassingly fully twenty years later. The Citadel was forced by public opinion to accept the first female cadet in 1995 and she was promptly run out by the Corps of Cadets in one week. After a massive campaign championing the former alumni and now famous writer Pat Conroy and a tremendous drop in enlistment numbers, the institution relented. VMI even defied a court decision to accept female "keydets" but also had to give in after the Department of Defense threatened to withdraw funds if the institute should remain to behave in an unconstitutional manner. The story is found in Philippa Strum, *Women in the Barracks: The VMI Case and Equal Rights* (Lawrence: University Press of Kansas, 2002).

114. U'Ren, *Ivory Fortress*, xi–xiv; Ed Berger et al., "ROTC, My Lai and the Volunteer Army," in *The Military and Society: A Collection of Essays*, ed. Peter Karsten (New York: Garland, 1998), 150.

115. U'Ren, *Ivory Fortress*, 19.

116. Ibid., 53.

117. The definition of the United States Naval Academy was much tighter and less slippery. Still, the Naval Academy's freshmen suffered from hazing, too. See David Edwin Lebby, "Professional

Socialization of the Naval Officer: The Effect of Plebe Year at the U.S. Naval Academy" (Ph.D. diss., University of Pennsylvania, 1970), 68–69. Unfortunately, Lebby's study is also not very critical regarding the phenomenon.

118. Reeder, *West Point Plebe*, 23–24.

119. Mullaney, *The Unforgiving Minute*, 36.

120. *West Point Demerit Book, 27 April 1912–9 August 1916*, Norman D. Cota Papers, Box 5, Dwight D. Eisenhower Library, Abilene, Kansas. The book shows numerous ridiculous reasons for demerits the first classmen put on the younger cadets. Norman "Dutch" Cota, USMA 1917, was only responsible for the last part of the book. He would become famous as assistant division commander of the 29th Infantry Division, when his leadership broke the stalemate on his part of the Normandy beaches where he had landed with the first waves on D-Day. Then and there he coined the famous motto that would be adopted by the Ranger Regiment, "Rangers lead the way," when he asked them to lead the charge at the beach fortifications. Cota was one of the few officers in the U.S. Army who had planned and war-gamed large-scale landing operations before the war. His fame would be hurt during the Battle of the Bulge when he commanded the 28th Infantry Division in what was thought to be an inflexible manner. Cota was approached by 20th Century Fox when the making of the famous war movie *The Longest Day* was planned. He refused to allow any character to play him for quite a time but finally relented when Robert Mitchum was selected for the role.

121. Holley, "Training and Educating Pre-World War I United States Army Officers," 27; *West Point Demerit Book, 27 April 1912 – 9 August 1916*.

122. Anders, *Gentle Knight*, 18.

123. Coffman, *The Regulars*, 176.

124. *Letter from James A. Van Fleet to J. Hardin Peterson, July 24, 1943*, James A. Van Fleet Papers, Box 42, Folder Postings—Fort Dix, New Jersey, Correspondence, July 1943, George C. Marshall Library, Lexington, Virginia.

125. Eisenhower, *Strictly Personal*, 36.

126. Ibid., 39.

127. *Letter from Joe Lawton Collins to his son Joseph "Jerry" Easterbrook,* July 30, 1943, Joe Lawton Collins Papers, Box 2, Folder 201 File— Personal Letter File—1943 (4), Dwight D. Eisenhower Library, Abilene, Kansas.

128. Holley, "Training and Educating Pre-World War I United States Army Officers," 28.

129. Reeder, *West Point Plebe*, 131–132. The roots for this dull and boring procedure, as well as for the fanatical focus on memorizing data, lay in the unfortunate "Thayer-System": John Philip Lovell, "The Cadet Phase of the Professional Socialization of the West Pointer: Description, Analysis, and Theoretical Refinement" (Ph.D. diss., University of Wisconsin, 1962), 34–36, 49–50. Lovell got, for this time, for his study a surprisingly high level of support from the United States Military Academy. That he was a West Pointer himself, USMA 1955, helped certainly as much as the fact that the plebe system is treated largely uncritically. His otherwise very interesting study defines professional socialization rather broadly and deals with questions of worldview rather than of military thinking and abilities. It is therefore not directly applicable to my findings.

130. Brown, *Social Attitudes*, 21.

131. Ganoe, *MacArthur Close-Up*, 97.

132. Nye, "Era of Educational Reform," 40.

133. Coffman, *The Regulars*, 147. Simpson would command the Ninth Army in World War II.

134. Jerome H. Parker IV, "Fox Conner and Dwight Eisenhower: Mentoring and Application," *Military Review* (July–August 2005): 93.

135. Miles, *Fallen Leaves*, 179.

136. Ibid.

137. Collins, *Lightning Joe*, 43.

138. Ibid.

139. Ibid.

140. Ridgway, *Soldier*, 32.

141. Miles, *Fallen Leaves*, 7. Miles cites then Captain J. Franklin Bell who would rise to position of chief of staff of the army. Bell made his statement in regard to the Spanish-American War.

142. "'Splendid, wonderful' says Joffre admiring the West Point cadets," *New York Times*, May 12, 1917; Ridgway, *Soldier*, 33. *Maréchal de France* Henri Philippe Pétain, the savior of Verdun in World War I, offered in private more criticism at West Point than his predecessor Joffre after his visit on October 25, 1931. He feared that "this monotony [of the teachings at West Point] must result in fixing the graduate's mind into a groove so rigid that elasticity becomes impaired." Mott, *Twenty Years*, 44.

143. Ridgway, *Soldier*, 33.

144. Genung, "Foreign Languages," 514–516.

145. Nye, "Era of Educational Reform," 189.

146. Frank J. Walton, "The West Point Centennial: A Time for Healing," in *West Point: Two Centuries and Beyond*, ed. Lance A. Betros (Abilene, Texas: McWhiney Foundation Press, 2004), 209.

147. Miles, *Fallen Leaves*, 168.

148. *Monk Dickson West Point Diary*. Entry from Sept. 21, 1917. Captain Harold Wood Huntley, USMA 1906, is listed as having been an instructor for mathematics at West Point only from 1910 to 1912. However, as there was only one Huntley as a mathematics instructor, Dickson is obviously right and the Register of Graduates is mistaken. See *Biographical Register of the United States Military Academy: The Classes, 1802–1926*. (West Point, New York: West Point Association of Graduates, 2002), 92.

149. Anders, *Gentle Knight*, 11. The description originates from Edwin Forrest Harding, who graduated in 1909, a classmate of George S. Patton, and rose to the rank of major general.

150. Holley, "Training and Educating Pre-World War I United States Army Officers," 30.

151. Nye, "Era of Educational Reform," 52–53.

152. *Annual Report of the Superintendent of the United States Military Academy*, 4–5.

153. Ganoe, *MacArthur Close-Up*, 61–63, 95–97.

154. Anonymous, "Inbreeding at West Point," *Infantry Journal* 16 (1919): 341.

155. *Annual Report of the Superintendent of the United States Military Academy*, 4.

156. Walter Crosby Eells and Austin Carl Cleveland, "Faculty Inbreeding: Extent, Types and Trends in American Colleges and Universities," *Journal of Higher Education* 6, no. 5 (1935): 262.

157. Ibid., 262. "Inbreeding" in this study is defined as hiring an individual for a teaching position who has earned at least one degree from the same institution.

158. Linn, "Challenge and Change," 246.

159. Ibid. The United States Naval Academy at Annapolis, Maryland, was at the same time doing much better in this respect. It featured three times as many faculty members with doctorates and nearly half of the faculty had at least a master's degree. These numbers even rose significantly five years later. See Lebby, "Professional Socialization of the Naval Officer," 83.

160. Holden, "The Library of the United States Military Academy, 1777–1906," 46–47. Holden, USMA 1870, was another of the inbred.

161. Norris, "Leslie R. Groves," 112.

162. Chynoweth, *Bellamy Park*, 70; Paul F. Braim, *The Will to Win: The Life of General James A. Van Fleet* (Annapolis, Maryland: Naval Institute Press, 2001), 15.

163. Chynoweth, *Bellamy Park*, 118.

164. Nye, "Era of Educational Reform," 108.

165. Ibid., 108–109.

166. Braim, *The Will to Win*, 14.

167. Eisenhower, *Strictly Personal*, 45–46.

168. Ronald P. Elrod, "The Cost of Educating a Cadet at West Point," (research paper submitted to the faculty of the United States Military Academy, History Department, West Point, New York, 1994), 9.

169. Eisenhower, *Strictly Personal*, 48.

170. A different opinion is found in Skelton, *Profession of Arms*, 167.

171. Mott, *Twenty Years*, 30.

172. Nye, "Era of Educational Reform," 337.

173. Ibid., 336–337.

174. It is an old cadet phrase and the "120" can be substituted by any number of years. See Stokam, Lori A. "The Fourth Class System: 192 Years of Tradition Unhampered by Progress from Within" (research paper submitted to the faculty of the United States Military Academy, History Department, West Point, New York, 1994). Stokam's paper is devastatingly critical toward the "plebe system." It is also a very courageous account. Though called a historical research paper, her work deals also with the recent changes in the "plebe system" and the lack of leadership at West Point.

175. Eisenhower, *Strictly Personal*, 98.

176. Eiler, *Mobilizing America*, 455–456.

177. Samuel A. Stouffer et al., eds. *The American Soldier: Adjustment during Army Life*, 4 vols., Studies in Social Psychology in World War II (Princeton, New Jersey: Princeton University Press, 1949), 1:56.

178. John Philip Lovell, "The Professional Socialization of the West Point Cadet," in *The New Military: Changing Patterns of Organization*, ed. Morris Janowitz (New York: Russell Sage Foundation, 1964), 135. The number is for the years from 1945 to 1960.

179. *Letter from John Raaen to Phil Whitney, July 8, 1944*, Norman D. Cota Papers, Box 1, Folder Personal File Correspondence 1944–1954 (2), 1, Dwight D. Eisenhower Library, Abilene, Kansas. Captain Raaen, USMA 1943, commanded a Ranger Company on D-Day, right at the side of Norman D. Cota, USMA 1917. Raaen would return to West Point as an instructor from 1945–1948 and many years later retire as a major general.

180. Ridgway, *Soldier*, 300.

181. *Letter of William R. Smith to Floyd L. Parks, December 27, 1937*, Floyd L. Parks Papers, Box 4, Folder Correspondence 1913-165, Dwight D. Eisenhower Library, Abilene, Kansas. Smith, USMA 1892, was at that time superintendent of the Sewanee Military Academy, Sewanee, Tennessee, and obviously anything but an agent of reform at this institution. He had been superintendent of West

Point from 1928 to 1932. Floyd L. "Parksie" Parks had not attended the USMA but his older brother Lyman graduated from the Academy in 1917.

182. MacArthur, *Reminiscences*, 81.

183. Harry N. Kerns, "Cadet Problems," *Mental Hygiene* 7 (1923): 689. Major Kerns was one of the first psychiatrists detailed to West Point. His speech was read at the 79th meeting of the American Psychiatric Association in Detroit, June 20, 1923, and remarkable because West Point always has shielded itself from the outside. His very frank—though often glorifying—remarks were deemed so important that they were published simultaneously in Mental Hygiene and the *American Journal of Psychiatry*. Interestingly, one of Kerns successor's fifty years later echoes many of his thoughts, which shows clearly how little has changed at the Academy. See: U'Ren, *Ivory Fortress*, 134–140.

184. Kerns, "Cadet Problems," 696.

185. Nye, "Era of Educational Reform," 295.

186. Stouffer et al., eds. *The American Soldier: Adjustment during Army Life*, 381.

187. Bland and Ritenour, eds., *"The Soldierly Spirit,"* 252.

188. Stouffer et al., eds. *The American Soldier: Adjustment during Army Life*, 380. A great part of the book deals with the problem. See especially chapter 8, "Attitudes toward Leadership and Social Control."

189. Bland and Ritenour, eds., *"The Soldierly Spirit."*

190. Brown, *Social Attitudes*, 22.

191. The report is cited in Stouffer et al., eds. *The American Soldier: Adjustment during Army Life*, 381. Exactly the same leadership problems that had been noted by Fosdick in World War I were noted by the sociologists in World War II.

192. Ibid., 381.

193. Bland and Ritenour, eds., *"The Soldierly Spirit,"* 455.

194. Ibid., 680. Marshall recommended Harold Roe "Pink" Bull, USMA 1914, as superintendent. Bull became in World War II the much-criticized G-3 or operations officer of Eisenhower at SHAEF.

195. Michael T. Boone, "The Academic Board and the Failure to Progress at the United States Military Academy" (research paper submitted to the faculty of the United States Military Academy, History Department, West Point, New York, 1994), 5.

196. In addition, physically fit cadets had it easier in general at West Point: Lloyd Otto Appleton, "The Relationship between Physical Ability and Success at the United States Military Academy" (Ph.D. diss., New York University, 1949).

197. *Charles L. Bolté interviewed by Arthur J. Zoebelein*, undated, Senior Officers Oral History Program, U.S. Army Military History Institute, Carlisle, Pennsylvania; Ridgway, *Soldier*, 27.

THREE "To Learn How to Die": *Kadetten* in Germany

1. Ernst von Salomon, *Die Kadetten* (Berlin: Rowohlt, 1933), 28–29. The greeting was in no way uncommon. A slightly different version is found in Emilio Willems, *A Way of Life and Death: Three Centuries of Prussian-German Militarism: An Anthropological Approach* (Nashville, Tennessee: Vanderbilt University Press, 1986), 78. I appreciate it that Ronald Smelser pointed this book out to me. See also Holger H. Herwig, "'You are here to learn how to die': German Subaltern Officer Education on the Eve of the Great War," in *Forging the Sword: Selecting, Educating, and Training Cadets and Junior Officers in the Modern World*, ed. Elliot V. Converse (Chicago: Imprint Publications, 1998).

2. Hans R. G. Günther, *Begabung und Leistung in deutschen Soldaten-geschlechtern*, Wehrpsychologische Arbeiten 9 (Berlin: Bernard & Graefe, 1940). The booklet contains racist idioms and Nazi jargon and tries to sound scholarly. The author was a professor at the University of Berlin and the study was created by an assignment from the Inspector General of the *Wehrmacht*. The study has no scientific background but simply names all the old German soldier families and their accomplishments and concludes that old soldiers' families with successful members are likely to produce more successful soldiers.

3. John McCain and Mark Salter, *Faith of My Fathers* (New York: Random House, 1999).

4. Holger H. Herwig, "Feudalization of the Bourgeoisie: The Role of the Nobility in the German Naval Officer Corps, 1890–1918," in *The Military and Society: A Collection of Essays*, ed. Peter Karsten (New York: Garland, 1998), 53, 55.

5. Daniel J. Hughes, "Occupational Origins of Prussia's Generals, 1870–1914," *Central European History* 13, no. 1 (1980): 5.

6. Horst Boog, "Civil Education, Social Origins, and the German Officer Corps in the Nineteenth and Twentieth Centuries," in *Forging the Sword: Selecting, Educating, and Training Cadets and Junior Officers in the Modern World*, ed. Elliot V. Converse (Chicago: Imprint Publications, 1998), 128.

7. Ibid., 128.

8. Bernhard R. Kroener, "Auf dem Weg zu einer "nationalsozialistischen Volksarmee": Die soziale Öffnung des Heeresoffizierkorps im Zweiten Weltkrieg," in *Von Stalingrad zur Währungsreform: Zur Sozialgeschichte des Umbruchs in Deutschland,* eds. Martin Broszat, Klaus-Dietmar Henke, and Hans Woller (München: Oldenbourg, 1988).

9. Clemente, "Making of the Prussian Officer," 56.

10. Nye, "Era of Educational Reform," 133–134.

11. Herwig, "Feudalization of the Bourgeoisie," 55.

12. In Prussia, Potsdam, the famous former residence of Frederick the Great, twelve miles southwest of Berlin; Wahlstatt, today in Poland and named Legnickie Pole; Bensberg, Nordrhein-Westfalen, just south of Bergisch-Gladbach; Oranienstein, at Diez, Hessen, between Frankfurt and Koblenz; Naumburg, Sachsen-Anhalt, between Jena and Leipzig; Köslin, a large coastal city in today's Poland and now named Koszalin; and Plön, Schleswig-Holstein, about sixteen miles south east of Kiel.

13. These are only the Prussian *Kadettenschulen*; other German states had their own facilities, like the Bavarians in München, for example.

14. Karl-Hermann Freiherr von Brand and Helmut Eckert, *Kadetten: Aus 300 Jahren deutscher Kadettenkorps*, 2 vols. (München: Schild, 1981), 1:156.

15. Ibid. These are numbers for the Prussian Army only and do not contain reserve officers. Torsten Diedrich, *Paulus: Das Trauma von Stalingrad* (Paderborn: Schöningh, 2008), 74.

16. *Generalfeldmarschall Werner von Blomberg,* War Minister; *Generalfeldmarschall* Fedor von Bock, Commander of *Heeresgruppe Mitte; Generalfeldmarschall* Walther von Brauchitsch, Commander in Chief (CinC) of the Army; *Generalfeldmarschall* Hans Günther von Kluge, Commander in Chief (CinC) West; *Generalfeldmarschall* Wolfram Freiherr von Richthofen, Commander of *Luftflotte 2; Generalfeldmarschall* Gerd von Rundstedt, CinC West; General Walther Wenck, *Generalfeldmarschall* Erwin von Witzleben, CinC West, Commander of 12. Army; *Generaloberst* Hans Jeschonnek, Chief of Staff (CoS) of the *Luftwaffe; Generaloberst* Johannes Blaskowitz, Commander of *Heeresgruppe* H; *Oberstgruppenführer* Paul Hausser, Commander of *Heeresgruppe* G; *Generaloberst* Hermann Hoth, Commander of 4. *Panzerarmee; Generaloberst* Alfred Jodl, *Chef des Wehrmachtsführungsstabes; Generaloberst* Kurt Student, CinC of the Paratrooper Forces; General Hasso von Manteuffel, Commander of 3. *Panzerarmee;* General Siegfried Westphal, CoS CinC West. The list contains only some of the most important and well-known commanders of World War II, who had been cadets. There is an equally impressive number for Germany's and Prussia's earlier wars, which indicates the importance of the *Kadettencorps.* For an exhaustive treatment of the alumni, see Brand and Eckert, *Kadetten,* vol. 1.

    Ibid. It should be noted that the officials Joachim Haupt and Reinhard Sunkel, who were responsible for establishing the Nazi elite schools—the *Nationalpolitische Erziehungsanstalten*—were former cadets. See Schmitz, *Militärische Jugenderziehung,* 12.

17. Herwig, "'You are here to learn how to die': German Subaltern Officer Education on the Eve of the Great War," 34.

18. Notable exception: John Moncure, *Forging the King's Sword: Military Education between Tradition and Modernization: The Case of the Royal Prussian Cadet Corps, 1871–1918* (New York: Lang, 1993). The author, USMA 1972, makes the same point in his introduction. His book is carefully researched and he turned up an astonishing

number of cadet memoirs. Clemente, "Making of the Prussian Officer." Clemente's work suffers from the author's intent to pack to much in one book and the fact that the author repeatedly falls victim to a host of Prussian clichés and the outdated historiography about Old Prussia.

See also Schmitz, *Militärische Jugenderziehung*. Schmitz deals exhaustively with the curriculum of the *Kadettenanstalten* but is less concerned with the daily lives of the cadets.

19. Moncure, *Forging the King's Sword*, 58.
20. Ibid., 207–209. Moncure answers with this correct statement his own earlier question about the reason for the existence of the *Voranstalten*.
21. Friedrich Franz von Unruh, *Ehe die Stunde schlug: Eine Jugend im Kaiserreich* (Bodensee: Hohenstaufen, 1967), 106.
22. Boog, "Civil Education, Social Origins, and the German Officer Corps," 82, 90–91.
23. Schmitz, *Militärische Jugenderziehung*, 123–124. The whole educational system of the *Kadettenschulen* and its historical developments as well as the public and internal discussion is covered in this work.
24. Ibid., 85.
25. Ibid., 89.
26. A detailed daily schedule for the *Voranstalt* Köslin in 1915 is found in Moncure, *Forging the King's Sword*, 110.
27. Manstein, *Soldatenleben*, 12–14. A brief discussion of the impact of his ancestry as well as a more detailed new assessment of von Manstein's command and leadership capabilities is found at Jörg Muth, "Erich von Lewinski, called von Manstein: His Life, Character and Operations—A Reappraisal," http://www.axishistory.com/index.php?id=7901.
28. Unruh, *Ehe die Stunde schlug*, 58.
29. Ibid., 60.
30. See the tables and explanations in Moncure, *Forging the King's Sword*, 61, 84, 90–91. Unfortunately, in the table of the father's occupation, the author does not distinguish the civil servant classes. This

would be very important because it determines if a son would originate from an officer-capable strata or not.

The significance is made quite clear in a detailed discussion in
Reinhard Stumpf, *Die Wehrmacht-Elite: Rang- und Herkunftsstruktur
der deutschen Generale und Admirale 1933–1945*, Wehrwissenschaftliche Forschungen, Abteilung Militärgeschichtliche Studien 29
(Boppard a. R.: Boldt, 1982), 204–229. Stumpf, however, is cited
in Moncure's bibliography.

31. Clemente, "Making of the Prussian Officer," 157–158; Schmitz,
    Militärische Jugenderziehung, 12.

32. Hans-Jochen Markmann, *Kadetten: Militärische Jugenderziehung in
    Preußen* (Berlin: Pädagogisches Zentrum, 1983), 42. For the impor-
    tance of being treated as an adult, see Salomon, *Die Kadetten*, 48.

    The author's account is remarkable because of its detail and
    enormous eloquence. The tale becomes especially gripping when war
    breaks out and only the youngest are left behind and immediately
    the first stories of the deaths of their comrades reach the *Kadetten-
    anstalt*. Later the wounded and maimed survivors come back to see
    again their younger comrades. Salomon missed World War I be-
    cause of his youth and volunteered for one of the infamous *Freikorps*
    roaming the Polish border and in the Baltic. After a year of fight-
    ing, he returned and helped build a "resistance movement," which
    sometimes supported the Nazis and created all kinds of mischief
    and even terrorism.

    When one of the resistance leaders proposed to kill German
    Secretary of State Walther Rathenau to set an example, Salomon
    agreed to help, despite his admiration for the writings of the politi-
    cian. At no cost would he let his friends down. He provided a driver
    for the car of the killers who was, however, sent away. This fact would
    later save him countless years in prison. The assassination succeeded
    and Salomon was later caught and sentenced to five years. During
    his prison time, his participation in an attempted *Fememord*—a mur-
    der of a supposed traitor—was discovered. Salomon, however, stopped
    the attempt after a vicious fight with the victim. He was sentenced to

264

another three years, which he did not have to serve, because the judicial branch wanted to play nice with the growing Nazi party and Salomon was considered a "political" prisoner and released after the initial five years. His story can be found in Salomon, *Die Geächteten*. Better than any history work, it helps to understand why the majority of a young generation fell for the Nazis.

When Hitler came to power, the men formerly considered murderers (only the driver and Salomon had survived) and their helpers became national heroes (Rathenau was also a Jew). Salomon ducked low and became one member of the silent majority who knew most of what was going on and did nothing during the horrible reign of the Third Reich. He was even able to cover for his Jewish girlfriend whom he displayed as his wife.

After World War II, he walked back into the limelight after writing *Der Fragebogen* (*The Questionnaire*), a book that dealt critically with the 131-page list of questions the Allies distributed to determine the level of guilt of a German. *Der Fragebogen* was an apologetic attempt with racist and xenophobic tendencies (already apparent in his earlier works) and became the first German postwar bestseller. For a very critical review, see "It Just Happened: Review of Ernst von Salomon's book *The Questionnaire*," *Time*, Monday, Jan. 10, 1955.

33. Brand and Eckert, *Kadetten*, vol. 1, 151, 167.

34. Clemente, "Making of the Prussian Officer," 225.

35. Felix Dhünen, *Als Spiel begann's: Die Geschichte eines Münchener Kadetten* (München: Beck, 1939), 17. Though Dhünen's account is written as a novel, he graduated from the *Kadettenschule* in München that he describes so vividly in his book. The author was born in Hessen and the reason he did not go to the Prussian institution was the higher level of education expected at the Bavarian school and a more easygoing daily life. It seems that his judgment was correct when his story is compared with the accounts in Markmann, *Kadetten*, and Brand and Eckert, *Kadetten*, vol. 1.

36. Schmitz, *Militärische Jugenderziehung*, 144.

37. Dhünen, *Als Spiel begann's*, 42; Brand and Eckert, Kadetten, vol. 1, 307; Leopold von Wiese, *Kadettenjahre* (Ebenhausen: Langewiesche, 1978), 67; Salomon, *Die Kadetten*, 89.

38. This custom existed in the Prussian Army since the days of Frederick the Great's father. See Muth, *Flucht aus dem militärischen Alltag*, 70–71.

39. Unruh, *Ehe die Stunde schlug*, 63, 87; Salomon, *Die Kadetten*, 60–63.

40. Salomon, *Die Kadetten*, 193; Unruh, *Ehe die Stunde schlug*, 62–64.

41. Markmann, *Kadetten*, 102; Unruh, *Ehe die Stunde schlug*, 132–133.

42. Ganoe, *MacArthur Close-Up*, 110.

43. Moncure, *Forging the King's Sword*, 182–184, 191–192.

44. Schmitz, *Militärische Jugenderziehung*, 145.

45. Though the topic of homosexuality was usually touched on by scholars who wrote about military academies when they were still exclusively male, there have been no further scholarly inquiries. Some assumptions about homosexual problems, however, disappear because the author was not able to read the language of the past properly. *"Zu Unsittlichkeiten verleitet werden"* (tempted to commit an immoral act) meant at this time "entice to masturbate" and not sexual intercourse with another male. See Markmann, *Kadetten*, 100–101. The same "problem" of masturbation in Wiese, *Kadettenjahre*, 69. Homoerotic encounters are spelled out crystal clear in Salomon, *Die Kadetten*, 194–195, 198. Wiese, *Kadettenjahre*, 85–86.

46. Dhünen, *Als Spiel begann's*, 56. Salomon, *Die Kadetten*, 33.

47. Unruh, *Ehe die Stunde schlug*, 62–64. At least five of the Unruh brothers attended the cadet schools. Obviously, the older brothers failed to prepare their younger siblings properly. Friedrich Franz (1893–1986), who wrote this memoir, stepped into the Badische Leib-Grenadier-Regiment No. 109 as an ensign right after finishing the cadet academy in 1911, which he had attended for six years. He fought in World War I, became decorated for valor, and rose to the rank of company commander in the same regiment. Like his

older brother Fritz (1885–1970), who also attended the *Kadetten-schule* and fought in the war, he became a known novelist and writer. Fritz's first drama, *Die Offiziere* (1912), dealt already with the military and the conscience of the commander and was highly successful in its time. Fritz fled Germany in 1932 and had the honor of his books being burned by the Nazis, which usually meant they were good and critical. He returned publicly only in 1948 when he gave the controversial and highly emotional *Rede an die Deutschen* (speech to the Germans) in which he damned the society and education in the emperor's Germany, including the *Kadettenschulen*, making him lots of enemies in the ranks of former cadets. Interestingly, at the *Kadettenschule*, Fritz was an elder—he would speak for the whole group of cadets—in the same class that Erich von Manstein attended. Manstein describes him as a *Musterkadett* (cadet role model). Fritz achieved several awards and even became *Erziehungskamerad* (education comrade) of the Prussian Prince Oskar, an assignment an ordinary cadet would not get. Though Manstein himself is not uncritical toward the cadet schools, he is greatly annoyed by the extreme statements of Fritz describing them as a mixture of "poet's fantasy, resentment, originating from his political development, and ungratefulness." See Manstein, *Soldatenleben*, 21–23.

48. Markmann, *Kadetten*, 32.

49. Wiese, *Kadettenjahre*, 37. It apparently caused no problem when they went to the frontlines. See Salomon, *Die Kadetten*, 211.

50. Brand and Eckert, *Kadetten*, vol. 1, 313.

51. Only three at the *Kadettenschule* in München, four in Karlsruhe. Another translation would be "censor class": Moncure, *Forging the King's Sword*, 190. Though the basic educational and disciplinary system was the same in all schools, each had its own identity. Snowball fights were encouraged in Berlin-Lichterfelde but forbidden in Wahlstatt. The latter seemed to have had the greatest leadership problems and was the least desirable for cadets. In Karlsruhe, the servants were not allowed to help the *Kadetten* to tend their uniforms.

52. Brand and Eckert, *Kadetten*, vol. 1, 179; Unruh, *Ehe die Stunde schlug*, 100.

53. Markmann, *Kadetten*, 42.

54. Moncure, *Forging the King's Sword*, 202–203. Company commanders got 4 *Reichsmark* a month, NCOs, 3; privates, 1,5; and regular cadets, 1.

55. Salomon, *Die Kadetten*, 206; Wiese, *Kadettenjahre*, 89–90.

56. Moncure, *Forging the King's Sword*, 190–191.

57. Mott, *Twenty Years*, 25.

58. Kroener, *Generaloberst Friedrich Fromm*, 225.

59. Ibid., 225.

60. Salomon, *Die Kadetten*, 50.

61. Markmann, *Kadetten*, 140.

62. *Charakterologie* is the pseudoscience invented by *Wehrmacht* psychologists. See Max Simoneit, *Grundriss der charakterologischen Diagnostik auf Grund heerespsychologischer Erfahrungen* (Leipzig: Teubner, 1943). All of those works of Wehrmacht psychologists and those from the series of *Wehrpsychologische Arbeiten* have strong racist and Nazi-supporting tendencies. Challenged after the war, the former head of the *Wehrpsychologische Institut*, Hans von Voss, and one of his leading psychiatrists, Max Simoneit, claim that "the *Wehrmacht* psychology has even after 1933 not become a national socialist institution.": Hans von Voss and Max Simoneit, "Die psychologische Eignungsuntersuchung in der deutschen Reichswehr und später der Wehrmacht," *Wehrwissenschaftliche Rundschau* 4, no. 2 (1954): 140. Simoneit seems to think that his many publications during the Third Reich have been forgotten. Sixteen years earlier, in one of those, he stated, "The here for psychological reasons developed requests [on the character of an officer aspirant] for self education conform with the general ideals of the national socialist Reich.": Max Simoneit *Leitgedanken über die psychologische Untersuchung des Offizier-Nachwuchses in der Wehrmacht*, Wehrpsychologische Arbeiten 6 (Berlin: Bernard & Graefe, 1938), 29.

63. Moncure, *Forging the King's Sword*, 186.

64. Constantly confused in Clemente, "Making of the Prussian Officer," 87, 92–94, 161, 167.

65. Hermann Teske, *Die silbernen Spiegel: Generalstabsdienst unter der Lupe* (Heidelberg: Vowinckel, 1952), 28. Teske's relatively sober account of his time as a General Staff officer stands in stark contrast to his jubilant and Nazi-friendly earlier book: Hermann Teske, *Wir marschieren für Großdeutschland: Erlebtes und Erlauschtes aus dem großen Jahre 1938* (Berlin: Die Wehrmacht, 1939).

66. Simoneit, *Leitgedanken über die psychologische Untersuchung des Offizier-Nachwuchses in der Wehrmacht*, 18, 26–27.

67. This feature of the German officer corps got its own book title. See Ursula Breymayer, ed. *Willensmenschen: Über deutsche Offiziere*, Fischer-Taschenbücher (Frankfurt a. M.: Fischer, 1999).

68. H. Masuhr, *Psychologische Gesichtspunkte für die Beurteilung von Offizieranwärtern*, Wehrpsychologische Arbeiten 4 (Berlin: Bernard & Graefe, 1937), 18–20, 25, 32.

69. Anne C. Loveland, "Character Education in the U.S. Army, 1947–1977," *Journal of Military History* 64 (2000).

70. Salomon, *Die Kadetten*, 28–29. See also Marcus Funck, „In den Tod gehen—Bilder des Sterbens im 19. und 20. Jahrhundert," in *Willensmenschen*: Über deutsche Offiziere, ed. Ursula Breymayer (Frankfurt a. M.: Fischer, 1999).

71. Salomon, *Die Kadetten*, 40.

72. Bucholz, *Delbrück's Modern Military History*, 61.

73. Stephen E. Ambrose, *Citizen Soldiers: The U.S. Army from the Normandy Beaches to the Bulge to the Surrender of Germany, June 7, 1944–May 7, 1945* (New York: Simon & Schuster, 1997), 165–166. Similar observations have been made by various war correspondents.

74. *Letter from Major General M. G. White, Assitant Chief of Staff, to John E. Dahlquist, March 11, 1944*, John E. Dahlquist Papers, Box 1, U.S. Army Military History Institute, Carlisle, Pennsylvania.

75. Stouffer et al., eds. *The American Soldier: Adjustment during Army Life*, 193, 196–197, 201, 368–374.

76. Peter S. Kindsvatter, *American Soldiers: Ground Combat in the World Wars, Korea and Vietnam* (Lawrence: University Press of Kansas,

2003), 235–236, 238, 242. The book unfortunately suffers from the great spectrum it tries to cover. None of the good leaders who are cited have a rank higher than captain. Interestingly, the author has not used Stouffer's surveys for his book.

77. Stefanie Schüler-Springorum, "Die Legion Condor in (auto-)biographischen Zeugnissen," in *Militärische Erinnerungskultur: Soldaten im Spiegel von Biographien, Memoiren und Selbstzeugnissen*, ed. Michael Epkenhans, Stig Förster, and Karen Hagemann (Paderborn: Schöningh, 2006), 230.

78. Karl-Heinz Frieser, *Blitzkrieg-Legende. Der Westfeldzug 1940*, Operationen des Zweiten Weltkrieges 2 (München: Oldenbourg, 1995), 337–339.

79. This fact was frequently noted by Allied intelligence on all levels. See, for example, *Intelligence Notes No. 54, Allied Forces Headquarters, April 11, 1944*, RG 492, Records of Mediterranean Theater of Operations, United States Army (MTOUSA), Box 57, Folder Intelligence Notes & Directives, C 5, National Archives II, College Park, Maryland.

80. R. D. Heinl, "They Died with Their Boots on," *Armed Forces Journal* 107, no. 30 (1970). Russell K. Brown, *Fallen in Battle: American General Officer Combat Fatalities from 1775* (New York: Greenwood Press, 1988). R. Manning Ancell and Christine Miller, *The Biographical Dictionary of World War II Generals and Flag Officers: The U.S. Armed Forces* (Westport, Connecticut: Greenwood Press, 1996). The poor state of research on the American officer corps is shown in the contradiction of numbers of the fallen. Literature above has numbers from sixteen to twenty-one and in some cases the rank is even unclear. The phrases used muddy the water even more. While "killed in combat" or "combat fatality" is pretty clear, "killed in action" stretches the possibilities. Brown's study seems to be the most solid. He counts twenty-one, but in my view William O. Darby has to be excluded because he was promoted to brigadier general posthumously. Brown counts only thirty-four wounded in action, including generals from the Marine Corps, pp. 203–205.

81. French L. Maclean, *Quiet Flows the Rhine: German General Officer Casualties in World War II* (Winnipeg, Manitoba: Fedorowicz, 1996). MacLean has written some other rather "popular" history about the Wehrmacht and Waffen-SS. He relies heavily on the problematic Josef Folttmann and Hans Möller-Witten, *Opfergang der Generale*, 3rd ed., Schriften gegen Diffamierung und Vorurteile (Berlin: Bernard & Graefe, 1957). Folttmann, a retired *Generalleutnant* of the *Wehrmacht*, wrote his pamphlet while the discussion about the "new" officer corps of the just-founded *Bundeswehr* was raging in Germany and he has the clear agenda of reestablishing the prestige of the German officer corps. The foreword was written by *Generalfeldmarschall* Gerd von Rundstedt. There was considerable resistance against the employment of Hitler's generals for the Federal Republic of Germany. Not the least, the pressure of the American military was responsible for the fact that finally 100 percent of all generals of the *Bundeswehr* had served in the *Wehrmacht*. The number I have given is a very conservative estimate and about 45 below that given by Folttmann.

82. Aleksander A. Maslov, *Fallen Soviet Generals: Soviet General Officers Killed in Battle, 1941–1945* (London: Cass, 1998). Maslov gives the number of 230. I did not, however, have time to check closely on the statistics of the book. I appreciate it that Yan Mann pointed this work out to me.

83. Harmon, MacKaye, and MacKaye, *Combat Commander*, 113.

84. Van Creveld, *Fighting Power*, 110. The author points out on the following page that "whereas in Germany it was more difficult for officers than for other ranks to earn the higher decorations, this was not the case in the U.S. Army."

85. *Combat Awards*, undated article draft, Bruce C. Clarke Papers, Combined Arms Research Library, Fort Leavenworth, Kansas.

86. Ganoe, *MacArthur Close-Up*, 146.

87. Stouffer et al., eds. *The American Soldier: Adjustment during Army Life*, 164–166. Compare the small percentage of U.S. Army officers who have seen combat. Obviously, casualties are not included in the survey. However, the survey shows a clear tendency.

88. Hans Joachim Schröder, *Kasernenzeit: Arbeiter erzählen von der Militärausbildung* (Frankfurt: Campus, 1985), 38. Hans Joachim Schröder, ed. *Max Landowski, Landarbeiter: Ein Leben zwischen Westpreußen und Schleswig-Holstein* (Berlin: Reimer, 2000), 35, 45.

89. Schröder, ed. *Max Landowski, Landarbeiter*, 53.

90. Förster, "The Dynamics of *Volksgemeinschaft*," 208–209.

91. Arnold Krammer, "American Treatment of German Generals During World War II," *Journal of Military History* 54, no. 1 (1990): 27.

92. Maclean, *Quiet Flows the Rhine: German General Officer Casualties in World War II*, 99. Presents this notion and also suggests that the *Wehrmacht* would have fought more effectively if a lesser number of generals had died. Exactly the opposite is the case.

93. Cited in Oetting, *Auftragstaktik*, 188.

94. Ibid., 284.

95. Cited in van Creveld, *Fighting Power*, 129.

96. Millett, "The United States Armed Forces in the Second World War," 76.

97. Eiler, *Mobilizing America*, 165–166.

98. Gerald Astor, *Terrible Terry Allen: Combat General of World War II: The Life of an American Soldier* (New York: Presidio, 2003), 270.

99. Van Creveld, *Fighting Power*, 168.

100. Stouffer, Samuel A., et al., eds. *The American Soldier: Combat and its Aftermath*, 4 vols., Studies in Social Psychology in World War II (Princeton, New Jersey: Princeton University Press, 1949), 2:124.

101. Stouffer et al., eds. *The American Soldier: Adjustment during Army Life*, 273.

102. Astor, *Terrible Terry Allen*, 257. The book is unfortunately a hagiographic account of Allen's life, like so many other biographies of American generals. While Allen was the controversial commander of the 1st Infantry Division in World War II and known for his drinking problem and boastful speeches, the fact that he was at the frontlines with his troops is undisputed. He was relieved of command for various controversial reasons but would later command the 104th Infantry Division in Europe.

103. *The American Field Officer*, Walter B. Smith Papers, Box 50, Folder Richardson Reports, 1944–1945, Dwight D. Eisenhower Library, Abilene, Kansas. Richardson was a veteran sergeant and war correspondent traveling the battlefields. He filed short essays on topics he deemed important directly to the highest places, namely Walter B. Smith, Ike's chief of staff, who trusted Richardson completely and occasionally took immediate action because of the contents of Richardson's reports. Such a procedure demonstrates the strength of the army of a democracy and was unthinkable in the *Wehrmacht*.

104. *Morale*, Walter B. Smith Papers, Box 50, Folder Richardson Reports, 1944–1945, Dwight D. Eisenhower Library, Abilene, Kansas.

105. *Memorandum of Discussion with Subordinate Commanders, CG Matthew B. Ridgway, XVIII Airborne Corps, January 13, 1945*, Matthew B. Ridgway Papers, Box 59, Folder XVIII Airborne Corps War Diary, United States Army Military History Institute, Carlisle, Pennsylvania. Ridgway targeted especially Major General Leland S. Hobbs, commander of the 30th Infantry Division, who tried to answer with a string of excuses ranging from bad weather to traffic problems but was cut off by Ridgway. Such a harsh and decisive treatment of subordinate commanders was a rarity in the U.S. Army. In the following memoranda, the topic of lacking leadership comes up again repeatedly. See also correspondence about the same problem in Boxes 17 and 21.

106. Letter from Jacob L. Devers to George C. Marshall, unreadable date [April/May 1944], Jacob L. Devers Papers, Box 1, Folder [Reel] 2, Dwight. D. Eisenhower Library, Abilene, Kansas. For the very reason of his critique Devers became an eternal enemy to Mark Clark, the commanding general of the theater of operations in Italy. See also the statement of Walter Bedell Smith about the general unwillingness of American officers to undertake counter attacks: Letter from Walter Bedell Smith to Thomas T. Handy, January 12, 1945, Thomas T. Handy Papers, Box 1, Folder Smith, Walter Bedell, 1944–1945, B-1/F-7, George C. Marshall Library, Lexington, Virginia.

107. At its greatest expansion in World War II, the U.S. Army fielded only eighty-nine divisions in twenty-four corps.

108. Wilson A. Heefner, *Patton's Bulldog: The Life and Service of General Walton H. Walker* (Shippensburg, Pennsylvania: White Mane Books, 2001), 91. Here Walker, one of Patton's corps commanders, complains about the regimental and battalion leadership in his corps after Patton had already voiced criticism. The lack of quality especially of the regimental commanders was a constant topic in the correspondence of the generals, especially when the fighting was hard. The story of the Battle of the Bulge is unfolded in Charles Brown MacDonald, *A Time for Trumpets: The Untold Story of the Battle of the Bulge* (Toronto, Ontario: Bantam Books, 1985). MacDonald's account is unique because he participated in the battle as a company commander before he became a historian for the U.S. Army. Shortly after the war he had already published his wartime memoir which has become a classic: Charles Brown MacDonald, Company Commander (Washington, D.C.: Infantry Journal Press, 1947).

109. *War Diary, XVIII Airborne Corps, 27 Dec., 1944, 0855 hrs*, Matthew B. Ridgway Papers, Box 59, U.S. Army Military History Institute, Carlisle, Pennsylvania. More problems with the fitness for command of regimental commanders: *Letter from John E. Dahlquist to Brigadier General Clyde L. Hyssong, April 29, 1944*, John E. Dahlquist Papers, Box 1, U.S. Army Military History Institute, Carlisle, Pennsylvania.

110. Schifferle, "Anticipating Armageddon," 50–51.

111. Coffman, *The Regulars*, 396–397; Schifferle, "Anticipating Armageddon," 153.

112. *Letter from George S. Patton to Thomas T. Handy, December 5, 1944*, Thomas T. Handy Papers, Box 1, George C. Marshall Library, Lexington, Virginia. Even the usually so direct Patton uses verbal gymnastics to get rid of one of his finest division commanders, John Shirley "P" Wood, USMA 1912, but at the same time tries not to hurt his career. Because Wood had made too many enemies along the way, including Omar N. Bradley and Manton S. Eddy, he went on to command a training center in the U.S. for two years and then retired.

113. Astor, *Terrible Terry Allen*, 149.

114. Wolfgang Lotz, *Kriegsgerichtsprozesse des Siebenjährigen Krieges in Preußen. Untersuchungen zur Beurteilung militärischer Leistungen durch Friedrich den II.* (Frankfurt a. M.; n.p., 1981).

115. Moncure, *Forging the King's Sword*, 263.

116. The course of a *Fähnrichsexamen* in the year of 1870 described in ibid., 236–237.

117. For more examples of questions asked at the exam, see the appendixes in Clemente, "Making of the Prussian Officer." Just like the examples in Moncure, however, they are from the nineteenth century.

118. Unruh, *Ehe die Stunde schlug*, 82. *Charakterisert* means the *Fähnrich* was not to be put into a regular chain of command yet—he was still an "apprentice ensign." In the Old Prussian Army most officers or officials of the same rank working for the military, like auditors (law counselors) and doctors, were allowed to carry sabers. The *Portepee* was a small rope of braided fabric that formed a loop for the wrist, so in the heat of the battle the saber would not get lost. Therefore, only the line officers who actually went into battle used it and distinguished themselves with it from other officials wearing uniforms. In the nineteenth century, it had become an ornamental status symbol for the officers, still marking those who would go into battle.

     The translation "brevet ensign" by Moncure comes close enough but does not grasp the title completely. An officer in the U.S. Army could command according to his brevet rank; a *charakterisierter Portepee-Fähnrich* could not. See Moncure, *Forging the King's Sword*, 16. The most important fact about this rank was that it marked the cadet as a serious officer aspirant—with a new and different uniform—who had shown that he will be an officer in the future if he did not seriously foul up and that granted him enormous prestige in Prussian and German society.

119. Highly biased but interesting because one of the very first treatises in German military sociology: Franz Carl Endres, "Soziologische Struktur und ihre entsprechenden Ideologien des deutschen Offizierkorps vor dem Weltkriege," *Archiv für Sozialwissenschaft und Sozialpolitik* 58 (1927).

The most modern research is found in Marcus Funck, „Schock und Chance: Der preußische Militäradel in der Weimarer Republik zwischen Stand und Profession," in *Adel und Bürgertum in Deutschland: Entwicklungslinien und Wendepunkte*, ed. Hans Reif (Berlin: Akademie, 2001). For data on the posting of cadets, see also Moncure, *Forging the King's Sword*, 242–256. Johannes Hürter, *Hitlers Heerführer: Die deutschen Oberbefehlshaber im Krieg gegen die Sowjetunion 1941/1942* (München: Oldenbourg, 2007), 619–669.

120. Unruh, *Ehe die Stunde schlug*, 106–107.

121. Moncure, *Forging the King's Sword*, 67.

122. Salomon, *Die Kadetten*, 243–248, 257–260.

123. Diedrich, *Paulus: Das Trauma von Stalingrad*, 43.

124. Ibid., 44.

125. Masuhr, *Psychologische Gesichtspunkte*, 22–24.

126. Brand and Eckert, *Kadetten*, vol. 1, 183.

127. Unruh, *Ehe die Stunde schlug*.

128. Brand and Eckert, *Kadetten*, vol. 1, 183, 188.

129. Moncure, *Forging the King's Sword*, 143, 147. It should be noted that Upton made his observation in the early 1870s when a regular *Abitur* from the *Hauptkadettenanstalt* was not yet possible. The reorganization to the schedule of a *Realgymnasium* took place in 1877. In contrast, in 1912, 65 percent of all German officer candidates held the *Abitur*, which carries more weight than a B.S. from West Point. A good discussion of the educational quality is in Moncure's chapter 5. The faculty at the *HKA* had obviously a much higher quality than that of the USMA.

130. Compare the statements of former cadets in Markmann, *Kadetten*, passim. The same words come up immediately in the introduction of Brand and Eckert, *Kadetten*, vol. 1. Also: Unruh, *Ehe die Stunde schlug*, 88. Manstein, *Soldatenleben*, 22; Salomon, *Die Kadetten*, 56.

131. Unruh, *Ehe die Stunde schlug*, 98.

132. Brand and Eckert, *Kadetten*, vol. 1, 314–315.

133. Ibid., 309.

134. Manstein, *Soldatenleben*, 22.

135. Ibid., 16.

136. This notion is supported by the fact that von Manstein in later years, even as a relatively junior officer, thought he could get away with basically everything. Oliver von Wrochem, *Erich von Manstein: Vernichtungskrieg und Geschichtspolitik* (Paderborn: Schöningh, 2009), 36. Manstein, *Soldatenleben*, 90–91, 114–115.

137. Brand and Eckert, *Kadetten*, vol. 1, 177, 186.

138. Salomon, *Die Kadetten*, 249.

139. Unruh, *Ehe die Stunde schlug*, 96.

140. Salomon, *Die Kadetten*, 21, 90.

141. Boog, "Civil Education, Social Origins, and the German Officer Corps," 125.

142. Schmitz, *Militärische Jugenderziehung*, 149–150.

143. Salomon, *Die Kadetten*, 46–47.

144. Schmitz, *Militärische Jugenderziehung*, 161.

145. Eisenhower, *Strictly Personal*, 44.

146. Salomon, *Die Kadetten*, 254.

147. Afflerbach, *Falkenhayn*, 11.

148. Wiese, *Kadettenjahre*, 41; Salomon, *Die Kadetten*, 21. One of the points most often made is that the cadets who were ten or twelve years old were just too young for a harsh disciplinary system, which is undoubtedly correct. However, an aspirant could enter the *Voranstalt* as well as the *Hauptkadettenanstalt* at any time; it was therefore not necessary to send him when he was so young.

    Only Wiese's account stands out with his total negativity and it consists of fewer than ninety pages and describes nothing but atrocities. Obviously the author (1876–1969) was thoroughly traumatized by his experiences at the *Kadettenschule*, which leads to obvious exaggerations in the account. It seems that the worst for young Leopold was not the facility itself but that he pleaded to his mother in heart-wrenching letters to take him away from the *Kadettenschule*, but she did not listen and kept him there for seven and a half years. The relatives put some additional pressure on her because Leopold had a reputation for "falsehood" as a child. Therefore, what Wiese perceived as lack of motherly love and understanding, and certainly felt as personal rejection, weighed much heavier in his account than daily life at the military facility.

It is one of the problems of the historiography about the *Kadettenschulen* that Wiese's accounts have been considered as representative of other cadets' experiences. Without putting them into context of his writings, they were deemed "factual," "reliable" and "unbiased": Schmitz, *Militärische Jugenderziehung*, 2. Wiese published his first book about the *Kadettenschulen* in 1924 when the discussion about reopening the *Kadettenschulen* came up despite the fact that they were forbidden by the Versailles Treaty. He obviously wanted to gain publicity against this undertaking. The author was at the time already a professor of economics and would later become famous as the "German founder of sociology."

149. Salomon, *Die Kadetten*, 9. Ernst von Salomon (1902–1972) was a tough kid who found it "unbearable" at home and immediately recognized upon entering the *Kadettenschule* in Karlsruhe that this was an institution where you have to "defend your skin," which is a German expression for taking no crap from the elders. More "volunteers" in Moncure, *Forging the King's Sword*, 81–83. Clemente, "Making of the Prussian Officer," 204–206.

150. Schmitz, *Militärische Jugenderziehung*, 131. In their accounts, however, just like in those of their West Point counterparts, the names of other persons are usually altered even when they are displayed favorably.

151. *Letter of William R. Smith to Floyd L. Parks, December 27, 1937.* The book ridiculed by Smith is Mott, *Twenty Years.* Colonel Mott, USMA 1886, became a tactical officer at West Point a few years after graduation and later kept close track of everything that happened at his beloved alma mater even after he went overseas. Mott's two chapters on West Point can be counted among the best and most reflective contemporary accounts about the Academy. Mott, however, had a stinging way of expressing the truth when he stated for example that "during the first three years hardly one military subject is taught in the classroom. Intellectually they [the cadets] are, during those

years, as little in contact with military ideas as the girls at Miss Spence's School." See Ibid., 38.

The then chief of staff, Major General Leonard Wood, who was not a graduate of West Point, urged Mott after a private talk to send his suggestions for improvements directly to the Academy where they were "politely" received—most likely only because of the chief's endorsement—and then buried. Mott foresaw precisely the reactions to his book and articles about West Point: "If any other graduate should find fault with the place they would say he was befouling his own nest." Ibid., 330. Similar apprehensions were written by another officer who criticized the selection and teaching methods at West Point: Sanger, "The West Point Military Academy," 134.

FOUR The Importance of Doctrine and How to Manage: The American Command and General Staff and the Overlooked Infantry School

1. Ridgway, *Soldier*, 27.
2. Nenninger, *The Leavenworth Schools and the Old Army*, 23–24.
3. Schifferle, "Anticipating Armageddon," 141.
4. Nenninger, *The Leavenworth Schools and the Old Army*, 27.
5. Booth, *My Observations*, 85, 92. Booth always had the dream of becoming an officer and even canceled a successful business career for his commission. He is one of those who did not attend the Leavenworth school for ticket-punching purposes. During the fighting in the Philippines in 1899, he went forward with a lieutenant who had the order to draw a map of the region. Booth was amazed by the accuracy of the map, which was finished after six hours. After asking the lieutenant where he had learned that skill, he was told at the Infantry and Cavalry School and then and there decided to attend that school. Ewing indeed made it into the course that began in 1902, the first after the Spanish-American War. He would graduate with honors and later return for several years as an instructor. The practice of graduating officers with honors was abandoned around the mid-1920s.
6. Nenninger, *The Leavenworth Schools and the Old Army*, 35.

7. Booth, *My Observations*, 87.

8. Abrahamson, *America Arms for a New Century*, 33.

9. On Wagner, see the brief T. R. Brereton, *Educating the U.S. Army: Arthur L. Wagner and Reform, 1875–1905* (Lincoln: University of Nebraska Press, 2000).

10. Nenninger, *The Leavenworth Schools and the Old Army*, 45. The opinion that there was a thirty-year backlog in U.S. Army didactics appears repeatedly in the memoirs of former instructors: Mott, *Twenty Years*, 18.

11. The German roots and some explanations are found in in Christian E. O. Millotat, *Das preußisch-deutsche Generalstabssystem. Wurzeln-Entwicklung-Fortwirken*, Strategie und Konfliktforschung (Zürich: vdf, 2000), 87–88.

12. The statement to that effect was made by General Kurt Brennecke, who graduated from the German substitute for the forbidden *Kriegsakademie* in 1925. Cited in Hackl, ed. *Generalstab*, 248–249.

13. Jason P. Clark, "Modernization without Technology: U.S. Army Organizational and Educational Reform, 1901–1911" (paper presented at the Annual Society of Military History Conference, Ogden, Utah, April 18, 2008), 2. This correct assessment by Major Clark is rather diplomatically phrased.

14. Robert M. Citino, *The Path to Blitzkrieg: Doctrine and Training in the German Army, 1920–1939* (Boulder, Colorado: Lynne Rienner, 1999), 64–67. The subtitle of his book is misleading because a doctrine in the American sense of the word did not exist in the German Army. This fact is overlooked or misunderstood in much of the Anglo-American literature about the German Army. Citino offers an expert translation—a rarity by Anglo-American scholars—and analysis of a typical German *Kriegsspiel* packed into a series of map problems. Characteristically for such a German exercise, the author of the *Kriegsspiel—Oberstleutnant* Friedrich von Cochenhausen— maintains that his attached solution is only one possible way to solve the exercise and by no means the only one. Cochenhausen was one of the officers who edited the famous *Wehrkreis-Prüfung* periodicals that will be discussed later in this chapter.

15. Coffman, *The Regulars*, 183.
16. *Letter from Captain Walter S. Wood to George C. Marshall, October 29, 1934, with enclosure of field problem for Reserve and National Guard officers*, George C. Marshall Papers, Box 1, Folder Illinois National Guard, Correspondence, General, 1 of 31, October 29–31, 1934, George C. Marshall Library, Lexington, Virginia. Wood was an instructor for the 130th Infantry, Illinois National Guard.
17. Cockrell, "Brown Shoes and Mortar Boards," 172.
18. Clark, "Modernization without Technology," 8.
19. Schifferle, "Anticipating Armageddon," 187–188.
20. Luvaas, "The Influence of the German Wars of Unification," 611.
21. Pogue, *Education of a General*, 96. Bell was commandant of Leavenworth from 1903 to 1906 and after that chief of staff of the Army.
22. Simons, ed. *Professional Military Education in the United States: A Historical Dictionary*, 50–51.
23. Clark, "Modernization without Technology," 7.
24. Nye, "Era of Educational Reform," 131. A different opinion is found in Cockrell, "Brown Shoes and Mortar Boards," 44. Cockrell claims that "Military history was deemed so important that for several years at the College almost fifty percent of the instructional time was taken up with it." The author is alone in this statement about the CGSS curriculum. Scholars and former students alike agree that military history was neglected. Cockrell's claim makes only some sense when map problems based on historical battlefields are counted as military history. I can, however, not follow such an argument. Cockrell's whole thesis is rather descriptive but features a very ingenious and valuable chapter in which he assesses the application of Leavenworth doctrine by U.S. commanders on the battlefield in Italy in World War II.
25. Cockrell, "Brown Shoes and Mortar Boards," 79.
26. Miles, *Fallen Leaves*, 229.
27. Mark Ethan Grotelueschen, *The AEF Way of War: The American Army and Combat in World War I* (New York: Cambridge University Press, 2007), 351. The author refers to the senior commanders and staff of the AEF but the statement is as true for the instructors at Leavenworth.

28. Nenninger, *The Leavenworth Schools and the Old Army*, 140. The fact is emphasized in Grotelueschen, *The AEF Way of War*, 350.

29. Nenninger, "Leavenworth and Its Critics," 201.

30. Cited in Schifferle, "Anticipating Armageddon," 178.

31. William G. Pagonis and Jeffrey L. Cruikshank, *Moving Mountains: Lessons in Leadership and Logistics from the Gulf War* (Boston: Harvard Business School Press, 1992). Lieutenant General Pagonis was responsible for arming, feeding, and fueling the huge army General H. Norman Schwarzkopf had amassed for Operation Desert Storm. Pagonis's book and the incorporated leadership lessons have become very popular in the business world. It is evident that "even" logistics needs leadership.

32. *Letter from J. H. Van Horn to George C. Marshall, May 16, 1938*, George C. Marshall Papers, Box 4, Folder Vancouver Barracks Correspondence, General, 1936–1938, May 8–16, 1938, George C. Marshall Library, Lexington, Virginia. A similar fear is expressed in *Letter from John McAuley Palmer to George A. Lynch, May, 25, 1938*.

33. For a different point of view, see Nenninger, "Leavenworth and Its Critics," 203. It is important to judge the opinions from former instructors or staff of Leavenworth—who were unsurprisingly often positive—differently than those from others.

34. Ibid., 203.

35. Cockrell, "Brown Shoes and Mortar Boards," 193.

36. Kirkpatrick, "The Very Model of a Modern Major General," 271.

37. Schifferle, "Anticipating Armageddon," 217.

38. *Letter from Walter B. Smith to Lucian K. Truscott, December 15, 1943*, Walter B. Smith Papers, Box 27, Folder 201 File, 1942–1943, Dwight D. Eisenhower Library, Abilene, Kansas.

39. "Does A Commander Need Intelligence or Information?," undated article draft, Bruce C. Clarke Papers, Box 1, Combined Arms Research Library, Fort Leavenworth, Kansas.

40. *Letter from Edward H. Brooks to Paul M. Robinett, January 2, 1942*, Paul M. Robinett Papers, Box 11, Folder General Military Correspondence, January 1942, B-11/F-35, George C. Marshall Library, Lexington, Virginia.

41. *Letter from Dan Hick [?] to Paul M. Robinett, July 23, 1941,* Paul M. Robinett Papers, Box 11, Folder General Military Correspondence, June–July 1941, B-11/F-40, George C. Marshall Library, Lexington, Virginia.

42. *Letter from Paul M. Robinett to Lieutenant-Colonel John A. Hettinger, December 23, 1940,* Paul M. Robinett Papers, Box 10, Folder General Military Correspondence, November–December 1940, B-10/F-11, George C. Marshall Library, Lexington, Virginia.

43. *Schedule for 1939–1940—Regular Class,* (Ft. Leavenworth, Kansas: Command and General Staff School Press, 1939), no page number.

44. Schifferle, "Anticipating Armageddon," 82.

45. Ibid., 161. See Schifferle's indispensable study for many more revealing numbers and statistics about Leavenworth.

46. Timothy K. Nenninger, "Creating Officers: The Leavenworth Experience, 1920–1940," *Military Review* 69, no. 11 (1989): 66–67.

47. An example is Garrison "Gar" Holt Davidson, USMA 1927, who did not attend the CGSC or the AWC. He made his mark as Patton's chief engineer in North Africa and Sicily and later held the same position for the whole Seventh Army. After again fighting, this time in the Korean War, Davidson not only became commandant of the CGSC from 1954–1956, but also superintendent of West Point from 1956–1960. For the Academy he devised some of the most far-reaching curriculum changes, which were badly needed, and gave the cadets more scholarly choices. Davidson retired as a lieutenant general without ever having attended one of the ticket-punching schools.

48. Bland and Ritenour, eds., *"The Soldierly Spirit,"* 516–517. Letter from General Malin Craig to George C. Marshall, December 1, 1936.

49. Booth, *My Observations,* 84–85.

50. Pogue, *Education of a General,* 96.

51. Harmon, MacKaye, and MacKaye, *Combat Commander,* 52–53.

52. Larry I. Bland and Sharon R. Ritenour Stevens, eds., *The Papers of George Catlett Marshall: "The Right Man for the Job"—December 7,*

1941–May 31, 1943, 6 vols.,(Baltimore: Johns Hopkins University Press,1991), 3:350. Letter from George C. Marshall to Major General Harold R. Bull, September 8, 1942.

53. Cockrell, "Brown Shoes and Mortar Boards," 128.
54. Chynoweth, *Bellamy Park*, 115.
55. Hofmann, *Through Mobility We Conquer*, 90. A very good description of Chynoweth's character and his problems is found in Theodore Wilson, ""Through the Looking Glass": Bradford G. Chynoweth as United States Military Attaché in Britain, 1939," in *The U.S. Army and World War II: Selected Papers from the Army's Commemorative Conferences*, ed. Judith L. Bellafaire (Washington, D.C.: Center of Military History, U.S. Army, 1998).
56. Schifferle, "Anticipating Armageddon," 142–144.
57. *Letter from Major General Stephen O. Fuqua, Chief of Infantry, to Lieutenant Colonel George C. Marshall, November 25, 1932*, George C. Marshall Papers, Box 1, Folder Fort Screven, Correspondence 1932, Nov 17–25, 1932, 1 of 4, George C. Marshall Library, Lexington, Virginia. Marshall recommended several officers who had served under him at Fort Benning but was informed that now only those with an efficiency rating of "superior" were admitted to the CGSS this year; a feeble "excellent" was no longer sufficient.
58. *Letter from George C. Marshall to Captain Walter S. Wood, November 8, 1934*, George C. Marshall Papers, Box 1, Folder Illinois National Guard, Correspondence, General, 1 of 33, November 2–15, 1934, George C. Marshall Library, Lexington, Virginia.
59. *Letter from Major Clarke K. Fales to George C. Marshall, Sept. 25, 1934*, George C. Marshall Papers, Box 1, Folder Illinois National Guard, Correspondence, General, 1 of 28, September 1934, George C. Marshall Library, Lexington, Virginia.
60. *Letter from Malin "Danny" Craig Jr. to Paul M. Robinett, February 26, 1934*, Paul M. Robinett Papers, Box 11, Folder General Military Correspondence, January 1934, B-11/F-24, George C. Marshall Library, Lexington, Virginia.
61. Schifferle, "Anticipating Armageddon," 147.

62. Ibid., 95. See also chapter 4 of the dissertation about the faculty of the CGSS. I did, however, interpret the numbers slightly differently than the author. The quotations provided there about the quality of the faculty are in the majority from the faculty or staff themselves. See his chapter also for more valuable numbers and statistics about the development of the faculty until World War II.

63. Cited in ibid., 100.

64. Cockrell, "Brown Shoes and Mortar Boards," 80.

65. Allan Reed Millett and Peter Maslowski, *For the Common Defense: A Military History of the United States of America*, Rev. and expanded ed. (New York: Free Press, 1994), 357.

66. Cited in Grotelueschen, *The AEF Way of War*, 44.

67. Schifferle, "Anticipating Armageddon," 164; Collins, *Lightning Joe*, 56. For a different view, see Nenninger, "Leavenworth and Its Critics," 203–207. The author is one of the leading experts on Leavenworth. However, of those whom he cites as having a positive opinion about the school, some have also voiced negative sentiments, notably Collins and Patton, both cited in the text. It has also to be distinguished between the contemporary sources and the memoirs and those officers who later became instructors at Leavenworth and then changed to promote the "party line." The point will be discussed further in the concluding chapter.

68. Harmon, MacKaye, and MacKaye, *Combat Commander*, 50. A variety of collected accounts is found in Coffman, *The Regulars*, 179–181.

69. Cockrell, "Brown Shoes and Mortar Boards," 99–101. Cockrell offers a good discussion on the stress for the officers and hints, like many other scholars and former graduates of Leavenworth, at the rumors of suicides caused by the pressure put on the students. The suicides, however, seem indeed to have been only rumors and will be dealt with in detail in Peter Schifferle's forthcoming book about Leavenworth based on his fine dissertation. I appreciate the author's taking time to discuss the matter with me.

70. A Young Graduate [Dwight D. Eisenhower], "The Leavenworth Course," *Cavalry Journal* 30, no. 6 (1927).

71. Larry I. Bland, Sharon R. Ritenour, and Clarence E. Wunderlin, eds., *The Papers of George Catlett Marshall: "We Cannot Delay"—July 1, 1939—December 6, 1941*, 6 vols. (Baltimore: Johns Hopkins University Press, 1986), 2:65. George C. Marshall agrees here for once with the chief of infantry.

72. Coffman, *The Regulars*, 176–177.

73. Lewis Sorley, *Thunderbolt: From the Battle of the Bulge to Vietnam and Beyond: General Creighton Abrams and the Army of His Times* (New York: Simon & Schuster, 1992), 25.

74. Pogue, *Education of a General*, 97.

75. *Letter from George S. Patton to Floyd L. Parks, January 26, 1933*, Floyd L. Parks Papers, Box 8, Dwight D. Eisenhower Library, Abilene, Kansas. Emphasis in the original. They make clear that Patton's admiration for the CGSS was limited. Having mastered the paperwork and a sound learning schedule, Patton graduated with honors. Years before, Patton had already sent his friend Dwight D. Eisenhower his notes and suggestions.

76. Holley, "Training and Educating Pre-World War I United States Army Officers," 26.

77. Bland, Ritenour, and Wunderlin, eds., *"We Cannot Delay,"* 64. In the same memorandum from September 26, 1939, for the assistant chief of staff, G-3 [Andrews], Marshall much praised his old teacher in tactics at Leavenworth, Morrison, who left obviously a great impression on him but had otherwise a rather mixed reputation. See Clark, "Modernization without Technology," 13.

78. Bland, Ritenour, and Wunderlin, eds., *"We Cannot Delay,"* 192. Letter from George C. Marshall to Brigadier General Lesley J. McNair, April 9, 1940.

79. Ibid. The change of mind in later years Marshall supposedly had in regard to Leavenworth remains unconvincing because of thin evidence. See Nenninger, "Leavenworth and Its Critics," 207.

80. Chynoweth, *Bellamy Park*, 124.

81. Pogue, *Education of a General*, 98.

82. Schifferle, "Anticipating Armageddon," 239. These surveys were rare and have to be assessed with a wary eye because officers might

not have trusted the anonymity of the survey and therefore might have been reluctant to voice negative observations that might jeopardize their careers. The attendance and successful completion of the CGSS was a paramount step in an officer's career. Special care has to be taken with questions like "Are you yourself in accord with school doctrines?" to which 76 percent answered predictably with "yes," 19 percent with "yes with qualifications," and only 5 percent with "no." See Nenninger, "Creating Officers: The Leavenworth Experience, 1920–1940," 64.

83. Hofmann, *Through Mobility We Conquer*, 232.

84. *How an Early Bird Got an "F,"* Bruce C. Clarke's Papers, Box 1, Combined Arms Research Library, Fort Leavenworth, Kansas. The article appeared in the *Engineer Magazine* on page 9, but there is no date on the copy in Clarke's papers.

85. Ibid. Amazingly, U.S. Army armored doctrine states basically the same 60 years later: David Zucchino, *Thunder Run: The Armored Strike to Capture Baghdad* (New York: Grove, 2004), 65.

86. Clarke was so impressed by his battalion commander, who also rose to high rank, that he published some anecdotes about him in *ARMOR* that displayed the great character of his former subordinate.

87. *How an Early Bird Got an "F."*

88. Bland, Ritenour, and Wunderlin, eds., *"We Cannot Delay,"* 182.

89. Ibid., 181–182.

90. Ambrose, *Citizen Soldiers*, 166–167.

91. Citino, *The Path to Blitzkrieg*, 58.

92. Porter B. Williamson, *Patton's Principles* (New York: Simon and Schuster, 1982), 10–11. Williamson, then a lieutenant, became acting G-4 (logistics and supply officer), for Patton's whole I Armored Corps during the South Carolina maneuvers in November 1941. His superior had quit his job out of fear of not being able to cope with Patton, leaving the junior officer in command of this vital position. Williamson, however, subscribed regularly to *National Geographic* and was thus in all topographic and geographic matters way ahead of his fellow officers, including Patton.

93. Nenninger, "Creating Officers: The Leavenworth Experience, 1920–1940," 63.

94. Schifferle, "Anticipating Armageddon," 203.

95. Cockrell, "Brown Shoes and Mortar Boards," 203.

96. Kirkpatrick, "Orthodox Soldiers," 113.

97. Cited in ibid., 103. The verse was found in the files of the Coast Artillery School.

98. Schifferle, "Anticipating Armageddon," 259–264. See the author's rather positive discussion of the school solution.

99. Major J. P. Cromwell, "Are The Methods of Instruction Used at this School Practical and Modern?, 1936. Cited and discussed in Cockrell, "Brown Shoes and Mortar Boards," 159–163.

100. Ibid., 162.

101. Chynoweth, *Bellamy Park*, 121. Chynoweth's memory may have failed him here in some small detail. The grade was supposed to be "SX" which translated into Leavenworth lingo as "exceptional": Nenninger, "Creating Officers: The Leavenworth Experience, 1920–1940," 61.

102. Chynoweth, *Bellamy Park*.

103. Collins, *Lightning Joe*, 56–57. Heintzelman was commandant from 1929 to 1935.

104. Ibid., 57.

105. Nenninger, "Leavenworth and Its Critics," 227.

106. A Young Graduate [Dwight D. Eisenhower], "The Leavenworth Course," 591.

107. Schifferle, "Anticipating Armageddon," 101.

108. The lack of knowledge of laws and procedures on the part of the responsible persons at the Combined Arms Research Library (CARL) at Fort Leavenworth greatly hindered my research. Despite the fact that I had stated my enterprise in advance and asked for assistance, my access to the special archives was suddenly barred because I was labeled a "civilian." I was saved by my "personal" archivist at the Dwight D. Eisenhower Presidential Library, David Haight, who provided me with the archive laws to gain access by pressure. I wish to

thank him for his assistance and help beyond the call of duty. A journey to Fort Leavenworth without any result would have been a financial catastrophe for an already poor graduate student.

109. Some of the very few dealing with relevant contemporary topics: Cpt. J. L. Tupper, "The German Situation" (This is an orientation subject), Group Research Paper No. 42, Group VI, 1931–1932, G-2 File, CGSS; Lt. Col. Ulio, "Is the Present Russian Army an Efficient Fighting Force? Could Russia Prosecute a Long War Successfuly?," Individual Research Paper, No. 78, 1931, G-2 File, CGSS; Cpt. Bonner F. Fellers, C.A.C., "The Psychology of the Japanese Soldier," Individual Research Paper No. 34, 1935, CGSS; Cpt. Hones, "The German Infantry School," Individual Research Paper No. 120, 1931, G-2 File, CGSS.

110. Fifteen officers contributed to the *opus magnum*, among them Major Mark Wayne Clark, later CG of Fifth Army in Italy and Walter Bedell Smith, later Eisenhower's chief of staff in World War II.

111. Capitals in the original.

112. Chynoweth, *Bellamy Park*, 68.

113. The grading system would change several times over the years. After World War I, letter grading was in fashion. See Nenninger, "Creating Officers: The Leavenworth Experience, 1920–1940," 61–62.

114. Pogue, *Education of a General*, 96.

115. A Young Graduate [Dwight D. Eisenhower], "The Leavenworth Course," 593.

116. Coffman, *The Regulars*, 282.

117. Joseph W. Bendersky, *The "Jewish Threat": Anti-Semitic Politics of the U.S. Army* (New York: Basic Books, 2000), 25. Bendersky has written a very important book. However, he failed to put the racist views of the American officer corps into the context of the general views and beliefs of the society at that time and he falls prey to the writings of the G-2 (intelligence) officers about their own work. They generally did not represent the best and the brightest the U.S. Army had to offer at that time. More on racism in the U.S. Army is found in Coffman, *The Regulars*, 124–131, 295–298.

118. Brown, *Social Attitudes*, 212. See chapter 5 of the book for more examples.

119. LeRoy Eltinge, *Psychology of War*, revised ed. (Ft. Leavenworth, Kansas: Press of the Army Service Schools, 1915), 5. Eltinge served in World War I and became a brigadier general. The examples cited in the text are only the "highlights" of his rants.

120. Brown, *Social Attitudes*, 213.

121. Eltinge, *Psychology of War*, 43.

122. Ibid., 43.

123. Ibid. Appendix "Causes of War," p. 8.

124. Ibid. Appendix "Causes of War," p. 32 + 23.

125. Joseph W. Bendersky, "Racial Sentinels: Biological Anti-Semitism in the U.S. Army Officer Corps, 1890–1950," *Militärgeschichtliche Zeitschrift* 62, no. 2 (2003): 336–342.

126. Brown, *Social Attitudes*, 213.

127. A brief but good discussion of the racism of the civilian elites is found in Allsep, "New Forms for Dominance," 230–236. For racism in the army, see Coffman, *The Regulars*, 124–132.

128. Bendersky, *Jewish Threat*, 7.

129. See, for example, Collins, *Lightning Joe*, 111, 358. Miles, *Fallen Leaves*, 292–294. Albert C. Wedemeyer, *Wedemeyer Reports!* (New York: Holt, 1958). See Wedemeyer's whole foreword, which shows a wholly distorted worldview that borders on schizophrenia. Wedemeyer is an enigma in the U.S. Army. As a mere major he was tasked with the drafting of the strategic Victory Plan dealing with a possible war in Europe and he did an outstanding job. Throughout the war he was highly regarded in the whole U.S. Army officer corps for his intelligence and courage. He is one of the very few American officers who asked for a demotion—he was a brigadier general then—so he could command a regiment and fight the Germans.

130. Hürter, *Hitlers Heerführer: Die deutschen Oberbefehlshaber im Krieg gegen die Sowjetunion, 1941/1942*, passim. There are quite a few books dealing with the racism in the German army's officer corps but Hürter's is of special relevance because he cites an enormous number of the contemporary letters and diaries of the generals of

his sample who—from their upbringing and socialization—are representative of the German generals of that time. See also, Andreas Hillgruber, "Dass Russlandbild der führenden deutschen Militärs vor Beginn des Angriffs auf die Sowjetunion," in *Das Russlandbild im Dritten Reich*, ed. Hans-Erich Volkmann (Köln: Böhlau, 1994). Wette, *The Wehrmacht*, 17–89; Mulligan, *The Creation of the Modern German Army*, 172–173, 208–209.

131. Coffman, *The Regulars*, 283–284.

132. Fröhlich, "'Der vergessene Partner.' Die militärische Zusammenarbeit der Reichswehr mit der U.S. Army 1918–1933," 86.

133. Smelser and Davies, *The Myth of the Eastern Front*, 64–73. See also chapter 1 of this study.

134. *Letter from Paul M. Robinett to the Chief of Military History, Sept. 23, 1974*, Paul M. Robinett Papers, Box 5, Folder B-5/F-28, General Correspondence, Halder-Keating, 1962–1974, George C. Marshall Library, Lexington, Virginia.

135. Bernd Wegner, "Erschriebene Siege: Franz Halder, die 'Historical Division' und die Rekonstruktion des Zweiten Weltkrieges im Geiste des deutschen Generalstabes," in *Politischer Wandel, organisierte Gewalt und nationale Sicherheit, Festschrift für Klaus-Jürgen Müller*, eds. Ernst Willi Hansen, Gerhard Schreiber, and Bernd Wegner (München: Oldenbourg, 1995); Smelser and Davies, The Myth of the Eastern Front, 56, 62–63.

136. The story of The Infantry School is found in Peggy A. Stelpflug and Richard Hyatt, *Home of the Infantry: The History of Fort Benning* (Macon, Georgia: Mercer University Press, 2007).

137. Collins, *Lightning Joe*, 44.

138. Anonymous [A Lieutenant], "Student Impression at the Infantry School," *Infantry Journal* 18 (1921). The article from the beginning of The Infantry School shows that the first steps were not easy but the spirit appears to have been already different from the CGSS. One reason might be the hands-on practical training.

139. Coffman, *The Regulars*, 263.

140. Bland and Ritenour, eds., *"The Soldierly Spirit,"* 583–585. Letter from George C. Marshall to Lieutenant-Colonel Guy W. Chipman,

March 16, 1938. Chipman, USMA 1910, and Marshall had served together before the war. Because Chipman would be an instructor for the Illinois National Guard, he characteristically asked Marshall for advice in teaching matters. See also Bland, Ritenour, and Wunderlin, eds., *"We Cannot Delay,"* 190–192. Letter from George C. Marshall to Brigadier General Lesley J. McNair, April 19, 1940, [Washington, D.C.].

141. Bland, Ritenour, and Wunderlin, eds., "We Cannot Delay," 190–192. Letter from George C. Marshall to Brigadier General Lesley J. McNair, April 9, 1940 [Washington, D.C.].

142. Anders, *Gentle Knight*, 122.

143. Bland and Ritenour, eds., *"The Soldierly Spirit,"* 583. Letter from George C. Marshall to Lieutenant-Colonel Guy W. Chipman, March 16, 1938.

144. That "youth and vigor were key assets" was also the opinion of his old friend and mentor General John J. Pershing, who commanded the American Expeditionary Force in the Great War: Timothy K. Nenninger, "'Unsystematic as a Mode of Command': Commanders and the Process of Command in the American Expeditionary Force, 1917–1918," *Journal of Military History* 64, no. 3 (2000): 748. See also Simons, ed. *Professional Military Education in the United States: A Historical Dictionary*, 350.

145. Bland, Ritenour, and Wunderlin, eds., *"We Cannot Delay,"* 192–193. Marshall made that testimony in front of the Senate Military Affairs Committee, April 8, 1940, when he argued for new promotion guidelines. His proposed bill passed.

146. Kirkpatrick, "The Very Model of a Modern Major General," 262.

147. Pogue, *Education of a General*, 248.

148. Ibid., 249.

149. Omar Nelson Bradley, *A Soldier's Story* (New York: Holt, 1951), 20.

150. Anders, *Gentle Knight*, 122.

151. Bland and Ritenour, eds., *"The Soldierly Spirit,"* 320.

152. Pogue, *Education of a General*, 260.

153. Ibid., 250–251.

154. Fröhlich, "'Der vergessene Partner.' Die militärische Zusammenarbeit der Reichswehr mit der U.S. Army, 1918–1933," 91.

155. Anders, *Gentle Knight*, 131.

156. Adolf von Schell, *Battle Leadership: Some Personal Experiences of a Junior Officer of the German Army with Observations on Battle Tactics and the Psychological Reactions of Troops in Campaign* (Fort Benning, Georgia: Benning Herald, 1933).

157. Lanham, ed. *Infantry in Battle.*

158. Bland and Ritenour, eds., *"The Soldierly Spirit,"* 479, 489–490.

159. Rommel's book is available in numerous English editions: Erwin Rommel, *Infantry Attacks* (London: Stackpole, 1995).

160. Hofmann, *Through Mobility We Conquer*, 203; Adolf von Schell, *Kampf gegen Panzerwagen* (Berlin: Stalling, 1936).

161. *Letter from Lieutenant-Colonel Truman Smith to George C. Marshall, November 20, 1938*, George C. Marshall Papers, Box 43, Pentagon Office, 1938–1951, Correspondence, Skinner-Sterling, Folder Smith, Tom K.—Smith, W. Snowden, 43/1, George C. Marshall Library, Lexington, Virginia. Truman Smith would forever write Schell's first name incorrectly as "Adolph."

162. *Letter from Oberst Adolf von Schell to George C. Marshall, January 5, 1939*, George C. Marshall Papers, Box 47, Pentagon Office, 1938–1951, Correspondence, General, Usher-Wedge, Folder Von Neumann—Von Schilling, 47/24, George C. Marshall Library, Lexington, Virginia. It is characteristic for German officers who initially resisted the Nazis and Hitler personally to write about him as "*Herr* Hitler," even denying him the title of *Reichskanzler*. That soon changed after the political and military victories in the first years and nearly every officer would call him "*Führer*" in their letters.

163. Kroener, *Generaloberst Friedrich Fromm*, 250–251. In the lingo of the typically boastful Nazi bureaucracy, von Schell's title was *Generalbevollmächtigter für das Kraftfahrwesen*, which translates directly as "Plenipotentiary for all Automotive Matters."

164. Förster, "The Dynamics of *Volksgemeinschaft*," 183.

165. Hofmann, *Through Mobility We Conquer*, 203–209. A picture of von Schell is on page 145.

166. Kroener, *Generaloberst Friedrich Fromm*, 593.

167. *Correspondence regarding Help for Adolf von Schell*, George C. Marshall Papers, Box 138, Secretary of State, 1947–1949, Correspondence, General, Sun Li Jen-Webb, Folder Von Schell-Vroom, 138–39, George C. Marshall Library, Lexington, Virginia. Von Schell would stay in contact with Marshall and send him heartwarming letters of gratitude until the great American's death in 1959.

168. Bland and Ritenour, eds., *"The Soldierly Spirit,"* 552. Letter from George C. Marshall to Lieutenant-Colonel (*Oberstleutnant*) Adolf von Schell, July 7, 1937, Vancouver Barracks, Washington.

169. Ibid., 321.

170. Ridgway, *Soldier*, 199.

171. Collins, *Lightning Joe*, 50.

172. Coffman, *The Regulars*, 264.

173. Schifferle, "Anticipating Armageddon," 234–237.

174. Kirkpatrick, "Orthodox Soldiers," 103. More accounts in are found in Coffman, *The Regulars*, 264–265.

175. Bland and Ritenour Stevens, eds., *The Papers of George Catlett Marshall: "The Right Man for the Job"—December 7, 1941—May 31, 1943*, 349–350. Letter from Major General Harold Roe Bull to George C. Marshall, September 14 and October 1, 1942. Bull had been a member of the faculty during Marshall's time at The Infantry School. Thus in the army culture it is possible that he might have whitewashed information about the school. It is, however, unlikely that his report tells anything but the truth. It was well known that Marshall disliked schmoozers and any inaccuracies would have brought Bull, who was already on the fast track at this time, only disadvantages. Bull also reports about the CGSS that indeed some commanders probably had been "palming off" mediocre officers there, though apparently the practice was decreasing and that the school still had problems getting "qualified instructors" especially from the Air Corps. It is apparent that the CGSS still suffered from the same problems as thirty years ago.

176. Eisenhower, *Strictly Personal*, 74.

177. Collins, *Lightning Joe*, 44.

178. *John A. Heintges interviewed by Jack A. Pellicci, transcript, 1974,* Senior Officers Oral History Program, Volume 2, U.S. Army Military History Institute, Carlisle, Pennsylvania. Heintges was the only officer of German stock I know of who made it to the frontlines to fight against the Germans. Two U.S. Army officers of German origin had claimed that the War Department's personnel section during World War II deliberately sent all those officers of German stock who qualified as troop leaders to the Pacific theater of war. First, I could not believe such a claim, but since then I checked in passing every U.S. officer whom I knew was of German descent and they indeed ended all up in the Pacific. The senior command and staff in the Pacific was even known as "MacArthur's Germans." Such a policy did certainly did not have the endorsement of the chief of staff, who repeatedly expressed that he had no doubts about the loyalty of all U.S. Army officers of German origin. Heintges only made it to North Africa with extraordinary tenacity, by bending the rules, and calling in favors. Obviously, later officers of German origin made it to Europe but rather as intelligence officers or interpreters rather than combat leaders. American junior officers who expressed any sympathy with the Nazis were generally left behind: Benjamin A. Dickson, *Algiers to Elbe—G-2 Journal*, Monk Dickson Papers (West Point, New York: West Point Library Special Archive, unpublished), 1–2.

179. Coffman, *The Regulars*, 265.

180. George C. Marshall's testimony in front of the Truman Committee, named for its chair Harry S. Truman, March 1, 1941. Bland, Ritenour, and Wunderlin, eds., *"We Cannot Delay,"* 482–483.

181. Pogue, *Education of a General*, 249.

182. The Infantry School needs the same high-quality number–crunching analysis that Peter Schifferle has forwarded for the CGSS. The problems to produce it will be considerably higher because more of its files have been destroyed.

FIVE The Importance of the Attack and How to Lead:
The German *Kriegsakademie*

1. Cited in Hofmann, *Through Mobility We Conquer*, 150. Hofmann
   offers a solid account of his topic. It is, however, totally incomprehensible that nearly every second German word is incorrectly
   typed or even garbled in his book. It should be no problem for the
   author or the publisher to get a German student to read the manuscript for a few dollars to ensure the foreign language used is
   correct. It should be considered standard procedure by a renowned
   author and a university press. Such negligence is unfortunately
   no rarity in American books that deal with German Army topics.

2. Erfurth, *Die Geschichte des deutschen Generalstabes von 1918 bis 1945*,
   127. Erfurth was a member of the General Staff with the rank of
   general and possessed a Ph.D. in history. He led one of the first research centers that the U.S. Army Historical Division established
   for former German officers to help write the history of World War II.
   The thousands of studies that were published changed the historiography considerably for decades because the German officers
   were successful in putting all the blame on Hitler. See Wegner,
   "Erschriebene Siege: Franz Halder, die 'Historical Division' und die
   Rekonstruktion des Zweiten Weltkrieges im Geiste des deutschen
   Generalstabes." Wette, *The Wehrmacht*, 229–235.

3. Nakata, *Der Grenz- und Landesschutz in der Weimarer Republik*, 220.

4. Cited in Citino, *The Path to Blitzkrieg*, 123.

5. Gordon, *The Reichswehr and the German Republic, 1919–1926*, 175.
   Gordon is a former U.S. Army officer and was able to talk to several German protagonists. Their view heavily influenced the whole
   book. Gordon goes so far as to insist that the education of General
   Staff officers and the existence of a General Staff corps were legal
   (p. 180). However, articles 160 III, 175 and 176, of the Versailles
   Treaty clearly state otherwise.

6. Detlef Bald, *Der deutsche Generalstab 1859–1939. Reform und Restauration in Ausbildung und Bildung*, Schriftenreihe Innere Führung,
   Heft 28 (Bonn: Bundesministerium der Verteidigung, 1977), 37.

7. Millotat, *Generalstabssystem*, 118–120.

8. Citino, *The Path to Blitzkrieg*, 94.

9. Fröhlich, "'Der vergessene Partner.' Die militärische Zusammen-arbeit der Reichswehr mit der U.S. Army 1918–1933," 14.

10. Bucholz, *Delbrück's Modern Military History*, 34.

11. Colonel A. L. Conger, Third Division Officers' School, March 7, 1928, and appendixes cited in Citino, *The Path to Blitzkrieg*, 93–94, 102–103.

12. Ibid., 98.

13. Model, *Generalstabsoffizier*, 32. Model's account is the best available about the staff officer's education in Germany. In addition to available publications of that time, he draws from original documents, interviews with former General Staff officers, and the studies written by German officers for the U.S. Army Historical Division. The latter, however, are highly glorified, as is Model's book, because he was a General Staff officer himself.

14. The German term was *"charakterliche Fehler."* Statement by General Hans Speth, cited in Hackl, ed. *Generalstab*, 261. The claim is believable because Speth had unusual insight—he was responsible for the preparation of the *Wehrkreis-Prüfung* in *Wehrkreis* IV in 1931.

15. The same might have happened at the *Fähnrichsexamen*: Moncure, *Forging the King's Sword*, 238–239.

16. Model, *Generalstabsoffizier*, 27.

17. Citino, *The Path to Blitzkrieg*, 74. Unfortunately, Citino discusses only the weaponry part of the *Wehrkreis-Prüfung* and not the applied tactics.

18. Bearbeitet von einigen Offizieren [prepared by some officers], *Die Wehrkreis-Prüfung 1924* (Berlin: Offene Worte, 1924). See foreword. The officers, however, were often members of the *Truppenamt*.

19. Teske, *Die silbernen Spiegel*, 36. Teske was trained as a General Staff officer and attended the *Kriegsakademie* in the fateful years from 1936 to 1938. He found himself in historic company. Among his classmates were three of the main perpetrators in the plot against Hitler, Claus Graf Schenk von Stauffenberg, Mertz von Quirnheim,

and Eberhard Fink, and last but not least the American exchange student Albert Wedemeyer. Teske's rather sober and critical account, with unfortunately little candor in regard to his classmates, stands in stark contrast to the Hitler and Nazi "hurrah" book he published at the end of his war academy time: Teske, *Wir marschieren für Großdeutschland.*

20. Afflerbach, *Falkenhayn,* 14.

21. Teske, *Die silbernen Spiegel,* 45.

22. Citino, *The Path to Blitzkrieg,* 101.

23. Bearbeitet von einigen Offizieren [prepared by some officers], *Die Wehrkreis-Prüfung 1924,* 18–19, 22, 24.

24. Williamson, *Patton's Principles,* 22.

25. Herr was chief of cavalry from March 23, 1938, to March 9, 1942. For his destructive influence and some of his remarks that bordered on psychosis, see Hofmann, *Through Mobility We Conquer,* 236, 289, 293. Harmon, MacKaye, and MacKaye, *Combat Commander,* 57. See also Herr's weird book: John K. Herr and Edward S. Wallace, *The Story of the U.S. Cavalry, 1775–1942* (Boston: Little, Brown, 1953). Fuqua was Chief of Infantry from March 28, 1928, to May 5, 1933. He continued his destructive work as military attaché to Spain from 1936 to 1939 when he sent misleading reports about the use of tanks during the Spanish civil war without hardly ever observing a battle: George F. Hofmann, "The Tactical and Strategic Use of Attaché Intelligence: The Spanish Civil War and the U.S. Army's Misguided Quest for a Modern Tank Doctrine," *Journal of Military History* 62, no. 1 (1998).

26. Bearbeitet von einigen Offizieren [prepared by some officers], *Die Wehrkreis-Prüfung 1924,* 49–55. *The Bewaffnung und Ausrüstung* was later renamed *Waffenlehre* (weapons craft).

27. Teske, *Die silbernen Spiegel,* 37.

28. Bearbeitet von einigen Offizieren [prepared by some officers], *Die Wehrkreis-Prüfung 1924,* 56.

29. Bearbeitet von einigen Offizieren [prepared by some officers], *Die Wehrkreis-Prüfung 1921* (Berlin: Offene Worte, 1921), 52.

30. Bearbeitet von einigen Offizieren [prepared by some officers], *Die Wehrkreis-Prüfung 1929* (Berlin: Offene Worte, 1930), 66.

31. Bearbeitet von einigen Offizieren [prepared by some officers], *Die Wehrkreis-Prüfung 1931* (Berlin: Offene Worte, 1932), 81.

32. See the statement of General Erich Brandenberger, cited in Hackl, ed. *Generalstab*, 211.

33. Bearbeitet von einigen Offizieren [prepared by some officers], *Die Wehrkreis-Prüfung 1924*, 66.

34. Bearbeitet von einigen Offizieren [prepared by some officers], *Die Wehrkreis-Prüfung 1931*, 81.

35. Bearbeitet von einigen Offizieren [prepared by some officers], *Die Wehrkreis-Prüfung 1921*, 76.

36. Teske, *Die silbernen Spiegel*, 37.

37. Bearbeitet von einigen Offizieren [prepared by some officers], *Die Wehrkreis-Prüfung 1929*, 66.

38. Bearbeitet von einigen Offizieren [prepared by some officers], *Die Wehrkreis-Prüfung 1930* (Berlin: Offene Worte, 1931), 70.

39. Bearbeitet von einigen Offizieren [prepared by some officers], *Die Wehrkreis-Prüfung 1924*, 87.

40. Bearbeitet von einigen Offizieren [prepared by some officers], *Die Wehrkreis-Prüfung 1933* (Berlin: Offene Worte, 1933), 79.

41. *Handbuch für den Generalstabsdienst im Kriege*, 2 vols. (Berlin: n.p., 1939), 1:34.

42. Bearbeitet von einigen Offizieren [prepared by some officers], *Die Wehrkreis-Prüfung 1937* (Berlin: Offene Worte, 1937), 4–6; Model, *Generalstabsoffizier*, 73. Model is obviously in error here because he still talks about reinforced regiments.

43. Model, *Generalstabsoffizier*, 71.

44. Ibid., 32, 74. That's the number most of the literature maintains. Erfurth states in contrast that the ratio of washouts to accepted became nearly reversed in the late 1930s. He does, however, present no evidence for that claim. There exists no study about the German General Staff that passes scholarly standards. Even those who attended the *Kriegsakademie* and were selected for the General Staff could not know the final numbers. Only those who were in-

volved in the selection process would know. For Erfurth's version, see Erfurth, *Die Geschichte des deutschen Generalstabes von 1918 bis 1945*, 171–172. The study of *Generalmajor* Horst Freiherr Treusch von Buttlar-Brandenfels states that before 1935 about 30 to 40 percent were washed out while after 1935 it was only 10 to 15 percent. These numbers pertain to those selected for the General Staff *after* successfully finishing the *Kriegsakademie*. See Hackl, ed. *Generalstab*, 183. Another different set of numbers—30 to 40 percent, sometimes 50 percent—washed out after the *Kriegsakademie*—in the statement of *Generalmajor* Peter von Groeben in Hackl, 313. It is important to remember that those who attended the *Kriegsakademie* were further weeded out and only a fraction of them would finally reach the General Staff.

45. Statement by General Erich Brandenberger is found in Hackl, ed., *Generalstab*, 210. It is apparent that American historians have viewed the Prussian-Bavarian military relations through rosy glasses. See David N. Spires, *Image and Reality: The Making of the German Officer, 1921–1933*, Contributions in Military History (Westport, Connecticut: Greenwood, 1984), xi.

46. Statement by *Generalmajor* August-Viktor von Quast in Hackl, ed., *Generalstab*, 269; Statement by General Hans Speth in Hackl, 261.

47. *Military Attaché Report, Subject: Visit to the German Armored (Panzer) Troop School at Wünsdorf, October 4, 1940*, RG 165, Records of the WDGS, Military Intelligence Division, Box 1113, Folder Correspondence 1917–1941, 2277-B-43, National Archives II.

48. *M.I.D. Report, GERMANY (Combat), Subject: The German General Staff School* (Kriegsakademie), Record Group 165, Records of the WDGS, Military Intelligence Division, Box 1113, Folder 2277-B-44 [Hartness Report], National Archives II, College Park, Maryland.

49. Harmon, MacKaye, and MacKaye, *Combat Commander*, 126–127. Harmon, then a division commander, made the late officers pay a fine of $50. In his memoir he surmised that his "severity" was a mistake. A German officer late for a briefing because of laziness had a good chance to be demoted.

50. Ibid., 50.

51. Teske, *Die silbernen Spiegel*, 50.

52. Model, *Generalstabsoffizier*, 38.

53. Andreas Broicher, "Betrachtungen zum Thema "Führen und Führer,"" *Clausewitz-Studien* 1 (1996): 121.

54. *M.I.D. Report, GERMANY (Combat), Subject: The German General Staff School* (Kriegsakademie). Captain Hartness emphasized the outstanding teaching ability of his German instructors several times. The same was done by his comrade Captain Wedemeyer.

55. Erfurth, *Die Geschichte des deutschen Generalstabes von 1918 bis 1945*, 126.

56. See the statement by General Hans Speth about his time as a *Hörsaalleiter* at the *Kriegsakademie* from 1936–1939, in Hackl, ed., *Generalstab*, 262–264. Also, see Teske, *Die silbernen Spiegel*, 45.

57. *M.I.D. Report, GERMANY (Combat), Subject: The German General Staff School* (Kriegsakademie).

58. Pogue, *Education of a General*, 97.

59. Statement by *Generalmajor* Peter von Groeben, is found in Hackl, ed., *Generalstab*, 308.

60. *Memorandum for the Adjutant General, Subject: German General Staff School* (Kriegsakademie), Record Group 165, Records of the WDGS, Military Intelligence Division, Box 1113, Folder 2277-B-48 [Wedemeyer Report], National Archives II, College Park, Maryland.

61. Model, *Generalstabsoffizier*, 81–82.

62. Diedrich, *Paulus: Das Trauma von Stalingrad*, 96–97.

63. Chynoweth, *Bellamy Park*, 123.

64. *M.I.D. Report, GERMANY (Combat), Subject: The German General Staff School* (Kriegsakademie).

65. Diedrich, *Paulus: Das Trauma von Stalingrad*, 99. Printed here in part from the periodical of the class of 1931–1932 and their assessment of their instructor in war history, then Major Friedrich Paulus, whom they nicknamed the "*Cunctator*" (Latin for Delayer, Hesitator), after Quintus Fabius Maximus, a Roman consul who did not dare attack Hannibal during the Second Punic War. Paulus would rise to command the 6th Army, despite knowing full well that it was under-

supplied in every aspect, "lead" it to take Stalingrad, where it was surrounded and finally destroyed. In hesitating to order a breakout of the encirclement and make his perilous situation crystal clear to his superiors, he showed that the nickname he had earned more than ten years earlier was well deserved.

66. Model, *Generalstabsoffizier*, 77.
67. Williamson Murray, "Werner Freiherr von Fritsch: Der tragische General.," in *Die Militärelite des Dritten Reiches: 27 Biographische Skizzen*, eds. Ronald Smelser and Enrico Syring (Berlin: Ullstein, 1995), 154.
68. Model, *Generalstabsoffizier*, 79–80.
69. Mark Frederick Bradley, "United States Military Attachés and the Interwar Development of the German Army" (master's thesis, Georgia State University 1983), 52.
70. Bald, *Der deutsche Generalstab, 1859–1939*, 88.
71. Ibid., 88.
72. Richard R. Muller, "Werner von Blomberg: Hitler's "idealistischer" Kriegsminister," in *Die Militärelite des Dritten Reiches: 27 biographische Skizzen*, eds. Ronald Smelser and Enrico Syring (Berlin: Ullstein, 1997), 56.
73. Bald, *Der deutsche Generalstab 1859–1939*, 103.
74. *M.I.D. Report, GERMANY (Combat), Subject: The German General Staff School* (Kriegsakademie).
75. Citino, *The Path to Blitzkrieg*, 184.
76. Ibid., 18, 24.
77. Teske, *Die silbernen Spiegel*, 45.
78. Oetting, *Auftragstaktik*, 263.
79. Teske, *Die silbernen Spiegel*, 48.
80. Statement by *Oberst* Hans Georg Richert, cited in Hackl, ed., *Generalstab*, 330.
81. Boog, "Civil Education, Social Origins, and the German Officer Corps," 123.
82. Cited in Luvaas, "The Influence of the German Wars of Unification," 618. The statement was made by Brevet Major General Wesley Merrit, USMA 1860.

83. The examples are numerous and range from the Spanish-American War until today: *Transcript of telephone conversation with John McAuley Palmer, Oct. 15, 1947, OCMH (Office of the Chief of Military History) Collection*, Box 2, U.S. Army Military History Institute, Carlisle, Pennsylvania.

84. Stouffer et al., ed. *The American Soldier: Adjustment during Army Life*, 57.

85. Ibid., 259.

86. Ibid., 264. Emphasis in the original. See also the whole chapter "'Bucking' for Promotion," which sheds more light on the issue.

87. Dwight D. Eisenhower, "A Tank Discussion," *Infantry Journal* (November 1920).

88. *Letter from Dwight D. Eisenhower to Bruce C. Clarke, September 17, 1967, Gettysburg, Pennsylvania*, Bruce C. Clarke Papers, Box 1, Combined Arms Research Library, Fort Leavenworth, Kansas.

89. Coffman, *The Regulars*, 277.

90. Boog, "Civil Education, Social Origins, and the German Officer Corps," 122.

91. For the student of military history and any staff ride, the Battle of Fehrbellin is of special relevance. Not only does it teach an enormous variety of aspects of military history—from leadership decisions to the cunning use of artillery—but Fehrbellin is the only battlefield in Germany that is nearly completely intact. Germany does not possess a battlefield preservation law like other countries.

92. Robert M. Citino, *The German Way of War: From the Thirty Year's War to the Third Reich* (Lawrence: University Press of Kansas, 2005), 14–22. Citino offers a slighty different version of the battle but his book includes battle maps and a detailed account of Brandenburg's military history. The author's book is invaluable for understanding the "German Way of War."

93. Wing adjutants were young, educated, and dynamic staff officers who were granted wide responsibilities and power by Fredrick the Great.

94. There are, as usual when it comes to legendary events, somewhat different versions of the story. The reply is slightly different in

Christopher Duffy, *The Military Life of Frederick the Great* (New York: Atheneum, 1986), 167.

95. It is most likely that nothing would have happened even if Marwitz had not resigned on his own. Though Fritze had a fiery temper he usually respected the opinion of his officers.

96. Yorck was neither a count then nor a "von Wartenburg." He was showered with titles and decorations later, after everything went well. I use his later name here for better recognition.

97. Förster, "The Dynamics of *Volksgemeinschaft*," 193.

98. Ibid., 201.

99. Oetting, *Auftragstaktik*, 198.

100. See, for example, Timothy A. Wray, "Standing Fast: German Defensive Doctrine on the Russian Front during World War II—Prewar to March 1943." (Fort Leavenworth, Kansas: U.S. Army Command and General Staff College, 1986), http://purl.access.gpo.gov/GPO/LPS58744; Timothy T. Lupfer, *The Dynamics of Doctrine: The Changes in German Tactical Doctrine during the First World War*, Leavenworth Papers (Ft. Leavenworth, Kansas: Combat Studies Institute, U.S. Army Command and General Staff College, 1981); Citino, *The Path to Blitzkrieg*. In Citino's book the doctrine shows only up in the subtitle (*Doctrine and Training in the Germany Army*) and unfortunately in the chapter about von Seeckt, who was anything but doctrine-oriented. The author, however, discusses the development of the German Army in a very flexible and knowledgeable way.

101. For a discussion of that, see the all-time classic, Hans von Seeckt, ed. *Führung und Gefecht der verbundenen Waffen* (Berlin: Offene Worte, 1921). In the opinion of the author it ranks in importance among the works written by Carl von Clausewitz and Sun Tzu.

102. Oetting, *Auftragstaktik*, 283.

103. Millett, "The United States Armed Forces in the Second World War," 65.

104. Manstein's position is not to be confused with the "Chief of Staff of Operations." Kurt Freiherr von Hammerstein-Equord was *Chef der Heeresleitung* during 1930–1934. Some of the war games mentioned here—inauspiciously called *Truppenamtsreisen*, literally "troop

office journeys"—are printed in Karl-Volker Neugebauer, "Operatives denken zwischen dem Ersten und Zweiten Weltkrieg," in *Operatives Denken und Handeln in deutschen Streitkräften im 19. und 20. Jahrhundert*, ed. Günther Roth (Herford: Mittler, 1988). Interestingly, the war games were played against Czechoslovakia, Poland, and France. Not all of them, however, had an offensive character.

105. Manstein, *Soldatenleben*, 109, 127, 241.

106. Wrochem, *Erich von Manstein*, 41.

107. For more on Manstein's leadership problems as well as a reappraisal of his operational abilities, see Muth, "Erich von Lewinski, called von Manstein: His Life, Character and Operations—A Reappraisal." See also Marcel Stein, *Field Marshal von Manstein, the Janus Head: A Portrait* (Solihull: Helion, 2007).

108. Nick van der Bijl and David Aldea, *5th Infantry Brigade in the Falklands* (Barnsley: Cooper, 2003), 70. The authors feature a brief but interesting discussion. The absence of "directive control" and the use of the contrasting "restrictive control" made things occasionally unnecessarily hard for the subordinate commanders and troops of the British Army during the Falklands campaign.

109. See Millotat, *Generalstabssystem*, 41 for more attempts in French and English. The author is very uncritical toward the German General Staff system and its members.

110. Oetting, *Auftragstaktik*, 320.

111. Hofmann, *Through Mobility We Conquer*, 149. The latter translation proposal is from Adolf von Schell, a German exchange officer who studied and lectured at The Infantry School, Fort Benning, Georgia. More on Schell below. See also the concise and correct explanation of *Auftragstaktik* in Citino, *The Path to Blitzkrieg*, 13. There are many more examples to illustrate the command concept in Oetting, *Auftragstaktik*.

112. Van Creveld, *Fighting Power*, 36. Van Creveld also offers some excellent examples for the explanation of *Auftragstaktik*.

113. Teske, *Die silbernen Spiegel*, 71. *Grenadier* is the old-fashioned word for a private.

114. Stouffer et al., ed. *The American Soldier: Adjustment during Army Life*, 65.

115. *Memorandum for the Adjutant General, Subject: German General Staff School* (Kriegsakademie).

116. Kielmansegg, "Bemerkungen zum Referat von Hauptmann Dr. Frieser aus der Sicht eines Zeitzeugen," 152. Kielmansegg was *Ib*—logistics officer —for the *1. Panzerdivision* and present when the words were spoken. Kielmansegg commented on Frieser's presentation, out of which the latter made his now famous book: Frieser, *The Blitzkrieg Legend*.

117. Harmon, MacKaye, and MacKaye, *Combat Commander*, 80.

118. Oetting, *Auftragstaktik*, 246.

119. Hofmann, *Through Mobility We Conquer*, 152.

120. Astor, *Terrible Terry Allen*, 81; Van Creveld, *Fighting Power*, 37.

121. Captain Harlan Nelson Hartness, USMA 1919, from 1935 to 1937; Captain Albert Coady Wedemeyer, USMA 1919, from 1936 to 1938; Lieutenant Colonel H. F. Kramer from 1937 to 1939; and Major Richard Clare Partridge, USMA 1920, from 1938 to 1939. Most went through the two-year courses, Partridge received a shortened education because of the outbreak of the war. Hartness became a brigadier general in World War II and assistant commandant of the CGSS from 1948 to 1950, retiring as a major general.

   Wedemeyer commanded U.S. Armed Forces in China in 1945 as lieutenant general and went on to four stars. Kramer commanded the 66th Infantry Division in World War II as a major general. Partridge commanded the 358th Infantry in World War II and retired later as a major general. Hartness, Wedemeyer, and Partridge had excellent reputations among their comrades and were regarded as outside-the box thinkers and can-do-types. See, for example, Dickson, *Algiers to Elbe: G-2 Journal*, 5–6; Collins, *Lightning Joe*, 185.

122. Wedemeyer, *Wedemeyer Reports!*, 49. Wedemeyer left the army in 1951 prematurely because he was unhappy with the direction in which it went and because of dissent in regard to the U.S. China

policy. His comments have to be viewed in this context. Nenninger, "Leavenworth and Its Critics," 216. Nenninger provides as usual one of the densest accounts but overlooks in this case Wedemeyer's emphasis on pedagogy and the cultural differences at the schools.

123. Citino, *The Path to Blitzkrieg,* 157–164.

124. Nenninger, "Leavenworth and Its Critics," 216.

125. Ibid., 215–216.

126. *Memorandum for the Adjutant General, Subject: German General Staff School* (Kriegsakademie). See the letter by Lieutenant Colonel Charles Manly Busbee, USMA 1915, who worked at the G-2 of the General Staff, attached to the report for the statement that a copy was forwarded to the CGSS. The low relevance assigned to these priceless reports becomes obvious when Busbee only "suggests" that Wedemeyer's report should also be forwarded to the Army War College "for notation."

127. *M.I.D. Report, GERMANY (Combat), Subject: The German General Staff School* (Kriegsakademie). Hartness offers two chapters dedicated to the quality of the instructors and the positive student contact, 17–19.

Wedemeyer: "The instructors are carefully selected, not only because they have splendid military records, but also became of their proven ability to instruct" (p. 2).

"The instructors are officers of exceptional ability [...]" (p. 12).

"Practically all of the instruction is imported through Troop Leading" (p. 12).

"There is no arbitrariness or restraint in the relations between instructors and students"(p. 13).

"In general the German Field Orders are not so schematic nor so specific as the American" (p. 78).

"The most important point under the subject instruction, I believe to be the method of presenting map problems. I found them realistic and practical" (p. 139).

"Students [...] conduct themselves exactly as they would in the field" (p. 139).

"The Germans emphasize that a commander must not only know *how* to arrive at a decision but also *when*" (emphases in the original, p. 139).

128. Ibid., 8. The same "real-life" feeling that came across during German war exercises was reported by numerous other foreign observers: Citino, *The Path to Blitzkrieg*, 66.

129. *M.I.D. Report, GERMANY (Combat), Subject: The German General Staff School* (Kriegsakademie). Hartness explicitly praised the "no school solution" teaching system of the Germans again in the conclusion on page 24 of his report.

SIX Education, Culture, and Consequences

1. Louis Abelly, *The Life of the Venerable Servant of God: Vincent de Paul*, 3 vols. (New York: New City Press, 1993), 2:375. St. Vincent de Paul was a Catholic monk living in the seventeenth century. In contrast to most of his peers, he lived in complete poverty and helped the poor all his life. Even during his lifetime he became a legendary figure because of the humility and wisdom he displayed. The quote is paraphrased in the biography cited above. I greatly appreciate the assistance of Nathaniel Michaud for helping me track down the quote.

2. Cited in Manstein. The original: "Vorschriften sind für die Dummen."

3. Afflerbach, *Falkenhayn*, 105, 134.

4. Bernhard R. Kroener, "Strukturelle Veränderungen in der militärischen Gesellschaft des Dritten Reiches," in *Nationalsozialismus und Modernisierung*, eds. Michael Prinz and Rainer Zitelmann (Darmstadt: Wissenschaftliche Buchgesellschaft, 1991); Bernhard R. Kroener, „Generationserfahrungen und Elitenwandel: Strukturveränderungen im deutschen Offizierkorps, 1933–1945," in *Eliten in Deutschland und Frankreich im 19. und 20. Jahrhundert: Strukturen und Beziehungen*, eds. Rainer Hudemann and Georges-Henri Soutu (Oldenbourg, 1994).

5. Dillard, "The Uncertain Years," 339. Exceptions were the few wartime classes that early "recognized" the plebes as cadets out of necessity because of the time restrictions.

6. Stephan Leistenschneider, "Die Entwicklung der Auftragstaktik im deutschen Heer und ihre Bedeutung für das deutsche Führungsdenken," in *Führungsdenken in europäischen und nordamerikanischen Streitkräften im 19. und 20. Jahrhundert*, ed. Gerhard P. Groß (Hamburg: Mittler, 2001), 177. The author found various names, among them *Auftragsverfahren, Freies Verfahren, Auftragskampf, Individualverfahren, Dispositionstaktik, Initiativverfahren*, etc.

7. Ibid., 189.

8. Clemente, "Making of the Prussian Officer," 174.

9. Ibid., 140. Clemente claims that German officer candidates were commissioned at all costs but there is no evidence for such an assertion because German officers clearly demonstrated scholarly abilities on all levels.

10. Moncure, *Forging the King's Sword*, 235.

11. Clemente, "Making of the Prussian Officer," 172.

12. Ernst von Salomon, without having completed his education at the *HKA* because it was disbanded in accord with the Versailles Treaty, became a machine-gun-section leader in a *Freikorps* and was perfectly able to handle his weapons in all situations. He was seventeen at that time. See his detailed account in Salomon, *Die Geächteten*.

13. Bland, Ritenour, and Wunderlin, eds., *"We Cannot Delay,"* 65. Marshall's memorandum to the assistant chief of staff G-3, September 26, 1939.

14. Schmitz, *Militärische Jugenderziehung*, 54–55.

15. Mott, *Twenty Years*, 35.

16. Lori A. Stokam, "The Fourth Class System: 192 Years of Tradition Unhampered by Progress from Within" (research paper submitted to the faculty of the United States Military Academy, History Department, West Point, New York: 1994), 9.

17. Mott, *Twenty Years*, 25. Joe Lawton Collins, who graduated twenty-one years after Mott, wrote, "I was one of those rare cadets who enjoyed West Point [...]." Collins, *Lightning Joe*, 6.

18. Schmitz, *Militärische Jugenderziehung*, 141. The original—in this case hard to translate—German word is *abwechslungsreich*.

19. Clemente, "Making of the Prussian Officer," 168. Clemente is on the wrong track, again making the mistake of assessing only curriculum hours and not taking into account didactics and pedagogics. See the more detailed and balanced chapter about *Kadetten* education in Moncure, *Forging the King's Sword*.

20. Nye, "Era of Educational Reform," 200–201.

21. John A. Logan, *The Volunteer Soldier of America* (New York: Arno, 1979), 441–458. Logan was a distinguished major general in the Union Army during the Civil War. Observing his comrades from West Point, he noted that the education they had received did not help them with soldering. He also pointed out that West Pointers did not show a better performance as officers than their comrades who received their commissions elsewhere. I appreciate it that Mark Grimsley pointed this book out to me.

22. Nye, "Era of Educational Reform," 233. Statement from General Committee on Revision of Courses, which was made up of West Point senior faculty, February 3, 1908. The report defeated another attempt to revise the curriculum. Dillard, "The Uncertain Years," 290–291.

23. Unruh, *Ehe die Stunde schlug*, 147–148.

24. LaCamera, "Hazing: A Tradition too Deep to Abolish," 12.

25. Mott, *Twenty Years*, 44.

26. See the conclusion of Richard C. U'Ren who worked as a psychiatrist at West Point: U'Ren, *Ivory Fortress*.

27. Kenneth S. Davis, *Soldier of Democracy: A Biography of Dwight Eisenhower* (Garden City, New York: Doubleday, 1946), 131.

28. Sorley, "Leadership," 138.

29. Mullaney, *The Unforgiving Minute*, 347. The author graduated in 2000 and is just one example of many.

30. Clemente, "Making of the Prussian Officer," 174.

31. Nye, "Era of Educational Reform," 183.

32. *John A. Heintges interviewed by Jack A. Pellicci, transcript, 1974.* Heintges was a West Pointer himself and therefore his honest statement critiquing other former graduates carries special weight.

33. *Charles L. Bolté interviewed by Arthur J. Zoebelein, undated.* Bolté was not a West Pointer but a very successful officer. He got four stars and became commander in chief of U.S. forces in Europe in 1953.

34. Nenninger, "Leavenworth and Its Critics."

35. Chynoweth, *Bellamy Park*, 85.

36. Schifferle, "Anticipating Armageddon," 79.

37. Cockrell, "Brown Shoes and Mortar Boards," 360; Schifferle, "Anticipating Armageddon," 61.

38. Williamson, *Patton's Principles*, 103.

39. Mullaney, *The Unforgiving Minute*, 23. The motto "cooperate and graduate" is from a cadet who graduated from West Point in 2000, but it seems to be a historical one.

40. Kirkpatrick, "The very Model of a Modern Major General."

41. Clemente, "Making of the Prussian Officer," 262.

42. Oetting, *Auftragstaktik*, 253.

43. Dirk Richhardt, "Auswahl und Ausbildung junger Offiziere 1930–1945: Zur sozialen Genese des deutschen Offizierkorps" (Ph.D. dissertation, University of Marburg, 2002), 28. Richardt's diligently researched dissertation offers an enormous amount of numbers for the German officer corps.

44. Bland, Ritenour, and Wunderlin, eds., *"We Cannot Delay,"* 112. Marshall, then chief of staff, testified before a special session of the House Appropriations Committee regarding the necessity of Congress providing a supplemental appropriation of $120,000,000 for fiscal year 1940 to facilitate more maneuvers and realistic training.

45. Ibid., 611. Marshall's speech to the American Legion, September 15, 1941, Milwaukee, Wisconsin.

46. U.S. War Department, ed. *German Military Forces*, ii. Stephen E. Ambrose made the statement in his foreword to the reprint of this classic.

47. Leonard Mosley, *Marshall: Organizer of Victory* (London: Methuen, 1982).

48. *Letter from Walter Bedell Smith to Thomas T. Handy, February 9, 1945,* Thomas T. Handy Papers, Box 1, Folder Folder Smith, Walter Bedell,

1944–1945, B-1/F-7, George C. Marshall Library, Lexington, Virginia.

49. *George S. Patton Diary, September 17, 1943*, George S. Patton Library, West Point Library, Special Archives Collection, West Point, New York.

50. *Letter from John McAuley Palmer to George A. Lynch, May, 25, 1938*.

51. Chynoweth, *Bellamy Park*, 296. Emphasis in the original.

52. Berlin, *U.S. Army World War II Corps Commanders*, 13–14. Memorandum to General Lesley McNair, December 1, 1942.

53. Ridgway, *Soldier*, 160. *Letter from Matthew B. Ridgway to Robert T. Stevens, Secretary of the Army*, Matthew B. Ridgway Papers, Box 17, United States Army Military History Institute, Carlisle, Pennsylvania; *Letter from Jacob L. Devers to H. F. Shugg, March 21, 1942*, Jacob L. Devers Papers, Box 2, Folder [Reel] 10, Dwight D. Eisenhower Library, Abilene, Kansas.

54. Kent Roberts Greenfield and Robert R. Palmer, *Origins of the Army Ground Forces General Headquarters, United States Army, 1940–1942* (Washington D. C.: Historical Section—Army Ground Forces, 1946), 26.

55. *Armistice Day Address to the American Legion by Paul M. Robinett, 1943, Mountain Grove, Missouri*, Paul M. Robinett Papers, Box 12, Folder Orders and Letters (bound), George. C. Marshall Library, Lexington, Virginia.

56. Chynoweth, *Bellamy Park*, 186.

57. Dickson, *Algiers to Elbe: G-2 Journal*, 37. The officers, however, were in their late thirties and early forties. Fredendall was then fifty-nine years of age. He entered West Point in 1905 but failed two times in mathematics and other topics and was "separated" from the Academy. He nevertheless took the officer's exam and gained a commission in 1907. Fredendall's name became synonymous with the defeat at Kasserine Pass. For many he became just the "goat" to cover up massive problems in the command structure and unclear strategic aims. It is undeniable, however, that Fredendall wasted an enormous amount of manpower and resources to build—in a war of movement—a command post into a mountain.

58. *Letter from Walter B. Smith to Lucian K. Truscott, December 15, 1943.*

59. *Dwight D. Eisenhower's official assessment of Thomas T. Handy for the years 1945/1946,* Thomas T. Handy Papers, Box 2, Folder Handy, Thomas T., B-2/F-36, George C. Marshall Library, Lexington, Virginia.

60. Handy became famous in privy circles for signing the order to bomb Hiroshima and for pardoning many of the *Wehrmacht* generals who were then imprisoned in Landsberg when he was commander in chief of U.S. forces in Europe in 1954.

61. Omar Nelson Bradley and Clay Blair, *A General's Life: An Autobiography* (New York: Simon and Schuster, 1983), 108–109.

62. Messerschmidt, "German Military Effectiveness between 1919 and 1939."

63. Martin van Creveld, *The Training of Officers: From Military Professionalism to Irrelevance* (New York City: Free Press, 1990), 25.

64. Clemente, "Making of the Prussian Officer," 293.

65. Brown, *Social Attitudes*, 83.

66. Ibid., 6–7.

67. Pogue, *Education of a General*, 114.

68. Citino, *The Path to Blitzkrieg*, 127.

69. Allsep, "New Forms for Dominance," 200.

70. See the pictures in Eisenhower, *Strictly Personal*. Bland, Ritenour, and Wunderlin, eds., *"We Cannot Delay"*.

71. Bland, Ritenour, and Wunderlin, eds., *"We Cannot Delay,"* 452.

72. Clemente, "Making of the Prussian Officer," 276.

73. The CCC was a program for youth employment created under New Deal legislation and lasted from 1933 to 1942. The volunteering young men were gathered in camps run by army officers all over the countryside and set to work in nationals parks and forests and planting and harvesting. The manpower mobilization for this program even dwarfed that of World War I.

74. Letter from Colonel Morrison C. Stayer to George C. Marshall, December 16, 1939, is found in Bland, Ritenour, and Wunderlin, eds., *"We Cannot Delay,"* 130.

75. Chynoweth, *Bellamy Park*, 80.

76. Mott, *Twenty Years*, 355.

77. Citino, *The Path to Blitzkrieg*, 223–224; Oetting, *Auftragstaktik*, 182–183.

78. Michael W. Sherraden, "Military Participation in a Youth Employment Program: The Civilian Conservation Corps," *Armed Forces & Society* 7, no. 2 (1981): 240. For more problems with the officers and their relationship with the civilians in the CCC camps and the National Guard, see the first three volumes of the published Marshall Papers and Pogue, *Education of a General.*

A work comparing the CCC with the *Reichsarbeitsdienst* (RDA): Kiran Klaus Patel, *Soldiers of Labor: Labor Service in Nazi Germany and New Deal America, 1933–1945* (Washington, D.C.: Cambridge University Press, 2005). Comparative studies are always intriguing but the title of the book is misleading. The title refers just to the aspect that is the least comparable between both mass programs, something the author admits in his otherwise fine work (pp. 153, 181). Considering the high desertion rate, the absence of any military drill until 1942, and the notorious laxness of the CCC in contrast to the explicit paramilitary training and later total integration into the German military system of the RDA, the military or "soldierly" aspect for the individual is negligible. However, the CCC gave the army the chance to practice managing huge numbers of men. See also Charles William Johnson, "The Civilian Conservation Corps: The Role of the Army" (Ph.D. dissertation, University of Michigan, 1968). Johnson's study rather portrays the internal struggle of the army with the program. Unfortunately, it is not very critical in its assessment. In addition, the author cites whole record groups from the National Archives, which is not good scholarship because the documents in question could only be found with an enormous effort and luck.

79. Johnson, "The Civilian Conservation Corps: The Role of the Army," 89.

80. *Memorandum from George C. Marshall to Chief of Staff, Sixth Corps Area, regarding officers' efficiency reports, May 31, 1934,* George C. Marshall

Papers, Box 1, Folder Illinois National Guard, Correspondence, 1 of 24, May 15–31, 1934, George C. Marshall Library, Lexington, Virginia. Here, the efficiency report of Cpt. Philip A. Helmbold, Commander CCC Company (training civilians), 8th Infantry, July 1, 1933 to Oct. 20, 1933.

81. Brown, *Social Attitudes*, 323.

82. *Letter from Major Clarke K. Fales to George C. Marshall, Sept. 25, 1934.* Fales had already been "stuck" with the National Guard for five years.

83. Pogue, *Education of a General*, 307–308.

84. Ibid., 346.

85. Kirkpatrick, "Orthodox Soldiers," 109.

86. Wette, *The Wehrmacht*, 2–3, 23.

87. Diedrich, *Paulus: Das Trauma von Stalingrad*, 134.

88. Förster, "The Dynamics of *Volksgemeinschaft*," 180, 206.

89. Ibid., 207.

90. Gerd R. Ueberschär, *Dienen und Verdienen: Hitlers Geschenke an seine Eliten*, 2nd ed. (Frankfurt a. M.: Fischer, 1999); Norman J. W. Goda, "Black Marks: Hitler's Bribery of His Senior Officers during World War II," *The Journal of Modern History* 72 (2000).

91. Geoffrey P. Megargee, "Selective Realities, Selective Memories" (paper presented at the Society for Military History Annual Conference, Quantico, Virginia, April 2000).

92. Förster, "The Dynamics of *Volksgemeinschaft*," 200.

93. *Spires, Image and Reality*, 2. Such a statement is basically to be found in any book about the *Reichswehr*.

94. Oetting, *Auftragstaktik*, 178.

95. Erfurth, *Die Geschichte des deutschen Generalstabes von 1918 bis 1945*, 151.

96. That had been already suggested anonymously in the most important post-war military journal in Germany. At the time the discussion was already ongoing over who the generals of the new German army—the *Bundeswehr*—should be and how they should be selected. The vehement replies from the ranks of former General Staff corps officers and psychiatrists responsible for the officers' selec-

tion soon quieted the dissenting voices: Anonymous, "Rechter Mann am rechten Platz: Versuch eines Beitrages zum Problem der 'Stellenbesetzung,'" *Wehrwissenschaftliche Rundschau* 1, no. 8 (1951); Voss and Simoneit, "Die psychologische Eignungsuntersuchung in der deutschen Reichswehr und später der Wehrmacht."

Kurt Weckmann, "Führergehilfenausbildung," *Wehrwissenschaftliche Rundschau* 4, no. 6 (1954); Otto Wien, "Letter to the Editor as Answer to the Critique of Theodor Busse on his Article 'Probleme der künftigen Generalstabsausbildung,'" *Wehrkunde* V, no. 1 (1956); Theodor Busse, "Letter to the Editor as Critique to the Article 'Probleme der künftigen Generalstabsausbildung,' by Otto Wien in WEHRKUNDE IV/11," *Wehrkunde* 5, no. 1 (1956).

97. See the collection in the outstanding book, Hürter, *Hitlers Heerführer: Die deutschen Oberbefehlshaber im Krieg gegen die Sowjetunion 1941/1942.*

98. Yingling, "A Failure in Generalship."

99. I borrowed the phrase from the excellent article by John T. Kuehn, "The Goldwater-Nichols Fix: Joint Education is the Key to True 'Jointness'" *Armed Forces Journal* 32 (April 2010).

100. Miles, *Fallen Leaves*, 282. The German version of that proverb reads in its translation nearly identical: "No report, no matter how good it is, can replace personal observation." Cited in Citino, *The Path to Blitzkrieg*, 58.

101. Bland and Ritenour Stevens, eds., *The Papers of George Catlett Marshall: "The Right Man for the Job"—December 7, 1941—May 31, 1943*, 62. Memorandum by George C. Marshall for Assistant Chief of Staff [Brig. Gen. John H. Hilldring], G-1, January 14, 1942, Washington, D.C.

102. Grotelueschen, *The AEF Way of War*, 364.

103. Michael R. Gordon and Bernard E. Trainor, *Cobra II: The Inside Story of the Invasion and Occupation of Iraq* (New York: Vintage, 2006), 431.

104. Zucchino, *Thunder Run*, 6.

105. Ibid., 38.

106. Ibid., 15.

107. Weigley, *Eisenhower's Lieutenants*, 594.

108. Gordon and Trainor, *Cobra II*, 450.

109. Ibid., 451.

110. Ibid., 453.

111. Zucchino, *Thunder Run*, 154.

112. Gordon and Trainor, *Cobra II*, 461.

113. Michael E. Fischer, "Mission-Type Orders in Joint Operations: The Empowerment of Air Leadership" (School of Advanced Air Power Studies, 1995).

114. Zucchino, *Thunder Run*, 241. The quote is from Major Roger Shuck, the operations officer of one of the Spartan Brigade's battalions.

115. Correlli Barnett, "The Education of Military Elites," *Journal of Contemporary History* 2, no. 3 (1967): 35. Barnett calls that diplomatically "undue respect for orthodox doctrine, and an unwillingness to deviate on his own responsibility from standard procedure." He had foreseen many of the effects of the American officers education forty years ago.

116. Grotelueschen, *The AEF Way of War*, 352.

117. Mullaney, *The Unforgiving Minute*, 189.

118. Gordon and Trainor, *Cobra II*, 354.

119. Ibid.

120. Ridgway, *Soldier*, 206–207.

Author's Afterword

1. I appreciate Edward M. Coffman and Dennis Showalter suggesting this afterword. It has been a good idea.

2. Ten years ago an expert already pointed that out but his words remain unheard: Murray. "Does Military Culture Matter?," 145–149.

Selected Bibliography

Archival Evidence/Documents

CARL (Combined Arms Research Library), Fort Leavenworth, Kansas

Course Material, Command and General Staff School
Regular Courses, 1939–1940, Misc., G-1, Vol. 1.
Regular Courses, 1939–1940, Misc., G-2, Vol. 11.
Regular Courses, 1939–1940, Misc., G-5, Vol. 19.
Individual Research Papers, 1934–1936.

Oral Histories
Armed Forces Oral Histories, World War II Combat Interviews,
2nd Armored Division.

Senior Officers Oral History Program
Ennis, William Pierce. Transcript.
Grombacher, Gerd S. Transcript.

Personal Papers
Clarke, Bruce C. Papers.
Hoge, William M. Papers.
Warnock, Aln D. Papers.

U.S. Military Intelligence Reports, Combat Estimates: Europe, Bi-Weekly
Intelligence Summaries 1919–1943

Dwight D. Eisenhower Presidential Library, Abilene, Kansas
Allen, Terry de la Mesa. Papers [fragments].
Bull, Harold R. Papers.
Collins, Joe Lawton. Papers.
Cota, Norman D. Papers.
Devers, Jacob L. Papers.
Eisenhower, Dwight D. Pre-Presidential Papers.
Norstad, Lauris. Papers.
Paul, Willard S. Papers.
Smith, Walter B. Papers.
Ryder, Charles W. Papers.
Woodruff, Roscoe B. Papers.

George C. Marshall Library, Lexington, Virginia

Interviews
Marshall, George C. Interview by Forrest Pogue, Nov. 15, 1956.
Smith, Truman. Interview by Forrest Pogue, Oct. 5, 1959.

Papers
Handy, Thomas T. Papers.
Marshall, George C. Papers.
McCarthy, Frank. Papers.
Robinett, Paul M. Papers.
Truscott, Lucian K. Papers.
Van Fleet, James A. Papers.
Ward, Orlando. Diary, March 25, 1938–Aug. 25, 1941

Harry S. Truman Presidential Library, Independence, Missouri
Baade, Paul W. Papers.
Quirk, James T. Papers.

National Archives II, College Park, Maryland

Collection of Twentieth-Century Military Records, 1918–1950

Series I—USAF Historical Studies
The Development of the German Air Force 1919–1939, German Air Force
Operations in Support of the Army, The German Air Force General Staff,
Box 38.

USAF Historical Studies: No. 174, Command and Leadership in the German Air Force, Box 39.

Record Groups
Record Group 38, (Chief of Naval Operations), Entry 99, Office of Naval Intelligence, Secret Naval Attaché's Reports 1936–43. Estimate of Military Strength, Summaries War Diary Berlin, Probability of War Documents E, War Diary Naval Attaché Berlin, Vols. 1–2, Boxes 1–5.

Record Group 165, Records of the War Dept. General and Special Staffs, Entry 194, Office of the Director of Intelligence (G-2) 1906–1949, "Who's Who" data cards on German Military, Civilian, and Political Personalities, 1925–1945: Army Officers, foreign volunteers, Army, *Generalfeldmarschall, Generaloberst*, NM-84 E 194, Box 3.

Record Group 165, Entry 65, Military Intelligence Division Correspondence, 1917–41, 2657-G-830/16 to 2657-G-842/135, Boxes 1473, 1672.

Record Group 165, Entry 65, Microfilm Publication No. 1445, Correspondence of the Military Intelligence Division relating to General, Political, Economical, and Military Correspondence in Spain, 1918–41, Rolls 6–12.

Record Group 165, Entry 65, Records of the WFGS [sic] [War Department General Staff], Military Intelligence Division, Correspondence, 1917–41, 2277-B-43 to 2277-C-22, Boxes 1113, 1177.

Record Group 218, Records of the U.S. Joint Chiefs of Staff, Chairman's File, Admiral Leahy, 1942–48, Folder 126, HM 1994, Memos to the President from General Marshall.

Record Group 226, Records of OSS, Research and Analysis Branch, Central Information Division, Name and Subject Card Indexes to Series 16, Alpha Name index (I) Sar–Jol, Box 18.

Record Group 226, Entry 14, Name Index (II), Boxes 22, 23.

Record Group 226, Entry 14, Records of the OSS, Research and Analysis Branch, Central Information Division, Name and Subject Card Indexes to Series 16, Country: Germany, Boxes 199, 200, 202, 228, 229, 230, 231, 232.

Record Group 226, Entry 16, Records of OSS, Research and Analysis Branch, Intelligence Reports ("Regular" Series) 1941–45, Boxes 1543, 1626, Interrog. Guderian.

Record Group 331, (Allied Operational and Occupation Headquarters, WW II), SHAEF, General Staff, G-2 Division, Intelligence Target ("T") Sub-Division, Decimal File 000.4 to 314.81, Box 156, no decimal file.

Record Group 331, (Allied Operational and Occupation Headquarters, WW II), Entry 12A, SHAEF, General Staff, G-2 Division, Operational Intelligence Sub-Division, Aug. 1944–May 1945, Decimal File 004.05–385.2.1, Box 15, G-2 Meetings, Personalities, Intelligence on Germany, Enemy Forces General.

Record Group 331, (Allied Operational and Occupation Headquarters, WW II), Entry 13, SHAEF, General Staff, G-2 Division, Operational Intelligence Sub-Division, Intelligence Reports 1942–45, Intelligence Notes 17 to 61, Boxes 25, 26, 29, 31,30.

Record Group 331, Records of Allied Operational and Occupation Headquarters, WW II, Entry 13, Office of the Chief of Staff Secretary, General Staff, Decimal File
Box 46, May 1943–Aug. 1945, 322.01 G-5 Vol. II to 322.01 PWD;
Box 47, May 1943–Aug. 1945, 332.01 PS to 327.22.

Record Group 498, Records of the Headquarters, ETOUSA, Historical Division, Program Files, First U.S. Army, G-2 Periodic Reports, Reports, Memos, Instructions, Notes, Combat Operations, 1943–1945, Boxes 1–4 and Annexe.

Record Group 498, Records of the Headquarters, ETOUSA, U.S. Army (WW II), Entry ETO G-2 Handbook, Military Intelligence, Box 1.

U.S. Army: Unit Records, 1940–1950
2nd Infantry Division.
79th Infantry Division.
101st Airborne Division.
103rd Infantry Division.

U.S. Army Military History Institute, Carlisle, Pennsylvania

Army War College Curricular Archives
1939–1940, G-2 Course, File No. 2-1940A, 1-28, Lecture by Percy Black, Seminar Study on Germany, "The German Situation"; Lecture by Dr. W. L. Langer, Harvard.

OCMH (Office of the Chief of Military History) Collection
ID 2, Army General Staff Interviews.

Personal Papers
Dahlquist, John E. Papers.
Heintges, John A. Papers.

Koch, Oscar. Papers.
Ridgway, Matthew B. Papers.
Smith, Truman, and Katherine A. H. Papers.
Wedemeyer, Albert C. Papers [fragments].

Senior Officers Oral History Program
Bolté, Charles L. Transcript.

West Point Library Special Archives Collection, West Point, New York
Dickson, Benjamin Abbott "Monk." Papers.
Krueger, Walter. Papers.
Murphy, Audie. Collection.
Palmer, Williston Birkheimer. Papers.
Patton, George S., Jr. Patton Collection.

Dissertations, Research Papers, and Unpublished Literature

Alexander, David R., III. "Hazing: The Formative Years." Research paper submitted to faculty of United States Military Academy, History Department, West Point, New York, 1994.

Allsep, L. Michael, Jr. "New Forms for Dominance: How a Corporate Lawyer Created the American Military Establishment." Ph.D. dissertation, University of North Carolina at Chapel Hill, 2008.

Appleton, Lloyd Otto. "The Relationship between Physical Ability and Success at the United States Military Academy." Ph.D. dissertation, New York University, 1949.

Atkinson, Rick. "Keynote: In the Company of Soldiers." Paper presented at Teaching about the Military in American History conference, Wheaton, Illinois, March 24–25, 2007.

Bernd, Hans Dieter. "Die Beseitigung der Weimarer Republik auf 'legalem' Weg: Die Funktion des Antisemitismus in der Agitation der Führungsschicht der DNVP." Ph.D. dissertation, University of Hagen, 2004.

Boone, Michael T. "The Academic Board and the Failure to Progress at the United States Military Academy." Research paper submitted to faculty of United States Military Academy, History Department, West Point, New York, 1994.

Bradley, Mark Frederick. "United States Military Attachés and the Interwar Development of the German Army." Master's thesis, Georgia State University, 1983.

Clark, Jason P. "Modernization without Technology: U.S. Army Organizational and Educational Reform, 1901–1911." Paper presented at Society of Military History annual conference, Ogden, Utah, April 18, 2008.

Clemente, Steven Errol. "'Mit Gott! Für König und Kaiser!': A Critical Analysis of the Making of the Prussian Officer, 1860–1914." Ph.D. dissertation, University of Oklahoma, 1989.

Cockrell, Philip Carlton. "Brown Shoes and Mortar Boards: U.S. Army Officer Professional Education at the Command and General Staff School, Fort Leavenworth, Kansas, 1919–1940." Ph.D. dissertation, University of South Carolina, 1991.

"Combat Awards." Article draft, undated. Bruce C. Clarke Papers. Combined Arms Research Library, Fort Leavenworth, Kansas.

Combined British, Canadian and U.S. Study Group, ed. *German Operational Intelligence*, 1946.

Dickson, Benjamin A. *Algiers to Elbe: G-2 Journal.* Unpublished. Monk Dickson Papers. West Point Library Special Archive, West Point, New York.

Dillard, Walter Scott. "The United States Military Academy, 1865–1900: The Uncertain Years." Ph.D. dissertation, University of Washington, 1972.

"Does a Commander Need Intelligence or Information?" Article draft, undated. Bruce C. Clarke Papers, Box 1. Combined Arms Research Library, Fort Leavenworth, Kansas.

Elrod, Ronald P. "The Cost of Educating a Cadet at West Point." Research paper submitted to faculty of United States Military Academy, History Department, West Point, New York, 1994.

"Faith—It Moveth Mountains." Article Draft. John E. Dahlquist Papers, Box 2, Folder Correspondence, 1953–1956, 13. U.S. Army Military History Institute, Carlisle, Pennsylvania.

Fröhlich, Paul. "'Der vergessene Partner': Die militärische Zusammenarbeit der Reichswehr mit der U.S. Army, 1918–1933." Master's thesis, University of Potsdam, 2008.

"The German General Staff Corps: A Study of the Organization of the German General Staff, prepared by a combined British, Canadian and U.S. Staff," 1946.

Grodecki, Thomas S. "[U.S.] Military Observers, 1815–1975." Center of Military History, Washington, D.C., 1989.

"History in Military Education." Paul M. Robinett Papers, Box 20, Folder: Articles by Brig. Gen. P. M. Robinett (bound). George C. Marshall Library, Lexington, Virginia.

Johnson, Charles William. "The Civilian Conservation Corps: The Role of the Army." Ph.D. dissertation, University of Michigan, 1968.

Jones, Dave. "Assessing the Effectiveness of "Project Athena": The 1976 Admission of Women to West Point." West Point, New York: Research Paper submitted to faculty of United States Military Academy, History Department, 1995.

Keller, Christian B. "Anti-German Sentiment in the Union Army: A Study in Wartime Prejudice." Paper presented at Society for Military History annual conference, Ogden, Utah, April 17–19, 2008.

Koch, Scott Alan. "Watching the Rhine: The U.S. Army Military Attaché Reports and the Resurgence of the German Army, 1933–1941." Ph.D. dissertation, Duke University, 1990.

LaCamera, Trese A. "Hazing: A Tradition too Deep to Abolish." Research paper submitted to faculty of United States Military Academy, History Department, West Point, New York, 1995.

Lebby, David Edwin. "Professional Socialization of the Naval Officer: The Effect of Plebe Year at the U.S. Naval Academy." Ph.D. dissertation, University of Pennsylvania, 1970.

Lovell, John Philip. "The Cadet Phase of the Professional Socialization of the West Pointer: Description, Analysis, and Theoretical Refinement." Ph.D. dissertation, University of Wisconsin, 1962.

Lucas, William Ashley. "The American Lieutenant: An Empirical Investigation of Normative Theories of Civil-Military Relations." Ph.D. dissertation, North Carolina at Chapel Hill, 1967.

Megargee, Geoffrey P. "Connections: Strategy, Operations, and Ideology in the Nazi Invasion of the Soviet Union." Paper presented at Society for Military History annual conference, Frederick, Maryland, 2007.

———. "Selective Realities, Selective Memories." Paper presented at Society for Military History annual conference, Quantico, Virginia, April 2000.

Muth, Jörg. "Gezeitenwechsel mit dem Machtwechsel?: Die Entwicklung der Bundeswehr bis zur Ära Brandt, und das Entscheidungsverhalten des ersten sozialdemokratischen Verteidigungsministers Helmut Schmidt an den Beispielen seines Krisenmanagements und der Reform der Offizieraus-bildung." Unpublished term paper, Universität Potsdam, 2000.

Nye, Roger H. "The United States Military Academy in an Era of Educational Reform, 1900–1925." Ph.D. dissertation, Columbia University, 1968.

"Observations on Military History." Paul M. Robinett Papers, Box 20, Folder: Articles by Brig. Gen. P. M. Robinett (bound). George C. Marshall Library, Lexington, Virginia.

"Personnel Relations in the French, Swiss, Swedish, British, German, and Russian Armies." Folder R-15152, Intelligence Research Project No. 3199. Combined Arms Research Library, Fort Leavenworth, Kansas.

Richhardt, Dirk "Auswahl und Ausbildung junger Offiziere, 1930–1945: Zur sozialen Genese des deutschen Offizierkorps." Ph.D. dissertation, University of Marburg, 2002.

Robertson, William Alexander, Jr. "Officer Selection in the Reichswehr, 1918–1926." Ph.D. dissertation, University of Oklahoma, 1978.

Robinett, Paul M. "The Role of Intelligence Officers." Lecture, Fort Riley, Kansas, March 17, 1951. Paul M. Robinett Papers, Box 20, Folder P. M. Robinett Lectures January, 11, 1943–January, 31, 1957. George C. Marshall Library, Lexington, Virginia.

————."Information Bulletins, GHQ, U.S. Army, December 18, 1941– March 7, 1942." Washington, D.C.

Schifferle, Peter J. "Anticipating Armageddon: The Leavenworth Schools and U.S. Army Military Effectiveness, 1919 to 1945." Ph.D. dissertation, University of Kansas, 2002.

————. "The Next War: The American Army Interwar Officer Corps Writes about the Future." Paper presented at Society for Military History annual conference, Ogden, Utah, April 17–19, 2008.

————. "The Prussian and American General Staffs: An Analysis of Cross-Cultural Imitation, Innovation and Adaption." Master's thesis, University of North Carolina at Chapel Hill, 1981.

Segal, David R. "Closure in the Military Labor Market: A Critique of Pure Cohesion." Paper presented at the annual meeting of the American Sociological Association, Anaheim, California, 2001.

Skirbunt, Peter D. "Prologue to Reform: The 'Germanization' of the United States Army, 1865–1898." Ph.D. dissertation, Ohio State University, 1983.

Stokam, Lori A. "The Fourth Class System: 192 Years of Tradition Unhampered by Progress from Within." Research paper submitted to faculty of United States Military Academy, History Department, West Point, New York, 1994.

Literature

Abelly, Louis. *The Life of the Venerable Servant of God: Vincent de Paul*. 3 vols. Vol. 2. New York: New City Press, 1993.

Abrahamson, James L. *America Arms for a New Century: The Making of a Great Military Power*. New York: Free Press, 1981.

Afflerbach, Holger. *Falkenhayn: Politisches Denken und Handeln im Kaiserreich*. München: Oldenbourg, 1994.

Allendorf, Donald. *Long Road to Liberty: The Odyssey of a German Regiment in the Yankee Army; The 15th Missouri Volunteer Infantry*. Kent, Ohio: Kent State University Press, 2006.

Ambrose, Stephen E. *Citizen Soldiers: The U.S. Army from the Normandy Beaches to the Bulge to the Surrender of Germany, June 7, 1944–May 7, 1945*. New York: Simon & Schuster, 1997.

————. *Duty, Honor, Country: A History of West Point*. Baltimore: Johns Hopkins Press, 1966.

————. *Eisenhower: Soldier, General of the Army, President-elect, 1890–1950*. 2 vols. Vol. 1. New York: Simon & Schuster, 1983.

———. *Eisenhower: President, 1952–1969*. 2 vols. Vol. 2. New York: Simon & Schuster, 1984.

———. *The Supreme Commander: The War Years of General Dwight D. Eisenhower*. 1st ed. Garden City, New York: Doubleday, 1970.

Ancell, R. Manning, and Christine Miller. *The Biographical Dictionary of World War II Generals and Flag Officers: The U.S. Armed Forces*. Westport, Connecticut: Greenwood Press, 1996.

Andrae, Friedrich. *Auch gegen Frauen und Kinder: Der Krieg der deutschen Wehrmacht gegen die Zivilbevölkerung in Italien, 1943–1945*. 2nd ed. München: Piper, 1995.

Andreski, Stanislav. *Military Organization and Society*. 2nd ed. London: Routledge, 1968.

Annual Report of the Superintendent of the United States Military Academy. West Point, New York: USMA Press, 1914.

Anonymous. "Inbreeding at West Point." Editorial. *Infantry Journal* 16 (1919).

Anonymous. "Politisierung der Wehrmacht?" Editorial. *Militär-Wochenblatt* 116, no. 1 (1931): 1–5.

Anonymous. "Rechter Mann am rechten Platz: Versuch eines Beitrages zum Problem der 'Stellenbesetzung.'" *Wehrwissenschaftliche Rundschau* 1, no. 8 (1951): 20–23.

Anonymous [A Lieutenant]. "Student Impression at the Infantry School." *Infantry Journal* 18, (1921): 21–25.

Anonymous. "'Versachlichte Soldaten.'" *Militär-Wochenblatt* 116, no. 8 (1931): 287–290.

Astor, Gerald. *Terrible Terry Allen: Combat General of World War II; The Life of an American Soldier*. New York: Presidio, 2003.

Aufnahme-Bestimmungen und Lehrplan des Königlichen Kadettenkorps. Berlin: Mittler, 1910.

Badsey, Stephen, Rob Havers, and Mark Grove, eds. *The Falklands Conflict Twenty Years On: Lessons for the Future*. London: Cass, 2005.

Bald, Detlef. *Der deutsche Generalstab, 1859–1939: Reform und Restauration in Ausbildung und Bildung*, Schriftenreihe Innere Führung, Heft 28. Bonn: Bundesministerium der Verteidigung, 1977.

———. *Der deutsche Offizier: Sozial- und Bildungsgeschichte des deutschen Offizierkorps im 20. Jahrhundert*. München: Bernard & Graefe, 1982.

Barnett, Correlli. "The Education of Military Elites." *Journal of Contemporary History* 2, no. 3 (1967): 15–35.

Bartov, Omer. *The Eastern Front, 1941–45: German Troops and the Barbarization of Warfare*. New York: St. Martin's Press, 1986.

———. "Extremfälle der Normalität und die Normalität des Außergewöhnlichen: Deutsche Soldaten an der Ostfront." In *Über Leben im Krieg. Kriegserfahrungen in einer Industrieregion 1939–1945*, edited by Ulrich Borsdorf and Mathilde Jamin, 148–161. Reinbek b. H.: Rowohlt, 1989.

———. *Hitler's Army: Soldiers, Nazis, and War in the Third Reich*. New York: Oxford University Press, 1991.

Bateman, Robert. "Soldiers and Warriors." *Washington Post*, Sept. 18, 2008.

Baur, Werner. "Deutsche Generale: Die militärischen Führungsgruppen in der Bundesrepublik und in der DDR." In *Beiträge zur Analyse der deutschen Oberschicht*, edited by Werner Baur and Wolfgang Zapf, 114–135. München: Piper, 1965.

Bearbeitet von einigen Offizieren [prepared by some officers]. *Die Wehrkreis-Prüfung 1921*. Berlin: Offene Worte, 1921.

———. *Die Wehrkreis-Prüfung, 1924*. Berlin: Offene Worte, 1924.

———. *Die Wehrkreis-Prüfung, 1929*. Berlin: Offene Worte, 1930.

———. *Die Wehrkreis-Prüfung, 1930*. Berlin: Offene Worte, 1931.

———. *Die Wehrkreis-Prüfung, 1931*. Berlin: Offene Worte, 1932.

———. *Die Wehrkreis-Prüfung, 1932*. Berlin: Offene Worte, 1932.

———. *Die Wehrkreis-Prüfung, 1933*. Berlin: Offene Worte, 1933.

———. *Die Wehrkreis-Prüfung, 1937*. Berlin: Offene Worte, 1937.

———. *Die Wehrkreis-Prüfung, 1938*. Berlin: Offene Worte, 1938.

Bellafaire, Judith L. *The U.S. Army and World War II: Selected Papers from the Army's Commemorative Conferences*. Washington, D. C.: Center of Military History, U.S. Army, 1998.

Bender, Mark C. *Watershed at Leavenworth: Dwight D. Eisenhower and the Command and General Staff School*. Fort Leavenworth, Kansas: U.S. Army Command and General Staff College, 1990.

Bendersky, Joseph W. *The "Jewish Threat": Anti-Semitic Politics of the U.S. Army*. New York: Basic Books, 2000.

———. "Racial Sentinels: Biological Anti-Semitism in the U.S. Army Officer Corps, 1890–1950." *Militärgeschichtliche Zeitschrift* 62, no. 2 (2003): 331–353.

Berger, Ed, et al. "ROTC, My Lai and the Volunteer Army." In *The Military and Society: A Collection of Essays*, edited by Peter Karsten, 147–172. New York: Garland, 1998.

Berlin, Robert H. *U.S. Army World War II Corps Commanders: A Composite Biography*. Fort Leavenworth, Kansas: U.S. Army Command and General Staff College, 1989.

Betros, Lance A., ed. *West Point: Two Centuries and Beyond*. Abilene, Texas: McWhiney Foundation Press, 2004.

Bijl, Nick van der, and David Aldea. *5th Infantry Brigade in the Falklands*. Barnsley, UK: Cooper, 2003.

Biographical Register of the United States Military Academy: The Classes, 1802–1926. West Point, New York: West Point Association of Graduates, 2002.

Bird, Keith W. *Erich Raeder: Admiral of the Third Reich.* Annapolis, Maryland: Naval Institute Press, 2006.

Birtle, Andrew J. *Rearming the Phoenix: U.S. Military Assistance to the Federal Republic of Germany, 1950–1960.* Modern American History. New York: Garland, 1991.

Bland, Larry I., and Sharon R. Ritenour, eds. *The Papers of George Catlett Marshall: "The Soldierly Spirit," December 1880–June 1939.* 6 vols. Vol. 1. Baltimore: Johns Hopkins University Press, 1981.

Bland, Larry I., Sharon R. Ritenour, and Clarence E. Wunderlin, eds. *The Papers of George Catlett Marshall: "We Cannot Delay," July 1, 1939–December 6, 1941.* 6 vols. Vol. 2. Baltimore: Johns Hopkins University Press, 1986.

Bland, Larry I., and Sharon R. Ritenour Stevens, eds. *The Papers of George Catlett Marshall: "The Right Man for the Job," December 7, 1941–May 31, 1943.* 6 vols. Vol. 3. Baltimore: Johns Hopkins University Press, 1991.

Blank, Herbert. "Die Halbgötter: Geschichte, Gestalt und Ende des Generalstabes." *Nordwestdeutsche Hefte* 4 (1947): 8–22.

———. *Preußische Offiziere.* Schriften an die Nation. Oldenburg: Stalling, 1932.

Blumenson, Martin. "America's World War II Leaders in Europe: Some Thoughts." *Parameters* 19 (1989): 2–13.

Böhler, Jochen. *Auftakt zum Vernichtungskrieg: Die Wehrmacht in Polen, 1939.* Frankfurt a. M.: Fischer, 2006.

Boog, Horst. "Civil Education, Social Origins, and the German Officer Corps in the Nineteenth and Twentieth Centuries." In *Forging the Sword: Selecting, Educating, and Training Cadets and Junior Officers in the Modern World,* edited by Elliot V. Converse, 119–134. Chicago: Imprint Publications, 1998.

Boog, Horst, Jürgen Förster, Joachim Hoffmann, Ernst Klink, Rolf-Dieter Müller, and Gerd R. Ueberschär. *Das Deutsche Reich und der Zweite Weltkrieg, Vol. IV: Der Angriff auf die Sowjetunion.* 2nd ed. München: Deutsche Verlags-Anstalt, 1993.

Booth, Ewing E. *My Observations and Experiences in the United States Army.* Los Angeles: n.p., 1944.

Borsdorf, Ulrich, and Mathilde Jamin, eds. *Über Leben im Krieg. Kriegserfahrungen in einer Industrieregion, 1939–1945.* Reinbek b. H.: Rowohlt, 1989.

Bradley, Omar Nelson. *A Soldier's Story.* New York: Holt, 1951.

Bradley, Omar Nelson, and Clay Blair. *A General's Life: An Autobiography.* New York: Simon & Schuster, 1983.

Braim, Paul F. *The Will to Win: The Life of General James A. Van Fleet.* Annapolis, Maryland: Naval Institute Press, 2001.

Brand, Karl-Hermann Freiherr von, and Helmut Eckert. *Kadetten: Aus 300 Jahren deutscher Kadettenkorps.* 2 vols. Vol. 1. München: Schild, 1981.

————. *Kadetten: Aus 300 Jahren deutscher Kadettenkorps.* 2 vols. Vol. 2. München: Schild, 1981.

Breit, Gotthard. *Das Staats- und Gesellschaftsbild deutscher Generale beider Weltkriege im Spiegel ihrer Memoiren.* Wehrwissenschaftliche Forschungen/ Abteilung Militärgeschichtliche Studien 17. Boppard a. R.: Boldt, 1973.

Brereton, T. R. *Educating the U.S. Army: Arthur L. Wagner and Reform, 1875– 1905.* Lincoln: University of Nebraska Press, 2000.

Breymayer, Ursula, ed. *Willensmenschen: Über deutsche Offiziere.* Fischer- Taschenbücher. Frankfurt a. M.: Fischer, 1999.

Brief Historical and Vital Statistics of the Graduates of the United States Military Academy, 1802–1952. West Point, New York: Public Information Office, United States Military Academy.

Broicher, Andreas. "Betrachtungen zum Thema 'Führen und Führer.'" *Clausewitz-Studien* 1 (1996): 106–127.

Broicher, Andreas "Die Wehrmacht in ausländischen Urteilen." In *Die Soldaten der Wehrmacht,* edited by Hans Poeppel, Wilhelm Karl Prinz von Preußen and Karl-Günther von Hase, 405–460. München: Herbig, 1998.

Broszat, Martin, Klaus-Dietmar Henke, and Hans Woller, eds. *Von Stalingrad zur Währungsreform: Zur Sozialgeschichte des Umbruchs in Deutschland,* Quellen und Darstellungen zur Zeitgeschichte 26. München: Oldenbourg, 1988.

Broszat, Martin, and Klaus Schwabe, eds. *Die deutschen Eliten und der Weg in den Zweiten Weltkrieg.* München: Beck, 1989.

Brown, John Sloan. *Draftee Division: The 88th Infantry Division in World War II.* Lexington: University Press of Kentucky, 1986.

Brown, Richard Carl. *Social Attitudes of American Generals, 1898–1940.* New York: Arno Press, 1979.

Brown, Russell K. *Fallen in Battle: American General Officer Combat Fatalities from 1775.* New York: Greenwood Press, 1988.

Bucholz, Arden. *Delbrück's Modern Military History.* Lincoln: University of Nebraska Press, 1997.

Burchardt, Lothar. "Operatives Denken und Planen von Schlieffen bis zum Beginn des Ersten Weltkrieges." In *Operatives Denken und Handeln in deutschen Streitkräften im 19. und 20. Jahrhundert,* edited by Günther Roth, 45–71. Herford: Mittler, 1988.

Burdick, Charles B. "Vom Schwert zur Feder. Deutsche Kriegsgefangene im Dienst der Vorbereitung der amerikanischen Kriegsgeschichtsschreibung über den Zweiten Weltkrieg." *Militärgeschichtliche Mitteilungen* 10 (1971): 69–80.

Burton, William L. *Melting Pot Soldiers: The Union's Ethnic Regiments.* New York: Fordham University Press, 1998.

Busch, Michael, and Jörg Hillman, eds. *Adel—Geistlichkeit—Militär.* Schriftenreihe der Stiftung Herzogtum Lauenburg. Bochum: Winkler, 1999.

Busse, Theodor. "Letter to the Editor as Critique to the Article "Probleme der künftigen Generalstabsausbildung," by Otto Wien in WEHRKUNDE IV/11." *Wehrkunde* 5, no. 1 (1956): 57–58.

Butcher, Harry C. *My Three Years with Eisenhower: The Personal Diary of Captain Harry C. Butcher, USNR, Naval Aide to General Eisenhower, 1942 to 1945.* New York: Simon & Schuster, 1946.

Campbell, D'Ann. "The Spirit Run and Football Cordon: A Case Study of Female Cadets at the U.S. Military Academy." In *Forging the Sword: Selecting, Educating, and Training Cadets and Junior Officers in the Modern World*, edited by Elliot V. Converse, 237–247. Chicago: Imprint Publications, 1998.

Caspar, Gustav Adolf, Ullrich Marwitz, and Hans-Martin Ottmer, eds. *Tradition in deutschen Streitkräften bis 1945*, Entwicklung deutscher militärischer Tradition 1. Herford: Mittler, 1986.

Chickering, Roger. "The American Civil War and the German Wars of Unification: Some Parting Shots." In *On the Road to Total War: The American Civil War and the German Wars of Unification, 1861–1871*, edited by Stig Förster and Jörg Nagler, 683–691. Washington, D.C.: German Historical Institute, 1997.

Chynoweth, Bradford Grethen. *Bellamy Park: Memoirs*. Hicksville, New York: Exposition Press, 1975.

Citino, Robert M. *The Path to Blitzkrieg: Doctrine and Training in the German Army, 1920–1939*. Boulder, Colorado: Lynne Rienner, 1999.

———, *The German Way of War: From the Thirty Year's War to the Third Reich.* Lawrence: University Press of Kansas, 2005.

Clark, Mark W. *Calculated Risk*. New York: Harper & Brothers, 1950.

Clausewitz, Carl von. *Vom Kriege*. Reprint from the original. Augsburg: Weltbild, 1990.

Cocks, Geoffrey, and Konrad Jarausch, eds. *German Professions, 1800–1950.* New York: Oxford University Press, 1990.

Coffman, Edward M. *The Old Army: A Portrait of the American Army in Peacetime, 1784-1898*. New York: Oxford University Press, 1986.

———. *The Regulars: The American Army, 1898–1941*. Cambridge, Massachusetts: Belknap Press, 2004.

Collins, Joe Lawton. *Lightning Joe: An Autobiography*. Baton Rouge: Louisiana State University Press, 1979.

Connelly, Donald B. "The Rocky Road to Reform: John M. Schofield at West Point, 1876–1881." In *West Point: Two Centuries and Beyond*, edited by Lance A. Betros, 167–197. Abilene, Texas: McWhiney Foundation Press, 2004.

Commandants, Staff, Faculty, and Graduates of the Command and General Staff School, Fort Leavenworth, Kansas, 1881–1933. Ft. Leavenworth, Kansas: Command and General Staff School Press, 1933.

Conroy, Pat. *The Lords of Discipline.* Toronto: Bantam, 1982.

——. *My Losing Season.* New York: Doubleday, 2002.

Converse, Elliot V., ed. *Forging the Sword: Selecting, Educating, and Training Cadets and Junior Officers in the Modern World.* Chicago: Imprint Publications, 1998.

Cooper, Matthew. *The German Army, 1933–1945: Its Political and Military Failure.* London: Macdonald and Jane's, 1978.

Corum, James S., and Richard Muller. *The Luftwaffe's Way of War: German Air Force Doctrine, 1911–1945.* Baltimore: Nautical & Aviation, 1998.

Crackel, Theodore J. *The Illustrated History of West Point.* New York: H. N. Abrams, 1991.

——. *West Point: A Bicentennial History.* Lawrence: University Press of Kansas, 2002.

——. "The Military Academy in the Context of Jeffersonian Reform." In *Thomas Jefferson's Military Academy: Founding West Point,* edited by Robert M. S. McDonald, 99–117. Charlottesville: University of Virginia, 2004.

——. "West Point's Contribution to the Army and to the Professionalism, 1877 to 1917." In *West Point: Two Centuries and Beyond.*, edited by Lance A. Betros, 38–56. Abilene, Texas: McWhiney Foundation Press, 2004.

"The Cream of the Crop: Selection of Officers for the Regular Army." *Quartermaster Review* (July–August 1946): 23–70.

Cullum, George W., and Wirt Robinson, eds. *Biographical Register of the Officers and Graduates of the U. S. Military Academy at West Point, New York, since its Establishment 1802.* Saginaw, Michigan: Seeman & Peters, 1920.

Daso, Dik Alan. "Henry. H. Arnold at West Point, 1903–1907." In *West Point: Two Centuries and Beyond,* edited by Lance A. Betros, 75–100. Abilene, Texas: McWhiney Foundation Press, 2004.

Dastrup, Boyd L. *The U.S. Army Command and General Staff College: A Centennial History* Manhattan, Kansas: Sunflower University Press, 1982.

Davies, Richard G. *Carl A. Spaatz and the Air War in Europe.* Washington, D.C.: Center for Air Force History, 1993.

Davis, Kenneth S. *Soldier of Democracy: A Biography of Dwight Eisenhower.* Garden City, New York: Doubleday, 1946.

Deist, Wilhelm. "Remarks on the Preconditions to Waging War in Prussia-Germany, 1866–71." In *On the Road to Total War: The American Civil War and the German Wars of Unification, 1861–1871,* edited by Stig Förster and Jörg Nagler, 311–325. Washington, D.C.: German Historical Institute, 1997.

Deist, Wilhelm, Manfred Messerschmidt, Hans-Erich Volkmann, and Wolfram Wette. *Das Deutsche Reich und der Zweite Weltkrieg, Vol. I: Ursachen und Voraussetzungen der deutschen Kriegspolitik.* München: Deutsche Verlags-Anstalt, 1979.

Demeter, Karl. *Das deutsche Heer und seine Offiziere*. Berlin: Reimar Hobbing, 1935.

————. *Das deutsche Offizierkorps in Gesellschaft und Staat, 1650–1945*. 4th ed. Frankfurt a. M.: Bernard & Graefe, 1965.

Department of Military Art and Engineering, United States Military Academy, ed. *Jomini, Clausewitz and Schlieffen*. West Point, New York: Department of Military Art and Engineering, United States Military Academy, 1945.

D'Este, Carlo. "General George S. Patton, Jr., at West Point, 1904–1909." In *West Point: Two Centuries and Beyond*, edited by Lance A. Betros, 59–74. Abilene, Texas: McWhiney Foundation Press, 2004.

Dhünen, Felix. *Als Spiel begann's: Die Geschichte eines Münchener Kadetten*. München: Beck, 1939.

Dickerhof, Harald, ed. *Commemorative Publication to the 60th Birthday of Heinz Hürten*. Frankfurt a. M.: Lang, 1988.

Diedrich, Torsten. *Paulus: Das Trauma von Stalingrad*. Paderborn: Schöningh, 2008.

Diehl, James M. *Paramilitary Politics in Weimar Germany*. Bloomington: Indiana University Press, 1977.

Doepner, Friedrich. "Zur Auswahl der Offizieranwärter im 100.000 Mann-Heer." *Wehrkunde* 22 (1973): 200–204, 259–263.

Doorn, Jacques van. *The Soldier and Social Change: Comparative Studies in the History and Sociology of the Military*. Sage Series on Armed Forces and Society. Beverly Hills, California: Sage, 1975.

Doughty, Robert A., and Theodore J. Crackel. "The History of History at West Point." In *West Point: Two Centuries and Beyond*, edited by Lance A. Betros, 390–434. Abilene, Texas: McWhiney Foundation Press, 2004.

Duffy, Christopher. *The Military Life of Frederick the Great*. New York: Atheneum, 1986.

Dupuy, Trevor Nevitt. *A Genius for War: The German Army and General Staff, 1807–1945*. Englewood Cliffs, New Jersey: Prentice-Hall, 1977.

————. *Understanding War: History and the Theory of Combat*. New York: Paragon, 1987.

Eells, Walter Crosby, and Austin Carl Cleveland. "Faculty Inbreeding: Extent, Types and Trends in American Colleges and Universities." *Journal of Higher Education* 6, no. 5 (1935): 261–269.

Ehlert, Hans, Michael Epkenhans, and Gerhard P. Groß, eds. *Der Schlieffenplan. Analysen und Dokumente*, Zeitalter der Weltkriege, Bd. 2. Paderborn: Schöningh 2006.

Eiler, Keith E. *Mobilizing America: Robert P. Patterson and the War Effort, 1940–1945*. Ithaca, New York: Cornell University Press, 1997.

Eisenhower, Dwight D. *Crusade in Europe*. Garden City, New York: Doubleday, 1947. Reprint, 1948.

[Eisenhower, Dwight D.]. A Young Graduate. "The Leavenworth Course." *Cavalry Journal* 30, no. 6 (1927): 589–600.

———. "A Tank Discussion." Infantry Journal (November 1920): 453–458.

Eisenhower, Dwight D., and Stephen E. Ambrose. *The Wisdom of Dwight D. Eisenhower: Quotations from Ike's Speeches & Writings, 1939–1969.* New Orleans, Louisiana: Eisenhower Center, 1990.

Eisenhower, Dwight D., and Robert H. Ferrell. *The Eisenhower Diaries.* New York: Norton, 1981.

Eisenhower, Dwight D., Daniel D. Holt, and James W. Leyerzapf. *Eisenhower: The Prewar Diaries and Selected Papers, 1905–1941.* Baltimore: Johns Hopkins University Press, 1998.

Eisenhower, Dwight D., George C. Marshall, and Joseph Patrick Hobbs. *Dear General: Eisenhower's Wartime Letters to Marshall.* Baltimore: Johns Hopkins Press, 1971.

Eisenhower, John S. D. *Strictly Personal.* New York: Doubleday, 1974.

Ellis, John. *Brute Force: Allied Strategy and Tactics in the Second World War.* New York: Viking, 1990.

———. *Cassino: The Hollow Victory.* New York: McGraw-Hill, 1984.

Eltinge, LeRoy. *Psychology of War.* Revised ed. Ft. Leavenworth, Kansas: Press of the Army Service Schools, 1915.

Endres, Franz Carl. "Soziologische Struktur und ihre entsprechenden Ideologien des deutschen Offizierkorps vor dem Weltkriege." *Archiv für Sozialwissenschaft und Sozialpolitik* 58 (1927): 282–319.

Epkenhans, Michael, Stig Förster, and Karen Hagemann, eds. *Militärische Erinnerungskultur: Soldaten im Spiegel von Biographien, Memoiren und Selbstzeugnissen.* Paderborn: Schöningh, 2006.

Epkenhans, Michael, and Gerhard P. Groß, eds. *Das Militär und der Aufbruch in die Moderne 1860 bis 1890: Armeen, Marinen und der Wandel von Politik, Gesellschaft und Wirtschaft in Europa, den USA sowie Japan.* Beiträge zur Militärgeschichte 60. München: Oldenbourg, 2003.

Erfurth, Waldemar. *Die Geschichte des deutschen Generalstabes von 1918 bis 1945.* 2nd ed. Studien und Dokumente zur Geschichte des Zweiten Weltkrieges. Göttingen: Musterschmidt, 1957.

Ernst, Wolfgang. *Der Ruf des Vaterlandes: Das höhere Offizierskorps unter Hitler; Selbstanspruch und Wirklichkeit.* Berlin: Frieling, 1994.

Exton, Hugh M., and Frederick Bernays Wiener. "What is a General?" *Army* 8, no. 6 (1958): 37–47.

Farago, Ladislas. *The Last Days of Patton.* New York: McGraw-Hill, 1981.

Feld, Maury D. "Military Self-Image in a Technological Environment." In *The New Military: Changing Patterns of Organization,* edited by Morris Janowitz, 159–188. New York: Russell Sage Foundation, 1964.

Ferris, John. "Commentary: Deception and 'Double Cross' in the Second World War." In *Exploring Intelligence Archives: Enquiries into the Secret State,* edited by R. Gerald Hughes, Peter Jackson and Len Scott, 98–102. London: Routledge, 2008.

Finlan, Alistair. "How Does a Military Organization Regenerate its Culture?" In *The Falklands Conflict Twenty Years On: Lessons for the Future*, edited by Stephen Badsey, Rob Havers and Mark Grove, 193–212. London: Cass, 2005.

Fischer, Michael E. "Mission-Type Orders in Joint Operations: The Empowerment of Air Leadership." School of Advanced Air Power Studies, 1995.

Foerster, Roland G., ed. *Generalfeldmarschall von Moltke: Bedeutung und Wirkung*. Beiträge zur Militärgeschichte 33. München: Oldenbourg, 1991.

Foerster, Wolfgang. "Review of 'Der deutsche Generalstab: Geschichte und Gestalt' by Walter Görlitz." *Wehrwissenschaftliche Rundschau* 1, no. 8 (1951): 7–20.

Foertsch, Hermann. *Der Offizier der deutschen Wehrmacht: Eine Pflichtenlehre*. 2nd ed. Berlin: Eisenschmidt, 1936.

Foley, Robert T. *German Strategy and the Path to Verdun: Erich von Falkenhayn and the Development of Attrition, 1870–1916*. Cambridge, UK: Cambridge University Press, 2005.

Folttmann, Josef, and Hans Möller-Witten. *Opfergang der Generale*. 3rd ed, Schriften gegen Diffamierung und Vorurteile. Berlin: Bernard & Graefe, 1957.

Förster, Jürgen E. "The Dynamics of *Volksgemeinschaft*: The Effectiveness of the German Military Establishment." In *Military Effectiveness: The Second World War*, edited by Allan Reed Millett and Williamson Murray, 180–220. Boston: Allen & Unwin, 1988.

———, ed. *Stalingrad: Ereignis—Wirkung—Symbol*. 2nd ed. München: Piper, 1993.

———. *Stalingrad: Risse im Bündnis, 1942/43*. Freiburg i. Br.: Rombach, 1975.

Förster, Stig. "The Prussian Triangle of Leadership in the Face of a People's War: A Reassessment of the Conflict between Bismarck and Moltke, 1870–1871." In *On the Road to Total War: The American Civil War and the German Wars of Unification, 1861–1871*, edited by Stig Förster and Jörg Nagler, 115–140. Washington, D.C.: German Historical Institute, 1997.

Förster, Stig, and Jörg Nagler, eds. *On the Road to Total War: The American Civil War and the German Wars of Unification, 1861–1871*. Washington, D.C.: German Historical Institute, 1997.

Freeman, Douglas Southall. *Lee's Lieutenants: A Study in Command*. New York: Scribner, 1942.

Friedrich, Jörg. *Das Gesetz des Krieges: Das deutsche Heer in Rußland, 1941 bis 1945; Der Prozeß gegen das Oberkommando der Wehrmacht*. Paperback ed. München: Piper, 2003.

Frieser, Karl-Heinz. *The Blitzkrieg Legend: The 1940 Campaign in the West.* Annapolis, Maryland: Naval Institute Press, 2005.

————. *Blitzkrieg-Legende. Der Westfeldzug 1940.* Operationen des Zweiten Weltkrieges 2. München: Oldenbourg, 1995.

Funck, Marcus. "In den Tod gehen: Bilder des Sterbens im 19. und 20. Jahrhundert." In *Willensmenschen: Über deutsche Offiziere,* edited by Ursula Breymayer, 227–236. Frankfurt a. M.: Fischer, 1999.

————. "Schock und Chance: Der preußische Militäradel in der Weimarer Republik zwischen Stand und Profession." In *Adel und Bürgertum in Deutschland: Entwicklungslinien und Wendepunkte,* edited by Hans Reif, 69–90. Berlin: Akademie, 2001.

Fussell, Paul. "The Real War, 1939–1945." *Atlantic Online* (August 1989). http://www.theatlantic.com/unbound/bookauth/battle/fussell.htm.

————. *Wartime: Understanding and Behavior in the Second World War.* New York: Oxford University Press, 1989.

Gabriel, Richard A., and Paul L. Savage. *Crisis in Command.* New York: Hill & Wang, 1978.

Ganoe, William Addleman. *MacArthur Close-Up: Much Then and Some Now.* New York: Vantage, 1962.

Gat, Azar. "The Hidden Sources of Liddell Hart's Strategic Ideas." *War in History* 3, no. 3 (1996): 292–308.

Geffen, William E., ed. *Command and Commanders in Modern Military History: The Proceedings of the Second Military History Symposium, U.S. Air Force Academy, May 2–3, 1968.* Washington, D.C.: Office of Air Force History, 1971.

Genung, Patricia B. "Teaching Foreign Languages at West Point." In *West Point: Two Centuries and Beyond,* edited by Lance A. Betros, 507–532. Abilene, Texas: McWhiney Foundation Press, 2004.

Geyer, Michael. "The Past as Future: The German Officer Corps as Profession." In *German Professions, 1800–1950,* edited by Geoffrey Cocks and Konrad Jarausch, 183–212. New York: Oxford University Press, 1990.

Goda, Norman J. W. "Black Marks: Hitler's Bribery of His Senior Officers during World War II." *Journal of Modern History* 72 (2000): 411–452.

————. "Justice and Politics in Karl Dönitz's Release from Spandau." In *The Impact of Nazism: New Perspectives on the Third Reich and Its Legacy,* edited by Alan E. Steinweis and Daniel E. Rogers, 199–212. Lincoln: University of Nebraska Press, 2003.

Gordon, Harold J., Jr. *The Reichswehr and the German Republic,* 1919–1926. Princeton, New Jersey: Princeton University Press, 1957.

Gordon, Michael R., and Bernard E. Trainor. *Cobra II: The Inside Story of the Invasion and Occupation of Iraq.* New York: Vintage, 2006.

Görlitz, Walter. *Der deutsche Generalstab: Geschichte und Gestalt.* 2nd ed. Frankfurt a. M.: Frankfurter Hefte, 1953.

————. *Generalfeldmarschall Keitel: Verbrecher oder Offizier?: Erinnerungen, Briefe, Dokumente des Chefs OKW.* Göttingen: Musterschmidt, 1961.

Görtemaker, Manfred. *Bismarck und Moltke. Der preußische Generalstab und die deutsche Einigung.* Friedrichsruher Beiträge. Friedrichsruh: Otto-von-Bismarck-Stiftung, 2004.

————. "Helmuth von Moltke und das Führungsdenken im 19. Jahrhundert." In *Führungsdenken in europäischen und nordamerikanischen Streitkräften im 19. und 20. Jahrhundert,* edited by Gerhard P. Groß, 19–41. Hamburg: Mittler, 2001.

Greenfield, Kent Roberts, and Robert R. Palmer. *Origins of the Army Ground Forces General Headquarters, United States Army, 1940–1942.* Washington, D. C.: Historical Division, Army Ground Forces, 1946.

Greenfield, Kent Roberts, Robert R. Palmer, and Bell I. Wiley. *The Army Ground Forces: The Organization of Ground Combat Troops.* The United States Army in World War II. Washington, D.C.: Historical Division, Department of the Army, 1947.

Grier, David. "The Appointment of Admiral Karl Dönitz as Hitler's Successor." In *The Impact of Nazism: New Perspectives on the Third Reich and Its Legacy,* edited by Alan E. Steinweis and Daniel E. Rogers, 182–198. Lincoln: University of Nebraska Press, 2003.

Groß, Gerhard P., ed. *Führungsdenken in europäischen und nordamerikanischen Streitkräften im 19. und 20. Jahrhundert.* Hamburg: Mittler, 2001.

Grotelueschen, Mark Ethan. *The AEF Way of War: The American Army and Combat in World War I.* New York: Cambridge University Press, 2007.

Guderian, Heinz. *Erinnerungen eines Soldaten.* Heidelberg: Vowinckel, 1951.

Günther, Hans R. G. *Begabung und Leistung in deutschen Soldatengeschlechtern.* Wehrpsychologische Arbeiten 9. Berlin: Bernard & Graefe, 1940.

Hackl, Othmar, ed. *Generalstab, Generalstabsdienst und Generalstabsausbildung in der Reichswehr und Wehrmacht, 1919–1945.* Studien deutscher Generale und Generalstabsoffiziere in der Historical Division der U.S. Army in Europa, 1946–1961. Osnabrück: Biblio, 1999.

Handbuch für den Generalstabsdienst im Kriege. 2 vols. Vol. 1. Berlin, 1939.

Harmon, Ernest N., Milton MacKaye, and William Ross MacKaye. *Combat Commander: Autobiography of a Soldier.* Englewood Cliffs, New Jersey: Prentice-Hall, 1970.

Hartmann, Christian, et al., eds. *Verbrechen der Wehrmacht: Bilanz einer Debatte.* München: Beck, 2005.

Hazen, William Babcock. *The School and the Army in Germany and France.* New York: Harper & Brothers, 1872.

Heefner, Wilson A. *Patton's Bulldog: The Life and Service of General Walton H. Walker.* Shippensburg, Pennsylvania: White Mane Books, 2001.

————. *Dogface Soldier: The Life of General Lucian K. Truscott, Jr.* Columbia: University of Missouri Press, 2010.

Heer, Hannes, ed. *Vernichtungskrieg: Verbrechen der Wehrmacht, 1941 bis 1944.* Hamburg: Hamburger Edition, 1995.

Heiber, Helmut, ed. *Lagebesprechungen im Führerhauptquartier: Protokollfragmente aus Hitlers militärischen Konferenzen, 1942–1945.* München: DTV, 1964.

Heider, Paul. "Der totale Krieg: Seine Vorbereitung durch Reichswehr und Wehrmacht." In *Der Weg der deutschen Eliten in den zweiten Weltkrieg*, edited by Ludwig Nestler, 35–80. Berlin, 1990.

Heinl, R.D. "They Died with Their Boots on." *Armed Forces Journal* 107, no. 30 (1970).

Heller, Charles E., and William A. Stofft, eds. *America's First Battles, 1776–1965.* Modern War Studies. Lawrence: University Press of Kansas, 1986.

Herr, John K., and Edward S. Wallace. *The Story of the U.S. Cavalry, 1775–1942.* Boston: Little, Brown, 1953.

Herwig, Holger H. "Feudalization of the Bourgeoisie: The Role of the Nobility in the German Naval Officer Corps, 1890–1918." In *The Military and Society: A Collection of Essays*, edited by Peter Karsten, 44–56. New York: Garland, 1998.

————. "'You are here to learn how to die': German Subaltern Officer Education on the Eve of the Great War." In *Forging the Sword: Selecting, Educating, and Training Cadets and Junior Officers in the Modern World*, edited by Elliot V. Converse, 32–46. Chicago: Imprint Publications, 1998.

Hesse, Kurt. "Militärisches Erziehungs- und Bildungswesen in Deutschland." In *Die Deutsche Wehrmacht, 1914–1939. Rückblick und Ausblick*, edited by Georg Wetzell, 463–483. Berlin Mittler, 1939.

Heuer, Uwe. *Reichswehr—Wehrmacht—Bundeswehr. Zum Image deutscher Streitkräfte in den Vereinigten Staaten von Amerika. Kontinuität und Wandel im Urteil amerikanischer Experten.* Frankfurt a. M.: Lang, 1990.

Heuser, Beatrice. *Reading Clausewitz.* London: Pimlico, 2002.

Heusinger, Adolf. *Befehl im Widerstreit: Schicksalsstunden der deutschen Armee, 1923–1945.* Tübingen: Wunderlich, 1957.

Higginbotham, Don. "Military Education before West Point." In *Thomas Jefferson's Military Academy: Founding West Point*, edited by Robert M. S. McDonald, 23–53. Charlottesville: University of Virginia, 2004.

Hillebrecht, Georg, and Andreas Eckl. *"Man wird wohl später sich schämen müssen, in China gewesen zu sein": Tagebuchaufzeichnungen des Assistenzarztes Dr. Georg Hillebrecht aus dem Boxerkrieg, 1900–1902.* Essen: Eckl, 2006.

Hillgruber, Andreas. "Dass Russlandbild der führenden deutschen Militärs vor Beginn des Angriffs auf die Sowjetunion." In *Das Russlandbild im Dritten Reich*, edited by Hans-Erich Volkmann, 125–140. Köln: Böhlau, 1994.

Hillman, Jörg. "Die Kriegsmarine und ihre Großadmirale: Die Haltbarkeit von Bildern der Kriegsmarine." In *Militärische Erinnerungskultur: Soldaten im Spiegel von Biographien, Memoiren und Selbstzeugnissen*, edited by Michael Epkenhans, Stig Förster and Karen Hagemann, 291–328. Paderborn: Schöningh, 2006.

Hofmann, George F. "The Tactical and Strategic Use of Attaché Intelligence: The Spanish Civil War and the U.S. Army's Misguided Quest for a Modern Tank Doctrine." *Journal of Military History* 62, no. 1 (1998): 101–134.

———. *Through Mobility We Conquer: The Mechanization of U.S. Cavalry.* Lexington: University of Kentucky, 2006.

Hofmann, Hans Hubert, ed. *Das deutsche Offizierkorps, 1860–1960.* Boppard a. R.: Boldt, 1980.

Hogan, Michael J. *A Cross of Iron: Harry S. Truman and the Origins of the National Security State, 1945–1954.* Cambridge, UK: Cambridge University Press, 1998.

Holden, Edward S. "The Library of the United States Military Academy, 1777–1906." *Army and Navy Life* June, (1906): 45–48.

Holley, I. B., Jr. "Training and Educating Pre-World War I United States Army Officers." In *Forging the Sword: Selecting, Educating, and Training Cadets and Junior Officers in the Modern World*, edited by Elliot V. Converse, 26–31. Chicago: Imprint Publications, 1998.

Horne, Alistair. *The Price of Glory.* New York: Penguin, 1993.

Hovland, Carl I., et al., ed. *Experiments on Mass Communication.* 4 vols. Vol. 3. Studies in Social Psychology in World War II. Princeton, New Jersey: Princeton University Press, 1949.

Hubatsch, Walther, ed. *Hitlers Weisungen für die Kriegführung, 1939–1945: Dokumente des Oberkommandos der Wehrmacht.* Frankfurt a. M.: Bernard & Graefe, 1962.

Hughes, Daniel J. "Occupational Origins of Prussia's Generals, 1870–1914." *Central European History* 13, no. 1 (1980): 3–33.

Hughes, David Ralph. *Ike at West Point.* Poughkeepsie, New York: Wayne Co., 1958.

Hughes, R. Gerald, Peter Jackson, and Len Scott, eds. *Exploring Intelligence Archives: Enquiries into the Secret State.* London: Routledge, 2008.

Hughes, R. Gerald, and Len Scott. "'Knowledge is Never Too Dear': Exploring Intelligence Archives." In *Exploring Intelligence Archives: Enquiries into the Secret State*, edited by R. Gerald Hughes, Peter Jackson, and Len Scott, 13–39. London: Routledge, 2008.

Huntington, Samuel P. *The Soldier and the State: The Theory and Politics of Civil-Military Relations.* Cambridge, Massachusetts: Belknap, 1957.

Hürter, Johannes. *Hitlers Heerführer: Die deutschen Oberbefehlshaber im Krieg gegen die Sowjetunion, 1941/1942.* München: Oldenbourg, 2007.

Hymel, Kevin, ed. *Patton's Photographs: War as He Saw It.* 1st ed. Washington, D.C.: Potomac Books, 2006.

Ilsemann, Carl-Gero von. "Das operative Denken des Älteren Moltke." In *Operatives Denken und Handeln in deutschen Streitkräften im 19. und 20. Jahrhundert*, edited by Günther Roth, 17–44. Herford: Mittler, 1988.

"It Just Happened: Review of Ernst von Salomon's book *The Questionnaire*." *Time*, Jan. 10, 1955.

Jackson, Peter. "Introduction: Enquiries into the 'Secret State.'" In *Exploring Intelligence Archives: Enquiries into the Secret State*, edited by R. Gerald Hughes, Peter Jackson, and Len Scott, 1–11. London: Routledge, 2008.

———. "Overview: A Look at French Intelligence Machinery in 1936." In *Exploring Intelligence Archives: Enquiries into the Secret State*, edited by R. Gerald Hughes, Peter Jackson, and Len Scott, 59–79. London: Routledge, 2008.

Janda, Lance. "The Crucible of Duty: West Point, Women, and Social Change." In *West Point: Two Centuries and Beyond*, edited by Lance A. Betros, 344–367. Abilene, Texas: McWhiney Foundation Press, 2004.

———. *Stronger than Custom: West Point and the Admission of Women.* Westport, Connecticut: Praeger, 2002.

Janowitz, Morris. "Changing Patterns of Organizational Authority: The Military Establishment." In *The Military and Society: A Collection of Essays*, edited by Peter Karsten, 237–257. New York: Garland, 1998.

———, ed. *The New Military: Changing Patterns of Organization.* New York: Russell Sage Foundation, 1964.

———. *The Professional Soldier: A Social and Political Portrait.* New York: Free Press, 1974.

Kaltenborn, Rudolph Wilhelm von. *Briefe eines alten Preußischen Officiers.* 2 vols. Vol. 1. Braunschweig: Biblio, 1790. Reprint, 1972.

Kaplan, Fred. "Challenging the Generals." *New York Times Magazine*, August 26, 2007.

Karsten, Peter, ed. *The Military and Society: A Collection of Essays.* New York: Garland, 1998.

———. "Ritual and Rank: Religious Affiliation, Father's 'Calling,' and Successful Advancements in the U.S. Officer Corps of the Twentieth Century." In *The Military and Society: A Collection of Essays*, edited by Peter Karsten, 77–90. New York: Garland, 1998.

Keegan, John. *The Battle for History: Re-fighting World War II.* New York: Vintage Books, 1996.

———, ed. *Churchill's Generals.* 1st American ed. New York: Grove Weidenfeld, 1991.

———. *Die Kultur des Krieges.* Berlin: Rowohlt, 1995.

———. *The First World War.* New York: Knopf, 1999.

Keller, Christian B. *Chancellorsville and the Germans: Nativism, Ethnicity, and Civil War Memory.* New York: Fordham University Press, 2007.

Kerns, Harry N. "Cadet Problems." *Mental Hygiene* 7 (1923): 688–696.

Kielmansegg, Johann Adolf Graf von. "Bemerkungen zum Referat von Hauptmann Dr. Frieser aus der Sicht eines Zeitzeugen." In *Operatives Denken und Handeln in deutschen Streitkräften im 19. und 20. Jahrhundert,* edited by Günther Roth, 149–159. Herford: Mittler, 1988.

Kindsvatter, Peter S. *American Soldiers: Ground Combat in the World Wars, Korea and Vietnam.* Lawrence: University Press of Kansas, 2003.

Kirkpatrick, Charles E. "Orthodox Soldiers: U.S. Army Formal School and Junior Officers between the Wars." In *Forging the Sword: Selecting, Educating, and Training Cadets and Junior Officers in the Modern World,* edited by Elliot V. Converse, 99–116. Chicago: Imprint Publications, 1998.

———. "'The Very Model of a Modern Major General': Background of World War II American Generals in V Corps." In *The U.S. Army and World War II: Selected Papers from the Army's Commemorative Conferences,* edited by Judith L. Bellafaire, 259–276. Washington, D.C.: Center of Military History, U.S. Army, 1998.

Kitchen, Martin. *The German Officer Corps, 1890–1914.* Oxford: Clarendon, 1968.

Klein, Friedhelm. "Aspekte militärischen Führungsdenkens in Geschichte und Gegenwart." In *Führungsdenken in europäischen und nordamerikanischen Streitkräften im 19. und 20. Jahrhundert,* edited by Gerhard P. Groß, 11–17. Hamburg: Mittler, 2001.

Kopp, Roland. "Die Wehrmacht feiert. Kommandeurs-Reden zu Hitlers 50. Geburtstag am 20. April 1939." *Militärgeschichtliche Zeitschrift* 62 (2003): 471–534.

Kosthorst, Erich. *Die Geburt der Tragödie aus dem Geist des Gehorsams: Deutschlands Generäle und Hitler; Erfahrungen und Reflexionen eines Frontoffiziers.* Bonn: Bouvier, 1998.

Krammer, Arnold. "American Treatment of German Generals during World War II." *Journal of Military History* 54, no. 1 (1990): 27–46.

Krassnitzer, Patrick. "Historische Forschung zwischen 'importierten Erinnerungen' und Quellenamnesie: Zur Aussagekraft autobiographischer Quellen am Beispiel der Weltkriegserinnerung im nationalsozialistischen Milieu." In *Militärische Erinnerungskultur: Soldaten im Spiegel von Biographien, Memoiren und Selbstzeugnissen,* edited by Michael Epkenhans, Stig Förster and Karen Hagemann, 212–222. Paderborn: Schöningh, 2006.

Kroener, Bernhard R. " Auf dem Weg zu einer 'nationalsozialistischen Volksarmee': Die soziale Öffnung des Heeresoffizierkorps im Zweiten Weltkrieg." In *Von Stalingrad zur Währungsreform: Zur Sozialgeschichte des*

Umbruchs in Deutschland, edited by Martin Broszat, Klaus-Dietmar Henke, and Hans Woller, 651–682. München: Oldenbourg, 1988.

———. *Generaloberst Friedrich Fromm: Der starke Mann im Heimatkriegsgebiet; Eine Biographie*. Paderborn: Schöningh, 2005.

———. "Generationserfahrungen und Elitenwandel: Strukturveränderungen im deutschen Offizierkorps, 1933–1945." In *Eliten in Deutschland und Frankreich im 19. und 20. Jahrhundert: Strukturen und Beziehungen*, edited by Rainer Hudemann and Georges-Henri Soutu, 219–233: Oldenbourg, 1994.

———. "'Störer' und 'Versager': Die Sonderabteilungen der Wehrmacht. Soziale Disziplinierung aus dem Geist des Ersten Weltkrieges." In *Adel— Geistlichkeit—Militär*, edited by Michael Busch and Jörg Hillman, 71–90. Bochum: Winkler, 1999.

———. "Strukturelle Veränderungen in der militärischen Gesellschaft des Dritten Reiches." In *Nationalsozialismus und Modernisierung*, edited by Michael Prinz and Rainer Zitelmann, 267–296. Darmstadt: Wissenschaftliche Buchgesellschaft, 1991.

Kroener, Bernhard R. , Rolf-Dieter Müller, and Hans Umbreit. *Das Deutsche Reich und der Zweite Weltkrieg, Vol. V/1: Organisation und Mobilisierung des deutschen Machtbereichs, 1939–1941*. München: Deutsche Verlags-Anstalt, 1988.

Kroener, Bernhard R., Rolf-Dieter Müller, and Hans Umbreit. *Das Deutsche Reich und der Zweite Weltkrieg, Vol. V/2: Organisation und Mobilisierung des deutschen Machtbereichs, 1942–1945*. München: Deutsche Verlags-Anstalt, 1999.

Kuehn, John T. "The Goldwater-Nichols Fix: Joint Education is the Key to True 'Jointness'" *Armed Forces Journal* 32 (April 2010).

Lanham, Charles T., ed. *Infantry in Battle*. Washington, D.C: Infantry Journal, 1934.

Larned, Charles W. "West Point and Higher Education." *Army and Navy Life and The United Service* 8, no. 12 (1906): 9–22.

Latzel, Klaus. *Deutsche Soldaten: nationalsozialistischer Krieg? Kriegserlebnis; Kriegserfahrung, 1939–1945*. Paderborn et al.: Schöningh, 1998.

Leistenschneider, Stephan. *Auftragstaktik im preußisch-deutschen Heer, 1871 bis 1914*. Hamburg: Mittler, 2002.

———. "Die Entwicklung der Auftragstaktik im deutschen Heer und ihre Bedeutung für das deutsche Führungsdenken." In *Führungsdenken in europäischen und nordamerikanischen Streitkräften im 19. und 20. Jahrhundert*, edited by Gerhard P. Groß, 175–190. Hamburg: Mittler, 2001.

Leon, Philip W. *Bullies and Cowards: The West Point Hazing Scandal, 1898–1901*. Contributions in Military Studies. Westport, Conneticut: Greenwood Press, 2000.

Lettow-Vorbeck, Paul von. *Mein Leben*. Biberach a. d. Riss: Koehler, 1957.

Liddell Hart, Basil Henry. *The Other Side of the Hill: Germany's Generals, Their Rise and Fall, with Their Own Account of Military Events, 1939–1945*. Enlarged and rev. ed. London, 1951.

————. *Strategy.* 2nd rev. ed. New York: Meridian Books, 1991.

————. *Why Don't We Learn from History?* New York: Hawthorn, 1971.

Lingen, Kerstin von. *Kesselrings letzte Schlacht: Kriegsverbrecherprozesse, Vergangenheitspolitik und Wiederbewaffnung; Der Fall Kesselring.* Paderborn: Schöningh, 2004.

Linn, Brian McAllister. "Challenge and Change: West Point and the Cold War." In *West Point: Two Centuries and Beyond,* edited by Lance A. Betros, 218–247. Abilene, Texas: McWhiney Foundation Press, 2004.

Lipsky, David. *Absolutely American: Four Years at West Point.* Boston: Houghton Mifflin, 2003.

Little, Roger W. "Buddy Relations and Combat Performance." In *The New Military - Changing Patterns of Organization,* edited by Morris Janowitz, 195–223. New York: Russell Sage Foundation, 1964.

Logan, John A. *The Volunteer Soldier of America.* New York: Arno, 1979.

Lonn, Ella. *Foreigners in the Union Army and Navy.* Baton Rouge: Louisiana State University Press, 1951.

Loßberg, Bernhard von. *Im Wehrmachtführungsstab: Bericht eines Generalstabsoffiziers* Hamburg: Nölke, 1950.

Lotz, Wolfgang. *Kriegsgerichtsprozesse des Siebenjährigen Krieges in Preußen. Untersuchungen zur Beurteilung militärischer Leistungen durch Friedrich den II.* Frankfurt a. M.,1981.

Loveland, Anne C. "Character Education in the U.S. Army, 1947–1977." *Journal of Military History* 64 (2000): 795–818.

Lovell, John Philip. "The Professional Socialization of the West Point Cadet." In *The New Military: Changing Patterns of Organization,* edited by Morris Janowitz, 119–157. New York: Russell Sage Foundation, 1964.

Lüke, Martina G. *Zwischen Tradition und Aufbruch: Deutschunterricht und Lesebuch im deutschen Kaiserreich.* Frankfurt a. M.: Lang, 2007.

Lupfer, Timothy T. *The Dynamics of Doctrine: The Changes in German Tactical Doctrine during the First World War.* Leavenworth Papers. Ft. Leavenworth, Kansas: Combat Studies Institute, U.S. Army Command and General Staff College, 1981.

Luvaas, Jay. "The Influence of the German Wars of Unification on the United States." In *On the Road to Total War: The American Civil War and the German Wars of Unification, 1861–1871,* edited by Stig Förster and Jörg Nagler, 597–619. Washington, D.C.: German Historical Institute, 1997.

Lynn, John A. *Battle: A History of Combat and Culture.* Boulder, Colorado: Westview Press, 2003.

MacArthur, Douglas. *Reminiscences.* New York City: McGraw-Hill, 1964.

MacDonald, Charles Brown. *Company Commander.* Washington, D.C.: Infantry Journal Press, 1947.

————. *A Time for Trumpets: The Untold Story of the Battle of the Bulge.* Toronto: Bantam Books, 1985.

Macksey, Kenneth. *Guderian: Panzer General.* London: Greenhill Books, 2003.

———. *Why the Germans Lose at War: The Myth of German Military Superiority.* London: Greenhill, 1996.

Maclean, French L. *Quiet Flows the Rhine: German General Officer Casualties in World War II.* Winnipeg: Fedorowicz 1996.

Manchester, William Raymond. *American Caesar: Douglas MacArthur, 1880– 1964.* Boston: Little, Brown, 1978.

Manstein, Erich von. *Aus einem Soldatenleben, 1887–1939.* Bonn: Athenäum, 1958.

———. *Lost Victories.* Novato, California: Presidio, 1982.

Manstein, Rüdiger von, and Theodor Fuchs. *Manstein: Soldat im 20. Jahrhundert.* Bonn: Bernard & Graefe, 1981.

Mardis, Jamie. *Memos of a West Point Cadet.* New York: McKay, 1976.

Markmann, Hans-Jochen. *Kadetten: Militärische Jugenderziehung in Preußen.* Berlin: Pädagogisches Zentrum, 1983.

Marshall, George C. "Profiting by War Experiences." *Infantry Journal* 18 (1921): 34–37.

Marwedel, Ulrich. *Carl von Clausewitz: Persönlichkeit und Wirkungsgeschichte seines Werkes bis 1918.* Militärgeschichtliche Studien 25. Boppard a. R.: Boldt, 1978.

Maslov, Aleksander A. *Fallen Soviet Generals: Soviet General Officers Killed in Battle, 1941–1945.* London: Cass, 1998.

Masuhr, H. *Psychologische Gesichtspunkte für die Beurteilung von Offizieranwärtern.* Wehrpsychologische Arbeiten 4. Berlin: Bernard & Graefe, 1937.

McCain, John, and Mark Salter. *Faith of My Fathers.* New York: Random House, 1999.

McCoy, Alfred W. "'Same Banana': Hazing and Honor at the Philippine Military Academy." In *The Military and Society: A Collection of Essays,* edited by Peter Karsten, 91–128. New York: Garland, 1998.

McDonald, Robert M. S., ed. *Thomas Jefferson's Military Academy: Founding West Point.* Charlottesville: University of Virginia, 2004.

McMaster, H. R. *Dereliction of Duty: Lyndon Johnson, Robert McNamara, the Joint Chiefs of Staff, and the Lies that Led to Vietnam.* New York: HarperCollins, 1997.

Megargee, Geoffrey P. *Inside Hitler's High Command.* Modern War Studies. Lawrence: University Press of Kansas, 2000.

Meier-Welcker, Hans. *Aufzeichnungen eines Generalstabsoffiziers, 1939–1942.* Einzelschriften zur militärischen Geschichte des Zweiten Weltkrieges. Freiburg i. Br.: Rombach, 1982.

Mellenthin, Friedrich Wilhelm von. *Deutschlands Generale des Zweiten Weltkriegs.* Bergisch Gladbach: Lübbe, 1980.

Messerschmidt, Manfred. *Die Wehrmacht im NS-Staat: Zeit der Indoktrination.* Truppe und Verwaltung 16. Hamburg: Decker, 1969.

———. "German Military Effectiveness between 1919 and 1939." In *Military Effectiveness: The Interwar Period*, edited by Allan Reed Millett and Williamson Murray, 218–255. Boston: Allen & Unwin, 1988.

———. "The Prussian Army from Reform to War." In *On the Road to Total War: The American Civil War and the German Wars of Unification, 1861– 1871*, edited by Stig Förster and Jörg Nagler, 263–282. Washington, D.C.: German Historical Institute, 1997.

Messerschmitt, Manfred. "Die Wehrmacht: Vom Realitätsverlust zum Selbstbetrug." In *Ende des Dritten Reiches: Ende des Zweiten Weltkriegs; Eine perspektivische Rückschau*, edited by Hans-Erich Volkmann, 223–259. München: Piper, 1995.

Meyer, Georg. *Adolf Heusinger: Dienst eines deutschen Soldaten, 1915 bis 1964.* Hamburg: Mittler, 2001.

Miles, Perry L. *Fallen Leaves: Memories of an Old Soldier.* Berkeley, California: Wuerth, 1961.

Millett, Allan Reed. *The General: Robert L. Bullard and Officership in the United States Army, 1881–1925.* Westport, Connecticut: Greenwood Press, 1975.

———. "The United States Armed Forces in the Second World War." In *Military Effectiveness: The Second World War*, edited by Allan Reed Millett and Williamson Murray, 45–89. Boston: Allen & Unwin, 1988.

Millett, Allan Reed, and Peter Maslowski. *For the Common Defense: A Military History of the United States of America.* Rev. and expanded ed. New York: Free Press, 1994.

Millett, Allan Reed, and Williamson Murray, eds. *Military Effectiveness: The Interwar Period.* 3 vols. Vol. 2. Mershon Center Series on Defense and Foreign Policy. Boston: Allen & Unwin, 1988.

———, eds. *Military Effectiveness: The Second World War.* 3 vols. Vol. 3. Mershon Center Series on Defense and Foreign Policy. Boston: Allen & Unwin, 1988.

Millotat, Christian E. O. *Das preußisch-deutsche Generalstabssystem. Wurzeln-Entwicklung-Fortwirken.* Strategie und Konfliktforschung. Zürich: vdf, 2000.

Möbius, Sascha. *Mehr Angst vor dem Offizier als vor dem Feind? Eine mentalitätsgeschichtliche Studie zur preußischen Taktik im Siebenjährigen Krieg.* Saarbrücken: VDM, 2007.

Model, Hansgeorg. *Der deutsche Generalstabsoffizier: Seine Auswahl und Ausbildung in Reichswehr, Wehrmacht und Bundeswehr.* Frankfurt a. M.: Bernard & Graefe, 1968.

Model, Hansgeorg, and Jens Prause. *Generalstab im Wandel: Neue Wege bei der Generalstabsausbildung in der Bundeswehr.* München: Bernard & Graefe, 1982.

Möller-Witten, Hans. "Die Verluste der deutschen Generalität, 1939–1945." *Wehrwissenschaftliche Rundschau* 4 (1954): 31–33.

Moncure, John. *Forging the King's Sword: Military Education between Tradition and Modernization; The Case of the Royal Prussian Cadet Corps, 1871–1918.* New York City: Lang, 1993.

Montgomery of Alamein, Bernard Law. *The Memoirs of Field Marshal Montgomery.* Barnsley: Pen & Sword, 2005.

Morelock, Jerry D. *Generals of the Ardennes: American Leadership in the Battle of the Bulge.* Washington, D.C.: National Defense University Press, 1994.

Morrison, James L. "The Struggle between Sectionalism and Nationalism at Ante-Bellum West Point, 1830–1861." In *The Military and Society: A Collection of Essays,* edited by Peter Karsten, 26–36. New York: Garland, 1998.

Mosley, Leonard. *Marshall: Organizer of Victory.* London: Methuen, 1982.

Mott, Thomas Bentley. *Twenty Years as Military Attaché.* New York: Oxford University Press, 1937.

———. "West Point: A Criticism." *Harper's* (March 1934): 466–479.

Mullaney, Craig M. *The Unforgiving Minute: A Soldier's Education.* New York: Penguin.

Muller, Richard R. "Werner von Blomberg: Hitler's 'idealistischer' Kriegsminister." In *Die Militärelite des Dritten Reiches: 27 biographische Skizzen,* edited by Ronald Smelser and Enrico Syring, 50–65. Berlin: Ullstein, 1997.

Müller, Rolf-Dieter. "Die Wehrmacht: Historische Last und Verantwortung; Die Historiographie im Spannungsfeld von Wissenschaft und Vergangenheitsbewältigung." In *Die Wehrmacht: Mythos Und Realität,* edited by Rolf-Dieter Müller, 3–35. München: Oldenbourg, 1999.

———, ed. *Die Wehrmacht: Mythos und Realität.* München: Oldenbourg, 1999.

Müller-Hillebrand, Burkhart. *Das Heer, 1933–1945. Entwicklung des organisatorischen Aufbaues.* 3 vols. Darmstadt: Mittler, 1954–1969.

Mulligan, William. *The Creation of the Modern German Army: General Walther Reinhardt and the Weimar Republic, 1914–1930.* New York: Berghahn, 2005.

Murphy, Audie. *To Hell and Back.* New York: Holt, 1949.

Murray, Williamson. "Does Military Culture Matter?" In *America the Vulnerable: Our Military Problems and How to Fix Them,* edited by John F. Lehman and Harvey Sicherman, 134-151. Philadelphia: Foreign Policy Research Institute, 1999.

———. "Werner Freiherr von Fritsch: Der tragische General." In *Die Militärelite des Dritten Reiches: 27 Biographische Skizzen,* edited by Ronald Smelser and Enrico Syring, 153–170. Berlin: Ullstein, 1995.

Muth, Jörg. "Erich von Lewinski, Called von Manstein: His Life, Character and Operations—A Reappraisal." http://www.axishistory.com/index.php?id=7901.

———. *Flucht aus dem militärischen Alltag: Ursachen und individuelle Ausprägung der Desertion in der Armee Friedrichs des Großen.* Freiburg i. Br.: Rombach, 2003.

Myrer, Anton. *Once an Eagle.* New York: HarperTorch, 2001.

Official Register of the Officers and Cadets of the U.S. Military Academy. West Point, New York: USMA Press, 1905.

Nakata, Jun. *Der Grenz- und Landesschutz in der Weimarer Republik, 1918 bis 1933: Die geheime Aufrüstung und die deutsche Gesellschaft.* Freiburg i. Br.: Rombach, 2002.

Nenninger, Timothy K. "Creating Officers: The Leavenworth Experience, 1920–1940." *Military Review* 69, no. 11 (1989): 58–68.

———. "Leavenworth and Its Critics: The U.S. Army Command and General Staff School, 1920–1940." *Journal of Military History* 58, no. 2 (1994): 199–231.

———. *The Leavenworth Schools and the Old Army: Education, Professionalism, and the Officer Corps of the United States Army, 1881–1918.* Westport: Greenwood, 1978.

———. "'Unsystematic as a Mode of Command': Commanders and the Process of Command in the American Expeditionary Force, 1917–1918." *Journal of Military History* 64, no. 3 (2000): 739–768.

Neugebauer, Karl-Volker. "Operatives denken zwischen dem Ersten und Zweiten Weltkrieg." In *Operatives Denken und Handeln in deutschen Streitkräften im 19. und 20. Jahrhundert,* edited by Günther Roth, 97–122. Herford: Mittler, 1988.

Niedhart, Gottfried, and Dieter Riesenberger, eds. *Lernen aus dem Krieg? Deutsche Nachkriegszeiten, 1918 und 1945.* Beiträge zur historischen Friedensforschung. München: Beck, 1992.

Norris, Robert S. "Leslie R. Groves, West Point and the Atomic Bomb." In *West Point: Two Centuries and Beyond,* edited by Lance A. Betros, 101–121. Abilene, Texas: McWhiney Foundation Press, 2004.

Nuber, Hans. *Wahl des Offiziersberufs: Eine charakterologische Untersuchung von Persönlichkeit und Berufsethos.* Zeitschrift für Geopolitik, Beiheft Wehrwissenschaftliche Reihe 1. Heidelberg: Vowinckel, 1935.

Nutter, Thomas E. "Mythos Revisited: American Historians and German Fighting Power in the Second World War." *Military History Online* (2004). http://www.militaryhistoryonline.com/wwii/armies/default.aspx.

Nye, Roger H. *The Patton Mind: The Professional Development of an Extraordinary Leader.* Garden City Park, New York: Avery, 1993.

Oetting, Dirk W. *Auftragstaktik: Geschichte und Gegenwart einer Führungskonzeption.* Frankfurt a. M.: Report, 1993.

O'Neill, William D. *Transformation and the Officer Corps: Analysis in the Historical Context of the U.S. and Japan between the World Wars.* Alexandria, Virginia: CNA, 2005.

Ossad, Stephen L. "Command Failures." *Army* (March 2003).

Overmans, Rüdiger. *Deutsche militärische Verluste im Zweiten Weltkrieg.* München: Oldenbourg, 1999.

Overy, Richard. *Why the Allies Won.* New York City: Norton, 1995.

Owen, Gregory L. *Across the Bridge: The World War II Journey of Cpt. Alexander M. Patch III.* Lexington, Virginia: George C. Marshall Foundation, 1995.

Pagonis, William G., and Jeffrey L. Cruikshank. *Moving Mountains: Lessons in Leadership and Logistics from the Gulf War.* Boston: Harvard Business School Press, 1992.

Paret, Peter, Gordon Alexander Craig, and Felix Gilbert, eds. *Makers of Modern Strategy: From Machiavelli to the Nuclear Age.* Princeton, New Jersey: Princeton University Press, 1986.

Parker, Jerome H., IV. "Fox Conner and Dwight Eisenhower: Mentoring and Application." *Military Review* (July–August 2005): 89–95.

Patel, Kiran Klaus. *Soldiers of Labor: Labor Service in Nazi Germany and New Deal America, 1933–1945.* Washington, D.C.: Cambridge University Press, 2005.

Patton, George S., and Paul D. Harkins. *War As I Knew It.* Boston: Houghton Mifflin, 1995.

Patton, George S., and Kevin Hymel. *Patton's Photographs: War as He Saw It.* 1st ed. Washington, D.C.: Potomac Books, 2006.

Pennington, Leon Alfred, et al. *The Psychology of Military Leadership.* New York: Prentice-Hall, 1943.

Pogue, Forrest C. *George C. Marshall: Education of a General, 1880–1939.* 3 vols. Vol. 1. New York: Viking Press, 1963.

Preradovitch, Nikolaus von. *Die militärische und soziale Herkunft der Generalität des deutschen Heeres, 1. Mai 1944.* Osnabrück: Biblio, 1978.

Prinz, Michael, and Rainer Zitelmann, eds. *Nationalsozialismus und Modernisierung.* Darmstadt: Wissenschaftliche Buchgesellschaft, 1991.

Purpose and Preparation of Efficiency Reports. 4th revised ed. Infantry School Mailing List. Fort Benning, Georgia: The Infantry School, 1940.

Rass, Christoph. *"Menschenmaterial": Deutsche Soldaten an der Ostfront - Innenansichten einer Infanteriedivision, 1939–1945.* Krieg in der Geschichte. Paderborn: Schöningh, 2003.

———. "Neue Wege zur Sozialgeschichte der Wehrmacht." In *Militärische Erinnerungskultur: Soldaten im Spiegel von Biographien, Memoiren und Selbstzeugnissen,* edited by Michael Epkenhans, Stig Förster and Karen Hagemann, 188–211. Paderborn: Schöningh, 2006.

Rass, Christoph, René Rohrkamp, and Peter M. Quadflieg. *General Graf von Schwerin und das Kriegsende in Aachen: Ereignis, Mythos, Analyse.* Aachener Studien zur Wirtschafts- und Sozialgeschichte. Aachen: Shaker, 2007.

Raugh, Harold E., Jr. "Command on the Western Front: Perspectives of American Officers." *Stand To!* 18, (Dec. 1986): 12–14.

Reeder, Red. *West Point Plebe.* Boston: Little, Brown, 1955.

Regulations for the United States Military Academy. Washington, D.C.: U.S. Government Printing Office, 1916.

Rickard, John Nelson. *Patton at Bay: The Lorraine Campaign, September to December, 1944.* Westport, Connecticut: Praeger, 1999.

Ridgway, Matthew B. *Soldier: The Memoirs of Matthew B. Ridgway.* New York: Harper & Brothers, 1956.

Ritter, Gerhard. *The Schlieffen Plan: Critique of a Myth.* New York: Praeger, 1958.

Röhl, John C. G. *Young Wilhelm: The Kaiser's Early Life, 1859–1888.* Cambridge: Cambridge University Press, 1998.

Rommel, Erwin. *Infantry Attacks.* London: Stackpole, 1995.

Rommel, Erwin, and Basil Henry Liddell Hart. *The Rommel Papers.* 14th ed. New York: Harcourt, Brace, 1953.

Roth, Günther, ed. *Operatives Denken und Handeln in deutschen Streitkräften im 19. und 20. Jahrhundert.* Herford: Mittler, 1988.

Salmond, John. *The Civilian Conservation Corps, 1933–1942: A New Deal Case Study.* Durham, North Carolina: Duke University Press, 1967.

Salomon, Ernst von. *Die Geächteten.* Berlin: Rowohlt, 1930.

———. *Die Kadetten.* Berlin: Rowohlt, 1933.

Samet, Elizabeth D. "Great Men and Embryo-Caesars: John Adams, Thomas Jefferson, and the Figure in Arms." In *Thomas Jefferson's Military Academy: Founding West Point,* edited by Robert M. S. McDonald, 77–98. Charlottesville: University of Virginia, 2004.

Sanger, Joseph P. "The West Point Military Academy: Shall its Curriculum Be Changed as a Necessary Preparation for War?" *Journal of Military Institution* 60 (1917).

Sassman, Roger W. "Operation SHINGLE and Major General John P. Lucas." Carlisle, Pennsylvania: U.S. Army War College, 1999.

Schedule for 1939–1940: Regular Class. Ft. Leavenworth, Kansas: Command and General Staff School Press, 1939.

Schell, Adolf von. *Battle Leadership: Some Personal Experiences of a Junior Officer of the German Army with Observations on Battle Tactics and the Psychological Reactions of Troops in Campaign.* Fort Benning, Georgia: Benning Herald, 1933.

———. "Das Heer der Vereinigten Staaten." *Militär-Wochenblatt* 28 (1932): 998–1001.

———. Kampf gegen Panzerwagen. Berlin: Stalling, 1936.

Schieder, Theodor. *Friedrich der Große: Ein Königtum der Widersprüche.* Frankfurt a. M.: Propyläen, 1983.

Schild, Georg, ed. *The American Way of War.* Paderborn: Schöningh, 2010.

Schmitz, Klaus. *Militärische Jugenderziehung: Preußische Kadettenhäuser und Nationalpolitische Erziehungsanstalten zwischen, 1807 und 1936.* Köln: Böhlau, 1997.

Schröder, Hans Joachim. *Kasernenzeit: Arbeiter erzählen von der Militärausbildung.* Frankfurt: Campus, 1985.

―――, ed. *Max Landowski, Landarbeiter: Ein Leben zwischen Westpreußen und Schleswig-Holstein.* Berlin: Reimer, 2000.

Schüler-Springorum, Stefanie. "Die Legion Condor in (auto-)biographischen Zeugnissen." In *Militärische Erinnerungskultur: Soldaten im Spiegel von Biographien, Memoiren und Selbstzeugnissen,* edited by Michael Epkenhans, Stig Förster, and Karen Hagemann, 223–235. Paderborn: Schöningh, 2006.

Schwan, Theodore. *Report on the Organization of the German Army.* Washington, D.C.: U.S. Government Printing Office, 1894.

Schwinge, Erich. *Die Entwicklung der Mannszucht in der deutschen, britischen und französischen Wehrmacht seit 1914.* Tornisterschrift des OKW, Abt. Inland, H. 46. Berlin: Oberkommando der Wehrmacht, 1941.

Scott, Len. "Overview: Deception and Double Cross." In *Exploring Intelligence Archives: Enquiries into the Secret,* edited by R. Gerald Hughes, Peter Jackson, and Len Scott, 93–98. London: Routledge, 2008.

Searle, Alaric. "Nutzen und Grenzen der Selbstzeugnisse in einer Gruppenbiographie." In *Militärische Erinnerungskultur: Soldaten im Spiegel von Biographien, Memoiren und Selbstzeugnissen,* edited by Michael Epkenhans, Stig Förster, and Karen Hagemann, 268–290. Paderborn: Schöningh, 2006.

―――. "A Very Special Relationship: Basil Liddell Hart, Wehrmacht Generals and the Debate on West German Rearmament, 1945–1953." *War in History* 5, no. 3 (1998): 327–357.

Seeckt, Hans von, ed. *Führung und Gefecht der verbundenen Waffen.* Berlin: Offene Worte, 1921.

Sherraden, Michael W. "Military Participation in a Youth Employment Program: The Civilian Conservation Corps." *Armed Forces & Society* 7, no. 2 (1981): 227–245.

Showalter, Dennis E. "From Deterrence to Doomsday Machine: The German Way of War, 1890–1914 " Journal of Military History 63, no. 2 (2000): 679–710.

―――. *The Wars of Frederick the Great.* Modern Wars in Perspective. London: Longman, 1996.

―――. *The Wars of German Unification.* Modern Wars Series. London: Arnold, 2004.

Simoneit, Max. *Grundriss der charakterologischen Diagnostik auf Grund heerespsychologischer Erfahrungen.* Leipzig: Teubner, 1943.

―――. *Leitgedanken über die psychologische Untersuchung des Offizier-Nachwuchses in der Wehrmacht.* Wehrpsychologische Arbeiten 6. Berlin: Bernard & Graefe, 1938.

———. *Wehrpsychologie: Ein Abriss ihrer Probleme und praktischen Folgerungen.* 2nd ed. Berlin: Bernard & Graefe, 1943.

———. *Wehrpsychologische Willensuntersuchungen.* Friedrich Mann's pädagogisches Magazin 1430. Langensalza: Beyer, 1937.

Simons, William E., ed. *Professional Military Education in the United States: A Historical Dictionary.* Westport, Connecticut: Greenwood, 2000.

Skelton, William B. *An American Profession of Arms: The Army Officer Corps, 1784–1861.* Lawrence: University Press of Kansas, 1992.

———. "West Point and Officer Professionalism, 1817–1877." In *West Point: Two Centuries and Beyond,* edited by Lance A. Betros, 22–37. Abilene, Texas: McWhiney Foundation Press, 2004.

Smelser, Ronald. "The Myth of the Clean Wehrmacht in Cold War America." In *Lessons and Legacies VIII: From Generation to Generation,* edited by Doris L. Bergen, 247–269. Evanston, Illinois: Northwestern University Press, 2008.

Smelser, Ronald, and Edward J. Davies. *The Myth of the Eastern Front: The Nazi-Soviet War in American Popular Culture.* New York: Cambridge University Press, 2007.

Smelser, Ronald, and Enrico Syring, eds. *Die Militärelite des Dritten Reiches: 27 Biographische Skizzen.* Paperback ed. Berlin: Ullstein, 1995.

Smith, Walter Bedell. *Eisenhower's Six Great Decisions: Europe, 1944–1945.* New York: Longmans, 1956.

Sokolov, Boris. "How to Calculate Human Losses during the Second World War." *Journal of Slavic Military Studies* 22, no. 3 (2009): 437–458.

Sorley, Lewis. "Principled Leadership: Creighton Williams Abrams, Class of 1936." In *West Point: Two Centuries and Beyond,* edited by Lance A. Betros, 122–141. Abilene, Texas: McWhiney Foundation Press, 2004.

Sösemann, Bernd. "Die sogenannte Hunnenrede Wilhelms II.: Textkritische und interpretatorische Bemerkungen zur Ansprache des Kaisers vom 27. Juli 1900 in Bremerhaven." *Historische Zeitschrift* 222 (1976): 342–358.

Spector, Ronald. "The Military Effectiveness of the U.S. Armed Forces, 1919–1939." In *Military Effectiveness: The Interwar Period,* edited by Allan Reed Millett and Williamson Murray, 70–97. Boston: Allen & Unwin, 1988.

Spires, David N. *Image and Reality: The Making of the German Officer, 1921–1933.* Contributions in Military History. Westport, Connecticut: Greenwood, 1984.

"Splendid, Wonderful,' Says Joffre Admiring the West Point Cadets." *New York Times,* May 12, 1917.

Stahlberg, Alexander. *Die verdammte Pflicht: Erinnerungen, 1932–1945.* Berlin: Ullstein, 1987.

Stanton, Martin. *Somalia on $5 a Day: A Soldier's Story.* New York: Ballantine, 2001.

Stein, Hans-Peter. *Symbole und Zeremoniell in deutschen Streitkräften: Vom 18. bis zum 20. Jahrhundert.* Entwicklung deutscher militärischer Tradition 3. Herford: Mittler, 1984.

Stein, Marcel. Die 11. *Armee und die "Endlösung" 1941/42: Eine Dokumentensammlung mit Kommentaren.* Bissendorf: Biblio, 2006.

———. *Field Marshal von Manstein: the Janus Head; A Portrait.* Solihull: Helion, 2007.

———. *Generalfeldmarschall Erich von Manstein: Kritische Betrachtungen des Soldaten und Menschen.* Mainz: Hase & Koehler, 2000.

Steinbach, Peter. "Widerstand und Wehrmacht." In *Die Wehrmacht: Mythos und Realität,* edited by Rolf-Dieter Müller, 1150–1170. München: Oldenbourg, 1999.

Steinweis, Alan E., and Daniel E. Rogers, eds. *The Impact of Nazism: New Perspectives on the Third Reich and Its Legacy.* Lincoln: University of Nebraska, 2003.

Stelpflug, Peggy A., and Richard Hyatt. *Home of the Infantry: The History of Fort Benning.* Macon, Georgia: Mercer University Press, 2007.

Stouffer, Samuel A., et al., eds. *The American Soldier: Adjustment during Army Life.* 4 vols. Vol. 1. Studies in Social Psychology in World War II. Princeton, New Jersey: Princeton University Press, 1949.

———, eds. *The American Soldier: Combat and its Aftermath.* 4 vols. Vol. 2. Studies in Social Psychology in World War II. Princeton, New Jersey: Princeton University Press, 1949.

———, eds. *Measurement and Prediction.* 4 vols. Vol. 4. Studies in Social Psychology in World War II. Princeton, New Jersey: Princeton University Press, 1949.

Strachan, Hew. "Die Vorstellungen der Anglo-Amerikaner von der Wehrmacht." In *Die Wehrmacht: Mythos und Realität,* edited by Rolf-Dieter Müller, 92–104. München: Oldenbourg, 1999.

Streit, Christian. *Keine Kameraden: Die Wehrmacht und die sowjetischen Kriegsgefangenen, 1941–1945,* Studien zur Zeitgeschichte. Stuttgart: DVA, 1978.

Strum, Philippa. *Women in the Barracks: The VMI Case and Equal Rights.* Lawrence: University Press of Kansas, 2002.

Stumpf, Reinhard. *Die Wehrmacht-Elite: Rang- und Herkunftsstruktur der deutschen Generale und Admirale, 1933–1945.* Wehrwissenschaftliche Forschungen, Abteilung Militärgeschichtliche Studien 29. Boppard a. R.: Boldt, 1982.

Sumida, Jon Tetsuo. *Decoding Clausewitz: A New Approach to 'On War.'* Lawrence: University Press of Kansas, 2008.

Taylor, John M. *General Maxwell Taylor: The Sword and the Pen.* New York: Doubleday, 1989.

Taylor, Telford. *Die Nürnberger Prozesse: Hintergründe, Analysen und Erkenntnisse aus heutiger Sicht.* 3rd ed. München: Heyne, 1996.

Teske, Hermann. *Die silbernen Spiegel: Generalstabsdienst unter der Lupe.* Heidelberg: Vowinckel, 1952.

———. *Wir marschieren für Großdeutschland: Erlebtes und Erlauschtes aus dem großen Jahre, 1938.* Berlin: Die Wehrmacht, 1939.

Thomas, Kenneth H., Jr. *Images of America: Fort Benning.* Charleston, South Carolina: Arcadia, 2003.

Trommler, Frank, and Joseph McVeigh, eds. *America and the Germans: An Assessment of a Three-Hundred-Year History.* 2 vols. Vol. 2. Philadelphia: University of Pennsylvania Press, 1985.

Tuchman, Barbara W. *The Guns of August.* New York: Macmillan, 1962.

Tzu, Sun. *The Art of War.* Translated by Samuel B. Griffith. New York: Oxford University Press, 1971.

U'Ren, Richard C. *Ivory Fortress: A Psychiatrist Looks at West Point.* Indianapolis: Bobbs-Merrill, 1974.

Ueberschär, Gerd R. "Die deutsche Militär-Opposition zwischen Kritik und Würdigung. Zur neueren Geschichtsschreibung über die Offiziere gegen Hitler." *Jahresbibliographie Bibliothek für Zeitgeschichte* 62 (1990): 428–442.

———. *Dienen und Verdienen: Hitlers Geschenke an seine Eliten.* 2nd ed. Frankfurt a. M.: Fischer, 1999.

Ueberschär, Gerd R., and Rainer A. Blasius, eds. *Der Nationalsozialismus vor Gericht: Die alliierten Prozesse gegen Kriegsverbrecher und Soldaten, 1943–1952.* Frankfurt a. M.: Fischer, 1999.

Unruh, Friedrich Franz von. *Ehe die Stunde schlug: Eine Jugend im Kaiserreich.* Bodensee: Hohenstaufen, 1967.

Upton, Emory. *The Armies of Europe and Asia.* London: Griffin & Co., 1878.

U.S. War Department, ed. *Handbook on German Military Forces.* Baton Rouge: Louisiana State University Press, 1990.

Van Creveld, Martin. *The Culture of War.* New York: Presidio, 2008.

———. *Fighting Power: German and U.S. Army Performance, 1939–1945,* Contributions in Military History. Westport, Connecticut: Greenwood, 1982.

———. "On Learning from the Wehrmacht and Other Things." *Military Review* 68 (1988): 62–71.

———. *The Training of Officers: From Military Professionalism to Irrelevance.* New York City: Free Press, 1990.

Vaux, Nick. *Take that Hill!: Royal Marines in the Falklands War.* Washington, D.C.: Pergamon, 1986.

Volkmann, Hans-Erich, ed. *Das Rußlandbild im Dritten Reich.* Köln: Böhlau, 1994.

Voss, Hans von, and Max Simoneit. "Die psychologische Eignungsuntersuchung in der deutschen Reichswehr und später der Wehrmacht." *Wehrwissenschaftliche Rundschau* 4, no. 2 (1954): 138–141.

Walton, Frank J. "The West Point Centennial: A Time for Healing." In *West Point: Two Centuries and Beyond*, edited by Lance A. Betros, 198–247. Abilene, Texas: McWhiney Foundation Press, 2004.

Warlimont, Walter. *Im Hauptquartier der deutschen Wehrmacht, 1939–1945: Grundlagen, Formen*, Gestalten. Frankfurt a. M.: Bernard & Graefe, 1962.

Weber, Thomas. *Hitler's First War: Adolf Hitler, the Men of the List Regiment, and the First World War*. London: Oxford University Press, 2010.

Weckmann, Kurt. "Führergehilfenausbildung." *Wehrwissenschaftliche Rundschau* 4, no. 6 (1954): 268–277.

Wedemeyer, Albert C. *Wedemeyer Reports!* New York: Holt, 1958.

Wegner, Bernd. "Erschriebene Siege: Franz Halder, die "Historical Division" und die Rekonstruktion des Zweiten Weltkrieges im Geiste des deutschen Generalstabes." In *Politischer Wandel, organisierte Gewalt und nationale Sicherheit, Festschrift für Klaus-Jürgen Müller*, edited by Ernst Willi Hansen, Gerhard Schreiber and Bernd Wegner, 287–302. München: Oldenbourg, 1995.

———, ed. *Zwei Wege nach Moskau: Vom Hitler-Stalin-Pakt bis zum "Unternehmen Barbarossa."* Serie Piper. München: Piper, 1991.

Weigley, Russell Frank. *The American Way of War: A History of the United States Military Strategy and Policy*. London: Macmillan, 1973.

———. *Eisenhower's Lieutenants: The Campaign of France and Germany, 1944–1945*. Bloomington: Indiana University Press, 1981.

———. "The Elihu Root Reforms and the Progressive Era." In *Command and Commanders in Modern Military History: The Proceedings of the Second Military History Symposium, U.S. Air Force Academy, 2–3 May 1968*, edited by William E. Geffen, 11–27. Washington, D.C.: Office of Air Force History, 1971.

Weinberg, Gerhard L. "Die Wehrmacht und Verbrechen im Zweiten Weltkrieg." *Zeitgeschichte* 4 (2003): 207–209.

———. "From Confrontation to Cooperation: Germany and the United States, 1933–1945." In *America and the Germans: An Assessment of a Three-Hundred-Year History*, edited by Frank Trommler and Joseph McVeigh, 45–58. Philadelphia: University of Pennsylvania Press, 1985.

———. "Rollen- und Selbstverständnis des Offizierkorps der Wehrmacht im NS-Staat." In *Die Wehrmacht : Mythos und Realität*, edited by Rolf-Dieter Müller, 66–74. München: Oldenbourg, 1999.

———. *A World at Arms: A Global History of World War II*. Cambridge: Cambridge University Press, 1994.

Weniger, Erich. *Wehrmachtserziehung und Kriegserfahrung*. Berlin: Mittler, 1938.

West, Bing. *No True Glory: A Frontline Account of the Battle for Fallujah.* New York: Bantam, 2005.

Westemeier, Jens. *Joachim Peiper: Zwischen Totenkopf und Ritterkreuz, Lebensweg eines SS-Führers.* 2nd revised and enhanced ed. Bissendorf: Biblio, 2006.

Westphal, Siegfried. *Der deutsche Generalstab auf der Anklagebank: Nürnberg, 1945–1948.* Mainz: Hase und Koehler, 1978.

Wette, Wolfram. *Deserteure der Wehrmacht: Feiglinge—Opfer—Hoffnungsträger? Dokumentation eines Meinungswandels.* Essen: Klartext, 1995.

———. *Die Wehrmacht: Feindbilder, Vernichtungskrieg, Legenden.* Frankfurt a. M.: Fischer, 2002.

———. *The Wehrmacht: History, Myth, Reality.* Cambridge, Massachusetts: Harvard University Press, 2006.

Wette, Wolfram, and Sabine R. Arnold, eds. *Stalingrad: Mythos und Wirklichkeit einer Schlacht.* Frankfurt a. M.: Fischer, 1992.

Wien, Otto. "Letter to the Editor as Answer to the Critique of Theodor Busse on his Article 'Probleme der künftigen Generalstabsausbildung'." *Wehrkunde* 5, no. 1 (1956): 110–111.

Wiese, Leopold von. *Kadettenjahre.* Ebenhausen: Langewiesche, 1978.

Wilhelm, Hans-Heinrich. *Die Einsatzgruppe A der Sicherheitspolizei und des SD, 1941/42.* Frankfurt a. M.: Lang, 1996.

Wilkinson, Spenser. *The Brain of an Army.* Westminster, UK: A. Constable, 1890. Reprint, 1895.

Willems, Emilio. *A Way of Life and Death: Three Centuries of Prussian-German Militarism; An Anthropological Approach.* Nashville, Tennessee: Vanderbilt University Press, 1986.

Williamson, Porter B. *Patton's Principles.* New York: Simon & Schuster, 1982.

Wilson, Theodore. "'Through the Looking Glass': Bradford G. Chynoweth as United States Military Attaché in Britain, 1939." In *The U.S. Army and World War II: Selected Papers from the Army's Commemorative Conferences,* edited by Judith L. Bellafaire, 47–71. Washington, D.C.: Center of Military History, U.S. Army, 1998.

Wilt, Alan F. "A Comparison of the High Commands of Germany, Great Britain, and the United States during World War II." In *The Impact of Nazism: New Perspectives on the Third Reich and Its Legacy,* edited by Alan E. Steinweis and Daniel E. Rogers, 151–166. Lincoln: University of Nebraska Press, 2003.

Wood, Gordon S. *The Radicalism of the American Revolution.* New York: Knopf, 1992.

Woodruff, Charles E. "The Nervous Exhaustion Due to West Point Training." *American Medicine* 1, no. 12 (1922): 558–562.

Wray, Timothy A. "Standing Fast: German Defensive Doctrine on the Russian Front during World War II, Prewar to March 1943." Fort

Leavenworth, Kansas: U.S. Army Command and General Staff College, 1986.

Wrochem, Oliver von. *Erich von Manstein: Vernichtungskrieg und Geschichtspolitik.* Paderborn: Schöningh, 2009.

Wünsche, Dietlind. *Feldpostbriefe aus China. Wahrnehmungs- und Deutungsmuster deutscher Soldaten zur Zeit des Boxeraufstandes, 1900/1901.* Berlin: Links 2008.

Yarbrough, Jean M. "Afterword to Thomas Jefferson's Military Academy: Founding West Point." In *Thomas Jefferson's Military Academy: Founding West Point*, edited by Robert M. S. McDonald, 207–221. Charlottesville: University of Virginia, 2004.

Y'Blood, William T., ed. *The Three Wars of Lt. Gen. George Stratemeyer: His Korean War Diary.* Washington, D.C.: Air Force History and Museum Program, 1999.

Yingling, Paul. "A Failure in Generalship." *Armed Forces Journal* (May 2007).

A Young Graduate [Eisenhower, Dwight D.]. "The Leavenworth Course." *Cavalry Journal* 30, no. 6 (1927): 589–600.

Zald, Mayer N., and William Simon. "Career Opportunities and Commitments among Officers." In *The New Military: Changing Patterns of Organization*, edited by Morris Janowitz, 257–285. New York: Russell Sage Foundation, 1964.

Zickel, Lewis L. *The Jews of West Point: In the Long Gray Line.* Jersey City, New Jersey: KTAV, 2009.

Ziemann, Benjamin "Sozialmilitarismus und militärische Sozialisation im deutschen Kaiserreich, 1870–1914: Desiderate und Perspektiven in der Revision eines Geschichtsbildes." *Geschichte in Wissenschaft und Unterricht* 53 (2002): 148–164.

Zuber, Terence. *Inventing the Schlieffen Plan: German War Planning, 1871–1914.* Oxford: Oxford University Press, 2002.

Zucchino, David. *Thunder Run: The Armored Strike to Capture Baghdad.* New York: Grove, 2004.

Index